HOLLYWOOD'S TEAM

GRIT, GLAMOUR, AND THE 1950S LOS ANGELES RAMS

HOLLYWOOD'S TEAM

GRIT, GLAMOUR, AND THE
1950S LOS ANGELES RAMS

Eloy,

*I hope you enjoy
this story abt frotball in a
special time ad place. Go Rams!*

JIM HOCK

WITH MICHAEL DOWNS

Publisher's Cataloging-in-Publication data

Names: Hock, Jim, author | Downs, Michael, 1964-, author.
Title: Hollywood's team : grit , glamour , and the 1950s Los Angeles
Rams / Jim Hock ; with Michael Downs.
Description: Includes bibliographical references. | First Hardcover
Edition | A Vireo Book | New York, NY ; Los Angeles, CA : Rare Bird
Books, 2016.
Identifiers: ISBN 978-1-945572-26-5
Subjects: LCSH Los Angeles Rams (Football team)—History. |
Football—United States—History—20th century. | BISAC SPORTS &
RECREATION / Football | HISTORY / United States / State & Local /
West (AK, CA, CO, HI, ID, MT, NV, UT, WY)
Classification: LCC GV956.L6 H63 2016 | DDC
796.332/64/0979494—dc23

My Everything: Kellie, John, and William

*My Inspiration: Dad #63, Mom and Jay, Mary, Sue, Lisa,
Anna, and Joe*

CONTENTS

Introduction

PART I

Chapter 1
The Rabbit Skinner Comes Home   15

Chapter 2
Training Camp   31

Chapter 3
"Git-gat-giddle with a geet-ga-zay!"   62

Chapter 4
Grids and Gridirons   87

Chapter 5
Safety   110

PART II

Chapter 6
The Weights   123

Chapter 7
Tomorrowland   148

Chapter 8
The Sweep   169

Chapter 9
Game Ball   182

Chapter 10
The Loser's Purse   206

Chapter 11
Those Strange Things Yet To Come   223

Chapter 12
Shuttle Guard   238

PART III

Chapter 13
A Special Invocation Honoring the Mothers   257
Chapter 14
Not A Very Nice Thing To Do   270
Chapter 15
LA Bums   283
Chapter 16
The Most Quiet Part   302
Chapter 17
Next Time   308
Chapter 18
Epilogue   322
Acknowledgments
Bibliography and Further Reading
Endnotes

INTRODUCTION

I REMEMBER THE WORDS as if it were yesterday: "If you don't do this I will kick your ass." As the youngest of seven kids, I had heard this kind of threat my entire childhood. But this time was different. Those words came from my brother Joe as he leaned over to talk to me at a memorial service for our father, John Hock, shortly after he passed away in 2000. Following the service, my siblings and I sat in rapt awe of the stories of former NFL greats Les Richter, Duane Putnam, and others. Tears and laughs. The stories provided comfort. Friends of our father, sharing memories of their dear friend and their days playing together for the Los Angeles Rams of the 1950s.

The "this" my brother referred to was to write and capture these stories, maybe even turn them into a book. I began writing it in 2002, and it took ten more years to finish. I started writing after the birth of our first son, I went in one direction and another, and in between started a company of my own. Honestly, the book was never meant for an audience wider than my mother and our immediate family. The Rams were an integral part of our parents' lives; they grew up just blocks away from the Los Angeles Memorial Coliseum that the team called home. Yes, the Rams loomed much larger than just a sports team in the Hock family. They represented something bigger: a way to connect and stay connected to the stories, our family history, and the history of Los Angeles, a city my parents loved.

Today, after twenty years in St. Louis, the Rams are back in their longtime home. Seems hard to believe. Some call their return to Los Angeles a relocation. Yet it's more like a restoration.

The Rams of the 1950s were innovative. They were glamorous. And most of all, they were exciting. And like the city itself, the Rams were comprised of both big stars and everyday workhorses like my dad—a quiet, humble, and stout offensive guard—that are needed to make things run.

The Rams were the first major professional sports team to move west of the Mississippi River. They were the first to integrate—roughly a full year before Jackie Robinson shattered major league baseball's color barrier. They were the first to paint a logo on their helmets. They were the first team to reach one million fans in a season. They were the first team with a television contract.

Their 1950s roster is a who's who of the NFL Hall of Fame. Names such as quarterback Norm "The Dutchman" Van Brocklin, wide receiver Elroy "Crazylegs" Hirsch, Bob Waterfield, split end Tom Fears, defensive back Dick "Night Train" Lane, and linebacker Les Richter. Other notables from the era include a wunderkind public relations man named Pete Rozelle who would go on to become the boy commissioner of the NFL at age thirty-three. Head Coach Sid Gillman was an architect of the modern passing game. Owner Dan Reeves was a genius in business, but troubled by alcohol. Heck, even the iconic comedian Bob Hope was a partial owner of the Rams at the time.

The Rams were Hollywood's team.

PART I

CHAPTER 1

The Rabbit Skinner Comes Home

CONSIDER THE WAY HOLLYWOOD would film the opening, this story of Los Angeles and professional football. Play at cinematography and place the cameras to show off our main character's best features. A giant, this guy, he wears an Army soldier's haircut, duffle bag strapped over shoulders that would fill a closet. For this—the movie version—he'd be wearing his Army uniform and corporal's stripes.

On location, outside a small bungalow in South LA, sunlight beats against the house's stucco. It's warm, this January day in 1953.

Imagine the camera shot from the sidewalk: our character's back fills the frame as he steps toward the house. He'd need to turn sideways to get through the front door. Who he is seems less important than where he's going, that house that seems too small. His age? Twenty-four, twenty-five. Yet he's slow up the two steps to the porch, walking as if his knees are stiff. He lingers to look around, enjoying all he has missed for so long. The camera tightens its focus, catches a glimpse of a name tag pinned to his chest. Then Corporal John Hock's parents open the door…

Cut to our hero's grown-man face as he peers out the side-by-side windows of his childhood bedroom, small and west-facing and so bright with January sun that you know the room would bake in summer. Big-chested at 230 pounds, he makes the window seem small. The glass reflects cars rushing by on Western Avenue. John Hock presses the palm of a hand against the pane as if to make certain the window is real. His eyes fix on a spot somewhere the camera can't see, and he searches the sky, a slight smile suggests that he's looking at all his best tomorrows.

Then he brings his hand to his jaw, that large hand with fingers thicker than most men's thumbs, thumbs wide as a Bible. He cups the chin as if he's taken by a thought.

Wait! the director shouts. *No! Not that!*

The jaw, you understand, John Hock's jaw, already draws enough attention to itself. Though Hock is big, blond, and blue-eyed, what separates him in any crowd or photograph, what people always remember, what you can't help but see, is that jaw.

Broad and long, with a cleft dead center in the chin, it's a jaw you could imagine was made of granite, a jaw God intended for Mount Rushmore. Its cousins are the jaws Disney Studios gave to Mighty Casey as he swung the bat in the 1946 cartoon, or years later to Paul Bunyan as he cleaved forests with his axe. Hock's profile makes Kirk Douglas's famous jaw forgettable.

So, hand on the windowpane, please—and then the camera draws back. Begins to build distance between itself and John Hock, shows the tiny house in its surroundings, only a few yards from the back door of a Roman Catholic church. From there, the camera rises high above the bungalow—a helicopter shot— John Hock and his world shrinking as the grid that is Los Angeles is revealed, streets and houses proliferating, endless sidewalks straight as sidelines, and palm trees tall as goalposts. At last the camera floats high enough to pan across several flat miles, and *there!* The Los Angeles Memorial Coliseum—just a long walk from the house where John Hock grew up.

The stadium sits empty now, in January, but a little film editing changes that. The picture grows hazy, and a fade-in fills the coliseum with tens of thousands of football fans who cheer and applaud. Under their roar is the grunting and thumping of men who fling their bodies hard against each other, a referee's whistle, a profanity shouted from a sideline. On the field, pass follows pass, touchdown follows touchdown. A newspaper headline spins into the picture to show a team familiar with glory (the banner reads: "THEY BEAT THE BROWNS! Rams win NFL Championship!"). And then, as if carved in marble, come the names of players who are already legendary: Van Brocklin, Tank, Crazylegs, Deacon Dan.

The future John Hock sees out his bedroom window has become clearer.

If everything happens as it can in the movies, in a few months John Hock will suit up in blue and gold, don a helmet decorated with the Rams' famous curling horns. When the starters rush from the sidelines for their first play of the season, he'll come with them, fall into a three-point stance on the offensive line and await the snap. With John Hock's brawn to shove aside a Colt here or a 49er there, the Rams will be on their way to another NFL championship.

Fittingly, this will all happen in his hometown. It is 1953, and the city he left for college seven years before has become something rare and strange, a place where the impossible can become real—a place so full of change that whole neighborhoods might seem unfamiliar to a man who has been so many years away.

This Los Angeles carries remnants of its Old West and Spanish colonial histories, but now strip malls and drive-in churches light the night with neon. Here, men design jet propulsion engines while others draw cartoons about sending a mouse into space. This Los Angeles is as fake as an African jungle on a stage set and as real as the concrete coliseum where a linebacker cracks the ribs of a quarterback; dangerous as big finned cars careening on a smooth highway, comforting as a suburb laid out in a perfectly predictable grid. Los Angeles is glamorous and middle class and poor. Full of promise, impossible to predict. It's a city so new that by the time the sun rises, it's already tomorrow.

The perfect sporting complement for that Los Angeles is the Rams: forward-thinking, impatient, innovative, gimmicky. Like their city, they are a feisty outlier challenging the nation's east-of-the-Mississippi establishment. From 1948 to 1951, the Rams played in the NFL's championship game, winning the last, and they hold just about every NFL record for passing and scoring. Yet those gaudy numbers aren't enough to satisfy Los Angeles, whose city leaders dream of something other than NFL football, who long to hear the crack of a major league bat and watch a summertime double play.

America's most exciting town. The nation's most exciting NFL team. And an affable giant of a man coming home and hoping to play for both.

A fast-talker could sell that script to Hollywood.

In the movie version, John Hock turns from the window. His mother is calling; she's fixed him dinner. Steak with potatoes, the meat broiled to medium with enough gristle to put "hair on your chest," she'd say—his favorite. Football will come soon enough. For now, he can enjoy being a regular guy, a GI happy to be in his parents' house, sipping a cold beer, and hopeful about a new job.

◆

WHEN JOHN HOCK FIRST left Harry and Elizabeth Hock's house for the University of Santa Clara in Northern California in 1946, he left behind a city still stunned by the Depression, exhausted by World War II. Seven years later and back from Army service during the Korean conflict in occupied Japan, he found that money and bulldozers and new ideas and new faces had scrubbed the city fresh.

People were betting on Los Angeles—and the bets were paying off. In truth, people had brought their hopes to Southern California since the turn of the century, but especially since the 1930s when Depression economies throughout the country convinced hundreds of thousands to move west. The Hocks were part of that migration, driving cross-country from ailing Pittsburgh in 1937 when John was nine years old. John's father, Harry, worked for US Steel and was one of thousands laid off and looking for work for month after month. Losing all hope, Harry had moved out a month before the wife and kids, telling young John that he'd see them soon in California. To the young John Hock, it must have felt like the other side of the planet.

The Rams themselves landed in 1946, having abandoned poor attendance and money problems in Cleveland to make themselves the first National

Football League team west of the Mississippi River. Not even the combination of a rookie star quarterback (Bob Waterfield) married to a movie star (Jane Russell) and an NFL championship in 1945 had drawn enough paying fans in Cleveland to offset that season's reported $50,000 loss. At first, NFL owners vetoed the move. Los Angeles was some two thousand miles farther than Chicago, the closest NFL city, and an airplane could take eighteen hours to cross the country. League owners saw long and expensive road trips. But Rams president Dan Reeves, then only thirty-three years old, is reported to have shouted at them, "And you call this a national league?" When that logic didn't convince, he won their approval for his move by agreeing to pay other teams' travel costs for games played in LA—an early indication that Reeves and the team wouldn't play the game as others did.

Both the Hocks and the Rams added to a Southern California population boom that would for decades shape the region and even the nation. In 1930, seven years before the Hocks arrived, the United States Census had counted about 2.2 million people in LA County. The population estimate for 1953? When John Hock's army service ended? More than double that at 4.6 million. *Four-point-six.*

During those years, Burbank added 70,000 residents and Long Beach, 110,000. In southeastern Los Angeles County, the area called Lakewood boomed from 980 people to an estimated 81,550—a spectacular growth rate of 8,221 percent.

LA, the city, also grew. The numbers for Van Nuys, where Rams quarterback Bob Waterfield and Jane Russell had met in high school, grew from a mere eleven thousand people in 1930 to about seventy-four thousand in 1953, the year Waterfield retired from the game. The Leimert Park neighborhood, just west of where the Hock family settled, doubled its population. As journalist Carey McWilliams wrote in 1946, "Every city has had its boom, but the history of Los Angeles is the history of its booms. Actually, the growth of Southern California since 1870 should be regarded as one continuous boom, punctuated at intervals with major explosions."

Many new residents had come from Texas, Oklahoma, Arkansas, and Missouri—states struck hardest by the Dust Bowl. Some people found work in the orange groves and agricultural fields east of the city, but perhaps six to seven hundred thousand came during World War II to work in factories to fuel America's war machine, such as those that manufactured aircrafts and parts in Long Beach and the San Fernando Valley. In a 1941 newspaper column, the famous reporter Ernie Pyle called them "Aviation Okies."

Other new residents were sailors and soldiers returned from World War II's Pacific Campaign. Many young men, aged nineteen or twenty or twenty-one—unmarried, looking for work—found that driving under a cloudless blue yonder was preferable to walking Boston's rain-splashed sidewalks, that tanning on a Santa Monica beach was more fun than shoveling snow from a Toledo stoop. Veterans found work building little houses that pimpled what had once been farm fields in Lakewood and other suburbs, and veterans bought those houses, too. In *Holy Land: A Suburban Memoir*, Lakewood resident D. J. Waldie writes of how the federal government threw money at veterans so they could buy homes—no down payment and 4 percent interest. Waldie's Lakewood subdivision added 17,500 of these houses in three years. They were small, built rapid-fire, and equipped, according to Waldie, "With a Waste King electric garbage disposal, oak floors, service porch, stainless steel kitchen counter, and a stainless steel double sink." He quotes what the subdivision's sales manager once said: "We sell happiness in homes."

Los Angeles drew more than its share of dreamers, too—the people who saw money in the marquees, who hoped for fame through film. Victor Mature arrived from Louisville, Kentucky; Hedy Lamarr came from Europe; and Bob Hope, who would one day own a share of the Rams, arrived in 1938 via Broadway and a deal with Paramount Pictures. For each film-famous face, thousands of others appeared only as gofers on stage sets or as servers in restaurants and bars. All told, their numbers were dwarfed in the population boom by the WWII veterans and the immigrants from the western South, but the most successful of the dreamers became the image LA showed the nation and the world—that beautiful, handsome, funny, perfectly lighted, and charismatic face of Hollywood.

◆

On an Army base outside Tokyo, in the summer of 1952—six months before he would muster out of the army—John Hock received a football player's version of a "Dear John" letter. His stateside team didn't want him anymore.

That team was the NFL's Chicago Cardinals, who had made him the ninety-ninth pick in the 1950 draft. He played in all twelve Cardinals games during his rookie season, when Chicago finished a less-than-mediocre 5–7. But then the government sent its own draft notice, so off Hock went.

First, the army sent him to Fort Ord in California for basic training and a season assigned to special services, the wing of the military meant to entertain the troops and raise morale. Hock's job, naturally, was to play football. From Fort Ord, he headed across the Pacific for more of the same: an assignment with Camp Drake's Bulldogs—the best team in the Far East Command. Hock, who had once faced the NFL's Eagles and Steelers, was now playing against Yokosuka Naval Base and the Tokyo Quartermaster Depot.

And that was fine. Heck, it was good. Each game provided a distraction for soldiers and sailors on R&R, a taste of stateside life, a safer violence. No complaints from Hock. Sure, he'd expected that service ball wouldn't match up to the NFL, that his teammates might be a bunch of deadpans. But they weren't. They acted like pros. Did what was expected without asking too many questions. That's what he told a reporter from *Pacific Stars and Stripes* on a late October day in 1952, in a damp locker room just after drills had ended. The reporter had done the fly-on-the-wall routine while the Bulldogs practiced, then followed players into the locker room with pen and paper to gather tidbits. He chatted with an all-American from Tennessee while nearby Camp Drake's coach painted stripes on game balls so they'd be easier to see. Another player was tightening new cleats onto his shoes. Hock stood at his locker, giving his knees a rest. Even at the University of Santa Clara they'd given him trouble—he'd worn a large knee brace for the team photograph his senior year. He didn't talk about the pains, but he knew he needed to take care. His career as an offensive lineman would last only as long as those knees. Could be years. Could be tomorrow. He babied them when he could.

Knowing Hock had played in the NFL, the reporter wandered over. He wanted to know what the pro thought of his new teammates.

Most of these boys have played some good college ball, Hock said. They do things right. They really surprised me.

And that was that. Stoic and humble, Hock had never been one to jabber.

If the reporter had pressed, though? If he'd asked more questions? Hock might have acknowledged that heck, well, sure it was better to be with Camp Drake than a team like Quartermaster Depot, which Drake had beaten, 74–0, the week before. Seemed every one of Drake's Bulldogs had scored a touchdown—even Hock, getting a turn on defense and falling on a dropped lateral in the end zone.

Seventy-four to zip? You didn't find such lopsided scores in the NFL.

Comparisons are a strange thing in wartime, though. You start making them, you can't stop, and each one added to the next seems to make less and less sense. If you start comparing the NFL to the Far East Command Football League and Camp Drake to Quartermaster Depot, you can't help but compare serving in Japan to serving in Korea, showering in a locker room to shivering in a foxhole. You take the field in a small stadium to cheers from guys who have battled back and forth across the thirty-eighth parallel, and you can't help but wish the Chinese and North Koreans could be swept 74–zip. And that's when you know none of it makes sense. Best, then, to put aside comparisons, follow orders, do what the United States government wants you to do, and be grateful to be spared bullets and bayonets and grenades.

Gratitude matters. Guys in foxholes sometimes get real "Dear John" letters. Cold, brief *sayonaras*. Hock's kiss-off from his team had been perfunctory, too. But it had come with a pretty big postscript.

Chicago didn't want him anymore, that was true. But the Cardinals had swapped him to Los Angeles for a rookie linebacker from Tennessee and a tackle out of Texas Tech. His new bosses had been willing to give up two players for him, and those boys could suit up right then, didn't have to miss one more season while playing the likes of Yokosuka Naval Base. Maybe that's why Chicago had traded him—for the chance to get help right away.

The Rams? They had wanted him even knowing they'd have to wait—like a sweetheart who takes your ring and says she won't date anyone while you're away.

◆

It was small, that bungalow on Fifty-Second Street at the corner of Western, so tiny he did not have a bedroom and slept on the back porch. Not much changed from when he was a boy, when he'd so often wake from a deep sleep to a tap on the siding or the window glass. Outside, a priest from neighboring St. Brigid's would motion with a finger, and John would know that some other altar boy hadn't shown for Mass. Within a few minutes, he'd be out the back door, past the Hocks' rabbit hutch, and into the sacristy, dressed in a surplice, ready to play his role. He knew the game plan: when to kneel, when to pour water over the priest's hands, when to ring the bell during the Eucharist. *Amen.*

Then, back home to do his part there, to feed and give water to the rabbits. Selling furs was how a boy could earn pocket change, maybe contribute to the family. Pittsburgh had been devastated by the Depression, so the Hocks had left, but Los Angeles didn't hand them thick rib eyes and an easy chair. In fact, answering the census worker who arrived at the door in 1940, the Hocks reported that only one person in the household held a job: daughter Ruth, ten years John's senior, who had worked the previous year as an office clerk for a credit collection bureau. Harry, the father, had been out of work for eighty-six weeks, nearly two years. His last job, the census worker noted, had been an assistant at a filling station.

John was twelve. He didn't have a job. He had rabbits.

Decades later, when he talked about the rabbits, the story would take a comedic turn—how young John sold rabbit skins! He'd tell the story and chuckle, and his kids, themselves grown, would consider the spectacle of some miniaturized version of their father, going door-to-door with a bag or a sack full of fur, or maybe to a shop somewhere, asking a nickel or a dime a pelt. *Dad did that? Can you imagine?*

Can you?

Take a moment and step up to the rabbit hutch with John Hock, the boy. It's morning, still cool. If the rabbits acknowledge him, it's difficult to tell; mostly they stay where they are, legs tucked beneath their bodies, whiskers twitching. He begins as his father taught him, reaching into the cage with one hand and grabbing one by the soft scruff, calming it with caresses as he takes it against his chest and with his free hand fastens the hutch door. Dumb, harmless—the rabbit knows nothing about the knife. He sets the rabbit down—on a table or on the ground—but doesn't let it go. Pets it, talks to it until it is calm. With his free hand, he grips the pipe, what he always uses. The blow needs to be quick and accurate, just as he was taught. Hit that spot behind the ears where the head meets the neck. Hit it hard, to stun. Now, move fast—knife to throat, slice. Blood spurts, and he doesn't want it on the fur, so he lifts the body by its rear legs, hangs it with wire or a peg, lets the blood drain. The rabbit is already dead, and soon the legs stop kicking, the body gives up its twitch. Now, with the knife, which must be sharp, he cuts circles around the rear legs and with his fingers yanks the fur down, first past the legs, then the torso. To knick the fur here and there with the knife makes everything easier. There's a soft tearing sound as the meat lets go of its skin. Some call this stripping the jacket, and when the job is finished, what's left is a handful of rabbit fur and a purplish carcass.

It's a small violence, maybe more than most boys could stomach. But John Hock isn't most boys. He'll never object to a chore, never complain about a job. It's in him to help his family, his church—later his teams and his country. It would always be in him to help, and he would do whatever needed doing. Show him the

Xs and Os of serving a Mass or skinning a rabbit or blocking a linebacker on a sweep left, and he'd follow the plan. It didn't matter whether he was sleepy, or the rabbit twitched, or his knees ached. In his quiet, you'd never know if he was troubled; he'd never say. He'd do what was expected.

These boys, he had told the newspaper reporter in Japan, *they act like pros, they do what's expected. They do things right.*

In January 1953, the man who had been that boy was home. He had become strong, quick. Having wrestled some in college, even good enough to go the Olympic trials, he had moves and balance. But the world was full of strong, quick men. Some with healthy knees. Not all of them made it in professional football. If he was to succeed with the Rams, John Hock needed something all the other strong, quick men didn't have. If he was to play for the NFL's most exciting team in what was probably America's most exciting city, he would need to bring to bear that talent he'd shown as a boy who skinned rabbits. It was perhaps his greatest gift: a willingness to take up any load, to tolerate any pain.

CHAPTER 2

Training Camp

THE SUMMER SUN, THROWING its first light from behind the San Bernardino Mountains, promised a sweltering day in Redlands. Seventy miles inland and planted amid desert brush and fruit orchards, Redlands often simmers ten to twenty degrees hotter than Los Angeles with its blessed ocean breezes. Mornings, though, can be cool, sixty-something, like this one in July 1953. Farmers checked irrigation systems, fed chickens. At the University of Redlands campus, inside Melrose Hall dormitory, John Hock and other football players slept. Outside their closed doors, coaches padded past; some might have grinned or suppressed a chuckle, knowing the ruckus to come.

At the controls of the dorm's public address system, a coach flipped a switch, spun up the volume, pressed a button.

"READY-SET-*HUT*-TWO-THREE-FOUR!"

Like a football version of reveille, the recorded voice boomed into every corner of Melrose Hall. Loud and fast, less a quarterback's voice, more an auctioneer's.

"READY-SET-*HUT*-TWO-THREE-FOUR! *HUT*-TWO-THREE-FOUR!"

It's six thirty in the morning, rookies. Welcome to training camp.

Up and down the hallways, players bolted awake, grumbling. John Hock stirred in his bed. You expected to rise early at training camp, but not to the crowing of a rooster this rude.

"*HUT*-TWO-THREE-FOUR! READY-SET-*HUT*-TWO-THREE-FOUR!"

In all Hock's years of football—high school, college, pro, and military—he'd never heard a snap cadence this fast. Or this loud. And never before coffee.

"*HUT*-TWO-THREE-FOUR!"

An air raid siren would be more melodious.

It had been almost six months since Hock's return to Los Angeles from Japan. Since then, he'd signed a contract with the Rams, rested his knees, and worked himself into shape for training camp. Though he had a year of NFL experience, the Rams' coaches wanted him to report early with the rookies. He was, after all, in his first year with the team, and he'd been out of the NFL for two years. So, on Monday he'd driven from Los Angeles, heading for that Redlands furnace where the Rams had held their annual training camp since '49. Their home for the next several weeks would be Melrose Hall with its thin mattresses and even thinner pillows. Like other dormitories at the University of Redlands, Melrose was built to take the edge off the heat: with high ceilings but only two stories, long and wide with shallow-pitched tile roofs, and lots of windows to open for a breeze. The long porch was sheltered, too, not for worry of rain, but to offer shade. Paired ionic columns framed the entry from the college's quad. Out back, a short stroll away, were the practice fields.

Hock had arrived with rookies who'd come from as far and wide as Spokane, Washington, and Lewisburg, Pennsylvania, hoping they might turn their love of a violent game into a paycheck. Among them was Verdese Carter, an offensive tackle who had been a Negro all-American at Wilberforce University, and who had lined up beside John Hock with the Camp Drake Bulldogs. Carter was taller than Hock by an inch and a half, outweighed him by twenty or so pounds. Together, they'd helped Camp Drake to the first-ever Far East Interservice championship game, what the military had called the Rice Bowl, as if it were an Asian cousin to the Rose Bowl or Orange Bowl. The military even scheduled the championship on New Year's Day, when all the big bowl games were played. The 1953 Rice Bowl pitted Hock and Carter's Bulldogs against the Yokosuka

Naval Base Sea Hawks, the teams meeting in a Tokyo stadium the Japanese had built but the Americans had commandeered and renamed for New York Yankee great Lou Gehrig.

Camp Drake scored first, near the end of the first half, then again at the start of the second, and eventually won, 25–6. A mere twenty days later, Corporal Hock had traveled the breadth of the Pacific Ocean, arrived at Fort Ord in California, and received his discharge papers. Now, he and Carter were competing for a spot on the offensive line where both had primarily played tackle.

Despite the name, an offensive tackle never tackled anyone. He played on the offensive line—that group of oversized men whose job was to be both battering ram and wall. On running plays, offensive linemen threw themselves at opponents in carefully choreographed patterns intended to clear paths that their fleet-footed teammates could rush through, carrying the ball. On passing plays, the line formed a protective circle around the quarterback, intending to give him an uninterrupted second or two to find an open man downfield to catch his pass.

In the middle of the offensive line were two guards and a center—men who were generally stouter, harder to move, but also gifted with better balance and dexterity. Imagine a dancing elephant, and you've got a guard. The two tackles, on either edge, needed to be rangier—generally bigger and taller—and needn't be so nimble-footed. After all, it's easier to walk on the edges of a crowd than it is to walk through the middle. Since college, John Hock had regularly played tackle on the left side, protecting the quarterback's blind side. So had Verdese Carter.

When Hock and Carter and other first-year players arrived at Redlands, they dressed out in Rams practice jerseys and helmets, then participated in a few easy drills and posed for newspaper photographers. Redlands locals gathered for the hubbub; ten- and eleven-year-old boys played at tackling the rookies, but mostly hung on their legs. That first day was a get-to-know-you affair. Tuesday would be the first true day of camp: workouts in hundred-degree heat.

But first:

"*HUT*-TWO-THREE-FOUR! READY-SET-*HUT*-TWO-THREE-FOUR!"

Though the recorded voice belonged to an assistant coach, the idea to wake the rookies this way came from the top man, Coach Hampton Pool. Beyond the welcoming prank, he wanted to make a point. Later that day, he would explain how every scoring record in the NFL belonged to the Los Angeles Rams, and he wanted the team to break its own marks. The way to do that, he theorized, was to speed up the offense. If you thought of a football team as a factory that manufactured points, and there were only sixty minutes in a game, the way to score more points was to speed up the production line. Every touchdown or field goal needed to come quickly and efficiently, so you'd sooner have an opportunity at another. Therefore, each play had to be quick—and each play started with the snap count.

"The faster you run off your plays, the more plays you can squeeze into a ball game," Pool told reporters, two of whom also stayed in Melrose Hall and were awakened with the rookies. "By increasing the tempo, you run less chance of being penalized for delaying the game. Also, the slower the cadence the more margin for error. If a player misses the beat by a fraction of a second, he can jam up the whole play."

Hamp Pool spoke as if what he'd come up with was an innovation that would change football.

Or was it a gimmick?

Maybe the rookies wondered themselves. For Hock, especially, and for other Angelenos, it was likely a familiar conundrum, an ongoing existential question, because in postwar Los Angeles every day seemed to bring a new something: gimmicks that could be innovations in disguise and innovations promoted with gimmicks. Which new things should you take seriously? Which could you ignore? Take, for example, night golf. A year before, a rich toy manufacturer hosted a golf-under-the-lights tournament at the Inglewood Country Club, hoping to prove that Americans in the Philippines or elsewhere could tee-up in equatorial jungles during the cooler after-hours. He paid Joe Louis, the former heavyweight champion, to play under a portable seven hundred thousand–beam candlepower lamp. "A light-bearer wears the spotlight on his head in a man-from-Mars effect," reported the *Los Angeles Times*, "and covers the course on a scooter-type affair." Take it seriously? Or laugh about it?

What about the humongous four-level stacked freeway *whatsit* opening that summer near downtown? The idea was to connect Highways 101 and 110, and politicians said it would be the first interchange of its kind—meant to use less land than a cloverleaf. An interchange for the future! Sure, but even drivers with a good inner compass struggled to understand how this ramp led to that direction. They merged lanes into the stack with a prayer on the lips: *Please, God, help me find a way out*. Would the interchange prove to be an innovation or a Rube Goldberg version of highway design? Or this: a few months before training camp, Warner Brothers Studios released the Vincent Price film, *House of Wax*, the first full-length 3-D stereoscopic film in color. Theatergoers had to wear flimsy red-and-blue cellophane-lensed paper eyeglasses to see that waxy-faced fellow in cape and hat run right toward them. Gimmick or innovation? Few, if any, were better than Hollywood at blurring the lines.

Was it money? Fancy? Optimism? Perhaps it was the newness of Los Angeles itself, all that originality generating new problems the way the city's pioneering highways had created smog a decade earlier. New problems called for new solutions. So, week in and week out, Los Angeles became a place where eager, hungry minds looked for problems to solve—and innovation and gimmicks thrived. Not only thrived, but were in demand. Because if you didn't have the next big innovation or a gimmick to sell, someone else did.

"However," wrote Frank Finch, the Rams' beat writer for the *Times*, "if they turn on that blasted recorder tomorrow at sunrise, I'm moving downtown."

◆

THIS TRAINING CAMP WAS Hamp Pool's first as head coach; maybe the wake-up call was him trying to make his mark. He couldn't have felt comfortable in his new position.

A year before, he'd been feuding with his one-time friend and his predecessor, "Jumbo" Joe Stydahar. Pool had won that go-around, and the head coaching job with it, but he was the Rams' fifth "boss coach" in eight seasons. All but one predecessor had been let go with a winning record; several had led the team to championship games, two had won it all.

Adam Walsh had coached the Rams in Cleveland and in their first Los Angeles season. Back east, he'd led the team to its first championship, beating Washington, 15–14, for the title in a game played in snow with a temperature around zero. Fans burned hay in barrels to stay warm. Players slipped around the field in rubber-soled shoes. But the next season, out in the sunny west, Walsh's Rams went 6–4. Dan Reeves, the team's principal owner and president, fired him.

The Rams promoted an assistant coach, Bob Snyder, who became at age thirty-four the youngest coach in the NFL. He went 6–6, but a four-game losing streak ended his first season. Following an exhibition-game loss the next season, he resigned, citing ulcers.

Clark Shaughnessy, another assistant and already admired as a football innovator, was next to plant his backside onto the hot seat. More than a decade earlier, Shaughnessy had needed only one season to coach Stanford University from a 1–7–1 joke into a 10–0 Rose Bowl champion. The change was so rapid that Shaughnessy's Stanford team became known as the "Wow Boys." Shaughnessy, nicknamed "Shag," worked that miracle by resurrecting an old, seldom-used offensive formation based on bulk and strength—the "T," which put three running backs behind the quarterback to make a shape like the capitalized letter. But instead of power running, Shaughnessy emphasized speed. The scheme confounded defenses relying on misdirection to mask which player would get the ball and which direction the play would go.

As head coach for the Rams, Shag kept innovating. He moved one of those "T" halfbacks up to the line of scrimmage so that particular halfback would be eligible to catch a pass. With that move, Shag created what was to become the wide receiver and the modern passing game. The change was so revolutionary and successful, especially with future Hall of Famers' Bob Waterfield and Norm Van Brocklin sharing quarterback duties, that other teams tried (and failed) to outlaw it at a meeting of the NFL rules committee. "There's nothing wrong with the play," Shaughnessy scoffed, "except some teams can't stop it!"

Yet after Shaughnessy's second season, with the Rams finishing 8–2–2, Rams president Dan Reeves fired Shag.

Reeves cited "internal friction," according to a *Times* report. The source of tension might have been an overly complex playbook that had begun to annoy the players. Or it might have been a postgame tongue-lashing Shag gave to some assistant coaches who had tippled in front of players after a game. Or it might have been all that and more. In *NFL Head Coaches: A Biographical Dictionary, 1920–2011*, author John Maxymuk describes Shaughnessy as "a milk shake drinker who neither drank nor smoked," and "aloof with a superior attitude and a penchant for cutting, sarcastic comments." Shaughnessy sued the Rams for more than $33,000, what he said was owed on his contract.

Reeves promoted Shag's assistant, the six foot four, 260-pound "Jumbo" Joe Stydahar. Said Shaughnessy, proving his cutting, sarcastic ways: "When Stydahar gets through coaching the Rams, I can take any high school team in the country and beat them."

Stydahar was no milk shake drinker. The son of a West Virginia coal miner, he was said to be capable of drinking whiskey while smoking a cigar and chewing tobacco, all at the same time. The press enjoyed his palaver. Stydahar took Shaughnessy's ideas about passing and, with the help of assistant coach Hampton Pool, pushed them further. In 1950, under Stydahar, the Rams scored sixty-four touchdowns. Van Brocklin threw for 554 yards in one game, breaking the record at the time by 86 yards (a record still standing more than six decades later). In two seasons under Stydahar, the Rams went 17–8 and won the 1951 NFL championship.

But even that couldn't save his job.

When Stydahar left the Rams at the start of his third season, he accused Pool of betrayal. The two had been teammates with the Chicago Bears, longtime friends, and Stydahar had given Pool oversight of the Rams' offense and defense. Pool, who had played offensive line but was a running back at heart, loved designing schemes and strategies based on speed. He had a master's degree in education from Stanford, and he relished study, staying up nights, and waking early to devise new game plans. The first photo of him as a Ram to appear in the *Times* showed him sitting at a desk with his necktie loose and with a sharp pencil in hand, reading an open three-ring binder. "Joe was a big, happy guy, the nice guy," Rams linebacker Don Paul later told Mickey Herskowitz, the author of *The Golden Age of Pro Football*. "Pool was the guy who worked his butt off."

Eventually, Stydahar came to believe he'd given away too much responsibility. "Pool wanted to run the club— the whole works—his own way," he told the *Associated*

Press. "I went to Dan Reeves on several occasions and asked him to do something about it. He refused. I asked for a showdown—and it went against me. That's well and good. It's probably good for the ball club. I'm glad I got out."

Professor Pool, as local sportswriters called him, finished that 1952 season, his first, with a 9–3 record. The Rams' last game was a playoff loss to the Detroit Lions. For the league's defending champs, it was a disappointing finish.

Now, it was training camp, and the professor needed to show something so that he could keep his job.

"READY-SET-*HUT*-TWO-THREE-*FOUR!*"

◆

BACK IN LOS ANGELES, football wasn't Rosalind Wiener's first concern. Probably, it wasn't even her twenty-second. Or eighty-ninth. Pick any number. Football wasn't on her agenda. Instead, Roz Wiener—staring hard into Los Angeles's future—saw baseball.

The Wednesday before the Rams training camp began, she had won an historic election to the Los Angeles City Council. At age twenty-two, she had become the youngest person ever elected to the job; like Van Brocklin's passing yards in a game, it is a mark that still stands. Nor had any woman served on the council since World War I, and no one Jewish since the turn of the century.

Months earlier, no one—not even Wiener—would have envisioned this happening. Though active in campus politics at the University of Southern California and with the local Democratic party, she had been thinking law school in 1953, not elected office. But she'd joined a committee to pick candidates who might run as Democrats for city council vacancies. "We didn't like anybody," she recalled years later. Then someone on the committee said to her, "You talk so much, why don't you run?"

So she did, fresh out of USC, where she had graduated with a degree in public administration. She had no platform when she started, no funds, no natural constituency. She filed her candidacy papers five minutes before the deadline. But Roz Wiener ran for LA's fifth council district as if she'd been preparing her whole life for the role—and perhaps she had been.

A photograph of a two-year-old Roz shows her standing by a billboard of Franklin D. Roosevelt. Her mother put the picture in her baby book. Mom and Dad were New Deal Democrats, and Sarah Wiener was a fierce champion for FDR, using the drugstore and soda shop she and Oscar owned on Western Avenue to campaign on Roosevelt's behalf. Roz grew up writing "Dear Mr. President" letters in the same tone she'd use to write an uncle. One of FDR's secretaries would write back: "Dear Roz, The President is very busy." When Roosevelt died, she—in her own words—went to pieces. She had loved FDR the way other girls loved Frank Sinatra.

To help fund Roz's city council campaign, her mother hosted card games. A nephew sold polliwogs and donated the money. Throughout her district, Wiener walked: door-to-door through the heart of central Los Angeles out to Sepulveda Boulevard, seven to eight hours a day, scheduling her visits around *I Love Lucy* episodes because the television show was so popular she knew people would be home watching. She walked so much she wore out thirteen pairs of shoes, which *LIFE* magazine captured in a photo published that year. The young woman who arrived at voters' doors showed herself to be energetic and full of ideas, a short brunette with green-brown eyes and an infectious smile. With voters, she left a bar of soap wrapped with a business card that read, "Let's Clean Up City Hall." On those cards, she put check marks next to her goals, including: "Bring Major League Baseball to Los Angeles."

As a native Angeleno, Wiener knew that in the eyes of the country—and even to many locals—Los Angeles was a second-class city. New York was the cream, the big brother with whom Los Angeles (and others) had a one-sided rivalry New Yorkers hardly noticed. After all, New York was busy being New York: catching theater on Broadway, enjoying a ticker-tape parade, spending Wall Street money to catch the Yankees in the World Series... Why would New York even notice Los Angeles?

Los Angeles cared what New York thought, but if Los Angeles wanted New York to come out and play, it needed a game worth The Big Apple's attention. If Los Angeles wanted to be a top-tier US city, Wiener believed, it needed Fortune 500 companies and a major opera house. Most of all, it needed major league baseball.

Los Angeles was home to the national pastime, but the Hollywood Stars and Los Angeles Angels played in the minor leagues. That put LA on a field with Oakland and Seattle, not Chicago and New York. Sure, the Rams played teams from back east, but in 1953 the National Football League was a sports afterthought. Maybe the Rams won championships and regularly drew some eighty thousand fans to games, but the nation didn't care. When the weekly *Sports Illustrated* was founded in 1954, it gave only about a page each fall issue to pro football. College football warranted several pages. So did horse racing, golf, boxing, and even fishing. Only professional ice hockey might have mattered less than the NFL.

If the Rams were at all useful to Los Angeles and Wiener in the effort to become top-tier, it was mostly as an example showing that pro sports could succeed in the Pacific Time Zone. No major league team played in a city farther west than St. Louis. Any baseball club would face a financial risk by packing up the moving trucks and driving out Route 66, just as Dan Reeves had taken a big chance when he moved the Rams from Cleveland.

But if an NFL team could succeed in Los Angeles, surely the Dodgers or Cubs would draw!

For her first act as a city councilwoman, Roz Wiener introduced a resolution encouraging the LA Memorial Coliseum's governing commission to let the local American Legion stage a baseball game in the coliseum. Though the coliseum had been used for track and field along with football, Wiener wanted to show major league owners and local skeptics that the great oval, Los Angeles's largest public gathering space, would serve well as a baseball venue.

The resolution was a gimmick, sure, but it was a gimmick with a purpose. Maybe it would take years to bring baseball west. (*Let's be realistic*, she might correct. *Probably it will take years*.) But she had to start her efforts somewhere.

That's how Roz Wiener began her quest to change Los Angeles sports history.

◆

NORM VAN BROCKLIN NICKNAMED him "Lantern Jaw," as in: "Hey, Lantern Jaw! Don't you know who you're supposed to block?" Other players called John Hock "The Hooker," playing off his last name. Tank Younger called him "Cotton" because he would sometimes foam at the edges of his mouth during games.

Perhaps more importantly, Professor Pool started called him an offensive guard, shifting Hock away from his familiar spot at left tackle. Maybe the Rams had too many tackles and too few guards. Big as Hock was, when compared to other Rams tackles he proved a few inches shorter and pounds lighter. Maybe the balance and footwork he'd learned as a college wrestler made him better suited for guard, especially in the system Pool wanted to use, emphasizing speed on the offensive line over size. Whatever the reason, shortly after training camp began, Pool told Hock to get used to playing one step to his right at guard, in the heart of the offensive line.

Naturally, Hock obliged.

Come serve the Mass, John. John, feed the rabbits. Ship out to Japan, Corporal Hock. Learn a new position, Hooker.

When you belong, Hock believed, you contribute. Family or church, country or team. If you think about it, it's a blessing to be instructed in that role, that liturgy, the military's regulations, the footwork and timing. It's a comfort. After depression and world war, and now with politicians talking about Soviets and city-destroying bombs, with so much changing so haphazardly—it's a blessing and a comfort to have directions to follow, a part to play, to know that some outcomes are predictable if you do your job.

John Hock turned the page in the playbook.

◆

THE NEXT TWO WEEKS of training camp, Hock's lessons were a combination of where to go and how to get himself there, who to hit and how to hit him. "When" to hit also mattered. In Pool's system, much of Hock's job would require clockwork timing, then violence: charging to his assignment and crashing into whatever snarling, roaring Eagle or Steeler or Giant he found there—before a Rams halfback arrived.

When lessons were over, there was running to be done. Coaches worshipped at the church of running. Leg strength was built by running. Endurance was built by running. Run laps. Run a mile. Run another. Run under the glare of that desert sun. Run through that desert heat. At training camp, no one escaped running. No one escaped the sun. There were no tents, no shelters. Sun glared off windows hundreds of feet away. It made the grass hot, the dirt dusty. It licked up sweat and burned skin. Sun burned in the players' eyes and in their mouths and ears; probably it burned in their dreams…while they ran.

Each night, a dinner. Maybe a letter written home. A game of cards on the dorm's porch. Days passed. Then, two weeks into camp, Van Brocklin and the veterans arrived.

With them came a different atmosphere. More joking, more insults, more pranks—all part of a shared history, a common language earned through years of bruises, ass-kickings and asses kicked, a shared expectation of the right way to win games. Van Brocklin, the quarterback known for what one sportswriter called his "carbonated remarks," might chew out the newbies.

Kinder players—like Duane Putnam, a guard playing on the right side of the line opposite Hock—offered tips.

Putnam, aka "Putter," had been the rookie sensation among linemen in camp the year before. Though at six feet he was smaller than most NFL guards, Putnam had drawn praise from his coaches. "Duane is a deadly blocker," Stydahar had said. "He not only has speed but he has quickness in getting to his man… [H]e can maintain a drive after the initial contact. Once he gets an opponent on the run, he chases him right out of the ballpark."

Putnam, already married and with a daughter, played guitar, dipped tobacco, and liked to laugh. He had dark hair buzzed flat on top and a face so boyish that when he tried to look mean people chuckled. He liked it when people laughed. Putnam, Stydahar had once said, knew how to have fun playing the game. But "he wants to be the best man at his position in the league. He doesn't come to you and tell you that, but that's the impression you get from watching him play." As guards on opposite sides of the line, Putnam and Hock weren't competitors so much as partners. They were like the two bishops on a chess board, lined up on either side of the king, greater if they worked in tandem than separately. Aside from playing guard, the men had other things in common. Both had played high school and college ball in California, and both had gone through tours in the Army. Both were in their second season as pros. Neither liked to talk much about himself. Both enjoyed a cold beer and someone else's jokes. Naturally, Putter and the Hooker hit it off.

One other very important thing changed when the veterans arrived. Putter and Van Brocklin and the rest? They knew about a little burgers-and-beer place outside town that could help a guy forget Redland's heat.

◆

HARRY PATTISON WAS A boy, probably twelve years or so, when fiery Jane Russell threw open the door of his parents' corner restaurant-bar and started yelling at her husband. Bob Waterfield, by then one of the best quarterbacks in the NFL, rose from his seat beside Van Brocklin at the end of the bar and headed outside.

"Bob Waterfield and Van Brocklin would always sit down by the far door there," Pattison says, recalling those summers the Rams sought refuge at Ed and Mary's, his parents' place.

He remembers how his mom once invited them all to the Pattisons' house up in the nearby mountains so they could taste her fried chicken. And the Rams came, too. A few went hunting for cottontails with Harry's dad.

Decades later, Harry still has a football that Rams players signed and gave him.

But when at the tavern his dad pulled him behind the counter and said, "Don't bother the players." Harry didn't.

He knew why the Rams ("the boys," he calls them) came out to Mentone, a tiny farm town a few miles east of the heart of Redlands. Down in Redlands, if the Rams stopped in at a bar, people would come by to gawk and not even buy beer, just try to chat up the Rams. What the players wanted to do was relax, forget the heat, and forget football.

At Ed and Mary's, everyone knew the house rule: no one bothers the boys.

"When the boys would come in," Harry says, some sixty years later, "my mom would have two or three of the waitresses working. 'Keep those pitchers coming,' my mom would say. 'Don't turn the taps off. Just keep 'em coming.'"

The Rams crowded around the bar, a small space maybe six feet wide and twenty feet long, room for a half dozen circle-tables.

Lucky Lager. Even now, if you ask Duane Putnam about Ed and Mary's, Lucky Lager is what he remembers.

"It was just so good," he says one morning at his house in Ontario, California. He cups his hands as if placing them around a mug. "It was so cold, the pitcher would end up with frost around it—and it was so *good*."

The Rams would come by Ed and Mary's after practice in the late afternoons, happy hour time. They needed to drink fast if they wanted to drink a lot, because they were always due back at the university for the team dinner. Harry remembers them ordering 7-Up soda, too, the green bottles standing amidst the beer glasses. "They liked to pour that into the pitcher after they took the first draw," Harry said. The Rams, apparently, believed 7-Up's carbonation made it so "they could belch louder and drink more beer."

*"READY-SET-*BURP-*NOW-*DRINK-*FOUR!"*

Bottles of 7-Up! Every new problem awaits its innovative solution.

◆

NOT ONLY WAS THIS summer Pool's first training camp as head coach, it was also the first time in eight seasons that the Rams had assembled for camp without Bob Waterfield, the UCLA legend and the team's top quarterback through two national championships. If there had ever been a Mr. Ram it was Waterfield: a physical marvel who not only played football but had been on the gymnastics team in college (in her autobiography, Jane Russell recalls him doing one-armed handstands on roof corners). During Waterfield's tenure he twice led the league in passing yards. He'd also kicked field goals and played defense. As a local boy who had led UCLA's Bruins to a Rose Bowl, he proved a big draw at the LA Coliseum. Wags often quipped that Dan Reeves moved the team from Cleveland to take advantage of Waterfield's celebrity and that of his movie-star wife.

Not that Waterfield enjoyed the spotlight. He didn't. Taciturn, stiff-jawed, more Humphrey Bogart than Cary Grant, Waterfield wanted to play football and drink beer with friends and not much else. Talk? He'd as soon tear his own tongue out. In the *Los Angeles Times*, one friend described a round of golf with Waterfield:

"He used to say to me just five words all day… On the first tee he'd say, 'Hi, Greek.' And on the eighteenth green he'd say, 'So long, Greek.'"

Nor did he say much during games. Waterfield, wrote legendary LA sportswriter Melvin Durslag in a 1953 *Colliers* magazine article, "bottled his emotions perfectly for eight years on the field and never exchanged a cross word with anyone."

That might explain why he only lasted eight seasons. In *Jane Russell: My Paths and Detours*, Waterfield's wife writes that a duodenal ulcer ended his career: "He took the responsibility for the team's success too personally," Jane Russell wrote, "and while it made him the great player he was, it could also kill him if he didn't get out."

So he got out. And the quarterback who remained was the anti-Waterfield.

Norm "Dutch" Van Brocklin couldn't run and didn't kick well. He couldn't play defense. It's unlikely he ever attempted a handstand.

"Afoot, he was very inept," recalls Durslag. "He had no speed."

For some old-school coaches, that meant Van Brocklin was a poser, one-dimensional, and not a true quarterback. Or as the legendary coach George Halas said: "Van Brocklin can throw. Period. In the full sense of the word, he is not a professional player."

Retorted Van Brocklin: "And Joe Louis wasn't a great fighter…all he could do was punch."

Van Brocklin could throw. Despite small hands with fat fingers, he tossed elegant, lofty, on-target passes—what Hall of Famer Elroy "Crazylegs" Hirsch compared to catching "floating bubbles." Another player at the time said Van Brocklin could make passes that "belong in a museum." His form was like that of a javelin thrower, his whole body making the pass rather than just his arm.

And, unlike Waterfield, he talked. You couldn't shut him up.

"His reaction to anything could have been almost anything," said Durslag, who covered the Rams as a columnist for the *Los Angeles Examiner*, which later became the *Herald-Examiner*. "He was a very erratic type of guy. He was an outstanding player. He was a little nuts, you know?"

But people liked him as often as they didn't. A giggler, he'd laugh at anyone's joke, no matter how schmaltzy. A teammate, Durslag once reported, called Van Brocklin "the man most likely to be babied by an airline hostess."

Charming, loquacious, vicious, mean, and unpredictable as Los Angeles itself. Any moment could give rise to a new Norm Van Brocklin. Hall of Famer Baltimore Colt Art Donovan and Van Brocklin would cuss so much across the line of scrimmage that players on both sides thought they were nuts.

Decades later, Durslag still remembered a time he was in the coliseum locker room after a game interviewing Van Brocklin. A radio reporter—"a nice guy," Durslag said—came over to ask for three minutes from Van Brocklin. Dutch grabbed the radio guy's shirt, pulled him near and growled, "One of these days I'm going to hit you so hard your ass will bounce like a golf ball down a paved road." Another time, Durslag recalled, Van Brocklin was riding in a taxi with a reporter who'd been given a championship ring by the Rams. "Where'd you get that?" Van Brocklin said, then asked to hold it for a closer look. The reporter slipped off the ring and handed it to Van Brocklin, who flung it out the cab window.

"You're talking about a guy that's a little cuckoo," said Durslag.

Harry Thompson, who played offensive line for the Rams, remembered Van Brocklin's reaction during a game when the quarterback heard the play Pool wanted him to run. "Where did he get that?" Van Brocklin asked his teammates in the huddle, "from his asshole?"

Reportedly, Coach Pool said, in turn, of Van Brocklin: "He is not a picture passer like Bob Waterfield…but he is the most skillful of all. He will break every record—if some lineman doesn't break his neck first."

Waterfield and Van Brocklin had competed against each other—while playing for the same team—for four seasons. Most NFL teams used one quarterback and kept another in reserve, but Waterfield and Van Brocklin were both too good to keep one on the bench for too long. They played fifty/fifty during games. Dutch played half and Waterfield had played the other half. The pair were more like coquarterbacks, a two-headed coin that paid off with three NFL championship games, including one victory. But neither man liked the herky-jerky nobody's-the-big-dog approach. Naturally, Van Brocklin was the one to complain. When he argued with "Jumbo" over playing time, Stydahar benched him for the 1951 championship game. But with eight minutes left and the Rams and Browns tied at seventeen, Stydahar knew Waterfield wasn't going to win the game for him. He needed Van Brocklin's arm. So Van Brocklin took the field, and three plays later, he tossed one of those floating bubbles to Tom Fears who caught it and scored. Pretty soon, Jumbo Joe was gone. Dutch stayed.

When Waterfield's ulcer finally settled the competition, Van Brocklin knew, as Durslag wrote in *Colliers*, that without him, their one remaining quarterback, "the Rams would be dead." Van Brocklin's contract was supposed to pay him $14,500 for the 1953 season. He wanted more. Durslag reported how the negotiations went.

First, a sportswriter quoted Van Brocklin as stating he would demand $25,000, an unprecedented figure for professional football. Then Norm got hold of an advertising folder which the Rams mail each year to their season-ticket prospects. He returned it to the club, writing under the section marked "Suggestions":

"Pay Van Brocklin one-and-a-half-milion dollars a year."

They settled, finally, for about $20,000, and since Norm felt he went too cheap, he insisted on a mere one-year contract, with the idea of asking for more in 1954.

This was the man John Hock—"Lantern Jaw"—hoped he'd be paid to protect.

◆

THE NFL IN THE 1950s was no way for anyone to get rich—not the owners and especially not the players. Most didn't earn anywhere near the five figures Van Brocklin made in 1953. Linemen like John Hock made five or six thousand dollars. Most needed off-season jobs to get by. Duane Putnam threw kegs in trucks for a Budweiser distributor. Woodley Lewis worked with juvenile delinquents through the LA police department. Andy Robustelli owned a sporting goods store in his native Connecticut. Because they were young men and athletic, some Rams showed up as extras in Hollywood films; Elroy "Crazylegs" Hirsch even starred in a couple (including a biopic of his own life and a prison flick that introduced the world to the famous ballad, "Unchained Melody"). New York Giant Hall of Famer Frank Gifford grew up in Los Angeles and spoke of his off-season routine, "You know, I wasn't even going to play pro football. I mean I could have made more money working as an extra and doing stunt work in the movies, which I did while I was at USC." Former Redskin and Giant Sam Huff was employed by the J. P. Stevens Textile Company selling men's fabrics reporting "I was there to learn how to deal and succeed in business. I learned how to maximize profit and such."

Fred Gehrke, a halfback with the Rams until 1949, had worked as an industrial illustrator for an aviation company. Putting paint on metal all day gave him the idea to paint sleek yellow Rams' horns on the players' helmets. Owner Reeves liked what he saw and paid Gehrke a dollar per helmet for his paint job—the first time any pro football team put an insignia on its hard hat. Creating an iconic logo, it was years before the rest of the NFL caught up.

At training camp in Redlands that summer, no player earned any money. That's how the contracts were structured. No pay until you play. Practice didn't count. Neither did those half a dozen or more games called "exhibitions," warm-ups that pit the Rams against other teams before the start of the real thing, the "regular" season.

So what happened if a coach says a guy's not good enough and sends him home from training camp? Sorry, Charlie. No money for you. What if a fella gets hurt in practice or an exhibition? It happened that summer to a rookie guard from the University of Houston. Rams players visited Frank James at Redlands Community Hospital, but if Frank got a penny for his troubles it was an aberration. Only those who made the roster for the regular season's opening kickoff could expect to get paid their contract salary.

Heading into the first exhibition game, John Hock was healthy and scheduled to start at left guard, a good sign even if not yet earning a paycheck. The Rams would face Fort Ord's football squad in a game to be played in Long Beach, a short drive southeast of Los Angeles. Fort Ord's defense didn't intimidate the Rams, but its offense featured Ollie Matson, a renowned running back who had led the nation in rushing yards as a college senior, then gone on to win a bronze medal in the four hundred meter and a silver in the four-by-four-hundred-meter relay at the 1952 Olympics in Helsinki.

That night at Long Beach, the Rams offense performed as if cockeyed, but Fort Ord and Matson didn't offer much of a threat, either, never getting closer to the end zone than the Rams' twenty-one-yard line. The Rams beat the soldiers, 24–0, before a small crowd of twelve thousand. The warm-up showed that the Rams were still a few spark plugs short of an engine. Even six days later, in a 72–19 rout of Navy and Marine all-stars, the pros didn't dazzle.

Probably the coaches would have liked a few more easy exhibitions to help new guys find their way and veterans shake the off-season stupor. But it didn't matter what anyone wanted. The next exhibition would be the Rams' first true test, less a simulation and more of a donnybrook.

The game had become an annual grudge match. Always, it was played for charity, but nothing charitable happened on the field. Always, it was the Rams' debut at LA Memorial Coliseum, one of football's historic palaces. Fans filled the stadium, wanting to be impressed by that year's team. Rookies hoped to impress coaches and coaches hoped to impress Reeves. For the first time, the Rams would match up against another NFL team. Always it was the same opponent: Washington's Redskins. Seven times the Rams and Redskins had met this way, and the Rams had won four.

Even without pay, players on each team hit each other as if this exhibition were the real thing. To heck with waiting for the regular season. This game *was* the real thing. In the previous year's match-up, Washington's star running back suffered a broken arm.

For John Hock, the *Times* Charities Football Game would be, in the words of TV personality Ed Sullivan, "a really big show." For the first time in two years, he'd be tested by a professional defensive line, pitting himself again players heavier, taller, faster, and meaner than those the Far Eastern teams had offered. Those boys across the line would be fighting for their jobs, too, wanting to knock Hock on his backside and crush Van Brocklin or any running back daring to carry the ball. That night, Hock would need to prove to Hamp Pool that he'd learned his plays, that he could hand out licks and take 'em, too.

And there was this, a tender prick to however much sentimentality resided in Hock's Irish Catholic heart:

for the first time he would dress out in the uniform of a professional football player, then run onto a grassy field under the lights in his hometown. He'd hear cheers from a crowd of eighty thousand fans welcoming its team, and maybe there'd be a few faces among them he'd recognize: his father, Harry, or a priest from St. Brigid's, maybe old high school chums. He'd look up into the blackness beyond the lights and know the particular thrill of game time. Feel how different it was from games in any other city, like Pittsburgh or Chicago, where he'd played his rookie year. This was Los Angeles in 1953. Maybe Los Angeles wasn't so special to merit major league baseball, but the Rams were still the best pro game in town—Hollywood's team and worthy of a five-star premiere, with celebrities on hand to make fans laugh, and a five-ring circus featuring aerialists and trampolinists and performing elephants and Hap Henry with his trick dogs.

John Hock, aka the Hooker, would fit his helmet with its golden horns over his head, snap in place the chin strap that stretched across his impressive jaw, then take the field and crouch in a three-point stance at the line—legs bent at the knees, fingers of his right hand in the grass and soft dirt. For a moment he'd become all heart and muscle, awaiting the "hut!" that would launch him like a rocket, his whole self exploding up and onward...

A night, as the shills like to say, to remember.

CHAPTER 3

"Git-gat-giddle with a geet-ga-zay!"

O N GAME DAY AT the Los Angeles Memorial Coliseum a groundskeeper finishes chalking the field's yard lines. Up high in the press box, a radio announcer stubs out a cigarette in an ash tray, lights another. He pencil-marks rosters, practices the pronunciation of names, especially those of Washington's Rykovich and Tershinksi and Ulinski. A wandering *Times* columnist notes the players from each team who have railroad nicknames: "Night Train Lane" and "Choo-Choo Justice," "Day Train Dwyer" and Chuck Drazenovich, aka the "Pennsylvania Flyer." Don't forget "Mule Train Heath," though his is not, technically, a railroad name.

No, Danny Kaye hasn't arrived yet, but don't worry, he's not performing until halftime.

Over on the southwest side of the stadium, circus folks are readying themselves for the pregame show, their trucks and wagons parked so they can roll equipment and animal cages down the ramp that cuts underneath the stadium and onto the field. Musetta, the heel-and-toe trapeze artist, touches up her mascara and chooses a lipstick to match her outfit, one a cigarette girl in Vegas might wear.

Fans come early, paying $3.90 for a reserved seat, a quarter for a game program. This morning's newspaper reported that the Russians have, for the first time, detonated a hydrogen bomb. Now we can blow them to smithereens, and they can send us to kingdom come. The uncertainty and worry is enough to make anyone want to get to the stadium and its distractions ahead of schedule. In the game program, a full-page advertisement from California Rent-A-Car promises that tonight somebody will win a two-door Ford sedan. "Your number is on the front of the program," it informs. A fan checks to see if his number looks lucky. It would be nice, like the ad says, to drive some cares away…

In the Rams locker room, a fellow in a T-shirt and slacks arranges bandages and wraps in case of injuries and checks to make sure there's plenty of ice for swollen ankles or shoulders. Hampton "Professor" Pool, the head coach, coughs and clears his throat. An ice pack might feel good to him right now, feverish and achy as he is with either a cold or the flu. Whichever, the sickbed will have to wait. He's got reminders to write on a chalkboard, players to coach.

First big game of the season, first big crowd. So who's nervous? Maybe the rookies. The Rams have nine. Some came straight out of college, but a few are NFL veterans new to this team, including Ben Agajanian, the kicker, there beside his locker, knotting the laces of his cleats—and likely the radio announcer is working his lips around that moniker, too. *AG-a-jay-nian? A-ga-JAYN-ian?* Maybe he'll just say "The Toeless Wonder," Ben's nickname since the accident. It involved a freight elevator, and it cost Ben four toes on his kicking foot. Now on one foot he wears size eleven. On the other, 7.5.

Agajanian is one of the rookies lucky enough—or good enough—to start tonight. The other two are Tom McCormick at halfback and John Hock, while not a rookie but first time as a Ram, at offensive guard.

No player wants to lose a knuckle catching a ring on someone else's equipment, so Hock, at his locker, slips a gold band off the finger where a married man would sport his wedding ring. It's big, sized for his thick finger, and an oval stone dominates the face—without facets, bright red as a cardinal and bigger than a dime. Embossed on the edge reads the Latin *Universitatis* harkening back to Hock's days with the Jesuits at Santa Clara University. He wears the ring as a matter of course, and it has become part of who he is. He wore it while in the military, and he wore it during his season with the

Chicago Cardinals. Santa Clara University, which had its beginnings in a simple Spanish mission dedicated to Saint Clare of Assisi, gave him an education and a degree in history so one day he might become a high school teacher. It deepened his appreciation of the Mass and its mysteries, and it provided an opportunity to excel in football. Santa Clara shaped him—body, mind, and soul—and had more to do with the man he became than either the military or the National Football League did. As a priest wears a collar and a police officer carries a badge, John Hock wears Santa Clara's ring, and, as far as he's concerned, he always will.

Today that ring is a reminder, too, of the last time he played in the LA Coliseum. It was nearly six years ago, on a Saturday—October 15, 1949. The Santa Clara Broncos were almost midway through Hock's senior season, with three victories against one loss, a team from a small school with players still unsure of how good they might be. At the coliseum, they were the visitors and the underdogs, facing UCLA's Bruins, who were 4–0 and predicted to be Rose Bowl–bound.

Tiny Santa Clara against mighty UCLA.

That was a good game. Turned into a heck of a season, too.

And because John Hock is a student of history, a man for whom history matters, he knows that in another part of the coliseum, in the visitor's locker room, there's a defensive back for Washington who might also be thinking about that game against the

Bruins. Hock knows that when the Rams take the field, the defense they face will include an Oklahoma-born halfback more familiar to him than most of his current teammates. Hall Gibson Haynes, dark-haired with an everyday handsomeness, was one of two team captains for the Santa Clara Broncos in that magical 1949 season.

John Hock, naturally, was the other.

◆

THWARTED, CURBED, FRUSTRATED—THAT WAS UCLA in 1949 against Hock, Haynes and the Broncos. Said Red Sanders, UCLA's first-year head coach: "We were simply outplayed by a tough team that earned its victory."

The teams had last met in Hock's freshman year, a 33–7 victory for UCLA. Perhaps the Bruins expected another easy go against a school so small it had cancelled its football program during World War II. If so, the Bruins were wrong.

When did they first consider that these Broncos were no easy mark? Maybe it was a few minutes into the game after UCLA recovered a Santa Clara fumble, giving the Bruins the ball thirteen yards away from a possible touchdown. Most teams would hope to keep the Bruins in check, give up a few yards, force them to settle for a three-point field goal rather than a six-point touchdown. But Santa Clara did better, driving UCLA *backward*—all the way to the forty-two-yard line. Neither field goal nor touchdown was an option from so far away. The Bruins punted.

Or maybe it was after the second time the Bruins recovered a Santa Clara fumble—this time even closer to the end zone, only nine yards. Three plays later, UCLA had nudged forward to the two-yard line. On the fourth down, the last chance to score, Coach Sanders opted against the field goal and the Bruins again tried to run. Santa Clara allowed them only a foot.

Nearing the end of the third quarter neither team had scored, and UCLA's defenders were gassed. The Santa Clara lines—offensive and defensive, each led by John Hock—had pushed and shoved and shoved and pushed until Bruins legs got wobbly. That's when Santa Clara scored the game's first points, the Broncos outmuscling UCLA on a quarterback sneak for the touchdown. Five minutes later, the Broncos scored again.

Final score? Santa Clara, 14; UCLA, zip.

"The statistics," wrote someone on the Santa Clara yearbook staff, "truly indicated the superiority of the fast-developing Broncos."

The nation noticed, too, and when Santa Clara finished the regular season at 7–2–1, the Broncos were ranked the fifteenth best college team in the country by the *Associated Press*. The committee for the renowned Orange Bowl sent an invitation, and Santa Clara accepted.

That Christmas night in San Jose, players and coaches, school officials, and some two hundred friends and family boarded a Southern Pacific Special with nearly twenty cars, bound for Miami. The trip lasted four days and covered 3,300 miles. The Bronco express arrived only a few days before the game, but according to Santa Clara–lore this was intentional. Coach Len Casanova had received a tip from one of his assistants that the fellow's father ran greyhounds at races in Florida and had discovered that the dogs fared better in the gauzy, steamy heat when he limited their workouts before a race. Maybe it was loopy to base a football team's future on what one man had to say about dogs, but Casanova took the advice seriously. In Florida, he kept workouts easy. Instead of sweating it out with tackling dummies, Casanova's young men hung around poolside in floral shirts and slacks, and they played shuffleboard like bona fide Florida pensioners.

Having arrived in early December, their opponent—the University of Kentucky Wildcats—had taken a different tack. That team's young coach worked his players hard. Bob Gain played on that team, and he'd eventually win the Outland Trophy for the nation's best college lineman. Years later, he recalled that Kentucky's coach, Paul "Bear" Bryant—who would one day become a college coaching legend and of the famous "Junction Boys" training camps of Texas A&M—brought the team to Cocoa Beach, woke the players each day at 5:00 a.m., and made them scrimmage twice a day. He squeezed practice sessions in between those. He forced his players to run wind sprints "like crazy, ten to twenty of those after practice," Gain said. The day after Christmas

Bryant told his players, "You ate like a bunch of pigs. You better run it off."

Apparently Bear Bryant had no connections at the dog track.

But he and Kentucky did have the nation's confidence. The Wildcats were ranked eleventh in the country by the *Associated Press*, and Las Vegas oddsmakers had deemed them an early thirteen-point favorite, even though that point spread shrank to 5.5 points by game day. A young Jimmy Snyder, already a successful gambler but not yet the famous television personality "Jimmy the Greek," bet $265,000 on Kentucky.

The smart-money guys had good reasons to favor the Wildcats. As an article in Santa Clara's alumni magazine noted sixty years later, Kentucky's advantages were obvious—starting with the team's helmets. The Wildcats protected their heads with streamlined, light, and durable white plastic—the latest technology. The Broncos, as if from the mists of history, strapped on leather headgear that John Hock used to say could "fit in your back pocket." To see the teams together on the field was like watching a horse-drawn wagon line up to race an Oldsmobile Rocket 88.

The most significant difference, though, might have been this: Bryant had two teams to Santa Clara's one.

In 1949, some coaches, including Bryant, had begun what would eventually become common practice: platooning their players. Traditionally, players had stayed on the field all the time, playing both offense and defense. Even for the Los Angeles Rams that year, Bob Waterfield was playing quarterback and defensive back (and punting and kicking field goals). The old system favored the best all-around athletes.

But coaches who platooned had decided that offense and defense required different skills and different mindsets. A good offensive lineman, for example, followed directions, cared about timing, protected his quarterback. But a good defensive lineman caused chaos, surprised and improvised, and played as if he were a wildly swinging wrecking ball. Players who platooned could focus on the particular skills and attitudes suited for their positions. As an added bonus, during games one group could rest while the other took the field.

Kentucky platooned; Santa Clara did not. John Hock played both offensive and defensive line. Hall Haynes, his cocaptain, was a halfback on offense who tried to break up passes on defense. Hardly a play went by with the captains on the bench. Oddsmakers must have figured Santa Clara's boys' would wear themselves out.

The Wildcats and Broncos met in the Orange Bowl on January 2, 1950, before some sixty-four thousand fans. The day promised a high of seventy-five degrees with humidity around 62 percent: less than sweltering, but still damper than the California air Hock and the other Broncos usually breathed.

As expected, Kentucky dominated the first half, building a statistical advantage in yards gained. But just as in the UCLA game, Santa Clara's defensive wall held. At halftime, Santa Clara trailed, 7–0, but the Broncos had ended the half by stopping the Wildcats just yards from the end zone. A Broncos' halfback, Bernie Vogel, spoke of that defensive stand sixty years later. "It was a big moment," he said, as quoted in Santa Clara's alumni magazine. "You could just feel it was starting to go our way."

Back on the field for the second half, the Wildcats fumbled on their own thirteen-yard line. A few plays later, Santa Clara tied the game with a touchdown. Later in that same quarter, Santa Clara, again, had the ball and worked its way to the Kentucky two-yard line. Vogel was correct. Something in the game *had* shifted. The Wildcats, though platooning, played as if exhausted—and they were. Santa Clara's boys, though they were playing both ways, didn't seem at all fatigued. An *AP* reporter later described them as "iron." Solid and unyielding.

When the next play began, John Hock lunged forward, taking a Wildcat low as the Broncos left end hit another man high. Both Wildcats toppled, and Haynes, taking the ball on a handoff, scooted around the block into the end zone. The nearest referee raised his hands to signal the touchdown and Santa Clara's lead. John Hock scrambled up from under a pile of Wildcats, hopping in celebration and clapping twice to punctuate the play.

Kentucky eventually scored on a pass play, though the Wildcats kicker missed his extra-point attempt. Then, with Santa Clara leading, 14–13, and less than thirty seconds left in the game, halfback Vogel took a handoff from quarterback Johnny Pasco and ran sixteen yards through a gang of flat-footed Wildcats for a final Bronco touchdown. Santa Clara, 21; Kentucky, 13.

The upstarts from California had won the Orange Bowl. It was a noteworthy victory—but only that. For people outside of Santa Clara it wasn't even the day's biggest college football story (not with Oklahoma and Notre Dame arguing about which of them should be awarded the national championship). In years to come, football historians would call the Santa Clara-Kentucky Orange Bowl an upset, but nothing in the Broncos' victory was history making—fancy or forward-looking. It wasn't a landmark contest that changed how football could be played. In a way, the Broncos had approached the game as Jesuits would have them do: traditionally, relentlessly, and with rigor—one group of young men throwing their bodies at another in proven ways, winning because they were tougher than their opponents, more rugged, able to endure. It was a playing style that suited John Hock's temperament and rewarded it, and it was satisfaction enough.

The train ride back home "was like a party from Miami to the Bay Area," recalled Len Napolitano, a reserve quarterback, in *Santa Clara* magazine. The Broncos were welcomed by more than ten thousand fans and with a victory parade. Cocaptains Haynes and Hock put on dark corduroy sport coats, and rode sitting atop the backseat of a convertible, California Governor (and future US Supreme Court Chief Justice) Earl Warren squeezed between them. Haynes wore his shirt collar and coat open. Hock, always aware of the right way to do things, kept his coat buttoned and wore a tie with a tight knot.

Three weeks later, NFL coaches and executives gathered to draft the best college players. Of Santa Clara's Broncos, five were taken, and three would go on to make NFL teams: Hall Haynes, the 19th pick for Washington; John Hock, 99th for Chicago's Cardinals; and Jerry Hennessy, 165th, also for the Cardinals. Hennessy and Hock must have been astonished to see themselves chosen by the same pro team. They'd been on the same team at Mount Carmel, a Roman Catholic high school in Los Angeles, then played together in college, and now had the chance to be teammates as pros.

In March, the new coach with the Chicago Cardinals traveled to Santa Clara to get Hennessy and Hock to sign contracts. Earl "Curly" Lambeau was as well-known a football ambassador as anyone could be. A frozen tundra named after him, he had played college ball under Coach Knute Rockne at Notre Dame, then in 1919 founded the Green Bay Packers for whom he played and coached over the next thirty years. The Cardinals hired Lambeau and gave him a piece of ownership at the twilight of his storied career. And now, he was sitting on the edge of a bed in John Hock's dorm room checking out the man for himself, then reciting for the young man the terms of a proposed professional football contract. But Hock, in a chair nearby, couldn't concentrate. He was thinking about the priests at Santa Clara and their rules, particularly the strick prohibition against smoking.

Because here was Curly Lambeau propped on the edge of Hock's neatly made bed, waving around a lit cigarette stuck into the kind of extended holder FDR had used, as he explained how life would be with the Cardinals in America's second city.

What did Curly Lambeau care that each day a priest came to inspect the student rooms? But Hock knew that the priest would check the bed, if made and crisp. What if he smelled the cigarette smoke? What if he saw that dusting of gray?

Open a window? That would be impolite, and a priest outside might notice the smoke.

Was there a dish to offer as an ashtray? Of course not; smoking wasn't allowed. Why would Hock keep an ashtray?

So he stayed where he was, his eyes moving from Lambeau to the tip of the cigarette to the growing gray-white ash, the now-spilling ash. Lambeau was oblivious. And whatever he was saying, Hock didn't really hear, distracted by a future that might have had him reciting a hundred "Our Fathers." Maybe two hundred. Maybe the priests would just expel him. Ashes to ashes, as they say.

In John Hock's life, a priest's direction would always trump that of an NFL coach. When Lambeau left Santa Clara, he had Hennessy's signature, but not Hock's. Hock would eventually study his contract and sign with the Cardinals, but his first priority had to be exorcising his room of Lambeau's transgression.

◆

ON GAME DAY IN 1953, the Los Angeles Memorial Coliseum is a small world within a small world. The NFL is a dozen teams, not the thirty-two it will one day become. Each of those twelve teams carries about thirty-six players on its roster, and when you add coaches that gives the league a population of about five hundred. The NFL in 1953 is not a city; it's not even a small town. It's a neighborhood.

Duane Putnam, for example—the guard who will start tonight for the Rams on the left side of the offensive line—played college football with Washington's five-foot-seven-inch quarterback, the "Little General," Eddie LeBaron. And Leon McLaughlin, the Rams center, played for UCLA the day the Bruins lost to Hock's Broncos. As Hock fits pads over his shoulders in the Rams locker room, his ash-spilling coach with the Cardinals, Curly Lambeau, is a quick walk away, now in his second season as Washington's head man. Jerry Hennessy—Hock's good friend and teammate from

Chicago, Santa Clara, and Mount Carmel High—is also in the visitor's locker room, having followed Lambeau from Chicago. Maybe John and Jerry will get together after the game. The hour will be late, but it would be pleasant to sit in the dark of the backyard next to St. Brigid's Church and listen to the city's night sounds and let Mother Hock's cooking and a few beers ease the aches and bruises.

So, yes, the NFL is a neighborhood—but it's a neighborhood of a particular kind. Only men live there, and they know each other not just by shared histories, but through weekly collisions, a repeated violent intimacy. Forget who mows the lawn each week and who doesn't, whose car left an oil stain in the driveway, and who voted for Eisenhower. What these men know about each other is deeper. They know each other's weight and speed, their breath and sweat. They know soft flesh and sharp bone. They know where each other has been broken. They know, especially if they are offensive linemen, that it is true what a poet will one day write: *they live in a closed world, a small space few can share*. It exists, that space, in moments. A few seconds of strain, of giving everything you've got, and then it's over. To live in that space requires you to live in it again and again, play after play, through practices and games, everything you've got, and then again, everything, and again. No matter how it hurts, you tolerate the pain, and you endure the repetition for only one reason: you feel alive in that small space, which becomes something like home.

Now, the five-ring circus is finishing its act. The tumblers have tumbled, the clowns clowned. Time for the players to don their helmets and jog out through a dark tunnel to emerge where the lawn is green and mown, the fans eager, and the stadium lights ablaze.

◆

THE RAMS KICK OFF, and Washington needs only four plays to get two first downs. On three of them the runner is Charley "Choo-Choo" Justice. In this same game a year before, Justice rampaged through Los Angeles's defense, averaging eighteen yards with each carry. That ended—along with much of his season—on a play in the third quarter when two Rams tackled him and his left wrist fractured. Now he's running right and left, shifting and shaking Rams defenders as if he wants payback. Add a pass from the Little General, and the visiting team has its first touchdown on its first possession, and a 7–0 lead, just that fast.

The Rams run right back—literally. In a series that doesn't include a single pass play, Los Angeles running backs follow blocks made by Hock, Putnam, and company. After a twenty-three-yard rumble by Paul "Tank" Younger puts the Rams in range, Professor Pool sends the Toeless Wonder out to kick a sixteen-yard field goal, and Los Angeles trails Washington, 7–3.

Back and forth they go, Younger and Justice leading each team's efforts. Now and then LeBaron and Van Brocklin try a pass, but their coaches call the plays, and tonight Lambeau and Pool seem most interested in the ground game.

But look at the Rams' jerseys! Those guys can't keep their shirts on. Turns out somebody with the organization had the not-so ingenious idea to save money with jerseys that would tear away rather than rip. Seems like every down the Rams are reattaching their uniforms. Betcha those won't catch on.

Wait. Look. There goes Skeet Quinlan for the Rams! Twenty-four yards and a touchdown! Los Angeles takes the lead, 10–7, heading into halftime.

Now the football players have cleared the field, and here's Art Linkletter, our master of ceremonies, to say a few words about the *Los Angeles Times* Charities and the *Times* Boys Club. More than 2,500 boys have enjoyed the lessons and activities they've found there, and this game, played annually since the Rams arrived in Los Angeles in 1946, has raised more than six hundred thousand dollars, which built the boys club, and now equips and maintains it.

A good man, that Mr. Linkletter. A gentle soul. He's like the next-door neighbor you wish you had. In fact, because of his radio and television programs, such as *Kids Say the Darndest Things*, people here at the coliseum do have a sense that they know him. He might be famous, but he's not untouchable like a Rockefeller or a Queen Elizabeth.

You could say the same for Ann Miller, who danced with Fred Astaire in *Easter Parade* and who is out there on the field performing now. She was raised by a single mother who moved with her daughter from Texas to right here in Los Angeles. One time, Ann might have *actually* been the little girl who lived next door. Her mother might have borrowed sugar from you.

And Danny Kaye? He's a stitch, with that nonsense "git-gat-giddle with a geet-ga-zay," sounding like something you'd get if you recorded a toddler trying to speak Yiddish and then sped up the voice ten or twelve times. But his parents were immigrants, his father a tailor. In that movie *Walter Mitty*, he played a Joe Schmoe who dreamed of ways his life could be different, and isn't that just like you and me?

Sure, they're celebrities, and maybe their lives are a little easier for all that, or maybe not. The Rams are celebrities, too, but Duane Putnam served in an army artillery unit just like any guy might have. And John Hock, he lives with his folks a few blocks from here and goes to Mass every Sunday.

Celebrity is a funny thing these days. It doesn't seem to mean you're untouchable. In fact, maybe it means you're more touchable. You're everybody's neighbor. Football player or movie star, you really are just like us.

◆

"A jester's chief employment is to kill himself for your enjoyment."

—*Danny Kaye*, The Court Jester, *1955*

THANKS TO BOB WATERFIELD and Jane Russell, the Rams arrived in Southern California already married to Hollywood.

Wags joked that President Dan Reeves had moved the team from Cleveland just to keep the Waterfields happy. Even if that wasn't true, Reeves must have recognized the advantage in publicity and ticket sales that could come with bringing a quarterback married to a silver-screen bombshell into Hollywood's backyard. Maybe their marriage also gave him an inkling how enterprises that seemed so severely different—showbiz and football—could make a connection as natural as the ocean with the beach.

After all, pro football and Hollywood's concerns met at the same place: the ticket booth. The common goal was to get Mr. and Mrs. Main Street through the turnstile and into the seats. Entertainment for the populace. Let high society have its tennis clubs and opera; football and showbiz were for everybody else.

And those folks at the movie theater on Saturday night, who might also be at the game on Sunday, got much the same thing from both experiences. Good guys to cheer and bad guys to boo, drama and stories, climactic moments, and a glimpse of people who could do what others only dreamed of. Tank Younger's footwork and Norm Van Brocklin's floating bubble passes were in their ways just as astonishing as Danny Kaye's inimitable "git-gat" and Ann Miller's super-speed tap dancing. Westerns demanded that actors ride horses, throw punches, get shot. Comedy depended on a poke in the eye, a bump on the noggin, a pratfall. As Kaye once sang in a film, his job was to kill himself for the audience's enjoyment. Football players did that, too. In the end, movie or television star, quarterback or offensive guard, they were all entertainers, all workers in an industry. They were labor, not capital.

This was an important distinction in LA society. Hollywood's talent, no matter how famous or rich, was more likely to chum around with a bunch of football players than with Los Angeles's wealthy elites. Historian Kevin Starr has described Los Angeles in the 1950s as a city shaped by an oligarchy, built and ruled by people who had money from sources other than Hollywood. Some had earned their fortunes through land development or railroads or oil. Others had inherited it from family, or brought it with them when they left the East Coast to retire to California. The oligarchs were often Wasp-ish, sometimes anti-Semitic, concerned with reputation and background. They were wary of a movie industry that still carried a whiff of immorality dating back to nineteenth-century burlesque and vaudeville, a taint kept alive by scandal sheets that reported Hollywood's crime, vice, and broken taboos. Even movie and television stars who remained scandal free might not find themselves mingling with the Pauleys or the

Firestones or the other movers and shakers. Having money was not the same as having a history of money, and many entertainers, like players for the Rams, had come from humble origins. Jane Russell's dad was an office manager. Art Linkletter left home after high school to hop freight trains, finding itinerant work as a meatpacker and busboy; before hitting it big, he broadcast from state fairs. Few Hollywood or television stars had been raised on art openings and opera and debutante balls.

But football? Many a marquee name could feel at home watching from the fifty-yard line.

In fact, even before the Rams arrived in Los Angeles, another pro football team had won the backing of some of Hollywood's biggest names. The Los Angeles Dons, part of an upstart league called the All-America Football Conference, played its first game in the Los Angeles Memorial Coliseum two weeks before the Rams kicked off their season. The Dons' owners included Bob Hope, Bing Crosby, Don Ameche, and Louis B. Mayer, the studio chief. But the Dons and the AAFC only lasted four years, and when the league shut down it left the Rams alone as Hollywood's Team.

Each party conveyed to the other a particular kind of celebrity. When Hollywood showed up for Rams games, it was as much an endorsement as when Elizabeth Taylor appeared in an ad for shampoo or John Wayne in one for cigarettes. A movie star in the stands or in the press box also brought a level of festivity and excitement to games.

For the movies, an industry based on faked sets and faked deaths and faked love, football players offered a sense of bruising physical reality to counter Hollywood's obvious artifice. A cameo from a handsome guy who really did get tackled, who really did suffer bruises and sprains, gave the movies grit and toughness. There was the novelty, too, of a football player acting—or trying to.

When the Rams held season-ending banquets, the entertainment could include Harry James and Betty Grable. Jerry Lewis and Bob Hope might make a few jokes at a player's expense. In the game program that night when John Hock made his Rams debut against Washington, special note was made that three Rams— Leon McLaughlin, Jim Winkler, and Tank Younger— earned off-season money working as extras in films. By 1953, Woody Strode, who played briefly for the Rams after their arrival in Los Angeles, was deep into a long film career that would see him in several westerns and as a gladiator who fights Kirk Douglas in *Spartacus*.

Twice, the entire Rams squad portrayed football teams in film, including in a 1949 effort called *Easy Living*, starring Victor Mature as a quarterback facing the end of his career and dealing with a wife who doesn't love has-beens. "Loving you is like getting kicked in the heart," Victor Mature seems to say on a poster advertising the movie, "—only in football, I get paid for it!"

And, of course, there was Jane Russell, sitting in section eight of the coliseum with the other Rams wives, then with them again at the locker room as they waited for their husbands to emerge.

"She was always with us after games," recalled Patty Putnam, Duane's wife, years later, "and she was just as common as anybody else. She never got all dressed up, she never put on airs."

Hollywood: at a Rams game, it was just the good-looking guy and gal next door.

◆

AT HALFTIME ON THIS night of the *Times* Charities Game against Washington, the Rams locker room is not a happy place. Sitting players look at their knees. Hamp Pool clears his throat. His team played as bad in the first half as he'd felt that morning.

No. The team played worse.

Sloppy. Jittery. Embarrassing. The Rams had been one of the league's best teams the season before, losing only three games and each of those to same team: the Detroit Lions. Washington had been one of the league's worst teams. Tonight's game should be a drubbing.

Yet Rams defensive tackles can't seem to catch anybody running in a burgundy uniform. Washington had used some nine different running backs, and it didn't matter who carried the ball, the Rams couldn't grab them. In fact, the visitors have already amassed 171 yards by running the ball, almost twice as much as the Rams. One hundred seventy-one! That's a good night for most teams, and there's still a half to play.

It's amazing, really, that the Rams even have the lead. For that, they can thank Washington's coach, Curly Lambeau. Leading 7–3 and poised five yards from the end zone, Washington and Lambeau were looking at fourth down and a decision. The conventional thinking is to take the easy points—kick the field goal—when your team holds the lead. Why risk trying for the touchdown and failing? But to Pool's surprise, Lambeau kept his place kicker on the bench. He was going to go for the touchdown. "Boy, there's a break," Pool said, turning to an assistant coach with him on the sideline. Then the two watched as Washington's LeBaron dropped back to pass for the touchdown, only nobody caught the ball. The visitors had squandered their opportunity.

Now, if only the Rams can rack up a few more points in the second half. Where's that speedy, high-scoring offense Pool envisioned in training camp? With the exception of Tank Younger, the Rams look as if they're playing in cement shoes. Worse, the offensive linemen have missed assignments and even blocked the wrong players. How many passes has Van Brocklin completed? Six? Only *six*? But how's he supposed to throw if he's got Washington's linemen chasing him all over the field. C'mon, guys, make your blocks. You play this badly in the second half, and Dutch might finish with only twelve pass completions.

When was the last time he completed only twelve passes? Fifth grade?

Maybe Waterfield would have made a difference, but Waterfield isn't here, and he's not coming back. The Rams have to learn to live without him. To win without him. To win a championship without him.

Halftime's almost over. Time to stop staring at those knees, boys. Rookies, you want a spot on this team? Earn it. Veterans, show them how. If you've got people in the stadium who know you, like Hock here, give them a reason to be proud. Now's the time. Get out there and hit somebody. Hit 'em hard.

And for God's sake, offense, make sure it's the *right* somebody.

CHAPTER 4

Grids and Gridirons

ALL THROUGH THE THIRD quarter and into the opening seconds of the fourth, Rams do indeed hit Redskins and Redskins hit Rams, but nothing much changes–especially not the score. But then, with his team trailing, 10-7, Washington's "Little General," Eddie LeBaron drops back to pass. It's a desperate ploy; he's only completed two passes all night, and there's no reason to believe he'll succeed this time.

LeBaron is tiny. Though the program lists him as five foot nine, he's really two inches shorter, something Washington's owner doesn't want the world—and especially opponents—to know. Thus, every program and roster sheet print the five foot nine lie. But reality is reality, and when a Ram rookie who is seven inches taller and some sixty pounds heavier crashes into LeBaron, the Little General sees stars. On the sidelines, the diagnosis is concussion, and Eddie LeBaron is out of the game.

Washington's coach, Curly Lambeau, has a rookie quarterback listed as LeBaron's back-up, but for some reason he keeps that youngster on the sidelines. Maybe the kid hasn't had time to learn the playbook, or maybe Lambeau just doesn't trust rookies. Whatever the reason, Lambeau sends in Harry Gilmer, a regular at running back who has in past seasons played some quarterback for Washington. In fact, as a sophomore at the University of Alabama, Gilmer gained some fame with an unconventional throwing style called the "jump pass." He'd leap before he threw, twisting his hips and snapping his body like a whip to add force to his throw. Tonight, though, Harry doesn't have much whip or jump. He has played every defensive down for Washington and half of the offensive ones. Bob Oates, reporting from the press box for the *Examiner*, watches Gilmer and sees a man so exhausted he can hardly bend over to take the ball on the snap. Once, Gilmer even drops it.

Two plays after LeBaron's brain bruise, Washington punts. Awaiting the ball for the Rams is Woodley Lewis, a Los Angeles native said to have the fleetest foot speed on the team. At the Rams' twenty-one-yard line, Lewis catches the ball, then darts and dodges. One tackler nearly grabs him, then a second and a third, but Lewis evades each to find the edge of the field. From there, it's an all-out sprint along the sideline, and no one is faster. Touchdown, Rams! The Toeless Wonder kicks the extra point, and Los Angeles now leads, 17–7.

The clock shows that there's time left, but everyone knows the game is decided. The fans know it, the reporters know it, the players do, too. Washington and Gilmer try, but for the rest of the game they can't manage even a single first down. The visitors are impotent, finished. Because they can, the Rams add a field goal. Final score: 20–7.

Fans applaud and cheer as the last seconds tick off, but it's not a full-throated whoop and holler. What they witnessed was far from the Rams' best effort. Wanting to test his new guys, Coach Hamp Pool tried out two, three, sometimes four players at every position except quarterback. John Hock played left guard, but so did two others. Trying to win that way is like trying to tune up a Chevy with parts from a Ford. And an Oldsmobile. Also a Buick. The fans know this, and they know the game was only an exhibition, more about charity and the Boys Club and a night of family entertainment than it was about top-notch football.

Nevertheless, the home team won, so the paying public shows its respect, then crowds the exits. For all the early hubbub, there's little reason to linger. It's late on a Wednesday night, after all. There's work tomorrow—at the factory, the office, the car dealership.

Outside the stadium, cars and charter buses inch from parking lots, drivers with feet tapping the brake pedal more often than the gas. Eventually, everyone will make it home—west to the valley, or northeast to Pasadena; a short drive to Echo Park, a long haul southeast to Orange County or directly south to Long Beach. As they go people will orient themselves, recalling the mountains that are north, and they'll know by the ancient grids of Los Angeles's streets, first mapped in 1781, how to get where they mean to go.

◆

"DRIVE FROM THE OCEAN to Los Angeles," writes D. J. Waldie in *Holy Land*, "and you'll stay on the same grid of streets. The drive passes through suburb after suburb without interruption."

Angelenos have mostly constructed their city as if it is a series of giant checkerboards with streets running north to south, east to west. Downtown is an exception, though a slight one: its grid is angled so on a map it looks like Xs. This street pattern helps drivers find their way. Keep in mind landmark roads—Wilshire Boulevard or Adams Boulevard, Vermont or Western Avenues—and you can't get lost. You can always find a road or an intersection that is familiar and from there trace the way home. There is nothing innovative about these grids, which have their origins in Spanish colonial history. They are utterly predictable, measured with precision. As an example, in Waldie's suburb of Lakewood:

"Every block is divided into the common grid of fifty-by-one-hundred-foot lots…

"The streets do not curve or offer vistas. The street grid always intersects at right angles…

"The sidewalk is four feet wide. The street is forty feet wide. The strip of lawn between the street and the sidewalk is seven feet. The setback from the curb to the house is twenty feet…

"This pattern—of asphalt, grass, concrete, grass—is as regular as any thought of God's…

"The necessary illusion is predictability."

For this generation of Angelenos, predictability is an asset. It is a virtue. It is a comfort. Thirty or forty years from now people of subsequent generations might call Los Angeles's map and its endless grids a monotonous sprawl, but in 1953 the grids offer a respite. The people who drive these roads have lived with economic uncertainty through the Depression. As soldiers during World War II, they island-hopped the Pacific from deadly beachhead to deadly beachhead. They've been warned that anyone might be a communist infiltrator—from government officials to the people who write screenplays for Hollywood films. Just today, they learned that the Soviets have the H-bomb, putting the world's future in doubt. For these people—including the eighty thousand driving home after tonight's Rams game, their cares lifted by Danny Kaye and the night's hero, Woodley Lewis—for them, the great Los Angeles grid is a boon, a simple way home.

Perhaps an affinity for what is simple and unambiguous offers another reason why these fans love football as they do, the tens of thousands who come to watch this sport played on a grid. Sportswriters call the football field a gridiron, a word with origins in a medieval torture device used to roast heretics—but really, it's a lovely field of green, neatly and precisely mapped. One hundred yards from end zone to end zone. Every three feet a new chalk line, every five yards a number—twenty-five, thirty, thirty-five—like addresses on a neighborhood block, clarifying the boundaries of what's allowed and what's not so that a player always knows where he is, where he needs to be (fans know, too). Teams must move ten yards for a first down, another try. The home team camps on one side of the field, the visitors on the opposite. This gridiron, flat as a valley floor, makes football predictable, defined and finite, limited in space. Here there are no H-bombs, and if there are Commie infiltrators, well, they're watching the game, too. On this field, the world is easily understood, and any surprise is a surprise on a human scale: Woodley Lewis dancing through tackles, a man without toes on one foot kicking field goals. These things seem grand, and they are, but only because so many people pay money to witness them. In football, the necessary illusion is significance, what the fans pay to watch is what only truly matters. Eighty thousand people gather, bound by an agreement that for these few hours, what happens on the gridiron is momentous, life's only essential thing.

◆

NOW THAT THE GAME has ended, let Hollywood's camera again find John Hock. The view is as if from the stadium's seats, but near enough to the field that we can make out his face as he laughs at something Duane Putnam leans near to say—some wry line, perhaps, about those silly tear-away jerseys. Sweaty and grass-stained, his forearms bruised from blocking, Hock keeps his head up, his massive chin lifted. Putter spits, his lip swollen with chaw. Then, a cutaway, and the picture is a close-up of Van Brocklin who barks and cocks a thumb, the signal from the captain that the boys need to hit the locker room. Cutaway once more, as en masse the players shift, then the camera eye focuses again on Hock in their midst. Even now, after his long night, there's power in his movement, there's momentum. This early in the season his legs recover quickly, so he jogs with his teammates into the lit tunnel that leads into the stadium's depths, the men's cleats clackety-clacking across the concrete.

They've earned a shower, these Rams, and maybe ice bags on sore shoulders and knees, and afterward a cold bottle of beer. Soon enough they'll be back to Redlands, that oven in the desert.

Tomorrow, though, at his parents' house, John Hock can sleep late. No coach will wake him with some prerecorded *ready-set-hut*, and he's past the age when an early tap on his bedroom window summoned him to serve the Mass. Should one of St. Brigid's priests stop by, he'll want only coffee and conversation about the game. John will say he's grateful for the win, but that the Rams know they can play better. He can play better, too. If pressed, he'll admit he got a few licks in, and he took a few. He'll offer brief answers to the priest's questions, hoping the subject will change. He'll have no complaints, though he knows why Van Brocklin had so little time to throw. Van Brocklin's linemen couldn't protect him because an offensive line needs machine-like teamwork and that's impossible to develop when coaches are switching players at a dizzying pace. Against Washington, the Rams tried out sixteen fellows at the five offensive line positions. No one found a rhythm, because there was no rhythm. No linemen could practice teamwork, because who were your teammates? But that's the exhibition season for you. Once the coaches could settle on a roster, once Hock lines up regularly with the Putter and Charlie Toogood and Leon McLaughlin—the starters—to play an entire game, maybe then the offense will become the scoring machine Coach Pool says he wants.

But he won't tell the priest any of that.

What he will say, if the priest stops by, is that this was only an exhibition. It's a long season, and yes, Father, you're right, who knows what might happen. A championship?

We've got as good a chance as any. You like cream with your coffee, Father, isn't that right?

◆

IN THE LOCKER ROOM, Rams players know that they have escaped something, and they know which players rescued them: Paul "Tank" Younger, whose pile driving runs kept the Rams advancing when nothing else worked; and Woodley Lewis, who scored the game-clinching touchdown. Rightly, the newspapers will laud the pair the next day. What the *Times* and the *Examiner* will not mention, though, is the irony that the Rams won, and the Redskins were beaten, because of two men not welcome on Washington's roster.

Nowhere in the NFL rule book does it prohibit black players like Younger or Lewis from suiting up for an NFL team. In the league's earliest years, rosters included players both white and black (and Native American, including Jim Thorpe with the New York Giants and Chicago Cardinals, among others). But in 1933, for reasons that are murky and may have been different for each team, NFL owners adopted an unwritten edict: no Negro players on the field.

In 1953, Washington's owner, George Preston Marshall, still lives by that rule.

Six seasons earlier, the Rams were the first to break it.

Throughout the 1940s and '50s, the Rams and President Dan Reeves proved themselves innovators in many ways—the move west from Cleveland, the execution of a high-scoring passing game like never before, the marketing of a brand when Fred Gehrke painted gold horns on the team's helmets—but none of those ground-breaking changes involved questions of justice, morality, or human dignity. Welcoming black players to their roster could be called another Rams' innovation; it changed the established way of fielding an NFL team. But for Reeves and the Rams, breaking the league's unwritten rule against black players was foremost a matter of political expedience, integration as a means rather than an end in itself. Presented with an opportunity to integrate their team and thus reintegrate the league, the Rams took it—not to make history or because it was the right thing to do, but to guarantee themselves a chance to play in Los Angeles's Memorial Coliseum.

◆

On Tuesday, January 15, 1946, a meeting happened at the coliseum offices that would change the course of professional football history.

To that meeting came Charles Walsh, nicknamed "Chile" (sometimes spelled "Chili"), a football alum and graduate of LA's Hollywood High School, who had decades earlier moved to the Midwest but who still called Los Angeles his hometown. Just shy of forty-three years old, he was also general manager of what had been, until a few days earlier, the Cleveland Rams. And he was at the pinnacle of his football career.

A month and a day ago he'd been in Cleveland, bundled up in below-zero temperatures, watching rookie Bob Waterfield lead the Rams past the Washington Redskins, 15–14, to win their first NFL championship. And three days before this trip to Los Angeles, Walsh had been at the Commodore Hotel in New York City cajoling NFL owners into letting their now league-champion Rams scamper off to the West Coast.

When that vote went the Rams' way, it meant the team had bested the league twice in one month: once on the field, once in owners' meetings, and Walsh had been central to both efforts. Now a third challenge awaited him here in Los Angeles. His assignment: to secure a lease so the team could play its games at the Los Angeles Memorial Coliseum, the city's crown jewel of sports venues.

Walsh's boss, Rams president Dan Reeves, wanted to call the coliseum home, and it's easy to understand why.

Consider its size. Built of reinforced concrete and expanded when Los Angeles hosted the 1932 Olympics, the coliseum could hold more than one hundred thousand people. One hundred thousand ticket-paying, program-buying, hot-dog-eating fans.

A crowd of forty-six thousand had been considered impressive in Cleveland.

Then, consider the coliseum's aesthetics. Modeled on the one built in ancient Rome, the elliptical stadium featured at its east end a series of columns and arches, topped by a triumphal arch upon which the Olympic Torch had once burned. The trappings gave any sport played in the coliseum the grand, legendary quality of an epic.

Then, understand its exclusivity. USC's mighty Trojans called the coliseum home, and UCLA played some football games there, too. The nine-man commission that governed the coliseum's use was known to favor its hometown college heroes and had never opened the stadium to any of the small-time professional football teams that in the 1940s and 1950s called Los Angeles home. The Trojans and the Bruins liked it that way.

To play in such a local landmark would confer immediate legitimacy. It would say: Behold, our new champions! Our *Los Angeles* Rams!

But both Reeves and Walsh knew it wouldn't be easy to win a lease, not with opposition from USC and UCLA. So Walsh, accompanied by the team's attorney, had come to his hometown bearing a gift for the commission and the city.

If granted the lease, Walsh promised, the Rams' first game in the stadium would be a headline-grabbing exhibition matchup: a replay of that winter's NFL championship against the Redskins. Moreover, the profits would go to charity. They'd call it the *Times* Charities Game, and if it was successful, the Rams and Redskins would play it every year. The offer was politically savvy given the power wielded in Los Angeles by the *Times*' owners, the Chandler family, and given patriarch Harry Chandler's influential role in the coliseum's financing and construction in the early 1920s.

How could the commission say no?

◆

THEY NUMBERED THREE, THE men—all African-American, all journalists writing for newspapers that served black communities—who came to the coliseum commission meeting that Tuesday in January 1946 to take on Chile Walsh and the Rams and through them the entire National Football League.

Herman Hill, who had played basketball at USC, worked as the West Coast editor of the *Pittsburgh Courier*, one of the nation's most prominent African-American newspapers. Abie Robinson oversaw the sports section at the *Los Angeles Sentinel*. And William Claire "Halley" Harding was a columnist for the *Los Angeles Tribune*, a man whose college career included football, basketball, and baseball—but who also boxed, acted, and fought with all his being against prejudiced whites (ofays, he called them) to create fair opportunities for black Americans. "God bless him," Herman Hill wrote years later in a letter to *Ebony* magazine, excerpts of which were published in 1970. "Halley used to tell ofays he got up every morning and proceeded to put his *boxing gloves* on as soon as he shaved and showered, to get ready to battle them and their prejudices!"

Hill, Robinson, and Harding sat together that day the coliseum commission considered the Rams' request for a lease. They were the only African-American men in the room—there to demand justice, to change history, to integrate professional football.

Professional football because it was not the Rams alone that day who wanted a lease to play pro football in the coliseum. An upstart league—the All-American Football Conference—had formed, and it included a Los Angeles franchise called the Dons, owned in part by Hollywood stars Don Ameche and Bing Crosby. Hill, Robinson, and Harding wanted to guarantee an integrated Dons, too.

The three sat listening while the teams made their pitches. Then, Commission Chairman Leonard Roach asked whether anyone else would like to speak regarding the teams' requests.

"That was our cue," Hill wrote in his letter to *Ebony*. "As a matter of fact, we had contacted Roach earlier and told him what we had planned to do—and he said, 'This will be your cue.'"

Halley Harding rose, metaphoric boxing gloves laced.

He spoke only a few minutes, and no record exists of his precise words. But those in the room remembered, and through their accounts published in books and magazines, the spirit of what Harding said survives.

Harding combined a journalist's brevity with a boxer's pugnacity to remind the commissioners—and Chile Walsh—that sports had long been integrated in California. Recall, he said, the UCLA team that featured future Rams quarterback Bob Waterfield playing alongside Kenny Washington and Woodrow Wilson Strode, both African-American and native to Los Angeles. Do not forget, he said, that the NFL was integrated at its start. He invoked the spirits of Fritz Pollard, who had coached an NFL team, and the famous Paul Robeson, who went from the Akron Pros and Milwaukee Badgers to a career in movies and theater. How can opportunity be denied to black players, Harding asked, when in the great war just won, black troops fought and died equally with their white fellows? Finally, he said, no public facility in Los Angeles ought to be leased to an organization that practices segregation. No organization that denies opportunities to people because of their race ought to be welcome in the City of Angels.

Chile Walsh hadn't expected this welcome home.

"He turned pale," Hill wrote, "and started to stutter."

Walsh denied that the Rams practiced discrimination. There's nothing in the rule book, he said, that bans black athletes.

Unwritten is not the same as nonexistent, said Harding. Look at the proof: no black man had played in the NFL in thirteen years. Kenny Washington, he noted, had been, arguably, the best football player in the country when he finished at UCLA, yet no NFL team drafted him or invited him to try out. Instead, he'd played football in Los Angeles for a team in a small regional league.

When Harding gave up the floor, the coliseum's commissioners began throwing their own punches. One asked whether the Rams would dare to bar Kenny Washington.

The Rams' attorney, according to Hill's letter, announced that "any qualified Negro could play with the Rams." Added Walsh: "Kenny Washington is invited by me at this moment to try out for the Los Angeles Rams."

Though the meeting ended without the commission granting a lease, Harding, Hill, and other African-American sportswriters kept pressure on Rams officials, even meeting with them at the Last Word Club on South Central Avenue at the heart of Los Angeles's black community. Negotiations continued, and the commission did eventually give both the Rams and Dons permission to use the coliseum.

The Rams then signed Kenny Washington to a contract, announced on March 21 at a press conference from the team's temporary headquarters, downtown's elegant Alexandria Hotel. A short while later, the team signed Woody Strode, Washington's friend and former UCLA teammate, in part to provide a roommate for Washington on road trips. When the Rams at last kicked off against the Redskins in the inaugural *Times* Charities Game—on the gridiron in Los Angeles's

Memorial Coliseum—for the first time since 1933 black men wore the uniform of an NFL team in a game between NFL teams.

But wear the uniform is about all they did.

In his book, *Goal Dust*, written with Sam Young, Woody Strode notes that Rams coaches sent Washington into that first exhibition game for only one play in the first half, then for a few more in the game's final minutes. Strode himself watched from the sidelines.

That pattern foretold their careers. Washington, a running back who relied as much on quickness as strength, had joined the Rams already having endured multiple knee surgeries. With number thirteen on his jersey, his weary expression suggested a man who had worked hard for too long a time, whose body had aged too fast. He carried the ball only twenty-three times in his first season, and his time in the NFL lasted a mere three years. As for Strode, the Rams cut him in his second season, just after the *Times* Charities Game. Believing he had the skill and athleticism to succeed in the NFL and that the Rams coaches intentionally misused him, Strode ended his historic career embarrassed and angry. Famously, he told a reporter from *Sports Illustrated*, "If I have to integrate heaven, I don't want to go."

As if to prove that signing Washington and Strode was a token gesture to win the coliseum lease and sell tickets to LA's black community—less an innovation in how NFL teams could be built, and more a gimmick to make money—a Rams assistant coach once said, "I doubt we would have been interested in Washington if we had stayed in Cleveland."

So if the reintegration of the NFL was a victory, it hardly belonged to the Rams, who did the right thing out of political expedience and with little gusto. No, the victory belonged to Los Angeles itself, its culture of integration in sports, its public officials who were willing to push for change, and especially to Harding, Robinson, and Hill. Without ever playing a down of NFL football, they changed the league forever.

◆

BY 1953, WHEN JOHN Hock had joined the Rams and the team played its ninth *Times* Charities Game against Washington, black players had not only been integrated, for the Rams, they had become integral.

Dick "Night Train" Lane's fourteen interceptions in 1952—his rookie season—set a league record that still stands more than sixty years later. What remains untallied were the number of players he knocked out of games. His hits were feral and feared, top-speed collisions pitting Night Train's forearm and shoulder against a receiver's head and neck. The Night Train Necktie, players called it, with equal parts admiration and apprehension—even after the league outlawed it.

Harry Thompson had started at right guard for the Rams in 1951, when they won the NFL championship by beating the Cleveland Browns. Now he was a substitute, suiting up in case any starting offensive lineman was ever hurt. Decades later, sportswriter Bob Oates would remember him in the pages of the *Times* as self-sacrificing, a man who almost always got cut, but somehow stayed on the roster.

Fleet-footed Woodley Lewis played halfback and defensive back, but he was most dangerous when awaiting a kick-off or punt. In an open field, he dazzled.

"Deacon" Dan Towler and Paul "Tank" Younger rumbled as part of what sportswriters had dubbed "The Bull Elephant Backfield." Each weighed nearly 230 pounds, making them as big—or bigger—than the linemen blocking for them.

But that was only five. Verdese Carter, John Hock's teammate at Camp Drake in Japan, would be cut before the start of 1953's regular season.

Five out of thirty-five. The Rams were still majority white, like the county in which they played, which had about one black and one Hispanic resident for every fifteen Caucasians—less integrated even than the Rams locker room.

In 1953, there were grids on the city's map that white people wanted to keep for themselves—bright white lines across which black people couldn't buy homes without incident or penalty. That June, even as the Rams entered training camp, the United States Supreme Court handed down a decision that declared it unconstitutional for white Los Angeles homeowners to sue Leola Jackson, their white neighbor, who violated her development's covenants by selling her house to a "non-Caucasian" family. That spring, the *California Eagle*, perhaps LA's most prominent African-American newspaper, reported that threats and attempts at intimidation greeted black families moving into then working-class-white Compton. White and black youths clashed in school yards. Black families armed themselves against crowds of whites gathering outside their homes chanting "protect our children." Black players who were welcome in the Rams' locker room and cheered by fans would likely have been shunned in majority white neighborhoods no matter how well they tackled or ran.

On the road, players still found themselves segregated. When they couldn't stay in a hotel with the rest of the team—as they couldn't in Pennsylvania, or for exhibition games in Arkansas and Alabama, or in Chicago where they stayed in Southside hotels while white players bedded down on the Gold Coast—black players stayed with people who opened their homes, or they bunked in separate hotels.

Back home was better. A little.

In a group photograph of the Rams Kick-Off Banquet at the Los Angeles Biltmore Hotel in 1954, there is a sea of white faces in the hall, hundreds of revelers, including players, smiling up toward the camera. One needs a magnifying glass to find faces that might be African-American. Way in the back there are two. Maybe.

The Rams, the NFL, and Los Angeles still had much work to do.

"I think every athlete had to be embarrassed in those times," said Sam Huff. "Bobby Mitchell was the first black [player] to come to the Washington Redskins and the team was the last to have a black player. I know it's part of history, but it's a part of history I don't like."

◆

But consider this: in 1953, John Hock and Duane Putnam, both white men playing the NFL's most anonymous positions, were throwing their bodies in harm's way to make spaces through which black men found touchdowns and glory and headlines and admiration.

◆

Was it a twist? A blow? Both?

Whichever, in his first season with the Rams, John Hock's knee had gotten wonky during one of the last exhibition games, and now he needed to give it ice and rest. It wasn't just pain. Pain, he could ignore. It was swelling, stiffness, the way the knee didn't quite work right.

He needed the joint for those quick side cuts—the Rams offense called for linemen who could shift side-to-side quick as a finger-snap. And he needed the knee to plant, to make a foundation that allowed him to hold his blocks. Rules kept offensive linemen from using their hands against a defender—no grabbing, no shoving, no nothing. Get caught with your palms out and you might cost your team a five-yard penalty. So technique called for linemen to raise their arms like chicken wings, hands near each other at the center of the chest, and push from the shoulders. As linemen go, Hock didn't have the strongest legs. His weren't ever going to be compared to coliseum pillars. No, his work depended on his upper body—shoulders, chest, abdomen, back. But he still needed to plant those knees, to brace his powerful torso. Knees were the cornerstones. If one wobbled, the building swayed.

Though not one to fret, Hock must have felt a twinge of concern. The team hadn't yet made its final cuts, and other players had been let go during exhibition seasons because of injuries. Coaches always sought reasons to trim the roster. And Hock was no Van Brocklin or Tank Younger, not a player who over several seasons had earned the right to be carried through injuries. With the Rams, Hock was a rookie. Worse, he was a lineman—the most interchangeable position in the sport.

So you never know.

But when the Rams finished their exhibition season in 1953 and began the regular season—the part of the schedule when games counted in the standings and players at last got paid—Hock's name was on the roster. Even though his knee kept him out of that opener against the New York Giants and Harry Thompson lined up in his spot, he had made the team. Of the final thirty-five, he was one.

Had he doubted? After two seasons away from pro football, he had reason to wonder whether he still had the speed, the skill, the strength, the know-how to play. But if he had doubts, those were gone. Hock had earned a spot with one of the best teams in football—even with his cranky knee.

So when the Rams played the Green Bay Packers in front of some twenty-three thousand people in Milwaukee's County Stadium, Hock was on the field, throwing blocks for Van Brocklin, Younger, and the others. The Rams won that day, and then they won the next week, beating their old nemesis Detroit, the team that had defeated them three times the previous season, including in a game to determine which team would move on to the NFL championship.

By midseason in 1953, the Rams had won five of their first six games and led in the NFL's Western Conference standings. They'd beaten Detroit twice, the last time at the Los Angeles Memorial Coliseum in front of ninety-four thousand fans—only eight thousand shy of filling the coliseum.

A championship? The priest from St. Brigid's might ask again, his coffee black, a ritual repeated.

Sure, Father, John Hock would say. *We've got as good a chance as any.*

CHAPTER 5

Safety

THE 1953 SEASON PROVED cruel to the Rams. At midpoint, they looked like world-beaters. If the NFL was a mountain, the Rams were like their big-horned namesakes, balanced powerfully on the tallest crag. They led the Western Conference standings with five victories against one defeat—and that loss had been only by one point. Twice, the Rams had beaten their chief nemesis, the defending NFL champions, the Detroit Lions.

Then they lost their footing.

A loss to San Francisco—the Rams' in-state rival since the 49ers joined the NFL in, coincidentally, 1949.

A tie with the Chicago Cardinals, perhaps the league's worst team.

Too late, the Rams finally won again, beating the Colts at Baltimore. Detroit had seized the conference lead, and the reigning champs weren't yielding the top spot. A third Rams loss, this time to the lowly Chicago Bears at Wrigley Field, had Rams fans and the team's owners looking toward the next season. The press blamed Van Brocklin, saying he was "struggling through the worst slump of his pro career." Recalling the speed with which Team President Dan Reeves had fired past coaches, sportswriters printed rumors that Hamp Pool's job was in jeopardy. The atmosphere mirrored that of the year's beginning, with players and coaches working to justify their jobs, but with one significant difference. In training camp, that need was coupled with optimism and hope for a season that shone with potential. Now, the work was spiced with disappointment and dissatisfaction over a bungled year.

Into that cauldron, the Baltimore Colts arrived for a game in Los Angeles.

Those poor Baltimore Colts.

A year before, they had been the hapless Dallas Texans, a team with only one victory to its name, so badly run that its owner ended the year having lost nearly a quarter million dollars. Now, as the Baltimore Colts, the players had a city that cared about them and a more successful owner in Carroll Rosenbloom, who would later own the Rams. But on the field, "hapless" still described them. Their starting quarterback had suffered a season-ending shoulder injury a few games before, and they'd already lost seven games, including that one to the Rams in Baltimore, 21–13.

Now, the two teams were to meet again in a game scheduled for a national television broadcast. The Los Angeles Almost-Was's against the Baltimore Never-Had-A-Chances.

Los Angeles fans couldn't generate much enthusiasm. Though ninety-four thousand had shown up to watch the Rams beat Detroit on November 1, that was when their team looked championship bound. Plus, that opponent was a rival and maybe the NFL's best team, a marquee draw in its own right.

Now, a month later, with almost no shot at the playoffs, and facing a lousy opponent with little name recognition, the Rams could muster only twenty-seven thousand fans on that beautiful, seventy-nine-degree afternoon.

That's about seven empty seats for every three taken. That's Rams coming out of the tunnel and being greeted by a vast emptiness, fans scattered here and there like beach sand blown across a Malibu parking lot.

Perhaps the small crowd embarrassed the Rams. Perhaps it angered them.

Because what those fans saw at the coliseum on December 5, 1953, was a one-sided butt-kicking. What those fans saw was a furious and proud Rams team, venting its frustration with a season turned sour. What those fans saw was Dutch Van Brocklin, on the first play of the game, throwing fifty yards to Skeet Quinlan, and only two plays later tossing a touchdown pass to Vitamin Smith.

What they saw was perfectly executed Rams football, just as Coach Hamp Pool had envisioned in training camp.

By the end of the first quarter, the Rams led, 14–0. The Colts' only opportunity to score in that quarter had been a field goal attempt, but Night Train Lane crashed through the Colts' linemen and sprang high to block the kick. And the Rams kept coming. Whatever adjustments Colts coach Keith Molesworth made to his game plan at halftime didn't matter. By the end of the third quarter, the Rams led, 45–0.

Forty-five to zip.

It was the most points the Rams had scored in a game all season. It doubled the scores of their previous two games.

But the afternoon wouldn't end perfectly. The Colts did eventually find some points, and the Hooker, John Hock—in the last game of his first season with his hometown team—played an unwitting role.

◆

LATE IN THE GAME, Hamp Pool decided to give Van Brocklin—and the Colts—a break. He brought Dutch to the bench and sent in a rookie back-up from USC named Rudy Bukich who promptly found himself running a play deep on the Rams' side of the field, so deep that when he dropped back to pass he was standing in his own end zone. Unable to find an open receiver and desperate with the knowledge that the Colts were about to grind him into the grass, Bukich cocked his arm and tossed what one report called a "throw-away."

If the Colts had tackled Bukich in the end zone, they would have been awarded two points—a safety. Embarrassing. A safety would mean Bukich and the Rams offense couldn't take care of business and move the ball forward. It would mean the defense had pushed them right off the field.

So Bukich threw the ball away. He tossed it to John Hock.

Hock was himself still in the end zone as Bukich's "throw-away" pass arrived. He had not practiced for this moment. In fact, if Hock had ever caught a ball in a game, it had probably been years ago. Catching passes had never been his job.

But he caught this one. Hock reached out, grabbed the ball, nestled it against his body. Now he needed to run and get the ball the heck out of the end zone.

Art Donovan meant to stop him.

Art Donovan: a future Hall of Famer, a crew-cut mass of fat and muscle some thirty pounds heavier than the Hooker, a man who famously joked in his Brooklyn accent that the only exercise he ever did was to "lift a twenty-four-ounce can of Schlitz" or "thirteen pushups in thirteen years" and who still managed to crush offensive linemen. "I told [then-coach] Weeb Ewbanks, do you want a gymnast or a football player?"

Donovan plowed into Hock. Another Colt piled on, and together they crumpled the Hooker in the end zone for the safety.

And that was how the game ended, a few minutes later, with the score, 45–2.

It's easy to picture John Hock chuckling after Donovan clambered up off of him. As a lineman, he was used to nobody paying any attention to what he did, except the quarterback, and maybe his father, Mr. Hock, in section eight, or a few friends and the coaches. But here, for one moment, all eyes in the stadium had been on number sixty-three. And in a game with no tension, with the season's smallest crowd, he gave everyone a final pratfall, a *hoop-de-doo* bit of comic relief. And that's the show, folks! Thanks for coming!

It's fun to imagine, too, what a laughing Van Brocklin had to say when ol' Lantern Jaw made it back to the sidelines.

Hey, Hooker! Maybe the Colts will give you their game ball!

◆

THE RAMS WON THEIR next game, too, the last of the season, beating Green Bay, 33–17. Maybe that, combined with the victory over the Colts, saved Hamp Pool's job, because the season ended, and he didn't get fired. His innovations—including that fast snap count—hadn't led to a championship, and Pool would need to come back with something new and better if the Rams were going to improve the results of this season.

In the national championship game, Detroit beat the Cleveland Browns, 17–16. Shortly after, the *Associated Press* named its all-pro team and about half the first-team players were from those two franchises. But there were also a few Rams, including Elroy "Crazylegs" Hirsch and defensive players Andy Robustelli and Don Paul. Several Rams earned Honorable Mention, including Dan Towler, Skeet Quinlan, Norm Van Brocklin, Woodley Lewis, Charlie Toogood, and Night Train Lane. Right up there with them was the Hooker, John Hock.

So, yes, the Rams still had the pieces. They still had the belief. They just needed another try. They needed 1954 to hurry up and arrive.

◆

BUT BEFORE 1954 BEGINS, step back once more to August 1953 and to that *Times* Charities Game featuring Danny Kaye at halftime, the game that put John Hock in the Memorial Coliseum for the first time as a Ram.

The next day in Los Angeles, newspaper sports sections were almost entirely taken up by the Rams, except for an important piece of newspaper real estate, the column written by the *Examiner*'s Vincent X. Flaherty. For most sportswriters, the biggest story the day before had been football, but Flaherty had baseball on his mind.

Flaherty, a Los Angeles transplant, had left a sportswriting job in Washington, DC to follow his older brother who had headed west to pursue an acting career. The younger Flaherty, a fan of the Washington Senators, was also zealous in his belief that Los Angeles needed major league baseball. Bringing baseball to LA had become for him a personal crusade.

And baseball is what he was writing about the morning after John Hock made his debut with the Rams at Memorial Coliseum.

"Del E. Webb," wrote Flaherty, "co-owner of the New York Yankees, is puzzled by the failure of Los Angeles to step up and make a strong organized bid for a major league baseball franchise."

Webb, a California native and famous real estate developer who would one day build Sun City, Arizona, was in Los Angeles overseeing construction of the $14 million Beverly Hilton Hotel on Wilshire Boulevard. He had been a principal owner of the Yankees for nearly a decade. Flaherty dedicated that day's column to Webb's thoughts about Los Angeles and the major leagues.

Webb told Flaherty that "Baltimore, Montreal, and Toronto also have pledged themselves ready to do anything to get a major league team, but Los Angeles has absolutely nothing. Los Angeles had better get a move on fast.

"If Los Angeles doesn't wake up and do something quick," he said, "this town just won't get a team."

That quote must have put Flaherty into a tizzy. In his book about O'Malley and the Dodgers, author Michael D'Antonio describes Flaherty as a "newspaperman, civic booster, and raconteur" who had "poured enormous amounts of time and energy into the cause of bringing the major leagues to Los Angeles" and who had become "a volunteer staff man for the self-appointed Los Angeles Citizens Committee for Major League Baseball. The leaders of this group included Howard Hughes, Conrad Hilton, Louis B. Mayer, and Reese Taylor, the president of Union Oil."

In fact, D'Antonio noted, Flaherty's efforts to consummate deals between the likes of major league owners, financiers from Texas, and Los Angeles's uber-wealthy citizens, drove him to exhaustion and a hospital bed that very August.

The next month, when major league baseball's owners gathered at the Commodore Hotel in New York City for their annual meeting, they listened to proposals from cities interested in winning a baseball team. In particular, the owners wanted to find a new home for the struggling St. Louis Browns. "Baltimore's presentation was the most complete," D'Antonio writes. "The LA group, headed by newly elected mayor Norris Poulson, said they could not put forward a specific ownership group but could raise the money to buy the club within a week." To prove this, Howard Hughes sent a $1 million check.

But Los Angeles's sketchy plans couldn't compete with Baltimore's careful proposal. The owners voted to let Baltimore have the Browns. The next season introduced a new city and team to major league baseball: the Baltimore Orioles.

In Los Angeles, Poulson, Flaherty, and others had to start again. They knew they had allies in both money and politics, including the young and energetic new city councilwoman Roz Wiener. Poulson was conservative, and liberal Wiener had opposed his appointment of a fellow to the library board because the man was a proponent of book burning. But it was clear she wanted Los Angeles to be a great city, and on that the mayor and she might find common ground.

There'd be other opportunities, after all. Los Angeles would have to be united in its effort. And better prepared.

But for now there was no major league baseball in Los Angeles, and the Rams remained safely atop the city's professional sporting world, unrivaled for the mantle of Hollywood's Team.

PART II

CHAPTER 6

The Weights

M R. AND MRS. JOHN Patrick Costello planned their daughter's wedding reception for the backyard. Card tables and folding chairs and a bar, and, because the Costellos had generous neighbors and expected plenty of guests, a second bar behind the house next door. The head table and wedding cake would go in the garage, which was a double garage, set toward the back of the lot, with enough room. That it was a garage didn't really matter. This was south central Los Angeles in June of 1955, and if Hollywood could turn a scrub brush stage set into a jungle or medieval castle for its cameras, then certainly the Costellos could transform their garage for a wedding. Build their own magic kingdom right there at Fourth Avenue and Forty-Eighth Street.

So the bride's uncle and aunt got to work. They lined the interior walls of the garage with vast sheets of pink paper, covering rough-cut two-by-four studs and oil cans. They unrolled strips of crepe paper, letting it sag from the ceiling like ribbon. They hung lacy paper wedding bells that unfolded like accordions. On the tables they arranged plastic daisies and tall tapered candles.

If Los Angeles taught any lesson, it was that a person with imagination could fool a camera, trick the eye. In years to come, when people looked back on photographs of Mr. and Mrs. John Hock posing by their wedding cake, no one would guess that the happy couple toasting with champagne saucers could be anywhere but a pleasant supper club in the valley or a Knights of Columbus banquet hall.

Los Angeles and Southern California kept you guessing that way, even in 1955. You might, for example, stroll down a street and into a gunfight between police and mobsters, only to learn the bullets were blanks and the blood fake. A Chinese temple rising along Hollywood Boulevard, you would come to understand, was only a movie house. The TV show, *Dragnet*, insisted that every episode's story of crime was true; the actor who portrayed the show's hero, Sergeant Joe Friday, was called in by the LAPD to help interview police academy applicants. In Los Angeles of 1955, fantasies and illusions and artifice offered a relentless challenge to reality, so much so that the nature of reality needed to be reconsidered. Even as Bernadette Costello and John Hock pledged on June 25, 1955, "I do," the animation impresario Walt Disney was overseeing the final touches on a $17 million 160-acre fantasy land, perhaps the world's greatest—if not most expensive—illusion, featuring moon trips and Mississippi River rides and a castle—all right there just over thirty miles away in Anaheim.

In such a place as Los Angeles in 1955, a short man becomes tall, a brunette becomes a blonde, a cartoon mouse dances with a snow-white princess. One day on a blind date, you might even step through a door for a St. Patrick's Day dance, as John Patrick Costello's daughter, Bernadette, did in 1954, and glimpse a fellow at the bar, an old friend. You wave to him with enthusiasm—the way you wave to a friend—and that's when you realize you don't recognize that man *at all*, and you just behaved in a very forward way with a stranger.

But a short while later, when that fellow at the bar looks at you again and stands, you aren't so troubled by your mistake. Because he stands and stands—he's so tall and broad-shouldered. Blond, too, with skin so Irish-fair it's pink. His eyes are bright-bright blue, visible from even over there—and what a jaw.

With a slight limp and a warm smile, he walks to meet you. Your blind date is about to not work out.

So much in Los Angeles depends on a trick of the eye.

◆

BERNADETTE WAS HER GIVEN name, same as her mother's, but the Costellos called her Micki. Born in 1930, she arrived in this world—so the story goes—with red hair and blue eyes, inspiring her Irish uncle Ray Heinen to say, "If that's not a Mick, I've never seen one."

That hair color changed through the years, sometimes more red, sometimes more blonde (and sometimes *nudged* toward the blonde). She had a small mouth and a small chin and mischief in her smile. "Bubbly," a friend would call her, years later. She grew up working-class Roman Catholic near South LA's Leimert Park neighborhood, in a craftsman-style bungalow that, for the area, was good-sized. Its second story and four bedrooms made it a rarity, though its one bathroom proved it still fit the neighborhood's working-class backdrop.

Micki's education began at St. Brigid's Catholic School, but a new parish opened in 1937 to accommodate the population boom. From then on, Micki switched school to where her family went to Mass, at the Church of the Transfiguration. For high school, she joined other Catholic girls at St. Mary's Academy, while her brothers attended the same all-boys Mount Carmel High as John Hock, where they played football. (She didn't much care for the sport except that her brothers played.) Wanting to be a schoolteacher, she studied education at Los Angeles State College, and by 1954, when she was twenty-three years old, she had responsibility for a classroom of kids at Woodcrest Elementary School.

That was when she, unmarried and living still with her parents, agreed to a blind date with a friend's cousin for St. Patrick's Day.

All three hit the town—Micki, her friend, Beverly, and Beverly's cousin, the Blind Date. The gals wanted to dance. So they found their way downtown to the Roger Young Auditorium where outside they could hear big band tunes, peppy stuff to make your feet tap and kick. Just inside the entrance, a crowd of twenty-somethings wearing green milled around, talking loud over the band's blaring horns. Our trio pushed through, hoping to find a table somewhere, and that's when Micki glanced at the bar and saw two fellas talking, and she recognized the one and waved.

He waved back. And that's the moment she knew she'd just been forward with a stranger.

"Oh, God," she told Beverley. "I didn't even really know him."

They found a table, ordered, and the Blind Date asked Micki to dance. A few songs later, he still hadn't generated much enthusiasm in her.

But that fellow at the bar, the stranger who had looked familiar, his eyes kept finding her through all the St. Paddy's green, through all the cigarette smoke and noise. A nice looking man, that's for sure. And then he rose from his stool and strolled to their table, blue eyes and shoulders, and now she knew she'd never met him before.

Micki, at five foot five, felt dwarfed. Even his hands were outsized. She explained her mistake. He smiled some more. They chatted a bit. He'd grown up in St. Brigid's Parish and still lived there. She knew that church; it wasn't far from her own house. That's where she'd started elementary school.

No, he said, he wasn't planning to dance. Hurt my leg at work. But tell me your last name again. Costello? Did your brothers go to Mount Carmel? Yes, I knew them.

He telephoned a few days later and invited her out. When he came to her parents' home to pick her up for the date, her father—a man who'd once worked as a boxing promoter—took his daughter aside.

"Well," John Costello told her, "this time you brought me a man."

That night, Micki and the man enjoyed a movie. Of course it would be a movie. This was Los Angeles, after all. But a movie would also serve as a conversation dodge, a way her date could avoid talking about himself. Though Micki didn't yet realize it, the familiar stranger didn't much like himself as a subject. So a movie was perfect: they could sit quietly for two hours, then afterward talk about the film, or he could ask about her, and bubbly as she was, they'd pass the night without him having to say much. In fact, after he dropped her off, she realized she didn't know much about him—except that he'd delivered her family's newspaper years before and that he would take her out again.

When later she told her oldest brother his name—John Hock—her brother said, "From Mount Carmel? You know he plays for the Rams?"

She did not. How could she have? John had never mentioned it.

◆

SHE COULD FILL A catalogue with all that he didn't say. He never said, for example, that he preferred red meat cooked well done. Instead, when Micki's mother served him a medium rare hamburger, he ate it up as if it were the world's only food and he a starving man. But later, when Micki asked privately how he had enjoyed the hamburger, he said:

"I'm accustomed to eating meat well done, but medium rare is growing on me."

Another time—the two of them on a date with people she knew—she began to introduce him by saying, "He plays for—" but she stopped mid-sentence when he nudged her gently. And without him saying, she understood that he'd rather be known as a fellow from the neighborhood who had delivered her newspaper rather than as a man who spent his Sundays cheered by tens of thousands.

He also kept to himself about the extent of his knee troubles. But they, too, eventually became clear.

John seldom wanted to walk far when on dates. Very few long, romantic strolls. No hikes into nearby mountain canyons. Not much, if any, dancing.

His right knee worked all right, but she knew it was also his weak spot. If the Greek hero, Achilles, was vulnerable at the heel, John could be undone by his knee. That's why he babied it, made few requests of it in day-to-day life—because he knew the demands he asked of it on the field. She learned to share his concern; they weren't a couple to fox-trot or Lindy Hop.

They became beach people, John and Micki, often taking afternoons at Santa Monica. There, the only long walk involved traversing the vast California beach—sometimes as long as a football field—to the water's edge. Once arrived, John and Micki could arrange towels and lie in the sun from afternoon into evening if they wanted, sip sodas from a cooler, eat a sandwich or two. If the sun beat too hard, they could step out past the breakers and let the buoyant ocean lift them. There, in cool water up to his chest, John walked as if he weighed no more than a teenager. The ocean pushed and pulled him, but its great gift was how it relieved his knee of its burden. The Pacific carried him.

Then, he'd come out of the water and towel off, the California sun high and bright above him, its light caught by water drops on those shoulders. Micki might not have given words to her thoughts, because she wouldn't have wanted him to feel self-conscious, but she must have thought the same thing other women did—and men, too—seeing John shirtless.

What those others thought?

Adonis. Greek god.

But that would describe a man stepped right out of a library's classics section. For an Irish-American kid growing up during the Depression, maybe the more accurate reference would be to a man who stepped out of a comic book advertisement.

Maybe the more accurate reference would be Atlas.

◆

CHARLES ATLAS MADE A fortune convincing American boys that to be the perfect man required the perfect physique—and that he knew how to build one. His iconic ads told over and over again the story of a skinny, pitiable man at the beach getting sand kicked in his face by a bully. But after "Mac" adopted Charles Atlas's system and built his brawn, he returned to the beach, smacked the bully's jaw, and became a man who could stride the world. And win the company of bikini-clad lookers.

John Hock tried what Atlas peddled—a system like isometrics. But John went far beyond that. He also pumped iron, lifted dumbbells and barbells. The results were Herculean.

It would have been blasphemous for Hock to say that he experienced something holy in the weight room. What he found, though, was familiar to what church provided. If not spiritual, lifting weights at least offered a particular kind of peace—or maybe calmness. Through the Mass, those qualities came from the repetition of words and motions, of kneeling and standing, counting the beads of a rosary, making the sign of the cross, humbling the self before the Father, Son, and Holy Ghost. In the weight room there was also ritual: the chalk on the hands, the measuring of weight, the lift, the drop, the squat, the curl, the counting of repetitions and sets. And if the weight room lacked as a spiritual place, it did make space for a quality in John Hock that Mass could not accommodate. In the weight room, he could be both meditative and fiercely physical. He could calm his mind while forcing his muscles to the point of pain, then through and past that point. The weights would always win in the end—he could never lift them all forever. What mattered was that with weights he could bring himself to a single teeth-gritting, jaw-clenching, muscle-popping moment—be ferocious and conquer. This toil touched in him what was old and elemental. Men had slung weight for centuries, and in a place like Los Angeles, where so much attention focused on the newest and the latest, the most dazzling and the falsest, the weight room took Hock deeply into true, old ways, to the beginning of things—not to their future.

It was also for many years a thing not to share with his coaches, an activity best practiced underground. Even by 1954, most NFL coaches disapproved of weightlifting. They still subscribed to a myth that pumping iron was bad for a player.

The coaches, though wrong, had reasons to think as they did. The game, and how it was played—even its rules—rewarded a balance of speed and brawn. Offensive linemen, in particular, needed quickness balanced with strength. That blocking technique that kept the arms tight in front of a player's body meant linemen couldn't reach out to shove someone. A block had to be made with the body—so the body had to react quickly to a defender's feints and dodges. Fat, slow men, no matter how powerful, got cut from the team. Mobility and endurance mattered. In the NFL of the 1950s, the ideal offensive lineman was less an unmovable mountain than he was a galloping bull, deft and solid—strength and speed in careful balance.

Too much strength, coaches feared, would upset that delicate equilibrium; thus the wariness regarding weightlifting. They looked at a fellow like Charles Atlas and saw someone "muscle-bound," that is, tied up by his own muscles.

So if a coach caught a player in a gym doing a clean-and-jerk, that player could get a chewing out or maybe worse.

That risk—especially for John Hock and his fellow lineman Duane Putnam—was necessary.

◆

THEY TALKED, THE LINEMEN did. Shared secrets. They talked about Frank Gifford. Gifford talked about his regimen, "what I did was run. I just ran everywhere. It was apples and oranges and nothing like they do today." The linemen were different. Through the 1953 season, the Putter had watched John Hock and noticed the advantages the Hooker gained from lifting weights. They'd both started the year listed at around 230 pounds, but by the season's end the Putter had dropped to a skinny 207. He feared the Rams would cut him if he returned the next year at that weight. No matter how nimble, a 207-pound Putter would get brushed aside by defensive linemen like Art Donovan and Leo Nomellini, future Hall of Famers with the Colts and 49ers, who each carried fifty more pounds than Putnam.

Not only in Charles Atlas' advertisements would big guys bully smaller men.

But look at Hock. By the end of the season he still came in around 230 pounds. And Hock, Putnam knew, lifted weights. You couldn't look like Adonis if you didn't.

So Putnam filed that information away until a day that spring on the UCLA campus where he was taking graduate courses in physical education. This was 1954 and the same spring when John and Micki started to date.

Putnam met a familiar face on campus: UCLA shot-putter Clyde Wetter. The Putter had put the shot himself for a few years in college and had come to know Wetter that way.

Wetter had heaved a sixteen-pound shot as far as fifty-four feet. He was one of the strongest men Putnam had ever seen. As the man chatted, Putnam explained his weight loss, his lack of strength. "Putter," Wetter said, "I guarantee you I can put twenty pounds on you if you'll work with the weights."

Let's give it a go, Putter said. Maybe coaches would chew him out if they discovered he was lifting weights, but if he didn't gain weight the coaches would cut him anyway. And if weightlifting gave him a body like Hock's—or sort of like his—the Putter couldn't imagine coaches complaining at all.

Working with Wetter twice a week through that spring, Putnam bulked up to 240 pounds. By the start of the Rams training camp, he could dead lift 400 pounds and curl 135. Now, like his buddy Hock, he was ready for those Donovans and Nomellinis.

And just to make sure he was still quick, the Putter dropped ten pounds. He felt stronger, quicker, faster.

No defensive linemen would kick sand in Duane Putnam or John Hock's faces.

❖

BUT THAT KNEE. JOHN Hock's danged knee. He could add power to his chest and shoulders, strengthen his quadriceps and calves, stretch his hamstrings…

The right knee still wobbled.

Through the 1954 training camp, he massaged it. Iced it. Sat in whirlpool baths. The team's athletic trainer rubbed and wrapped the knee. Yet if anything, it was getting worse, looser.

That August, when the time came for the 1954 *Times* Charities Game, Hock's second such, he gave his two complimentary tickets to a cousin and asked the cousin to bring Micki. Micki and Charles Grimes sat in section eight, near the thirty-five-yard line toward the southwest end of the stadium, where the guests of Rams players always sat—and for this game, so did Bob Hope, who now owned a small share of the team and was just a few seats away from Micki. The event proved festive, as the *Times* Charities Game always did, and the field play went well for Los Angeles, which beat Washington, 27–7. But the evening didn't go so well for John. Micki would always remember that in this, the first game she ever watched him play, he got hurt.

It was the knee, of course. The injury kept him out of the next exhibition game against the Cleveland Browns while doctors looked him over. A tendon in his right knee—likely the patellar, connecting the kneecap to the shin bone—wouldn't heal by itself, they said. If the knee were to be repaired, it would need surgery. The prognosis for recovery must have covered a range of possibilities—from a few weeks to much, much longer— because there was some hope and even an expectation among coaches and players that Hock could recover and return to the team in a few games.

He didn't. The knee met the knife in August, and that cost him all of 1954.

◆

"Fresh flesh."

Decades after his NFL career ended, that's how Art Hauser described the attitude of coaches and management toward players. One player goes down, gets tired, gets old, the team finds fresh flesh. A new body.

In that summer of 1954, his rookie year, Hauser wanted little else than to be a body the Rams could use. With a flat-nosed and flat-browed face that looked tough enough to break a brick, Hauser came into camp as a recent graduate from Xavier University in Cincinnati. He brought what he had: a Midwestern work ethic, a quick and powerful body, a suitcase, a few pairs of socks, and not much else. Rams coaches listed him third on their depth chart, behind the starters and the reserves. A third-string linemen, Hauser knew, seldom made the team. So his investment of time with the Rams carried a big risk. Players, after all, didn't get paid for training camp—not a penny—and Hauser's wife, Joanie, was eight months pregnant.

Each day he learned by his failures. In practice, across the line of scrimmage, crouched Duane Putnam and John Hock. Hauser had been a pass rusher in college. His job had been to tackle the quarterback. But now he'd try to headfake Putnam and Hock and they'd still get in his way. He'd spin, and they'd know where he was going. Maybe he was as strong as them, but these guys, they had technique.

He must have done something right, though. Cut after cut, the coaches kept Hauser around. But as the last exhibition game approached—the final cut to follow—he believed he was done. He counted, studied the line-up, figured which veterans the Rams would keep, and the calculations always ended with the same result: Art Hauser wouldn't make the team. There just wasn't room. Even when Rams coaches let him start in that last exhibition game against the Eagles, he figured his time was done.

The Rams had played that last exhibition game in San Antonio, then boarded a plane for Washington, DC where they would open the regular season. They brought Hauser along, but he knew the inevitable was coming. And in the nation's capital, in a meeting room at a hotel on Dupont Circle, Hauser gathered with the rest of the players, and prepared himself for the final word. Coach Hamp Pool stood before the group, looked around at the faces, and announced, "This is the Rams team for 1954."

Hauser looked around the room. Veterans stared back at him. Who was cut? What veteran was let go?

Later, everyone heard the explanation. No one got cut. But John Hock's knee surgery would keep him out for the season. Hauser, that fresh rookie flesh, won the Hooker's spot.

◆

IF THERE HAD BEEN any Rams season John Hock would do well to have missed while convalescing, 1954 was the best choice. No one could blame him for the mess.

The Rams finished 6–5–1, their worst record since 1948. That 6–5–1 record gave them fourth place in the NFL's six-team Western Conference. Given regular Rams' expectations, the 1954 season was a disaster.

The problems were myriad, though Coach Hampton Pool received the blame for many. He was in his third season as Rams coach and never under him had the team improved. He'd begun the 1954 season by making questionable trades—sending away Night Train Lane, for example—but once the season began, the "Ramanian Empire" (as one journalist called it) crumbled. Pool changed the offense every week to suit each new opponent, then raged against players who couldn't master a new system in time for Sunday. Players publicly complained after he railed against them during halftime of a game against the Lions in October, and several assistant coaches pledged to quit. Pool, chastened, apologized and said he would adopt a new attitude, that of a "Happy Warrior." He even brought Norman Vincent Peale's *The Power of Positive Thinking* to a team meeting and read aloud from it for an hour.

That didn't get a positive reaction.

But his ever-changing game plans remained, and it became clear that "Happy Warrior" wasn't Pool's style. He was a twenty-hours-a-day kind of worker, and what he demanded of himself he also demanded of his players and assistants. After a loss to the Chicago Bears on November 29, Pool again unleashed his temper.

During a film session in which he and players reviewed the previous game, he lambasted all-pro running back "Deacon" Dan Towler and berated as "a loafer" Tom Fears—a player on his way to the Hall of Fame. He warned everyone that the next two games would decide who was called back for the '55 season and how much money they'd earn. "I've been too easy on you guys," Pool reportedly said. "We're going to play this my way, again."

Players rebelled. "If Pool stays," one veteran star anonymously told the *Los Angeles Times*, "there are going to be some very good players who won't be back next year. All we want to do is win the championship, but we've gotten to the point where we don't think we can do it with Hamp Pool." Added a lineman: "That blow-up Wednesday was the worst I've ever seen in all my years of pro football. Players expect to get chewed out, but not when they haven't got it coming to them."

Through the public feuding, Rams president Dan Reeves insisted Pool would be his coach again in 1955. Then the 1954 season ended, and Rams assistant coaches resigned en masse—or maybe they were fired. Stories say both happened. A few days later, Pool was out, too. "I should have spent less time on the field, held fewer team meetings, kept everything simpler," Pool is quoted saying years later in Mickey Herskowitz's book, *The Golden Age of Pro Football: A Remembrance of Pro Football in the 1950s*. "I would change the offense every week to fit the opponent. I was a stickler for detail. Football should be a simple game, really."

Yet football isn't a simple game. It wasn't so in 1954, and it was becoming more complicated every season. A game can't really be simple when it involves precise technique and timing between eleven men, while another eleven wearing different color jerseys try to violently disrupt that timing. In such a game, details do matter; sticklers are welcome. Of the three aspects Pool considered to be at the root of his failure with the Rams, the one that rings most true is that he shouldn't have changed the offense every week.

The Rams' culture since the move west had been akin to Los Angeles's culture: one that encouraged the next new, best thing. Reeves hired men who could invent, innovate. He seemed to like the mad-scientist model of coach. But Pool had become less inventor and more nonstop tinkerer. An example: he'd brought back an innovation—the two-headed quarterback—introduced by his old mentor, "Jumbo" Joe Stydahar, except that tactic wasn't a surprise anymore. Worse, it angered Norm Van Brocklin who again had to share his job. If Dutch had endured that arrangement when the other quarterback was Mr. Ram, Bob Waterfield, now he was flat-out insulted that he had to share the ball with a *rookie*: Vanderbilt's Billy Wade.

What Pool did by changing the offense every week wasn't innovative, it was week-to-week problem-solving. He didn't create a surprising way to play football that would force other teams to react to the Rams. That's what had happened in the 1940s, when Rams coach Clark Shaughnessy moved a halfback to the line of scrimmage and introduced the position people now call a wide receiver. That change surprised teams, made the way they played defense irrelevant. Something similar happened when Stydahar put three two-hundred-plus-pound "bull elephant" fullbacks in the game at the same time, so they could rumble over opponents.

What Pool did was to react—weekly—to the Rams' opponents. In a way, he paid more attention to other teams than he did to the Rams or to football itself.

That pattern didn't appeal to players. They needed a playbook they could rely on, one to master. The playbook could offer something new; it just couldn't keep changing. As Pool kept awake into the wee hours devising his gambits and stratagems, he'd forgotten that a person could tinker so much with a car that it would never, ever drive right.

So Pool was out.

And Reeves started a nationwide search for his next new mad scientist.

◆

John Hock, meanwhile, had spent that lost 1954 season in pursuits other than learning Hamp Pool's playbook. When the cast came off, his leg was stiff and the muscles atrophied, so he began to stretch and exercise. Sometimes Micki helped, massaging the joint, rubbing the muscles around it. He kept the rest of his body in shape as best he could, lifting weights while taking care not to strain the knee. He lifted books, too, because he'd begun to take graduate courses in education at the University of Southern California.

He missed football, Micki could tell, though he seldom gave voice to how or why, and he never complained. He put himself to work, because missing the 1954 season was a reminder that he needed a plan for life after football. Even next season, when he rejoined the team, one good shot at his knee could end his career. Guys got hurt all the time, especially linemen. Broken noses and jaws and fingers and legs. Night Train Lane, after his trade to the Chicago Cardinals, suffered a fractured skull—in practice. In a game that fall against San Francisco, Bob Carey, a Rams offensive end, ran out to set a block for Skeet Quinlan and had his leg snapped for his troubles. His season ended at Queen of the Angels Hospital, and who knew whether he'd be back? And Stan West, a Rams defensive lineman, once got smashed in the face so hard his front teeth drove straight through his lip. Football hurt people, sometimes for good. The smart player had a back-up plan. John Hock's was to teach history to high school students. The salary would be about the same, and maybe he could coach a high school team for a little extra money. Get summers off, so he and Micki could spend them together at the beach.

◆

EIGHT DAYS AFTER HAMP Pool was fired, John Hock came to Micki's house with a little box in his pocket. With Mr. and Mrs. Costello busy in the kitchen preparing Christmas Eve dinner, and Micki seated on the couch in her parents' living room, John presented her with the engagement ring, her Christmas gift.

◆

JOHN FELT PLAYFUL THE day of the wedding, posing for a photograph with his best man—Micki's older brother, Jack—as if the two were late to the church. Jack gripped John's wrist with one hand and with the other pointed at John's watch. "*We have to go!*" John, gape-mouthed, raised his free hand to his forehead. "*Oh no! My wife will kill me—and we're not even married!*"

He wore a tuxedo with striped pants and an ascot, with a carnation as his boutonniere. When he met his bride that morning at Transfiguration Church, she wore a simple crown to hold her veil, a scoop-neck gown with a poofy skirt, and she carried a bouquet of roses. Inside the sanctuary, John and Micki stood under a dark, mahogany-stained ceiling, before the church's altar, whitewashed walls aglow with light that filtered through rose-shaped stained glass windows on the church's eastern wall. Ahead and above them, depicted in a mural and atop a mountain, a transfigured and radiant Jesus spread his arms, accompanied by prophets: Moses with God's commandments to the bride's side, Elijah on the groom's.

That day—June 25—was unseasonably cool, a day when gentlemen didn't mind keeping their suit coats buttoned and ties knotted tight: a good day for a wedding. In fact, that day three Rams were "deserting the bachelor ranks," as the *Times* put it. Along with John Hock, Les Richter, a first-year linebacker, married Miss Marilyn Shaw. Tom Dahms, a tackle from San Diego State, married Miss Diane Ewing.

At the Costellos' house, the wedding was small and simple, friends and family. The only NFL players to attend were men who had played with John in high school at Mount Carmel: Jerry Hennessy, who had suited up with Washington, and John Helwig who was with the Chicago Bears. Helwig served as a groomsman. Guests mingled in the garage and in the backyard, and when Micki tried to go to the one bathroom in the house, she found a line snaking down the stairs. Naturally, she was given priority.

"Get through this," Hock whispered to Micki in the midst of the toasts and the hubbub, "and then we're all right."

The party ended that afternoon. Mr. and Mrs. John Hock changed into traveling clothes, then met in the driveway. Her car, a fire-red Chevy convertible coupe, was packed and ready for their honeymoon. Plastered to the trunk were two signs reading "Just Married." The Hocks planned a few days up north, in the tiny beach town of Carpinteria, just south of Santa Barbara. John, after all, had been out of football for the past year. They couldn't pay for much more than that.

Nor were they rich in time. Training camp would begin in a few weeks, probably why so many Rams had scheduled their wedding days for June 25. John planned to report early. After having missed an entire season, he wanted to arrive in Redlands by July 12, get a jump on things. There was a new coach to learn, with a new system. The Rams had hired a college fellow from the Midwest, someone with no professional football coaching experience. The scuttlebutt said Sid Gillman was a kind of genius—a fellow who played jazz piano, wore a bow tie on the sidelines, and had come up with new ways of studying game films. Certainly he'd won plenty at the University of Cincinnati. But you never knew with a new man at the top how things would go. John wasn't the sort who liked too many surprises.

Two weeks and three days until then. Hardly much time at all. Just enough for that Carpinteria honeymoon. Just enough to move out of their parents' houses and into their new home (a small second-story two-bedroom apartment on Slauson Avenue; Micki's aunt lived underneath, but she owned the building and gave the newlyweds a deal). Just enough time for Micki to feed her husband chocolate cake, and steak cooked the way he liked it, and potatoes, and bring him coffee in a small cup, because he always liked to drink from the smallest cup in the cabinet. Just enough time to figure out how to share the bathroom, and for her to enjoy riding in the car's passenger seat, and to decide who gets what side of the bed. Just two weeks and three days to learn everything she would miss after he left for Redlands.

CHAPTER 7

Tomorrowland

THE SUMMER OF 1955 brought lots of news to Los Angeles, news that would usually grab people's imagination—but not this year. What people wanted to talk about was the opening in Anaheim, on July 17, of a magic kingdom built over land that a year earlier had been orange groves.

The Rams' training camp had opened with a new coach and new hope after the dismal 6–5–1 season, but so what? Roz Wiener Wyman, the now-married, young city councilwoman, was appointed by her colleagues to pursue the New York's Giants or Brooklyn's Dodgers—but who cared? Louise Brough of Beverly Hills won Wimbledon, but…

And it wasn't just people in Los Angeles excited about Disneyland. The whole nation had turned its eyes to Southern California.

The Washington Post: "22,000 Guests Attend Disneyland Premiere"

The Baltimore Sun: "CROWDS JAM DISNEYLAND OPENING DAY"

The New York Times: "Disneyland Is a Child's World of Fantasy Come True"

Hedda Hopper, the gossip column queen, wrote that there weren't "enough adjectives in Mr. Webster's book to describe the wonders of this playground."

Adjectives, perhaps not. But there were facts aplenty:

- From groundbreaking to grand opening took one year and a day
- The park cost $17 million to build and, with parking lots, covered 160 acres
- The King Arthur carousel was the world's largest with more than seventy horses
- To guarantee authenticity along Disneyland's jungle river, Walt Disney had arranged for trees from thirty to fifty years old to be shipped from Africa, South America, and southeast Asia, including Australia, New Zealand, and China
- The parking lots combined to cover three million square feet, all paved
- Construction required 3.5 million board feet of lumber

- Fifteen thousand people stood in line for the opening, four abreast, snaking a mile from the gate. Thirty thousand visited that day
- On opening day, the Santa Ana freeway leading to Disneyland was jammed for five miles—adding to skies already smoggy—until Disney officials opened their parking lots that morning
- Tickets were one dollar for adults, fifty cents for children
- Dishwashing machines broke down in one restaurant and a gas leak closed part of Fantasyland's castle, but both repairs were made in a short time

In the weeks before the opening, Walt Disney himself had overseen the final details of construction, flying by helicopter from his offices in Burbank so as to avoid the Santa Ana, which clogged with construction and supply trucks on their way to Disneyland. One problem he'd had to solve was the loss of construction workers.

Many had been drawn away from building Disneyland by the promise of bonuses to help construct nearby tract housing—part of Anaheim's Disneyland-fueled growth spurt. This was part of a new phenomenon in Southern California. Most growth in previous decades stemmed from manufacturing and wartime spending. Hollywood and the entertainment industry had helped to create an identity for the region and to bolster the economy and population, but the most powerful engines of economic expansion had come from those other sources. Now, with the nation out of wartime, Walt Disney was turning entertainment and tourism into major economic forces. If Hughes Aircraft had helped remake physical landscapes in past decades, now it was Mickey Mouse and Dumbo driving backhoes.

Or, more specifically, Peter Pan and Captain Nemo and Davy Crockett. Those had been Disney's biggest hits the previous three years, the latter appearing on a Wednesday night TV show on ABC and dominating that night's ratings. The TV show had debuted for the 1954–55 season, keeping the Disney brand in front of audiences year-round, and it had provided a weekly advertisement for the park, then under construction in Anaheim.

As a concept, Disneyland itself was like nothing the world had ever seen. It was not an amusement park like Coney Island. It was not a fair. People groped to describe it. Some called it a new wonder for the world. "An integrated juvenile world's fair of fantasy," *The New York Times* decided. "A juvenile fairyland," said *The Boston Globe.*

Though the park itself contained five "lands"— Main Street, USA; Fantasyland; Adventureland; Frontierland; and Tomorrowland—visitors could opt for only two experiences of time: the past or the future. At Disneyland, there was no present.

The park's backward glance took visitors to gas-lit streets (Main Street, USA), paddle-wheel riverboats

(Frontierland), and colonial jungles in Africa (Adventureland). For future dreams, Tomorrowland launched visitors on a rocket bound for the moon and drove them through a four-wheeled paradise called "Autopia." There, children steered while parents, as passengers, relaxed—an idealized view of a world with roads far less cluttered than the Santa Ana Freeway.

In his book, *The Hollywood Sign*, historian Leo Braudy notes that a characteristic of Hollywood has been to juxtapose the future with a sentimental past—and Disneyland did exactly that. Visitors could choose from two narratives. In one, the distant past was fun and thrilling, and safe and clean—and romanticized. In the other, the future promised technological achievement and societal perfection. In promoting Tomorrowland, the company line was that designers had been given the task of theorizing what the decades would bring—from the types of chairs to how people would dress. In actuality, they'd been given the task of creating an idealized future—a sentimental hope to equal a sentimental past.

Disneyland's concept of time was perhaps the greatest difference between this park and what Americans had known as "amusement parks." Places such as Coney Island, with their Tilt-A-Whirls and the Ferris wheels, were neither past nor future. They were about thrills, right now, relentlessly in the present.

The present lay outside Disneyland's walls. The present—its smog and traffic jams, its racial tensions, its Cold War enemies with their hammer and sickle, its sex symbols, its litter, its crime—was what people escaped at the gates of that fairytale kingdom, that national time machine, as seen each week on TV. The promise Disneyland made was that the present would one day vanish and make way for a perfect world where kids could drive safely. Perhaps even across the surface of the moon.

◆

TO ACCOMPANY ITS STORY headlining the news that the Rams had hired Sid Gillman as head coach, the *Los Angeles Times* chose a photograph of Gillman sitting beside a film projector. In the photo, his eyes are wide, as if he's been too long in the dark. His straightforward look suggests that he's focused on whatever that projector projects. Lacking the stereotypical football coach's square jaw or thick neck, Gillman in the photograph most resembles a Hollywood director reviewing a final cut. More Elia Kazan or Joseph Mankiewicz than Curly Lambeau or Jumbo Joe Stydahar.

Clearly, he's been posed by the photog. There's no light emanating from the projector. Gillman's probably looking at a blank screen. Nevertheless, the *Times* couldn't have chosen a better image.

David Gillman, Sid's father, had run movie theaters in Minneapolis when Sid was a boy. As a college football coach, Sid found a competitive edge in the film room, using the technology to see the game in new ways.

While other coaches studied game films from kickoff to final tick of the clock, Gillman cut them up, spliced them. With scissors and tape, he edited films by play or by player. He could then watch a dozen versions of the same trap or counter play over and over again, and by comparison discover what worked best and what didn't. He could isolate a quarterback and see under what circumstances the quarterback made accurate throws and when he didn't.

Then, he could take that information and teach.

Films helped him design his game plans, showed him his team's strengths and opponents' weaknesses. Films allowed him to "grade" his college players on their performance and to show them—right on the screen—what they'd goofed up and what they'd done right.

The nickname Van Brocklin gave his new coach—"the Rabbi"—was a poke at Gillman, who was Jewish. But from another angle the title fit, given that Gillman really was a teacher, though more interested in the lessons of football than of Judaism.

His football heritage had its roots in Ohio. He'd played and served as an assistant coach at Ohio State University under Francis Schmidt, an early adopter of the forward pass. Gillman eventually also coached at Denison University east of Columbus, and at Miami University on the state's western boundary, before he took the job at Cincinnati. Even his brief flirtation with professional football had been an Ohio affair. In 1936, a friend asked him to play for a fledgling team in an upstart league trying to challenge the NFL. Gillman agreed and played just that one season in Cleveland. That league would eventually fold, but the team, called the Rams, proved successful enough to be absorbed by the NFL.

Then those same Rams won the league championship in 1945. And then they moved to the West Coast.

Nearly twenty years later, in this different league and different city, and under different owners, Gillman had found his way back to the Rams.

Coming into training camp with them, he had already studied the films.

◆

A YEAR BEFORE, IN the summer of 1954, the summer before Disneyland opened, Joanie Hauser had been the young, eight-months pregnant wife of a Rams rookie, and the team seemed to her like a wonderful family. Kind and caring, the players and their wives: Micki and John Hock. Patty and Duane Putnam. Jean and Andy Robustelli. Lu and Tom Fears. Gloria and Dutch Van Brocklin. Everyone was so nice.

Coming to Los Angeles from Xavier University in Ohio, Joanie and Art Hauser didn't know what they'd find. *God kissed this place*, Joanie thought, as she and Art explored the mountains, the ocean, the Pacific Coast Highway. All the buildings seemed to be either white or pink or blue. It was all so exotic and beautiful.

What impressed her most, though, was the welcome she and Art received, how the Rams took in a young couple, especially when her husband had only just made the team because of John Hock's season-ending injury. Joanie had the impression that rookies received no special treatment, especially rookies who had made the team by a margin no bigger than a knee tendon.

And especially not the wives of rookies.

That's why she was so surprised when the team, which had been in the Midwest playing road games, offered to provide her a seat on their charter plane early in the season to bring her from Ohio to Los Angeles. Pregnant and sitting alone by a window, she was even more surprised when Elroy Hirsch came and asked to sit beside her. Here was a football player who was also a movie star—in 1953 he'd starred as himself in a biopic called *Crazylegs*. He was a Ram veteran, entering his ninth year in the NFL. A movie star and a star athlete! So why would he even talk to her, she who considered herself a "little rookie wife"?

But he did. Hirsch, like her husband, had grown up in Wisconsin, a fellow Midwesterner. He asked if she was excited to be going to games.

"Oh, I won't be going to the games," she said. She motioned toward her pregnant belly. She told him she'd need to care for the baby.

He protested. His wife, Ruthie, had come to games when she had a baby at home. The answer was as easy as having a great babysitter. "Let me have Ruthie call you," he said. "You can trust her sitter."

Other players and their wives were just as nice. Gloria and Norm Van Brocklin, for example, gave the Hausers' baby clothes their kids had grown out of. So Joanie, who had never lived anywhere but Cincinnati, felt welcomed and cared for. And she was able to attend games. Even better, the coaches gave Art lots of playing time, and he received a game ball for his work as a pass rusher in the season's final game.

Then all that Hamp Pool stuff came on like a big family squabble. Though some players had complained about Hamp, others took his side. "The man does a week's work every day," said Don Paul, the linebacker and a team captain. "It seems some of the Rams will never mature." Paul was one of Pool's drinking buddies. They'd get together with Bob Waterfield and Bob Kelley, the team's radio and TV announcer, and have a raucous time playing practical jokes on each other, like when Pool secretly delivered dozens of Christmas trees to Waterfield's house, or the time the others smeared Limburger cheese over Kelley's car engine before he took a long drive through 102-degree weather. Kelley kept having to pull to the side of the road to throw up.

Then Pool was fired and Gillman hired, so there wasn't a side to take.

So, in Redlands that summer when Disneyland opened, today was a better place than yesterday. Players could be easy with each other again. Play cards at night;

drink down at Ed and Mary's Tavern where the beer was so cold. Line up in practice, listen to the new coach's instructions. Behave like a family again and wait to see what tomorrow might hold.

◆

WHAT GILLMAN HAD SEEN as he studied his carefully edited films was a team too smitten with the grand gesture. What he'd seen was a passing game that a Hollywood critic would call melodramatic.

Norm Van Brocklin was the star of this picture show. There he was, in black and white on the screen, over and over again, cocking back his arm and chucking the ball as if wanting to throw it over the goal posts and out of the coliseum. Streaking wide receivers—Elroy Hirsch, Tom Fears, and especially Bob Boyd—scrambled to get under those passes. The ball flew from Van Brocklin's hand, spiraling without a hint of wobble, tracing an elegant arc from Van Brocklin to…

Well, that was the problem.

Opponents had figured out that Hamp Pool and the Rams liked to sling that ball as far downfield as often as they could. So, opposing coaches positioned their defensive backs far from the line of scrimmage, and when Dutch hefted those long passes the opponents had almost as good a chance of catching them as the Rams.

What Gillman was seeing were the downsides to Hamp Pool's "READY-SET-*HUT*-TWO-THREE-FOUR!" score-fast-so-you-can-score-again football. No matter the result of those long passes—a touchdown, an interception, a catch, a dropped ball—the plays lasted scant seconds and robbed the Rams defensive players of any time to rest. If the Rams threw such a pass on first or second down and the result was an interception— and too often it was—the Rams defense might have just reached the benches when it was time to get up and trudge right back onto the gridiron.

So, one of the first things Gillman changed in training camp: fewer long passes. Let's use the whole field, he told Van Brocklin. Throw to the sidelines. Throw shorter.

The next thing he changed? The defense. He emphasized its necessity and made a trade with San Francisco to help recapture what the team had lost with the departure of Night Train Lane. He moved Don Paul, known as a tough, nasty linebacker, up into the center of the defensive line, a position *Sports Illustrated*'s Jim Murray equated to serving as the defense's shock absorber.

Then he made endless hours of film part of training camp life. He even invited Bob Waterfield back to training camp as a special consultant. In addition to his work as quarterback, Waterfield had been the best placekicker in Rams history and still held several NFL kicking records. So Gillman put Waterfield in a dark room with four hundred feet of slow-motion footage showing the current Rams kicker, Les Richter, at work. *Study his technique*, Gillman said. *Let's make him better.*

Finally, he ran a different sort of training camp. Players found it to be rigorous, but more relaxed, better organized. They could offer suggestions and believe they were heard. "We're not asked to do something that can't be accomplished," Skeet Quinlan told the *Los Angeles Times*. "Just because it looks good on paper doesn't mean it will work in a game. Before we try anything in play it has to weather the test of trial and error."

When the exhibition season began, Gillman offered another surprise. Though the Rams had, in the last decade, fired at least one head coach after exhibition losses, Gillman argued that victories and losses in those games shouldn't matter. Why beat up your best players for games that didn't count toward the championship? An exhibition game was a learning tool, a classroom exercise. The score? Immaterial.

For the first time in years, the Rams lost to Washington in the *Times* Charities Game. Next, they faced the Cleveland Browns and Coach Paul Brown, who treated exhibition games in the same manner as Gillman. Brown usually played rookies and was reputed never to look at the scoreboard. So here was a game that neither coach cared to win. At the coliseum, though, were some thirty-five-thousand fans who wanted a victory, so the Rams mustered enough touchdowns to keep those paying customers happy.

But as the Rams left the coliseum field, Brown awaited them in the tunnel to the locker rooms. His teams had played in the last five NFL championship games, winning two, and he wanted to make sure these Rams understood that a victory over Cleveland's Browns in August meant as much as banking Monopoly money.

"Okay, okay," he shouted at Van Brocklin and Hock and bow-tied Sid Gillman as the Rams jogged past him toward the locker room. "But what about December?"

◆

Dear Mr. O'Malley...

The day before the Rams' non-game against Cleveland, Roz Wyman had written to Walter O'Malley, the president of the Brooklyn Dodgers. In her letter, the city councilwoman asked to meet with him. Later that month, it so happened, she'd be in New York with Councilman Edward R. Roybal on other LA-city business. They'd be happy to talk about the ways Los Angeles could accommodate the Dodgers, should the Dodgers like to move their operation west.

In writing to O'Malley, Wyman was following up on a telegram the city council had recently wired at Wyman's urging to let O'Malley know of the council's resolution, which read in part that "Los Angeles is seriously interested in making a home for a major league club and it would be appreciated if the gentlemen could come here for a serious conference and 'look-see' at our facilities." The council had also sent a similar telegram to O'Malley's opposite number with the New York Giants. Knowing that Wyman and Roybal had a trip east scheduled, the council agreed with her that it should empower Wyman and Roybal to meet with either owner.

O'Malley read Wyman's letter and wrote back. No, he couldn't meet. He was busy, his team was in a pennant race. And, he added—because that telegram the council had sent appeared in newspapers before he'd even received it—"I assumed it was part of a publicity stunt."

Thus, once again New York brushed off Los Angeles. Second-class LA. Kid brother LA.

"I was really mad, to put it mildly," Wyman said in an interview years later. "I thought it was pretty rude, to tell you the truth, the way you answer two elected officials. 'I thought this was a publicity stunt or something.' I felt O'Malley had dealt too long with New York politicians, and we were a little different out here. There were no Tammany bosses, and there was none of that in LA."

If O'Malley's letter stung with a kind of East Coast smugness, the prick may have felt worse, because East had just competed with West in one of the year's most-watched sporting events, a winner-take-all horse race pitting the nation's two best: Southern California's Swaps against Maryland-bred Nashua. The race on the last day of August had carried all the tensions and imagery of the East-West dichotomy. The western horse, Swaps, was owned and trained by cowboys, his jockey a young Willie Shoemaker from Texas. The eastern horse was owned by an heir to a banking fortune, his jockey a man who had won his first Derby nearly twenty years earlier. Prior to the match race meeting in Chicago, the two horses had met only once—at the Kentucky Derby, which Swaps had won. Nashua won the Preakness and Belmont Stakes that followed, but Swaps hadn't run in those, likely because his owner couldn't afford the fees. Yet, out west, Swaps continued to race undefeated, and it was clear to the country that these were the nation's top two horses. Their one-on-one rematch pitted western aspirations against eastern eminence.

A national television audience of some fifty million watched. It had rained in Chicago the night before, and Nashua's jockey, with years of experience on young Shoemaker, forced the western horse to the outside and into a muddy path where the run was troublesome and tiring. Nashua won by 6.5 lengths.

In its quest for major league baseball, though, the west would not be so easily pushed aside. Walter O'Malley, after all, had written back. Perhaps his tone was prickly, but he hadn't ignored Roz Wyman's letter.

Now, they were correspondents. Now, he knew who she was.

Very truly yours,
ROSALIND WIENER WYMAN
Councilwoman—5th District

◆

IT'S A SUNDAY MORNING, autumn, in any NFL city that's not Los Angeles. Maybe the Rams are in Detroit or Milwaukee. Maybe Chicago or Baltimore. This happened in all those places. So let's say Baltimore. Let's say it's November 20, 1955, a clear, windy, and cold day, with yesterday's snow blown into piles like dust against curbs and across lawns. Later this afternoon the Rams, with five victories against three losses, will play the Colts at Baltimore's Memorial Stadium.

But this morning, we'll station Hollywood's cameras inside a church sanctuary, the primary shot focused on the church's entry. There, framed by the doors and silhouetted by morning sunlight, a quartet of burly men cross the threshold, removing gloves to dip their fingertips in marble pedestal fonts filled with Holy Water, making the sign of the cross.

In real life, in any NFL city, this scene would likely be whatever church was within walking distance of whatever hotel houses the Rams. And John Hock could have rounded up more to attend Mass—or fewer. But for this scene in Baltimore, our Hollywood director has decided on four players, and he's chosen Baltimore's Basilica, in the heart of the city. Less well-known by its full name—the Basilica of the National Shrine of the Assumption of the Blessed Virgin Mary—the site is historic. It's the United States' first Cathedral, and it's the site where bishops created the Baltimore Catechism—so any visiting Roman Catholic would want to attend Mass there—and it's within walking distance of several hotels where the Rams might have stayed. But the primary reason for the director's choice is the interior of the Basilica—with high stained glass windows and two saucer dome ceilings, each decorated by pink rosettes, and at the highest point of the largest dome: a white dove sculpted and suspended below a golden radiance as if the bird flies from the heart of the sun.

(Later, the director will order establishing shots from outside, show the church's columns, its neoclassical style, then add those frames in the editing room.)

For now, though, the camera follows our burly quartet—the Pope's Rams. These men used to space and speed and collisions, long strides across one hundred yards of open grass. But here? In this Sunday-morning church crowd? They shuffle. They "pardon me." They teeter and tilt and try not to bump other parishioners or step on their feet. They are especially wary near the older ladies. People stare, they know these robust, shy strangers who draw attention to themselves by trying not to draw attention to themselves.

It's comical as the four squeeze into a pew, shoulder-to-shoulder, rump-to-rump.

By now we recognize them: Andy Robustelli, the defensive all-pro with his Italian-olive complexion and that off-kilter look to his face, the left eye sitting a little lower than the right; Art Hauser, the Midwesterner in his second year, with his flat face that looks tough enough to break a brick; and John Hock.

The fourth, on the end, is Duane Putnam, and it's clear from his actions that he's the outlier, the non-Catholic in the bunch. He fidgets. He looks around too much. He studies his teammates, tries to imitate what they do. At the threshold, when they dipped fingers, he dipped fingers. When they genuflected at the pew, he genuflected. When they picked up a book, he peered over Hock's shoulder for the page number.

When the times comes for them to drop cash in a plate, he drops cash in a plate. A pipe organ blares, and in a minute or so, another plate passes. The teammates drop cash. The Putter drops cash.

"How many times is that coming around?" he whispers to Hock, his roommate on the road.

Hock grins.

And when they kneel, Putnam kneels, too. Four big guys and not nearly enough space for all the ways their legs want to go. Mo, Larry, Schemp, and Curly would do it funnier, but only just.

Putter whispers, "Playing for the pope is pretty hard on those stumps. And all this time you've been blaming football."

Hock grins at that, too. "Might have been part of it," he says. But the camera, focusing on his face, can't detect a grimace or a twitch. He'll kneel or rise as the Mass requires, and he'll carry that soreness, that twinge. Behind them, on a wall, is a portrait of Christ's descent from the cross, his side pierced, his feet broken. If a man can't take a little pain for God, well, how can he share a holy space like this one, with his Son?

The four stand, they kneel, they stand again. The Putter says, "We don't even have to warm up for the game, we're getting up and down so many times."

◆

SOMETIMES, DUANE PUTNAM COULD hear a grinding come from John Hock's knees, probably the kneecap grinding on the bones behind it, the cartilage all worn down. Sometimes, John couldn't hide the pain the knees caused him, and he winced as he moved. Putnam probably knew Hock's knees better than anybody outside of the sawbones and Micki. On the road, they were roommates. At home, their lockers sat near each other. After games, John would set plastic bags filled with ice on his knees to check the swelling. Before games, though, that's when you had to admire him. He kept a box of bottles, and in each bottle was a red liniment of some sort. He'd rub that stuff into his knees, say, "I'll get it. Don't worry. I'll be there."

"John's knees," Putnam recalled years later, "were so bad."

◆

IN 1955, THE ICE and the liniment and the surgery held those knees together. And with them, John Hock started every game. The Rams, under their new coach with his new philosophy, won their first three games, then went on a win-loss yo-yo until that cold, cold day in Baltimore. That one was a tie, 17–17. Then, the Rams won in Philadelphia and headed home to Los Angeles with two games to go, a 6–3–1 record, and good odds to win the Western Division champion.

Awaiting them on the schedule were two rematches with teams that had gotten the better of the Rams. First, they'd face Baltimore again. Then, the Green Bay Packers would come into the coliseum, having beaten Los Angeles earlier that season by scoring a game-winning field goal in the last minute.

Avenge themselves on both teams, and the Rams would secure a spot in the NFL championship game.

"We should never have been beaten by the Packers nor tied by the Colts," Van Brocklin told a reporter. "We owe both Baltimore and Green Bay real good whippings."

CHAPTER 8

The Sweep

IN 1955, NO STUNTMEN played for Hollywood's Team. But there were actors—and one self-proclaimed villain.

Like many villains, he presented an appealing smile (dimpled!) and a friendly manner. He proved loyal to friends. Probably he was kind to dogs and children. His new restaurant, the Ram's Horn, had just opened that November on Ventura Boulevard in Encino, and he greeted patrons like there was no one else he'd rather have visit. He'd happily fetch the menu's newest cocktail, the "Middle Guard." *Give it a taste*, was the joke. *You'll want to tackle and block.*

But not hurt anyone. The Rams' Don Paul said he never intentionally hurt players from other teams. He acknowledged that the NFL did include some really awful human beings who tried to hurt other players. *Vipers*, he called them. He knew of one who stomped the hands of men who, having been tackled, lay helpless on the grass.

Villains (like him), said Paul, only want to harass, frustrate, intimidate, bully, and bedevil. Villains, he said, want to be hated. Specifically, he, Don Paul, wanted players—be they Lions or 49ers or Browns or Bears—to hate him with such blood-red fury that they would forget everything but their hatred. He wanted their hatred to swell until it pressed from inside against their skulls and the backs of their eyes and made them forget whether it was first down or fourth, or that they were supposed to run a post pattern, or that punching someone (say, Don Paul) leads to a fifteen-yard penalty.

Many in the league did not seem to appreciate Paul's carefully considered distinction between a viper and a villain. Many just called Don Paul "dirty." In *TIME* magazine the previous season, several Detroit Lions were quoted saying that nobody in football played dirtier than Don.

The 1955 season was Paul's eighth with the Rams, and he had played for no other team. He'd played linebacker and middle guard, and he admitted to throwing an elbow here and there when referees weren't looking. Yes, he baited other players into shoving him— after he warned a ref that so-and-so was giving poor Don the business. He studied, and when possible, adopted the techniques of other villains he admired. In a *Sports Illustrated* article, published just as the Rams returned home for their last two games of the 1955 season, Paul spoke of his admiration for Art Donovan of the Colts. It happened that the Colts were coming to Los Angeles for a rematch of that that 17–17 tie in November. Donovan's specialty, Paul said, was to crush any running back playing the role of decoy—that is, any back pretending to have the ball when he doesn't. After the decoy got accordioned two or three times by Donovan and his 260-something pounds—without even carrying the ball!—the decoy tended to get timid, no longer faking with gusto. Then it was easy for every Colt to recognize who really carried the ball.

Another villain Paul cited was George Connor of the Chicago Bears, nicknamed "The Foot" because of the regularity with which other team's receivers tripped over George's feet. Once, Connor combined with a fellow Bear to harass Paul's teammate, Elroy "Crazylegs" Hirsch, until Hirsch made the wrong move and got sandwiched by the two Bears. As Hirsch picked himself up off the turf, Connor turned with mock disapproval to his teammate and said of the movie star at their feet, "Don't go messing up Hollywood like that."

All those villains, and Paul himself, specialized in defense. Offensive players—running backs, wide receivers, quarterbacks—had to master techniques to counter villainous antics. Among them:

1. Never show that a villain has rattled you; never show you are hurt

2. Make the villains look like fools. Send a fleet-footed decoy so far away from the real play that Art Donovan will look like a fat beagle chasing a rabbit

3. "Bumstead." Or, as Norm Van Brocklin puts it, "ham it up good"

No stuntmen played for the Rams in 1955, but there were actors, and Dutch Van Brocklin was one. Not a student of method acting, he instead learned his thespian craft at the Funny Pages School of Drama, particularly from the cartoon strip, *Blondie*. Whenever Blondie's husband, Dagwood Bumstead, tumbled or fell (often downstairs), he gyrated and his feet scrambled and his arms windmilled. Van Brocklin learned that whenever a villain so much as breathed on him, it was time to "Bumstead." Once, he Bumstead-ed after being brushed by George Connor, that Bear who called Hirsch, "Hollywood." When Dutch spilled, the ref called Connor for a penalty. Van Brocklin winked at Connor, who snarled, "Get up, you bum. You're not hurt." And Connor was penalized again—this time for unsportsmanlike conduct.

A lot of this theater, however, came with a real price. There were no stuntmen, after all. Part of football's allure—likely one reason for its popularity in Southern California where Davy Crockett and the Indians, no matter how many times they fight at Disneyland, always live to fight again—is that real bodies are at stake. If

Disneyland and Hollywood tell stories of adventure without risk, football reminds its fans that life is a struggle, that people are built to be hurt and to heal and get hurt again. Flesh-and-blood men risk bruises and ruptures of their own flesh, risk gashes and scrapes that draw their own blood. Everyone in the NFL knows that some pain is necessary, even sanctioned. But anything extra—anything dirty—in 1955 made players grumble. So, Otto Graham, a future Hall of Fame quarterback for the Browns, claimed dirty play that season after he suffered a concussion against the Giants. A growing number of players wore face guards with their helmets to keep from being punched or having their eyes poked. Said Detroit Lion halfback Doak Walker: "They're chiefly interested in protecting themselves against dirty football."

That term, "dirty football," was spit out by more coaches and players through the 1954–55 seasons than probably through all other NFL seasons combined. In Hamp Pool's last season, the 49ers' coach publicly accused the Rams of "dirty football." Pool said no, it was the 49ers who played dirty. Then Pool accused the Chicago Cardinals, led by his one-time boss, Jumbo Joe Stydahar, of dirty play. The managing director of the Cardinals shot back that Pool was "nothing but a crybaby." Et cetera, et cetera. Coaches throughout the league studied their own game films and made lists of fouls that no official had noticed and then complained to Bert Bell, the NFL's commissioner.

The problem wouldn't go away. That facemask designed to keep players from getting eyes gouged or noses smacked? Villains figured out that it was easy to grab the facemask and yank a runner to the ground. In another year, fearing broken necks, the NFL would make that technique illegal.

And in January 1957, Bert Bell would still hear so many gripes about dirty football that he'd have to defend the league, declaring in *Sports Illustrated*, "I don't believe there is dirty football... I don't believe there are any maliciously dirty players in the National Football League."

◆

NORM VAN BROCKLIN PLAYED several games of the 1955 season with a broken bone in his throwing hand. Andy Robustelli, a defensive all-pro, twisted a knee. Don Burroughs, a defensive back, suffered bruised ribs. Lineman Paul Miller *sprained his neck*. Other players knocked out for a game or more included Deacon Dan Towler, Bob Boyd, and Crazylegs Hirsch.

The Rams in 1955 suffered more injuries than in any other year the team's veterans could recall.

"Maybe twice as many as last year," Van Brocklin told a newspaper reporter that December, just before the Rams' late season rematch with Baltimore. "And yet, we've thought about it less." Gillman, he said, was not one to moan about injuries, "like some other coaches

I've known. He just keeps putting someone else in there to fill the gap and that player comes through."

But in the midst of this injury-riddled season, in this era of dirty football, three Rams at least never missed a game. And together the trio gave the Rams perhaps their most potent weapon.

One of them was John Hock. Given the tenuousness of Hock's knees, it must have seemed a miracle that game in, game out, he found his way onto the field. Another who never missed a kickoff was Duane Putnam. The third was a rookie halfback named Ron Waller, a slippery kid from a farming town in the mid-Atlantic.

Think of Hock and Putnam as Waller's bodyguards. Each game they led the way, running first into the fists and fury of the defense, throwing blocks, with Waller steps behind, scurrying his way to an all-pro season as a rookie.

"They helped me out a lot, I know that," Waller recalled decades later from his home in Delaware. "They were great guards, man. They were great pulling guards… It was Putnam leading and Hock behind him. They did a hell of a job."

◆

TOM FEARS, A VETERAN receiver for the Rams who had given Night Train Lane his nickname, decided Ron Waller would be called "the Rat."

"I don't know why he gave me that name," Waller said. "I guess because I scampered… I was a rookie. I didn't ask any questions."

Four years before, the Rat had been Delaware's high school athlete of the year, coming out of the tiny town of Laurel, known for sweet potatoes until a blight in the 1940s. The Rat's high school graduating class numbered forty-four. Waller didn't travel far for college, just across the Chesapeake Bay to the University of Maryland. Then the Rams used their second draft pick in 1955 to select him, and suddenly, the young halfback was Los Angeles–bound.

"The first time I walked into camp," he said, "there were about twenty-five halfbacks, and they were looking to replace one guy. I said, 'Shit, I'll never make this team.'"

That summer, the Rams coaches excused him from training camp to play in the national college all-star game, where he ended up on defense. Back in camp, the coaches tried him out at wide receiver, and he proved he could play there, too. Wide receiver, defensive back, halfback—that versatility worked in his favor. "In those days, they looked for guys who could play more than one position," he recalled. So the Rams offered him an $8,000 salary with a $1,000 bonus for signing his name to a contract. Waller signed. By the second game that season, a 17–10 victory over Detroit, the *Los Angeles Times* was calling him "one of the most graceful runners in Rams' annals." Later, the paper wrote that

Waller "has about five different gaits. He minces, he drives, he sprints…" The other two gaits must have been indescribable; the reporter never named them.

Game in, game out, no Ram carried the ball more often. None gained more yards. None scored more touchdowns. No one benefited more from having John Hock and Duane Putnam as teammates.

◆

IMAGINE MATCHING PILLARS OR bookends, jersey numbers sixty-three and sixty-one, Hock taller and Putnam thicker, one at right guard and the other at left, the Hooker and the Putter, with flecks of grass sticking to the sweat on their forearms and faces. Waller remembers the pair as quiet men, reserved, neither a seeker of attention. That both were fierce on the field, and tough, is a given—they played offensive line in the NFL. But to distinguish them, Waller gives the edge to Putnam. "I wouldn't ever want to get in a fight with him," he says. "He was really tough. John,"—the former altar boy who led Sunday morning visits to Mass—"was more mild-mannered."

That the two were great pulling guards, Waller says, means that they excelled at the play called the sweep. Rather than require Hock and Putnam to smash into whatever defender faced them across the line of scrimmage, the sweep required them to sprint—or *pull*—away from the line, out either to the right or the left. While running, they needed to make split-second decisions about who to hit in order to *sweep* clear an alleyway for Waller.

If the play went left, "Putnam would look to seal and start that alleyway," Waller says. "And then John Hock would go downfield and take out a cornerback or a safety—anybody supporting. I would stay right behind them, and they would hopefully create an alleyway for me." If the play went to the right side, the men would reverse roles.

Against Detroit in the second game that season, Waller ran behind Hock and Putnam to gain ninety-eight yards, eight more than the entire Lions team. In a second game against Detroit, he gained 132 yards, averaging nearly eight yards per carry—and, again, Hock and Putnam's blocking made it work. "Lions were flying all over the joint," the *Los Angeles Times* reported, "as Ron's interference lowered the boom."

Waller's talents included not only his speed, but an ability to slide between tacklers without losing speed. His new coach, Sid Gillman, compared him to "a piece of wire." An assistant coach noted that tacklers could seldom hit Waller head-on, and that probably saved the rookie from injuries. "Tacklers never get a square shot at him," the assistant coach said. "When they catch him, he's turned sideways."

By the time the Colts came to Los Angeles that December for a rematch after that 17–17 tie, Waller had established himself as the Rams' top running threat. The teams met on a soggy, drizzly December 4, the kind of day that surprises Angelenos so accustomed to reliable sunshine. Perhaps because of a lack of umbrellas or raincoats, only about thirty-seven thousand fans showed, the year's smallest crowd by some ten thousand souls. Those hardy fans watched, according to *The Baltimore Sun*, as a mud-splashed Waller "squirted around the Colts' flank" to gain 138 yards. Tank Younger scored two touchdowns, and the Rams won, 20–14.

Exactly a year before, the Rams had been in turmoil, arguing with their coach and suffering through one of the worst seasons in team history. Now, with a new coach emphasizing defense and a more patient offense, and with a knockout rookie running back, they had worked their way back to the top of the league. Maybe the victory over Baltimore wasn't the "good whipping" Van Brocklin had said the Rams owed the Colts, but it was the first of the two revenge victories Los Angeles needed to win the NFL's Western Conference title and a spot in the NFL championship game.

One remained. Beat Green Bay's Packers, and the Rams would play for the NFL's crown.

◆

THE RAMS AND PACKERS had first met that season in Wisconsin, a game waged in Milwaukee rain and mud and fifty-degree misery, the sort of day when players spent sideline time using wooden tongues to clean mud from between their cleats. The Packers won, 30–28, on a field goal with only twenty-four seconds left. The game had been, perhaps, Norm Van Brocklin's worst performance of the season, if not his career. The man who had once thrown for 544 yards in a single game managed only thirty-four. Three of his attempted passes were intercepted.

Dutch kept mum about it then, but that broken bone in his throwing hand troubled him. Already stubby-fingered for a quarterback, he found himself unable to grip the ball with his swollen mitt. He'd played anyway. That was the NFL code: play hurt. Show no pain. Stay on the field until the coach says you can't. After all, every player was hurt—all the time. "The only time you weren't hurt," Ron Waller recalled, "was at the beginning of the season." So, in Wisconsin rain, Van Brocklin tried to hold that ball and throw it where it needed to be. He tried until Gillman benched him for the second-string quarterback, Bill Wade. Gillman had known something was wrong with Van Brocklin's hand, because he was accustomed to hearing a sound—*zzt!*—when the ball left Dutch's fingertips. He hadn't heard that sound for a while.

For the second Packer-Rams game—this one in Los Angeles—the *zzt!* had returned. Weather forecasters called for the usual: clear and temperate, with a high around seventy. Oddsmakers gave the advantage to the Rams by 7.5 points. Based on pregame ticket sales, about fifty-thousand fans were expected for the 2:05 p.m. kickoff.

Then, the day of the game, people began lining up at the coliseum ticket windows. They lined up by the hundreds. They lined up by the thousands. Then tens of thousands. So many people wanted tickets that by the time the game began, hundreds of fans still waited to buy their way into the stadium.

In the end, some forty thousand tickets sold the day of the game. That brought the crowd to just over ninety thousand, about as many people as lived in Burbank and nearly a full house in the coliseum.

Through that 1955 season, there had never been a larger crowd to watch an NFL game.

"With gold and glory within their grasp," wrote the *Times'* Frank Finch, "I think we're going to see a top effort by the Rams today. They're long overdue."

CHAPTER 9

Game Ball

"Whatever LA is, it has a certain amount of entertainment sophistication."
    —Melvin Durslag, legendary Los Angeles sportswriter

I T'S NEVER EASY TO perform for the performers.

Take any Los Angeles crowd arriving at the coliseum to watch the Rams. Among them are film critics and publicists, makeup artists and lighting technicians, musicians and dancers, directors and animators. Be they award-winning or aspiring or merely adequate, many of those taking their seats are people accustomed to being in front of an audience, so being part of one presents less of a thrill. Their business is entertainment, and entertainment is their business.

They react to a performance—appreciate its virtues and failures—differently than people who build cars on assembly lines or run Laundromats or diagnose cancer.

Melvin Durslag is in a good position to explain the nature of Los Angeles fans. What others call fun and thrills—watching sports—was for him a job spanning six decades at Los Angeles newspapers including the *Herald-Examiner* and the *Times*. He knows what it means to appraise entertainment with a cool, professional detachment. He understands that it is in the character of an Angeleno to hold part of the self in reserve when watching a movie in a darkened theater, or when hearing a symphony at the Hollywood Bowl, or attending a football game at the coliseum.

What this means—when talking sports—is that LA's fans don't tend to paint their faces and scream until their jugular veins bulge, and they don't wear hog snouts over their noses or cheese wedges on their heads. They are not likely to rattle cowbells as if a cowbell may mean the difference between their team winning or losing. What is true today was true in 1955. Rams fans, no matter how many tens of thousands, never—in Durslag's memory—deafened a visiting quarterback with their roar.

To impress sophisticated Los Angeles, to bring it to its feet in an ecstasy of shouting and cheering, requires a performance that is rare, an occasion that overwhelms.

◆

IT WAS A COMPLICATED affair, the city's with the Rams during their first decade together.

By 1955, Los Angeles—in the person of Councilwoman Roz Wyman and columnist Vincent Flaherty, among others—courted baseball's Brooklyn Dodgers: flattered, proffered gifts, argued and flirted, cajoled.

But in 1946 when the Rams had arrived from Cleveland, they came—as did so much of Southern California's immigrant population boom—uninvited. Perhaps in some corners of Los Angeles the Rams were even unwelcome. The city already had two minor league football teams, and it had the Dons, a team from a league challenging the NFL: the All-American Football Conference. And what did the NFL matter anyway? If, in 1946, major league baseball was the national pastime, pro football was the national "maybe-we'll-care-if-we-have-the-time." On the gridiron, college football held the nation's affection, and that was especially true for longtime Angelenos who lined up to cheer USC's Trojans and UCLA's Bruins.

When Dan Reeves brought his team from Cleveland, it wasn't because Los Angeles wanted the Rams; it was because Reeves, the Rams president and owner, wanted Los Angeles.

Yet, eight seasons later, Rams players appeared in films and on TV shows; children and adults waited outside the locker room to get Crazylegs and Tank Younger and others to sign their names to photographs and game programs. The city and the Rams would set an NFL attendance record, drawing 93,751 to watch the home team play the Lions, more fans than had ever witnessed a single game. By 1955, they'd nearly match that number for their final regular season game against Green Bay.

What made the difference? How did the Rams attract headlines and popping flashbulbs and autograph-hungry crowds in a city where such attention was among the most valuable commodities?

It helped that the All-American Football Conference failed after four seasons and took the Dons with it. It helped that the Los Angeles sun shone more often than did the sun in Cleveland or Pittsburgh or Detroit and made a day at the game more inviting. It helped that when the Rams arrived from Cleveland, they were the reigning national champs and that their leader, Bob Waterfield, had prepped at Van Nuys High School, played for UCLA, and married a movie star. It helped that Los Angeles was in the midst of yet another population boom, the region growing annually by hundreds of thousands, so even a small percentage of Angelenos buying tickets meant *stacks and stacks* of tickets. It helped, too, that many of those immigrants— Sooners and Longhorns and Razorbacks—arrived with a love for football and no allegiance to either Trojan nor Bruin nor any pro team. Those folks might attend their first Rams game because they enjoyed football in general, not Rams football in particular. But maybe they'd come back for a second game or a third, because—man alive!—Tom Fears could run a great good-lord pass route, and did you hear the "*whoof!*" from that Packers running back when Andy Robustelli caught him shoulder-to-midsection? And the touchdowns! Who could keep track with the Rams scoring fifty-one points, or sixty-five…even seventy! That was just plain fun. That would get people through the turnstiles.

But Reeves seemed to understand that for the Rams to last in Los Angeles he needed more than people in the seats. He needed to make professional football part of the city's culture, to transform the Rams into an LA institution as significant as Sid Grauman's theaters or traffic jams or the Hollywood Bowl. He needed Angelenos to wake up during football season thinking about the Rams, to chat at lunch about that week's game, to schedule their lives around Sundays.

This was bigger thinking. Reeves was no Walt Disney, but what he wanted to build would require Disney–esque inventiveness and optimism and risk-taking. It would require a spirit and ambition to match that of Los Angeles itself.

Thus, his efforts to collaborate with the coliseum and the *Times*—because how better to become an institution than to affiliate with other institutions? The resulting *Times* Charities Game drew some eighty thousand fans to the coliseum each year. Then, Reeves took a risk and gave away seats—sometimes as many as twenty thousand—to children under twelve years old whose parents bought a ticket, calling the program "Free Football for Kids." Not only would this lead to children bothering their parents about the Rams, but in ten or fifteen years, Reeves figured, those kids would be back on their own. Fred Gehrke's idea to paint the Ram's horn logo onto helmets fit Reeves strategy, too, providing a way to brand the team.

Then there was television.

In 1947, people had yet to embrace TV. The nation's television manufacturers built only 178,000 sets. But that number grew to three million two years later. Those manufacturers had learned that sets sold faster if there was more and better content broadcast on TV. Sports—especially boxing—were popular. Football, with the rectangular shape of its field, its right-to-left and left-to-right action, appeared to be a sport well suited for the tube. So it made sense to Reeves when the Admiral Television Company offered to sponsor broadcasts of Rams home games to an LA audience. This was a groundbreaking idea; no NFL teams had ever broadcast home games. The upside? The Rams would work their way into the lives of more and more people. The risk? Reeves and his staff recognized it immediately. Why would fans pay for a ticket when they could watch a game at home for free? Given that, Reeves agreed to the deal with a condition: Admiral would subsidize ticket revenue lost during the season. Admiral agreed, and in 1950, Angelenos became the first in the country to watch their NFL team play home games on TV.

Attendance did fall. The Rams' previous average of nearly fifty-two thousand fans per game dropped to about thirty-one thousand. Admiral paid the shortfall, about $307,000.

But Reeves had the benefit of people watching from home in Pasadena or Pomona, perhaps even some who would never have come to a game. The broadcasts reminded Angelenos that Waterfield and Crazylegs and Tank and Dutch worked magic on the gridiron right down the highway from those houses in Pasadena and Pomona. These football players? They were neighbors.

With the Rams on TV every week, some people became accustomed to having the Rams in the living room or den. Maybe they even looked forward to a Sunday with the team, just as every week they looked forward to *Meet the Press* and Ed Sullivan and *Kukla, Fran and Ollie*—growing institutions, all.

The next year, the Admiral deal ended. The Rams again blacked out home game broadcasts, and attendance rose. By midway through 1953, John Hock's first season with the team, the Rams drew their record-setting crowd, those ninety-three thousand–plus.

That was a high. There were still lows. Later that same season only twenty-three thousand showed for a game against the Packers. Maybe they stayed away because it was cold that day, a high of forty-five degrees. Or maybe smog hung low, and few people wanted to spend hours outdoors, risking that telltale burn at the back of the throat. Maybe LA's fans didn't want to give much time to a team that was out of contention for a title, as the Rams were that year.

Any and all of those reasons.

Attendance continued to rise and ebb like the coastal tide, fluctuations that could doom a short-term endeavor like a movie or a television show. But institutions survive such shifts, and by 1955 the Rams had become an institution, had become part of the fabric of Southern California life. At banquets to honor the team, people paid ten dollars a plate. The "Ye Old Rams" fan club offered weekly luncheons. Bob Oates of the *Times* published a book chronicling "the story of the Rams...the finest book on professional football ever published." The Rams even sold Christmas gifts out of their game day programs. "Rooter caps" were two dollars each. For $1.50 you could drop a lapel pin in your husband's stocking, and for $8.50 a cuff link. Big spenders could unload $21.50 for a Rams blanket, good for use at the stadium or the beach, and "attractive for the den."

And the team's away games were regularly broadcast on KABC-TV.

The Rams had become such an organic part of Los Angeles that nationwide, they were among those institutions—including Disneyland, Hollywood, smog, and beaches—that people associated with Los Angeles. Melvin Durslag was writing about the Rams for national magazines such as *Vanity Fair* and *Sports Illustrated*. People throughout the country—from

Maine to Mississippi—could watch Rams players star in movies. In the consciousness of the country, the Rams had become Los Angeles's team; there was no other. Perhaps the best indication was that derisive name George Connor of Chicago's Bears had spat that day he and a teammate knocked over Crazylegs Hirsch, the word that equated player with place:

Don't go messing up Hollywood like that.

◆

TWENTY-EIGHT DEGREES. THAT WAS the high in Chicago on December 11, 1955, the last day of the NFL's regular season, when George Connors and the Bears met Philadelphia's Eagles. So chilly and bright was the afternoon that the Bears' coach, George Halas, wore sunglasses along with his fedora and heavy overcoat as he worked the sidelines at Wrigley Field. Halas, called Papa Bear, was one of the NFL's founding coaches; as a player-coach he'd brought the Bears to Chicago in 1921. Earlier in the 1955 season, he'd announced his plans to retire. When the Bears played their last game of the year, it would be his last—period. Now, taking the field, the Bears knew, as did their fans, that this one might be Papa's finale. They trailed the Rams in the NFL's Western Division, and a loss to the Eagles would end their season. But a chance remained. With the right combination of events, including a victory over Philadelphia, the Bears and Halas might yet play once more—in the NFL's Championship game.

So, that afternoon carried with it a particular poignancy. Newspaper photographers stalked Halas, capturing his every move: kneeling on the sideline, applauding a successful pass play, shaking his fist, listening to information from his assistant coaches. On the field, running and tackling with a combination of hope and desperation, Halas's Bears did their part, beating the Eagles, 17–10.

What remained for them now was to wait.

After interviews with reporters and showers and clean clothes and combed hair and cologne, Bears players, some fans, and Halas himself gathered at the Edgewater Beach Hotel, north of Wrigley and near the lakeshore. WGN radio sounded over the hotel's south terrace. The station was broadcasting a game from two time zones away: the Rams versus Packers at LA's Memorial Coliseum. Because the Bears had beaten Philadelphia, they had one remaining chance to win the Western Division Title and go on to the NFL championship game. One outcome in Los Angeles would extend Halas's legendary career and give the Bears a shot at a storybook ending to Papa Bear's fabled career.

That's why every Bear and every Bear fan was rooting for Green Bay to win and for Los Angeles to lose.

◆

TAKE STOCK, FOR A moment, of John Hock's life, that morning of December 11.

He's twenty-seven years old, an Army veteran, a devout Roman Catholic, educated in history by the Jesuits. Six months ago, he married a pixie of a girl who grew up a few blocks away from his boyhood house. Right-handed, he wears a college ring on his wedding-band finger. He is one of some 420 men in the entire country who play professional football for the NFL, and he is one of only 132 who start on offense. Only eleven other men start at right guard, his same position.

He's twenty-seven years old, and there are days his knees feel twice that age. Long scars run parallel along the outer edges of the right joint. He plays for the NFL team in his hometown, so his wife and father easily attend home games, like today's. He wears jersey number sixty-three. Teammates call him Lantern Jaw or the Hooker. The newspapers, when they mention him, often call him Johnny Hock as if he's still the teenager who impressed people while playing at Mount Carmel High School. He stands six foot two and 235 pounds, lifts weights, wears his blond hair neatly trimmed (when it needs the scissors he can tell because the tip of his widow's peak reveals a wave). He's no jabber mouth—sometimes he's quiet as stone—but he likes to laugh. A good time for him is watching other people have a good time. He does not like to draw attention to himself, though people notice when he enters a room. He and his wife, who is a schoolteacher, make their home in a small second-floor apartment owned by her aunt, who lives on the ground floor. The American city

Nine-year-old John Hock with mother Elizabeth and sister Ruth making their move from Pittsburgh to Los Angeles in 1937, where dad Harry was looking for work.

John Hock (left) taking part in basic training for his service in the Korean War in 1951.

Hall Haynes (left), former California Governor and Supreme Court Chief Justice Earl Warren (center), and John Hock (right), in the parade to celebrate the Santa Clara Broncos 1950 Orange Bowl victory over Paul "Bear" Bryant's University of Kentucky Wildcats. (Photo courtesy of Santa Clara University Archives.)

John Hock in high school at the now-defunct Mount Carmel (Los Angeles) circa 1945.

John Hock of the Los Angeles Rams in 1957.

The Chicago Cardinals team photo from 1950, John Hock's (#11) rookie season. Pictured in the center is legendary coach Earl Louis "Curley" Lambeau.

John Hock getting ready for the 1954 season with Hall of Fame receiver Tom Fears (right).

RAMS—1953

Volney "Skeet" Quinlan, V. T. "Vitamin" Smith, Tom McCormick, Duane
e Toogood, Stan West, Norman Van Brocklin, Don Paul (Captain), Dick
RD ROW: Hamp Pool (Head Coach), John Hock, Norb Hecker, Harland
" Hirsch, Howard "Red" Hickey (End Coach). REAR ROW: "Deacon" Dan
Brink, Frank Fuller, Bud McFadin, Tom Dahms, Bill Battles (Line Coach).

LOS ANGELES RAMS

RAMs

CONFERENCE CHAMPS — 4 TIMES
WORLD'S CHAMPS — 1951

LES RICHTER
LINEBACKER   LOS ANGELES RAMS

BILL WADE
QUARTERBACK   LOS ANGELES RAMS

DUANE PUTNAM
GUARD   LOS ANGELES RAMS

JON ARNETT
HALFBACK   LOS ANGELES RAMS

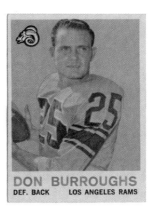

DON BURROUGHS
DEF. BACK   LOS ANGELES RAMS

The Hock family in 1976. Pictured left to right is Anna, Lisa, Sue, Mary, Jim, Joe, John, Micki, and Jay.

Micki and John Hock on their wedding day on June 25, 1955.

John and Micki Hock are toasted by family and friends before they embark on their honeymoon to Carpinteria.

John and Micki Hock celebrate their wedding reception in the backyard and garage of Micki's parents home in South Los Angeles.

where they live—his hometown—is glamorous and dramatic, intoxicating. Even its seedy and scandalous sides—the affairs, the murders, the feuds—fascinate people. On its way to being the entertainment capital of the world, his hometown might be the American city that most craves *and* captures the nation's attention (but don't tell that to New York). Whether people here are TV and movie stars at a party or neighborhood folks around a charcoal grill, they have a good time. John Hock, he enjoys watching them laugh, play pinochle or horseshoes.

In his twenty-seven years, he's faced many crucibles: the first Mass he ever served, the rabbit-skinning table in the backyard, the Orange Bowl while in college, basic training at Fort Ord, the Far East Bowl while serving in Japan, a season without football so his knee tendon might heal. In their ways, each of those made demands of him, put him under particular pressures. They required that he act with precision, that he practice patience, that he understand what he was called to do and put aside all other concerns. Those tests required him to focus on a single thing—when to ring a bell, where to cut with a knife, how to assemble pieces into a rifle, who to knock down—and only that thing.

He's twenty-seven, newly wed, and about to play the most important game of his career.

That day would start early, but not with an alarm clock. There'd be no reason. He and Micki were not people to stay up late or to sleep in; they'd wake early enough. Probably he'd have slept well. Seldom nervous, never overwrought, he would carry the weight of the coming game with an easy grace.

Maybe she'd make breakfast while he shaved. Bacon sizzling in a cast iron pan, eggs over-easy, toast patted with butter—and then more butter. A small glass of chilled juice, hot coffee from the percolator. At the table, with the Sunday paper, he'd set the sports section aside. What others had to say about his team's game held little interest for him.

Then, because it's Sunday morning, Mr. and Mrs. Hock would go to Mass, proclaim the mysteries of faith and share in the miracle of Christ's sacrifice. Soon after, he'd leave for the stadium. Micki would drop him off, so that later she could drive together with his dad and after the game they could all go home together. Or maybe she and Dad would come separately, because sometimes, after games, the Hocks and the Hausers, the Putnams and the Robustellis, would drive out to the valley for dinner at the Ram's Horn, Don Paul's restaurant. Today would be a nice day for that, especially if the Rams win. A festive way to celebrate.

Once at the stadium, John will join his teammates in stretching and light calisthenics. They'll practice a few formations. The trainers will tape players' ankles and knuckles and wrists. Players will screw cleats into the soles of their shoes. Today they'll wear their gold jerseys, the ones with blue numbers, and when they come onto the field, that gold will glow in the bright day's light. Ninety thousand people will rise to greet them. A Los Angeles crowd, sure, so maybe less vocal than others in Pittsburgh or Baltimore—but when ninety thousand people whisper it's a loud whisper, and when they shout, that sound cascades to the field, envelops the players, comes like late day heat—from everywhere and nowhere in particular. The players spill over the field, west to east across the grass, toward fifteen arches that decorate that end of the coliseum. Through those, this morning, the sun glared. Now it sits overhead as if it, too, wants to watch the game. The stadium sinks below grade, and its top rows are so high that from the field, the city is hidden from the players' view. All that the Rams can see are people filling the seats, and those arches recalling ancient Rome, and the Southern California sky unfolding forever, and footballs that spin and spiral against the unending blue. What else is there in the world?

Then, the Packers and the Rams line up for the kick-off.

◆

Up in his box, Dan Reeves watches. What a strange week it has been for him. Six days ago he met with his fellow Rams stockholders. Years back, when the Rams were losing money, he and his partner Frederick Levy Jr., had sold stakes in the team for a dollar to a few others willing to help absorb the financial losses with the promise of profits later. Now, with a stake in the team of 33 1/3 percent, Reeves needs to sign a contract each year keeping him as president. This year, though—six days ago—the other owners balked. They told him he was spending too much time on his Beverly Hills brokerage firm and not giving enough attention to the Rams. Fred Levy, who owned 22.5 percent of the team, said the owners wanted Reeves to work full time for the Rams or not at all. Continue as an owner, yes, of course, but if he couldn't give himself fully to the job of president, they wanted him to give up the role.

This must have rankled.

Reeves had purchased the Rams with Levy in 1941, with Reeves controlling the team's operations. He'd come to football using money inherited from his father, the owner of a New York–area grocery store chain, and through the years he'd parlayed that wealth into even more as principal owner of the Rams and of Daniel Reeves & Company, his brokerage firm. Though he'd been an athlete at Georgetown University, he was not a big man. His nose came to a sharp point, and his oddly shaped ears looked as if they'd been used too often when he was a boy to yank him out of trouble. And he seemed often to be in an argument with someone: fellow NFL owners, his coaches, other owners of the Rams. Those arguments were often about Reeves' ideas for modernizing the NFL or his team.

A team about to play for the Western Division Title.

The Western Division Title. In front of ninety thousand people.

And his fellow Rams owners believed he wasn't doing enough.

Said Reeves to the press: "After fifteen years as head of the Rams I have no intention of stepping out."

Answered Levy: "If he is able to devote enough time to the job, he may continue as president."

Levy, however, a man who had been Reeves' close friend since the Cleveland days, may have been speaking in a code only Rams insiders would understand. For years, Reeves had shown himself to be a binge drinker. Tex Schramm, who would go on to be the general manager of the Dallas Cowboys, and whose title with the team in 1955 was "assistant to the president," believed that Reeves had probably been drunk years before when he fired Hamp Pool. Sober and focused, Schramm knew, Reeves could solve any problem his team faced. Drunk, he became an unsolvable problem. Sometimes he would disappear for days at a time.

Years later, Melvin Durslag would remember the Rams' owners as a strange bunch, most of whom enjoyed parties, alcohol, and arguing—all a bit too much. He called Reeves "an alcoholic" who "fought it all his life."

"He was born on Fifth Avenue, and he got ill," Durslag said. "He was really a good guy, you see, but the guy had a drinking habit."

In other words, when the other owners said publicly that Reeves was spending too little time on the Rams, they may also have been saying to Reeves: "Sober up."

◆

ON THE GAME'S THIRD play, with only a minute and seven seconds elapsed and some late-arriving fans still clambering to their seats, Van Brocklin called for a sweep to the left. The Rams had reached their own forty-five-yard line, nearly midfield, and Waller was to receive the hand off.

On the snap, Putnam and Hock pulled left, Putnam leading the way, Hock a half-step behind. Van Brocklin tucked the ball into Waller's gut, and the Rat took off, chasing Putnam and Hock. The Putter rumbled into the first would-be tackler, and Waller deftly dodged that pileup. But another Packer loomed to grab him and keep him from a good gain. Hock, though, still charged ahead. He angled himself so he'd hit that Packer square on. He chicken-winged his arms, lowered his helmet, and—at precisely the right moment—uncoiled. The block was perfect, devastating. It raised the Packer player off his feet and Hock kept driving his legs, driving, driving, until the fellow went down, Hock rolling over him. It was the rare sort of block that even fans notice; teammates and coaches, too. Exquisite in its execution, timing, and result. "Crushing," the *Times* would call that block the next day.

Now Waller faced a mostly open field. A single player remained to beat: Doyle Nix, a defensive back who'd played college ball at Southern Methodist University and who, like Waller, was a rookie. Waller used Nix's momentum against him, cutting back to the right and twisting Nix's legs into such a knot that he tumbled to the turf. With Rams' lineman Charlie Toogood following a just-in-case half-step behind, Waller finished his run, covering fifty-five yards to the end zone. Les Richter kicked the extra point, and the Rams led, 7–0.

Green Bay kicked a field goal not long after to make it 7–3. The Rams came right back, driving all the way to the Packer one-yard line where they had a first down. One yard to go, with four tries to get it for a touchdown. Van Brocklin called on Tank Younger, the thick-muscled 226-pound back. Once, Tank rushed the Packer line, then twice. Neither time could Hock, Putnam, and the other Rams linemen budge the Packers, and Younger, plunging straight forward, was stopped with hardly an inch gained. On third down, Van Brocklin tried a pass play to Woodley Lewis, but a Packers linebacker knocked the ball to the turf.

That left fourth down. Van Brocklin was known to be a stubborn play-caller who had once insisted on the same play four straight times to prove it would work. This day, he must have believed in *Tank-straight-ahead*. Yet again, he called for a hand-off to Younger. Younger gripped the ball against his abdomen, lowered his shoulders and bulled toward the right side of the line.

Two men—270-pound Jerry Helluin and 240-pound Bill Forester—hit him. "Nailed Younger cold," reported the *Times*, "and shortened his neck a couple of inches, maybe." The series of downs was so impressive even Rams fans applauded Green Bay.

Dejected, the Rams' offense gave way to the defense. But the Packers, stuck back on their own one-yard line, weren't going to have an easy time of it, either. On their first play, quarterback Tobin Rote handed off to Breezy Reid who fumbled. Art Hauser of the Rams fell on the ball at the one-yard line. Rams ball! And Van Brocklin, Hock, Younger, and Co., came right back out on the field.

"We knew they were going to fumble as soon as they took over," Van Brocklin later quipped.

So here were the Rams, back where they'd started, on the one-yard line with four tries to score. Except this time Van Brocklin handed the ball to Waller, not Younger. And skinny, wiry Waller split two tacklers at the line of scrimmage and scampered into the end zone.

Now, with Les Richter's kick, the Rams led 14–3. A third Waller touchdown early in the second half made it 21–10, and at the Edgewater Hotel in Chicago, Bears fans began to despair. When Skeet Quinlan's fifty-five-yard punt return pushed the lead to 31–10, the outcome appeared certain.

In Chicago, Papa Bear Halas was shaking hands with myriad guests when someone mentioned to him the score. "Thirty-one to ten?" he said. "Is that what it is?"

◆

THOSE LOS ANGELES FANS. Those relaxed, detached observers of all things entertaining. When the gun cracked to end the game, and the Rams had won, 31–17, that sophisticated Los Angeles crowd gave up its whole self.

First came the roar, a resounding approval. And then came the fans themselves. Thousands spilled over the stadium walls onto the field. Wanting the euphoria to last, wanting to grip the joy the Rams had brought and not to let go, the fans tromped the grass, touched their champions, dry fingertips to sweaty shoulders and arms, patted their backs, engulfed them. If there had ever been any questions about Los Angeles's feelings for this uninvited team playing something less than the national sport, those were answered. The Rams belonged to Los Angeles, and Los Angeles belonged to the Rams.

In one section of the stadium, the team's band blew brass and thumped drums. Cheerleaders cheered. Gene Lipscomb, a Rams defensive tackle, and Don Paul, the Rams' villain, seized their bow-tied first-year coach, lifting Sid Gillman to their shoulders so awkwardly his pants legs rode up to his knees. They carried him that way, with other Rams gathered around as if they were Gillman's Praetorian guard and he their Caesar. They pushed through the mass of their own celebrating fans toward the edge of the field and into the tunnel, all the way to the locker room.

Dan Reeves was at the door to meet them. "Well done!" he said, and then again, "Well done!" shaking this player's hand, patting that one on the back. Then, with all the Rams safely tucked away in the locker room, they removed their helmets. Van Brocklin raised Gillman's arm, and John Hock, right beside them, lifted his right fist, and all the Rams mirrored him, shouting their triumph as one.

When they'd quieted, Tom Fears stood to speak. A tall, powerful man, he was a cocaptain and one of the most respected players on the team, known as much for the ferocity of his blocking as the precision with which he ran pass routes. He'd scored the winning touchdown the last time the Rams had won the NFL championship—in 1951, against the Browns—when he snatched a Van Brocklin pass from the air and ran nearly fifty-five yards to break a 17–17 fourth-quarter tie. Even in this, his eighth season in the league, he'd caught forty-four passes, more than any other Ram.

Now, in the dank, warm locker room, its bright lights shining down out of the ceiling, Fears took a football in hand. This was the ceremonial game ball, the award given to the man who provided the day's greatest contributions, chosen by his peers.

Fears looked first at his coach. When Gillman had come to training camp, he'd promised more defense and a more patient offense. Then, he'd improved the defense with a trade, and maybe as a result of that the Rams' Will Sherman led the league that season with eleven interceptions, while Don Burroughs was tied for second with nine. On offense, Gillman had cut back on the long pass plays, using the run more often and the shorter pass. The Rams ended up passing more often than the season before, but the yards they gained per pass dropped from 10.1 to 6.9. Even with a broken hand through much of the season, Van Brocklin threw fewer interceptions under the new system. Finally, Gillman had dealt with injuries by assuming that every player off the bench could contribute equally. With these changes, the Rams had won their way all the way to the NFL title game.

Fears held the ball forward so all could see. "We thought of giving this ball to Coach Gillman," he said. "But there's an even more important game coming up."

Everyone in the room knew what that meant: The Rams would give Gillman the game ball after they beat the Eastern champions, the Cleveland Browns, and captured the NFL title. It was a challenge Fears and Don Paul, as team captains, were making to their teammates and to themselves and even to Gillman. It was as if they were saying, "Lead us to one more victory, Sid; do that, and this ball is yours."

Then Fears turned back to his teammates.

"So today's award," he said, turning toward the man who had delivered the day's most bone-shivering block, "goes to John Hock for his fine play in the line."

He offered the game ball, and Hock took it in his big hands. He held it shyly, nodding his gratitude to his teammates, who applauded and cheered him. He understood how rare a gift this was, only twelve given a year on a team of thirty-five players, and even more rarely did it come to offensive linemen, those players who neither tackled nor scored touchdowns. It was a gift that said, "We saw you today. We saw how you opened the field for the Rat, but also every trap and counter, every sweep right or left. We saw how you protected Dutch. We saw how you pitted yourself against Green Bay's best and beat them. We saw all that you did and how well."

Amidst the cheers, Hock ducked away, back to his locker even as Putnam and Hauser and Robustelli and the others slapped his shoulders and back, grinned at him, shook his hand, recalled this play or that, how Hock dominated.

Then the players made their way to their own lockers or to George "Mother" Menefee, the athletic trainer, to grab a bag of ice for a shoulder or ankle. Reporters huddled around asking questions of Dutch and Gillman. Hock needed ice, too, for his knees. But in a quiet moment he looked at the ball. Someone, maybe Don Paul or Fears, had written across its face in indelible black ink, with a careful hand. "Western Division Champs, 1954" it read, just above the Rawlings stamp. And below that, "Green Bay Packers 17, LA Rams 31."

He rolled the ball over in his hand to read the other side: "Game Ball," it said, "to John J. Hock."

The attention attached to this prize was done, which was fine. What remained, what would last, was what the ball represented. A decade or so earlier, on the Mount Carmel High School football field a few miles south, John Hock had discovered the work for which he was best suited. Since then, he'd wanted little more than to be steady in that work and to do it well. It was never easy on his body or his will—and that, in part, was the reward. The work suited him because it tested him, just as it tested every man who played. Fans might not always understand that, not in the rough bone and sinew and gut where such understanding lived. Perhaps even coaches had forgotten the pain and sacrifice their players renewed each day. That's why this football mattered, the one John Hock held in his big hand. It came from the men who knew the work, who knew it today, who knew it now, who knew it in that place deeper than any bruise, past any broken part. They knew, and they had taken this moment to say, "Good job."

◆

As the Rams showered, reporters gathered around Gillman, who had pulled a cuff link from his pocket. The piece was big and new and shiny, with a gem like a diamond—maybe it was a diamond—at its center. Around the edge was an inscription:

"1955 World Champions" and "Chicago Bears".

A friend, Gillman said, had sent it from Chicago. "Someone back there jumped the gun," he said.

He was asked whether the Rams might order their own such.

"Let's wait until we get over the Cleveland Browns," Gillman said.

Practice, he added, would start again on Thursday.

CHAPTER 10

The Loser's Purse

REMEMBER PAUL BROWN'S TAUNT? The Rams did. It came after they had beaten the Browns, 38–21, in that exhibition game back in September. Everybody knew the results didn't matter, didn't indicate a thing. But Cleveland's coach couldn't let it go. As Hock and Van Brocklin and Waller and the rest jogged past him, he had challenged them: "Okay, okay, but what about December?"

What *about* December?

December was the Browns' month. They owned it in a way no other NFL team did. The franchise had existed for only nine years, born the season after the Rams left Cleveland. But in those nine years the Browns had played in nine league championship games: four as part of the All-American Football Conference, and then five in a row after that league folded and the Browns joined the NFL. Cleveland had won all four AAFC title games, and they'd won two in the NFL.

Now here came December: the day before Christmas, in the midst of the lunch hour, a plane carrying Coach Brown and his team touched down at Burbank's airport. Clouds like gray wool dropped sprinkles, which landed on the suit coats of Browns players as they descended from the plane to the tarmac. They might have hoped for sun, but it had been raining for days, so much so that at the coliseum the grounds crew had spread a new $16,000 tarp across the field to keep it in good condition. Still, the greeting Los Angeles's climate offered to the Browns was better than the hard, frigid cruelty they'd left behind in northeast Ohio where icy fields made practice hazardous.

Otto Graham, the Browns' quarterback, looked up into the dreary sky and deadpanned to reporters: "Unless you guarantee that the temperature will be at least fifty degrees, we won't play."

The last time Graham had been in Los Angeles was almost a year before, in more pleasant weather, as the starting quarterback for the East's squad in the NFL's Pro Bowl. Graham had an easy smile when making jokes—but when he pulled on a helmet his face changed. He wore a dark intensity like a mask; his glare looked as if it could cut glass. Perhaps more than any other player, perhaps even more than Coach Brown, Graham was responsible for the Browns' success. He'd been their quarterback since the team's founding in 1946, running his coach's preferred offense—the T-formation—better than anyone in the league. On any play, Graham might hand off to one of three running backs lined up behind him, or he might pass, or he might run himself—and at six foot one, two hundred pounds, he was tough to tackle. In the previous year's title game—a 56–10 thrashing of Detroit's Lions—Graham had thrown three touchdown passes and run for another three. After that game, he announced his retirement, wanting to end his career with a championship. But without him, the Browns lost a string of exhibition games to start 1955—including that game when Paul Brown taunted the Rams. The taunt was bold, given that Brown knew the primary reason his team had lost. Without Graham, there might be no December. So, just after that loss to the Rams, Brown telephoned Graham and set up a meeting at a restaurant in Aurora, Ohio. There, he offered his old quarterback a $25,000 salary—the highest pay in the NFL—to draw him out of retirement. It worked, and with Graham back, the Browns regained their old form and finished with a 9–2–1 record. Now, both odds-makers and bettors favored them to beat the Rams for the title, the line running as high as six points.

The Browns headed from the airport straight to a field nearby for practice. The next day was Christmas, and Coach Brown—a no-nonsense disciplinarian—

wanted his team to work right away. There wasn't time to waste. The day after Christmas, they'd meet the Rams.

And after that, no matter the outcome, Otto Graham planned to retire. For good this time.

◆

TWICE BEFORE, THE RAMS and Browns had clashed for the NFL title.

Each game had been decided in the final quarter. In 1950, the Rams had lost at Cleveland, 30–28, when Browns kicker, Lou "The Toe" Groza, kicked a field goal with twenty-eight seconds left.

The next year the Rams won at the coliseum, 24–17, on that long, fourth-quarter scoring pass that made a local legend of Tom Fears.

Four years had passed since Dutch-to-Fears won it all, and quite a few players from those days still wore Rams helmets: Tank Younger, Deacon Dan Towler, Don Paul, Andy Robustelli, Bob Boyd, and Crazylegs Hirsch, among them. All could remember what it meant to play a Cleveland Browns team at its best.

But most Rams, including John Hock, had only played Cleveland three times—all exhibition games. Since Hock had joined the team, the Rams and Browns had never played each other in a game that mattered— and certainly not in the NFL's pinnacle game with all its attendant spectacle.

It couldn't match the opening of Disneyland for national attention and economic upswing, but NBC had paid the league $100,000 for the rights to broadcast the game nationally. The contract prevented the game from being shown in Los Angeles because the NFL wanted to encourage the hometown fans to pay the five-dollars-a-ticket price and head out to the coliseum. By Christmas Eve, sixty thousand tickets had been sold, and coliseum officials expected to blow up the record for attendance at a championship game. It was a safe prediction, given that the previous best was 58,346, the number who watched the 1946 championship at the Polo Grounds in New York, pitting the Giants against Chicago's Bears.

Tickets sales mattered to players, too, who would receive bonuses based on the league's revenue earned from the game, sometimes as much as a couple thousand dollars. Each player would get the same fixed amount; the winners would earn a bit more than the losers. For a player with Otto Graham's highest-in-the-league salary, the bonus might seem small, perhaps 10 percent of his annual take.

That amount going to an offensive lineman, say to John Hock, might be half again his annual salary.

◆

THE X-RAYS SHOWED A hairline fracture cutting through a vertebrae bone in Tank Younger's neck, that same neck Frank Finch of the *Times* had described as "shortened" by all those failed one-yard runs against the Packers.

It was a smart-aleck comment—until it wasn't.

"This is not to be confused with a broken neck," said the Rams surgeon, Dr. Dan Fortmann, who himself had played offensive line for the Chicago Bears as he finished his medical degree. "The hairline fracture has started to knit. However, it is not deemed advisable to permit Younger to play."

In a season when the Rams had suffered more injuries than in recent memory, Sid Gillman had hoped that he could meet the mighty Browns with a team at full strength. Even Elroy Hirsch looked to return, who had limped through most of the season and spent about as much time in the team's whirlpool as he had on the field. To lose any starter, but especially to lose Younger, was disappointing news. That season, he had been the Rams' leading fullback and second-leading rusher after Ron Waller.

A mainstay of the Rams offense since 1949, he would spend his third NFL championship game on the sidelines in street clothes.

Younger had come to the Rams from Louisiana, raw and trim and tall, and already bearing the nickname, "Tank." He'd received the name while playing at tiny Grambling College, a school founded by black Louisianans as an agriculture and industry school for black students. When Paul Calhoun Younger signed his pro contract, he became the first player from an all-black college to sign with an NFL team. While the Rams had signed Kenny Washington and Woody Strode under pressure to integrate, the decision to

211

sign Younger, while historic, was based entirely on his quality as a player. That the Rams signed him as a free agent rather than selecting him with a precious draft pick was less a statement about him than it was about the attitudes NFL players and coaches had toward players from "Negro colleges." The Rams knew no other team would want Younger—they might not even know about him. So why waste the draft pick?

That the Rams knew about Younger was indicative of their cutting-edge scouting system. In the postwar 1940s, they knew more about potential players than any team in the league. It was another way Reeves leapt ahead of the NFL's old-guard owners and coaches. Those other teams spent little, if any, money on scouting. Mostly, each relied on good-ol'-boy networks, informed gossip from buddies and former teammates, thought it was still only gossip. Reeves organized a methodology.

In 1946, as the team headed for Southern California, he hired Eddie Kotal, a one-time running back with Green Bay's Packers, as a full-time scout, the first in NFL history. Kotal's job was to drive all over the country—from Louisiana to Oregon to Wisconsin to Connecticut—evaluating talent at football powerhouses such as Ohio State University or Notre Dame, but also in hideaways such as Scottsdale Community College, Arnold College, or Grambling College. He'd visited Tank Younger a few times, including once after Younger and Grambling played in the Vulcan Bowl, a premiere bowl game for black colleges. "Have you ever considered playing pro football?" Kotal asked Younger. "I've never given it a thought," Younger told him. When the time came for him to sign with a team, Younger knew he wanted the Rams. "By showing personal interest in me," Younger told *Ebony* magazine years later, "Kotal impressed me."

Kotal, bushy-browed and dapper and happy to play a hand of gin rummy, was the face of the Rams scouting operations. But those operations involved many more people than Kotal. Tex Schramm, Reeves' assistant, explained the system in detail years later to Michael MacCambridge, author of *America's Game*. Reeves had a network of some one hundred college coaches around the country whom he paid for twice-a-year reports. He paid honorariums to California high school coaches to visit the Rams headquarters in Beverly Hills and watch game films to evaluate potential players. Rams staff mailed questionnaires to players in their junior years and studied the responses. Reeves hung a wall map of the United States in his office and with pushpins marked the location of each four-year college that played football.

So, come draft day, when NFL owners and coaches would gather at a hotel, usually in New York City, the Rams would call out names of players no other owner or coach had heard of—or expected.

Andy Robustelli? Who? Where's Arnold College? Who have they played? The Sisters of Charity?

After a few years, though, chuckles gave way to something else. You can imagine the *oh-hell-not-again* dread. Soon, every team had hired its own Eddie Kotal with the hope of finding its own Tank Youngers.

In 1955, Curly Lambeau, the legendary Packers coach who had spilled cigarette ash on John Hock's dormitory bed, gave credit to Kotal and Dan Reeves for the Rams' ascendence to the NFL championship game. "I'm not taking anything away from Sid Gillman—he's done a wonderful job," Lambeau told the *Los Angeles Times*, "but I think Dan Reeves and Eddie Kotal deserve a lot of credit for obtaining the high type of player that represents Los Angeles in the National Football League."

But now Younger was out for the championship game, and the Rams would turn to "Deacon" Dan Towler, another of those scouting system successes. Towler, a little-known running back when the Rams drafted him (in the *twenty-fifth round*) from Washington & Jefferson College south of Pittsburgh, arrived the year after Younger made the team. Together, the two joined with Dick Hoerner from Iowa to make that legendary trio nicknamed "The Bull Elephant Backfield," because all of them stood taller than six foot two and weighed more than 220 pounds. The Rams often played all three fullbacks at once, and they trampled other teams.

Hoerner was traded after the 1951 season, breaking up the herd. Of the two who remained, Towler was the more successful runner, gaining almost nine hundred yards in the 1952 and 1953 seasons. Younger gained less than half as much, but also played linebacker on defense. The two presented much different personalities, as their nicknames suggested. Younger, well-liked on the team, could curse with the best of them. His struggles through a brief and unhappy marriage led to a fourteen-day jail sentence after he was accused of hitting his mother-in-law. He said she'd been drinking a vodka cocktail called a "Moscow Mule," which she threw at him, and she called him a "bum football player," so he pushed her and she fell. The Rams paid his $1,000 bail. Later, when his wife sued for divorce, she accused him of drinking too much, staying out late, gambling, using vulgar language, and, on occasion, hitting her, too. Younger said nothing during the divorce hearing. The judge granted the separation with no alimony and gave custody of a keeshond puppy named Jolie to Younger's now ex-wife.

Towler, on the other hand, carried the nickname "Deacon" because even as he played for the Rams, he studied at USC toward a graduate degree in theology with the goal of becoming a minister. He had, on occasion, called the team together and led pregame prayers. By special arrangement with Reeves, he was allowed to miss practices or training camp when he deemed it necessary for his studies. And still he'd gained more than 5.7 yards per carry over three seasons.

But in 1955, Deacon suffered a leg injury in the season's third game. Since then, he'd only carried the ball four times. He'd gained all of eight yards.

In Tank's absence, the Rams would need every bit of power and grace left in Deacon's legs.

◆

IF ANY TWO TEAMS were known for visionary work in professional football through the postwar decade, it was the Rams and the Browns. With Los Angeles, innovation began with Dan Reeves. With Cleveland, it started with Paul Brown.

Reeves hired the first year-round scout; Brown hired the first year-round assistant coaches. Reeves popularized branding the team through its helmets; Brown was first to add a single-bar face mask (trying to protect Graham, who had suffered a mouth wound that required fifteen stitches); Reeves had integrated the NFL; Brown, back in the AAFC days, made Cleveland the first pro team in the modern era to draft African-American players. Reeves moved a team from Cleveland. Brown built a new one there. Both made NFL history and would one day be voted into the league's Hall of Fame.

The NFL they dominated was in many ways still young, its rules comparatively few. The game's past was flat, solid ground. Upon it, strong skilled men struggled against each other in familiar ways. The results were often predictable, because it was easy for coaches and owners to see who was the strongest and most skilled. But clever minds willing to explore and dare could discover ample other ways to win. What Reeves and

Brown had done since 1946 was to open themselves to the future. The past asked who: Who was strongest? Who was best at this position? Who was the most motivational coach? Reeves and Brown asked "What if?" They imagined.

Because they did, each had won two NFL titles. Their teams were meeting for the third time in the league's top game. And that meeting would take place in Los Angeles, the city itself an engine of the imagination.

But some quality that had vaulted the Rams and Browns atop their peers had gone missing. Though they could claim to be the best of 1955, the teams lacked the snap and surprise of the forward-looking. The Rams had won through dependable, grind-it-out, blood-and-bone football. Gillman, the Rams coach, worked with film in new ways, but on the field he had turned his players back toward old ideas. Reeves, for so long an inventive and indulged autocrat, had slipped enough that there came a public rebellion from the rest of the Rams' ownership. As for Brown, he'd resuscitated his team's season not through anything new, but with a desperate and pricey plea to the past and what had worked before. And after this title game, the day after Christmas, that old quarterback, Otto Graham, who had transformed the Browns from losers to winners, would leave for good.

Maybe in a season to come Reeves and Paul Brown would rediscover that forward snap and surprise. Maybe they could find the creative energy to push not only beyond the way *things are done* but, more importantly, beyond the way the Rams and Browns had done them. Reeves was only forty-three years old; Brown only forty-seven.

Or maybe not. Each had built an institution; sustaining such a thing would require other skills, a different vision. Maybe the two men had become convinced that their way of winning was the only way, and the Rams and Browns would become as hidebound, stagnate, and entrenched in failed practices as musty as those of George Preston Marshall and his all-white Redskins.

Maybe the 1955 NFL championship was the great good end of the best their teams would ever be.

◆

WHEN HOLLYWOOD'S CAMERA NEXT finds John Hock, he's got the meaty side of a fist smashed against his helmeted head.

Why?

"There's an old theory," says Bob Gain, who played defensive lineman for the 1955 Cleveland Browns. "Wherever the head goes, the rest of the body follows. We could head slap. It was legal. I didn't really head slap. I punched."

So that's why. And that fist upside John Hock's head? Let's say it belongs to Bob Gain. Gain and Hock faced each other across the line of scrimmage in that 1955 championship game. The two men had history, though maybe even they didn't realize it. They'd lined up against each other nearly six years before, when Hock's Santa Clara Mustangs beat Gain's Kentucky Wildcats in the Orange Bowl.

So: Gain's fist. He's got huge hands, after all, maybe even bigger than Hock's. Hands like a grizzly's paws. Hands big as a cast iron pan. Though he and Hock match height, Gain outweighs the Hooker by some twenty-five pounds.

It's a fist and then chaos that the camera and audio capture. A hand there, a jaw there, another fist, a helmet. Mostly, it's sound. A growl and a huff, a crack when helmets hit, a thud, a pop, a rip. After so many days of rain, there's mud mixed with sweat and spit and snot. The only colors are the burnt orange of the Browns helmets; the shiny blue of the Rams; some jumble of dirt-smeared white and yellow—the jerseys.

The men line up to do it again. The camera pulls back a bit, giving a less intimate view and more context. The Rams try a pass play. Hock and Putnam and the other linemen step backwards, trying to catch the stampeding Browns, trying to stop Gain and company from reaching Van Brocklin.

Another pass play, and the lineman back up again.

A third play, and again it's a pass. Hock, Putnam and the rest are playing—literally—on their heels.

Finally, Van Brocklin zips one, and the camera follows the ball's arc as it travels through a gray sky, the stadium floodlights burning against that gloom. A

Brown reaches out and grabs the ball—interception—then collapses under a pile of Rams.

Hock and the rest jog to the sidelines, and if their heads aren't dipped, there's still something about their postures that suggests frustration. The interception's bad, sure, but worse is how the game is unfolding. The linemen will fall back as often as is called for, but they'd like to pull away from the line, too, run into open field, hit someone. That'll be rare in this game, and that's part by design and part by circumstance. Coach Gillman thought the Browns might be vulnerable to a passing game, so his strategy gives Van Brocklin plenty of tosses. When the camera catches the scoreboard, the circumstance is apparent: Browns seventeen, Rams seven, with just a few seconds left in the first half. Los Angeles trails and the fastest way to get points is by passing.

Now the camera pans the Rams sideline, and there's Van Brocklin jawing with one of the Browns who has hurried by while showing four fingers, one for each of Dutch's interceptions. The camera keeps going until it catches Hock, and there it stops. He's lifted his helmet, so it sits high on his head, the single-bar guarding making a shadow on his forehead. His cheeks are flushed, fists at his hips, chest expanding with heavy breaths. But his mouth isn't open. He's not panting. That big jaw is set. His eyes show the reality; he'll go out there on the field again, and he'll fight and grip and hold and work to keep Dutch out of trouble. He's not beaten, and neither are the Rams—and they won't be, not until the final gun cracks. But any clear-eyed pro can already see that that the Browns are the much better team. The Rams aren't beaten, no, but they will lose this game.

◆

Just about the time the game ended, the rain, which had threatened all afternoon, began to fall, a fitting coda for the Rams and their fans.

"We got our butts kicked," recalls Ron Waller, then the Rams rookie halfback.

"We ended up winning it pretty good," says Cleveland's Bob Gain.

Thirty-eight to fourteen was the final score, and—as the sportswriters say—it wasn't that close.

Van Brocklin threw six interceptions to tie an NFL record no quarterback would ever want. After Gillman benched Dutch, his replacement, Bill Wade, threw another to make it seven for the game. Waller managed only forty-eight yards on eleven carries.

For the Browns, Otto Graham had run for two touchdowns and thrown for two others. When Graham left the field, the Los Angeles crowd of nearly eighty-eight thousand—larger than any to ever have watched an NFL title game—rose as one and offered a loud and long ovation. A similar spirit waited at the Browns' locker room, where Don Paul—the Rams' infamous villain and cocaptain—congratulated each of the winning players.

And some eighty-eight thousand disappointed fans, many hiding under umbrellas, headed for the parking lots. They hadn't been able to help their Rams to victory, but they had staked the NFL to its largest net profit for any championship game—$431,538.88.

The players, by contract, would receive seventy percent of that. The Browns players—as winners—would each cash a record championship paycheck of about $3,500.

The loser's purse to each Ram? About $2,300.

"Hell, you could buy a new car for that," recalls Bob Gain, then corrects himself.

"Not all new cars, but—like—a Chevy."

CHAPTER 11

Those Strange Things Yet To Come

How could John Hock live in Los Angeles and not look forward to tomorrow? How could he, in that spring of 1956, be anything but optimistic? He'd always risen early, which served him well in the military and as an altar boy and at training camp with the Rams. Night scrubbed dust and grit from the world, and what had been tomorrow came quiet and fresh, rich with potential, so rich that if it carried a price tag no one could afford it, not even Howard Hughes. Yet those mornings belonged to him: a kid selling rabbit skins during the Depression, a GI in Japan, a football player making schoolteacher wages. Wake early, open his senses—that's all it took. So he'd rouse himself from sleep and listen to the day gather its energy: the sizzle and smokiness of bacon in a pan; a Western swing tune, staticky and thin on a radio; the surprise of a car backfiring; then the growing thrum as engines heated and people drove to work. It didn't matter whether his joints ached or his nose or a finger was broken. He would push through that, because pain mattered less than astonishment. Out there life waited, and it promised to thrill, because every day was all so new.

Los Angeles was like that, too, crisp and bright as his favorite minutes of morning, promising each day to astound him. All he had to do was venture from home, drive out to the beach, or to Rams headquarters on Beverly Boulevard, or up to Granada Hills with Micki, to visit the Putnams—Duane and Patty—for a cookout in the backyard of their tract home.

Drive. That's all he had to do.

Past that new Capitol Records building, built like a cylinder of stacked thirty-threes, and shake his head and marvel. First circular office building in the world, the newspapers said. Stop at a traffic light on Santa Monica Boulevard and stare at that massive new church the Mormons built and called a temple, that religion's largest in the world. Gawk at a donut shop with a giant donut on its roof, bigger even than Art Donovan and Big Daddy Lipscomb combined. Such sights made John Hock a tourist in his own hometown. He didn't have to pay for a ticket at Disneyland to be amazed. Every day it seemed the city offered something else to make him smile: a coffee shop that looked like it had been built on Venus, with arches bent over its roofline like comet tails of steel and plastic; a drive-in diner with enough angles to confuse a billiards whiz; a bowling alley just opened in Covina but straight out of Egypt by way of Polynesia (or Polynesia by way of Egypt, who knew?). And the colors! No one would call them subtle. Yellows and reds and blues, flat and bright and hot. Strange, those buildings, sure, but so danged cheerful and whimsical and surprising. Like morning every day.

He'd marvel for years, John Hock would, the astonishment present and palpable as in 1956. "It was all so new," he'd tell people again and again.

◆

"'WE CALL IT GOOGIE architecture,' said Professor Thrugg, 'named after a remarkable restaurant in Los Angeles called Googie's.'"

There actually was no Professor Thrugg. But there was a clever architecture critic from the East Coast named Douglas Haskell. And there was a Googie's. Haskell, driving through Los Angeles, came across a diner with a bright red roof that tilted upward, as if a giant red wafer cookie had been glued to the corner. A neon sign added eye-pupils into the Os in Googie's. The crassness of the design seemed to represent everything Haskell disdained in a new, popular style that, as yet, had no name.

So Haskell named it. His stand-in, Professor Thrugg, appeared in *House and Home* magazine's February 1952 issue, lecturing on the new architectural direction. Haskell transcribed an imagined conversation between Thrugg and a horrified student.

"'Do you mean then,' asked the student, 'that Googie is an art in which anything and everything goes?'"

"'So long as it's modern,' came back the Prof."

What Thrugg and Haskell were describing was the architecture that so overtook Los Angeles after World War II, what John Hock saw popping into view, new, it seemed, day after day. Alternately described as space age, uninhibited, incoherent, whimsical, dynamic, cartoonish, outlandish, and, as one journalist wrote in *Smithsonian Magazine*, so exaggerated and flamboyant that it is "almost beyond parody."

And it was inherently optimistic. It brought the promise of the future to Los Angeles's working and middle classes, to anyone who could afford a cup of coffee or ten frames of ten pin. The future, Googie said, is fun. The future can do anything! It tilts walls and turns triangles into birds and birds into triangles. It puts flagstone together with plastic and massive glass plates.

"It's too bad our taste is so horrible," Professor Thrugg concluded. The only benefit he acknowledged might come of Googie was that its jarring strangeness could someday prepare people "for those strange things yet to come which will truly make good sense."

Googie, from an East Coast point-of-view, was nonsense.

◆

How could John Hock drive around the palm trees and neon of Los Angeles in the spring of 1956 and feel anything but optimism? Micki was pregnant and expected their first child in June. John's knees had held up through an entire football season; the Rams had reached the title game; he had received two grand for the privilege. Seven of his teammates had been voted to the Pro Bowl, including the Putter, Hock's best friend on the roster, and he couldn't be happier.

All over the league, people were calling Duane Putnam one of the NFL's best guards. "If you'd take a 'toughest guy' poll among the [Rams]," wrote Frank Finch in the *Times*, "he'd win in a walk." How tough? Years later, Rams lineman John Houser would tell of a time when Putnam jumped off-sides on the first play of the game and head-butted Baltimore's Gene Lipscomb and bloodied his nose. Lipscomb, the man called "Big Daddy," was not only six inches taller and fifty pounds heavier than Putnam, he was a former teammate, who had helped carry Sid Gillman from the field after the Rams won 1955's Western Division title. "Aw shit, Putter, what'd you do that for?" Lipscomb said, according to the tale. Putnam didn't answer, just smiled, and according to Houser's story, "Lipscomb was putty in Putter's hands from then on."

Some said it was that toughness—what Ron Waller had called "feisty," the reason he'd never want to fight

Putnam—that made Putnam one of the league's top guards. Some cited the Putter's greater power since he'd started weight lifting, the beef added to his legs and shoulders. Others gave credit to Gillman and the new coaches. "He was good last year but he's absolutely great this season," said Skeet Quinlan. "The coaches studied him in films, changed him around a bit and capitalized on his potential. The result is that his blocking has been terrific." Feistiness, strength, or technique—Putnam's play had improved since he and John Hock had first paired as tandem guards back in 1953. That year, Hock was named honorable mention all-pro by the *Associated Press*. In seasons since, though, he had struggled with his knees, and he'd missed 1954, and, maybe because of all that he'd lost a step or two. Or maybe it was just that Putnam had improved so much. Regardless, near the end of the 1955 season, Gillman called Putnam, "the perfect guard."

That assessment would come into play the next season when Gillman changed how he used the Rams' offensive line and—consequently—threatened John Hock's career.

◆

How could any Los Angeles sports fan not be optimistic early in 1956? The city kept climbing in the sports world, and if it wasn't on top, it was close. From Swaps the summer before to the Rams finishing second in the NFL to the city hosting the annual NFL

Pro Bowl game, LA was making an argument for itself as a sports capital. Roz Wyman felt the momentum and kept it going by offering resolutions to the council—one congratulating Sid Gillman on his success with the Rams and another welcoming the NFL's East and West squads to the Pro Bowl, including the seven gentlemen from the hometown Rams.

Among those was young Ron Waller, who had also finished second in the league's Rookie of the Year voting to another running back, Baltimore's Alan Ameche.

After such a fine season, Waller decided he ought to be making more money. The Rams had signed him the summer before for $8,000, plus a $1,000 bonus. He asked to meet with Tex Schramm, and then Waller asked for a contract worth nearly double what he'd made the year before.

Fifteen thousand? asked Schramm.

Fifteen thousand, said Waller.

"Son," Schramm said, "you've got be in this league a long time before you make fifteen thousand."

So Waller signed for much less. But in reality, his pay no longer mattered much to his day-to-day life. Since his move to Los Angeles, he'd met and become engaged to a woman some five years his senior—a competitive swimmer, an aspiring actress and granddaughter to one of the country's wealthiest women.

A kid from Laurel, Delaware, where a sweet potato blight had a decade earlier devastated the local economy, was about to join the highest of societies.

◆

Won't you marry me, marry me, off to the altar please
carry me?
Give me combs for my curls, made of silver and pearls,
and a two-penny bridal bouquet...say!
Hurry up, hurry up, hitch that old horse to the surrey-up,
and I'll vow to be true to no one but you,
so marry me, marry me, do.
> —The Hudspeth sisters, including Pearl, played by
> Marjorie Durant, off-key and serenading Anthony
> Perkins in the film, *Friendly Persuasion*

IN HER FIRST FILM, in her first scene, she's splitting wood on a farm somewhere in what's supposed to be the rural Midwest, nearly one hundred years ago (but is really California in 1955). Her character lives with two sisters and her widowed mother, all four of them desperate for the company of men, which we'll learn shortly, because Gary Cooper and Anthony Perkins, playing father and son, rumble toward her in a wagon. Marjorie Merriweather Durant swings the axe like a pro, her long blonde braid flailing with it. When the blade sticks in a hunk of wood, she kicks it free like she's been splitting wood her whole life.

"HEY, MAW!" she bellows toward the farmhouse. "A COUPLE-A MEN TO SEE YA!"

It's a comic role lasting only ten minutes in a movie that stretches over two hours. She's physical in it, wielding that axe like Paul Bunyan, shoving Anthony

Perkins here and there as she ogles him, her inbred leer saying, "I will violate you in every way and enjoy it."

"Wanna smoke?" she later asks Perkins, who plays a thoughtful Quaker lad. When he demurs, she asks, "Wanna drink?"

Filming took place over autumn in 1955, even as the Rams worked their way toward the Western Division title and a date with Cleveland's Browns. The next April—seven months before the film's release—Marjorie Merriweather Durant, granddaughter and namesake of Marjorie Merriweather Post, heiress to a cereal fortune, married Ronald Bowles Waller at St. Thomas Episcopal Church in Washington, DC, near where the bride's mother raised thoroughbreds in Maryland. *The New York Times* gave the wedding eight inches on its society page. The article lists ten attendants in addition to the matron of honor. Among them was Mrs. Bud McFadin, whose husband played lineman and linebacker for the Rams.

Marjorie was no Jane Russell. She was more starlet than star. But her family wealth gave her social standing and celebrity, and her family history—her father had worked as a personal assistant to Charlie Chaplin—gave her Hollywood connections. She was represented by Allied Artists, the studio that produced *Friendly Persuasion*. That movie had done well, meaning Durant had a bit role in a picture that competed with *Giant, The Ten Commandments,* and *The King and I* for Best Picture at the Academy Awards. It won the Palme D'Or at the Cannes Film Festival. Altogether, Durant had enough of a resumé to reassert the Rams' connections to glamorous Hollywood.

She'd host parties at the home she and Ron shared in the Santa Monica mountains near the water. At the Wallers' home, Rams players could mingle with Hollywood actors the likes of Richard Boone, Tab Hunter, and Ty Harden, aka, Bronco Layne of the Western TV series *Bronco*. The Rams and their wives called their hostess Marge, and sometimes she was just as brash and sassy as Pearl Hudspeth from *Friendly Persuasion*.

When Micki Hock, pregnant with her first child and nauseated, decided to skip a Durant social event, Marge sought her out saying, "Micki! Why the heck aren't you coming to my party?" Once, at a game, sitting behind John Hock's father, Harry, Marge couldn't control her enthusiasm and kept kicking him in the back. When he finally turned to object, she teased him: "Old man, if I'm kicking you, well, you need to have your coat cleaned once in a while."

Not all Rams and their wives were comfortable sharing in that Hollywood life. For some it was too fast, too loud, too inebriated, too many ex-husbands and ex-wives, too many dramas. After a couple of seasons trying to live in Los Angeles, for example, Art and Joanie Hauser decided to live in the off-season back home near Cincinnati. "It was just really wild for us," Joanie Hauser recalled, years later. "We just weren't from that wild background… It was different, the Hollywood part."

It was different for Ron Waller, too. Less than a year before he'd been a rookie at training camp, worried that he'd get cut and be heading back to tiny Laurel, Delaware. Now he found himself visiting with his wife's grandmother at Mar-a-Lago, her mansion estate in Palm Beach, Florida. Mar-a-Lago, had well over 100 rooms, 20,000 roof tiles, and 2,200 black and white marble floor blocks in only the entrance hall, living and dining rooms. Laurel High School, with forty-four students in Waller's graduating class, was smaller.

"It was a big jump," he recalled. "I tell you…"

◆

THAT SAME SPRING, THE Rams signed Ron Miller, who had played end for USC. Also, he was Walt Disney's son-in-law. During the 1956 season, Diane Disney Miller sat with the other Rams' wives in the coliseum, and once Walt Disney joined them outside the locker room as they waited for their husbands to emerge. Diane and Ron were older—the military had kept him out of pro football for a while—and already had children. Now and then, Micki Hock babysat for Walt Disney's grandchildren.

But Ron Miller's football career didn't last long. Against Detroit at the coliseum during the 1956 season, he took a vicious hit across the face from Night Train Lane, now playing for the Lions. That collision broke

Miller's nose and knocked him unconscious. Walt Disney watched horrified from a seat in the stadium. It's easy to imagine Disney, with his visionary foresight, dreaming of a nightmare future in which Miller became crippled or worse. Later Disney demanded his son-in-law accept a prominent job in the family business, a chance to build a company and provide for his family rather than suffer broken bones. Miller accepted.

As a parting gift to his teammates, though, he arranged a deal for all those with whom he shared the locker room: bring the families through the gates of the Magic Kingdom in Anaheim—anytime, gratis.

◆

Sometimes, playing for the Rams in the 1950s, you said hello. Oftentimes you said goodbye. Sometimes, though, there wasn't much chance to say anything.

John Hock didn't get to say goodbye to Andy Robustelli that summer of 1956. Robustelli was one of Hock's best friends on the team—two soft-spoken and Roman Catholic men who surprised people with their ferocity. Robustelli, a stalwart on defense, hailed from a small college in Connecticut and seemed to be one of those necessary pieces for the Rams' success. He seemed one of those fellas Sid Gillman especially had in mind when he'd filled the locker room with praise after the Rams beat the Packers for the division title, saying: "You not only are the greatest players I've ever been with, but as a group, you're the greatest bunch of men."

So when John Hock and the Rams left to go their separate off-season ways, they shook hands and John knew that when Andy returned he'd get to meet John and Micki's firstborn child, expected in June. The men believed the next time they'd see Robustelli would be out in dry, dusty Redlands for training camp. Robustelli had been a regular Pro Bowler, and he was good for team morale. Ma Robustelli's spaghetti had stuffed more than a few Ram bellies. The team even announced in February that Robustelli, Norm Van Brocklin, and Bob Boyd had all signed new contracts. That was good news for Robustelli and his growing family. His wife, Jeanne, was pregnant with the couple's fourth child.

The baby was born on the eve of training camp, and Robustelli placed a long-distance call to Gillman to explain that he'd be late to report. He was needed at home. Three kids and a new baby and all.

It was not an unreasonable request given that, since Robustelli had joined the team, Dan Towler had been able to skip parts of training camp for his theology studies and Elroy Hirsch had missed days to finish up movie acting jobs. But Gillman, whose own children were often football orphans, reacted harshly. He ordered Robustelli to report, ASAP.

In his memoir *Once a Giant, Always…: My Two Lives with the New York Giants*, Robustelli recalled saying "Sid, I'll be out there as soon as my home situation is settled."

Soon after, Robustelli received a phone call from Wellington Mara, a co-owner of the Giants and the fellow in charge of their personnel. "I've been talking to the Rams about you," Mara said, "and they're willing to trade you. I know you're thirty years old, but do you think you could play two or three more years?"

Betrayals happen that fast in the NFL. One minute you're with a team, the next you learn that the team doesn't want you. But playing for the Giants would mean Robustelli could stay with his family in southwestern Connecticut year-round. Strange as it seemed, maybe Gillman was doing him a favor. Robustelli answered Mara honestly and quickly.

"I'll try to play as long as I can," he said. "But I don't know how long that will be."

"If you tell me you can play," Mara said, "or at least will try to play for that long, then I think I can make a trade for you."

Robustelli said, "Make the deal."

The announcement came on July 27. In return, the Rams received a high draft pick they could use after the 1956 season.

◆

SOME FOOTBALL JOURNALISTS HAVE speculated that the Rams let Robustelli go because Gillman believed a player lost zip after age thirty. Robustelli had celebrated the big three-oh that past December, and his dedication to his family gave Gillman a pretext for a decision

Gillman already wanted to make. But maybe it wasn't Gillman who believed that age thirty was bad news. After all, this was only his second season working with pros. As a college coach, his players were seldom older than twenty-one. Mara's concern about Robustelli's age suggests that in the NFL of the 1950s it was the practice to treat thirty as the beginning of the end. Otto Graham had retired for the first time at age thirty-three. Bob Waterfield quit when he was thirty-two. It makes sense that what Gillman believed about players at age thirty was only what others had told him.

In the spring of 1956, on March 15, Norm Van Brocklin blew out thirty candles on his cake.

It's easy to make the connection between that fact and what Gillman decided, going into training camp, involving Van Brocklin and John Hock. Gillman's plan was a dramatic shift in how the Rams operated and in who called the shots. Certainly his decision about Robustelli had hurt team morale, but this other decision—the one that threatened Hock's career—angered Van Brocklin.

And when had pissing off Dutch ever helped anything?

CHAPTER 12

Shuttle Guard

CALL THIS SID GILLMAN's perfect dream:

At the coliseum, the day sparkles as only a Los Angeles day can—clear and dry, warm but not too, a breeze clearing the smog, making way for the blue. Across the field, let's say, are Philadelphia's Eagles: a good matchup for the Rams, but nothing worthy of a ticker-tape parade. Because of that and the blue-breeze day, the crowd's only half strength, some fifty-five thousand. It's summer, after all, in Los Angeles. With a whole season to go, there's plenty of weekends to come when casual fans might catch a Rams' game. Sid, bow-tied as usual, doesn't mind the sparser crowd. It's not his job to put people in the seats.

It's his job to win ball games, and to that end he's got this new idea he's trying out today.

The Eagles start with the ball, but the Rams' defense holds, so Philadelphia punts. Now's Sid's moment: As the Rams' offense readies itself to take the field, Sid instructs his starting quarterback, Norm Van Brocklin. He's telling Dutch which play to run to start the game.

Though this has never ever happened before, though Dutch has *always* called his own plays, Van Brocklin nods. Maybe he even says, "Great call, Sid! I hadn't thought of that." (Remember, this is Sid's dream.)

Then Van Brocklin and the offense trot onto the field. The Rams run the play their coach wants, and perfectly—a twelve-yard gain, first down! Sid, straining to stretch his arm across the big shoulders of a second-string offensive lineman, tells him the next play. Then he gives the lineman a gentle shove toward the field. The substitute sprints to the huddle even as a starting lineman sprints out, his place taken by the man with Gillman's message. In the huddle, Van Brocklin listens as the lineman conveys the next play. Then Dutch glances to the sidelines, gives Gillman the thumbs up. Another first down for sure!

That's the dream version.

◆

GILLMAN BORROWED THE IDEA from Paul Brown who'd pioneered it and used it in the 1955 championship game when his quarterback took instructions from his coach on the sidelines via a steady rotation of linemen. Though stripped of the authority to call his own plays, quarterback Otto Graham threw two touchdown passes and ran for two more.

Gillman, across the field, watched helplessly as Van Brocklin decided which plays the Rams would run—and threw six interceptions.

The convention in the NFL had always been that coaches drew up the plays and crafted the strategies, but quarterbacks decided which plays to call, and when. This was often a practical matter. There had never been a foolproof method to get a message from the sidelines to the quarterback without the other team figuring it out. Then the NFL changed its substitution rules, allowing coaches to shuttle players in and out of games, and Paul Brown had his epiphany. He could choose the plays and send them via a substitute. He opted to use offensive linemen as his messengers, perhaps because offensive linemen were less specialized than players at other positions. They were necessary but interchangeable. Light bulbs on a movie set.

There were good reasons for a quarterback to call plays. He had the best view of the field. He knew what player might have been hurt on the last play. He could listen to guys in the huddle and adapt. But Brown had arguments for giving himself the job. Unlike the quarterback, he had a telephone line to the press box where assistant coaches with a bird's-eye view saw what no one on the field could see. He'd been the one to study game films and the opponents' tendencies, and he possessed decades more experience and insight into the game than his quarterback.

Gillman could claim several of those reasons, too—though Van Brocklin had played seven seasons in the NFL—so he understood the league in ways Gillman, a longtime college coach in his second season with the pros, was only just learning.

For example, unlike in college, an experienced NFL quarterback might get caught up in shenanigans. He might get annoyed at a defensive lineman's cheap shot, so call a play in which his blockers stepped aside so that lineman could charge unimpeded and the quarterback could throw the ball hard at the lineman's face.

Not that Van Brocklin ever did that, except for that time when he did. Hit the lineman right between the eyes.

Van Brocklin's way of choosing plays was not always cerebral, so Gillman—a professor of football, a teacher, a "rabbi" in Van Brocklin's lingo—decided to follow Brown's model. The big difference would be that Brown had assumed the role of play-caller from Otto Graham. Graham hadn't wanted to surrender the responsibility, but he—this future head coach at the Coast Guard Academy—respected authority. He followed Brown's orders.

Van Brocklin, since his first year in the league, had never shied from disagreeing with a coach—often via a creative and robust heaping of Anglo-Saxon invective.

For Dutch, calling plays wasn't just a responsibility he'd prefer to have. It was part of his natural self. His wife, Gloria, more than once woke to hear him in bed beside her mumbling and yipping. "Even at three a.m.," she says in the book, *The Golden Age of Pro Football*, "he was calling plays."

To take that role away from Dutch would be like cutting out his brain. The message would be, "You're an arm; leave the thinking to me." To insult Van Brocklin that way carried a risk, but Gillman wasn't going to get himself fired because his quarterback chose the wrong plays and the Rams lost. If Dutch didn't like this new reality, well, Gillman had an option other than a thirty-year-old who had thrown six interceptions in the one game when his play counted most. The Rams' backup quarterback, Bill Wade, had been named the most valuable player in the football-devoted Southeastern Conference while he played at Vanderbilt University. Tall, strong, talented, and young, he'd sat on the sidelines most of two seasons with the Rams. In some ways, he was the anti–Van Brocklin: polite while Dutch was crude, soft-spoken while Dutch was loud and profane. Dutch skipped optional Monday night meetings at Gillman's house; Wade always attended. Van Brocklin "would cuss and all that," recalled lineman Art Hauser. "Bill Wade, he was my roommate when we were rookies. At training camp in Redlands he'd sit down on the john and read quotes from the Bible."

Wade believed himself to be just as worthy to start as Van Brocklin and in better playing condition, and he thought he'd performed well enough in training camp to win the job outright. Sitting on the bench frustrated him, and he began to wonder whether there might be other reasons—even conspiratorial forces—that kept him off the field.

"It seemed like to me that there were certain elements in Los Angeles that did not want me to be the quarterback," said Wade, years later. "I hated it. Every minute of it. I mean, I wanted to play football. I was in good condition and better condition than my competitor. I could throw the ball eighty yards in the air. I didn't know how far he could throw it, and I didn't really care."

Wade had worked to be a good team player on the bench and wait for his chance. If running Gillman's plays meant he'd take the snaps, well, yes sir, he'd run those plays.

◆

WHAT WORKED IN CLEVELAND turned out to be disastrous in Los Angeles. Imagine it this way: a guy in the backseat tells one of the best drivers in the country when to turn, when to brake, when to merge into traffic. Sometimes the driver roars back that the directions are as useful as a "how to wipe your ass" manual written in Russian. Then, with the car stopped at a pumping station, the passenger pockets the keys and hands them to a fellow who'd spent two years changing the oil.

The worst part? No matter who drove, the car kept smashing—into donut shops and office buildings and other cars' big-finned rear ends.

By the first week of November, the Rams—the defending Western Conference champs—had played six games. They'd lost five.

Van Brocklin kept throwing too many interceptions. He threw his first in the season's opening game, with less than two minutes ticked away, and *zip*! Gillman benched him for Wade. Wade threw interceptions, too. In fact, he and Van Brocklin were each throwing more interceptions than touchdown passes. But Wade ran the plays Gillman wanted. Van Brocklin spent games fuming that Gillman sat him—or, when he played, scorning whatever plays Gillman wanted. That Van Brocklin sometimes ignored Gillman's calls frustrated the coach.

At Rams' weekly luncheons, fans complained—loudly. Some argued Gillman should return the play-calling responsibility to Van Brocklin—or Wade, whoever. Gillman sometimes snapped back his answers. The newspapers wrote regularly about the controversy. The locker room split.

Decades after, it was clear who Duane Putnam wanted in charge during the game.

"Sid wanted to be in control, to control everything, control the play," Putnam said one summer afternoon, sitting with his wife Patty at the dining room table in his home outside Los Angeles. "It was just his way of doing it."

"You mean he wouldn't let Dutch call his plays?" Patty asked.

"No." Putnam had a small pouch of tobacco in his lip and spit discreetly. "Quarterbacks knew what was going on more than the coach knew."

Then he praised Van Brocklin. "He was honest," Putnam said, "and he was a man about everything. He wasn't against anything or anybody. He was just out to get the game won. You like to be around people like that. They shoot straight."

During that dreadful 1956 season, insiders like Putnam knew the offense wasn't the only problem. The defense missed its captain, Don Paul, who had retired to run his restaurant. And it really missed Robustelli, whom Gillman had traded to the Giants. Robustelli's replacement, Frank Fuller, had suffered a broken leg during the exhibition season against the 49ers, leaving the Rams with what amounted to a third-stringer in Robustelli's spot. Meanwhile, the Giants, with Robustelli starting at defensive end, were 5–1 at midseason.

Play-calling, play-calling, play-calling! The fans, the press, Van Brocklin and Gillman, the Rams talking among themselves—it was a lot of noise. It was so loud, filling so much of every head that cared, hardly anyone could give a thought to the messengers, the shuttle guards who now carried the plays from Gillman to the quarterback.

In particular, hardly anyone gave a thought to the effect all this had on John Hock.

◆

WHY HOCK, OF ALL five starting offensive linemen?

Paul Brown had used guards, not tackles, and Gillman followed that lead. That gave him two guards from which to choose: Putnam or Hock. Putnam was all-pro. "A perfect guard," Gillman had said.

John Hock was a good, high-quality guard. Excellent, even. But Putnam was a shade better. If a coach is always working percentages to give himself and his team the best chance to win, he needs his best guard on the field as often as possible. That was Putnam.

Hock became the messenger.

◆

MAYBE IT DOESN'T SEEM like such a bad thing, to deliver a coach's plays from the sideline. Leave the field after a tough play, take the next one off. Sip water. For thirty seconds or so, no one hits you in the head.

But consider this: John Hock had only a few seconds to rumble on and off the field. He had to sprint. Usually, as a lineman, the most he'd run on a play is six or ten yards before he smashed somebody. As a shuttle guard he had to run from Gillman's side to the line of scrimmage wherever the heck that happened to be on the field. If it was at the five-yard line, Hock had to gallop thirty-five yards to get there. Then, he ran a play. And if the team gained no yards? He galloped thirty-five yards back. A short gain? Thirty yards to carry the next play. That's one hundred yards over two plays instead of the twenty to which Hock was accustomed. Hitting and being hit, that's what Hock expected—it's what he practiced. If he hadn't liked collisions, he would never have become an offensive lineman. Sprinting a hundred yards? That was for track and field guys, skinny fellas with batons and flimsy shorts. Hock wore cleats, not winged Mercury's sandals.

Something else bothered him about being a shuttle guard. It wasn't anything easy to explain, but through years as an offensive lineman, Hock had come to know and value the game's rhythms, how to pair his actions and reactions to its flows. A game was, what?, waves and tides?, and to live in its violence required a routine, a practiced sense of timing built over years snap-by-snap, block-by-block, so that when it became part of him it felt as if it has always been part of him. Then it wasn't thinking that told him how long to hold a block or when to let it go. It wasn't counting the seconds. He could just tell. The game—or its rhythms—lived in him, and he lived in them, and that gave him comfort, satisfaction.

Now, Paul Brown's innovation and Sid Gillman's imitation had broken that routine to pieces. Now it was in, then out. In, then out. A long sprint, a short sprint, a somewhere-in-the-middle sprint. Where does anybody find a routine in all that? Hock had become a yo-yo, one moment in hand, the next spinning uselessly in space.

◆

Each day of his football life—and with special care during the season—John Hock calibrated how he used his legs. It was as if he knew his knees had only a finite number of strides before they'd quit on him.

So, he wasn't much for walking. He didn't climb stairs if he could press an elevator button. He drove to the grocery store, even if it was only a few blocks. Better to use whatever was left of his knees on those sweeps and traps. Better to use them for football.

Not to play Western Union.

"He didn't like to take any extra steps, I remember that," Duane Putnam said, recalling those days. "He just didn't have the good pins under him. His stumps would get clanked every week. He'd have to rub them and put ice on them. They weren't skinny. They just weren't structurally strong to handle what he had on top."

Hock didn't grumble in the locker room or at the bars where players gathered to drink Schlitz. But playing shuttle guard took some of the joy away, and those who knew him could tell. At home, he'd sit in a chair with his feet up, or lie on the couch, his infant son, Jay, in his lap, a light from a table lamp falling across the boy's astonished face. Or maybe, Jay asleep and Micki sitting nearby, he'd have a magazine in his hand, the glow of the television flickering across his face. He'd find reasons to stay put, and though Micki could see that his knees hurt him, he'd never acknowledge it, even if she asked.

"I suppose," Micki wondered aloud so many years after, "he didn't want you to say, 'If it hurts, don't play.'"

◆

A FEW DAYS BEFORE the Rams' fifth loss that 1956 season, news broke in New York that Walter O'Malley, president of the Brooklyn Dodgers, had sold Ebbets Field, the team's home stadium, to a real estate developer for an undisclosed price "in seven figures."

O'Malley had long and loudly and publicly complained that Ebbets Field was "outmoded, dirty, and inadequate" and said his baseball team wouldn't play there after the 1958 season. Even so, the sale of the ballpark contained a provision that allowed the Dodgers to lease it back until the end of the 1961 season. And Marvin Krattner, the developer who bought the stadium, said he'd extend that lease as long as necessary if it meant the Dodgers would stay in the borough. "I would never do anything to keep the Dodgers from playing in Brooklyn," he said.

So far, though, O'Malley's efforts to arrange for a new home in Brooklyn had whiffed so badly, some people suspected a sham, that he didn't want New York at all. That season, O'Malley had scheduled more than half a dozen of the Dodgers' home games in Jersey City, New Jersey, and declared that the team would do the same the next season. Were the "Jersey City Dodgers," as some journalists called them, a trial separation for life away from Brooklyn, perhaps a gauge of how things might work even farther west?

Replied O'Malley: "Would you make a move to Los Angeles with a stop in Jersey City on the way?"

◆

IN JERSEY CITY, THE fans booed the Dodgers. Razzed 'em. Heckled. When a public address announcer mentioned that fans could buy a Dodgers yearbook, they booed the yearbook.

"They wouldn't applaud if you gave them free hot dogs," a Dodgers rep told William Conklin of *The New York Times.*

Players were flummoxed. Journalists scribbled stories. The reasons given most often for the Jersey cheer? Loyalty elsewhere. The Giants had kept a farm team in Jersey City for years, which cultivated a following for that Big League team. Jersey Citizens would buy tickets to Dodgers games just for the opportunity to boo the Giants' archrival: those bum carpetbaggers from Brooklyn. That's how much Jersey City loved its Giants.

Out in Los Angeles, a rivalry with San Francisco meant that Rams games against the 49ers regularly drew more fans than those against the Chicago Cardinals or Pittsburgh Steelers. Sports teams do unite the people of a city or region in ways little else does, and they often engender a fierce loyalty that makes a city seem inseparable from its team, and vice versa. So John Lardner, a sportswriter and son of the more famous

Ring Lardner, asked in *The New York Times* in 1956, "Would it still be Brooklyn? Without the Dodgers?" (The answer was no.)

A city comes to see in its team the qualities its people believe make them exceptional. Teams embody fans' aspirations and the narrative they tell about themselves. A team may even seem to take on the personality of its city. To watch their team play, Green Bay Packer fans in the 1950s proudly endured asphalt-cracking cold, frigid temperatures that would keep Rams fans home. But because the players also endured that cold, the shared suffering gave Packers fans the sense that they too were in games with the players, struggling with them. The fans' identities so melded with the guys wearing green and gold, they used plural personal pronouns to talk about the team: what "we" had to do to salvage the season, how the Bears always gave "us" trouble.

Likewise, Los Angeles fans could embrace "Crazylegs" Hirsch, who came from Wisconsin, and who was movie-star handsome with sculptured hair, who found his way into the pictures, and called the boys who crowded around for his autograph "Little Rams." ("A prima donna," Duane Putnam recalled. "He had LA in his fist.") And Ron Waller had married a high society starlet. And Bob Waterfield had wed a bombshell. And didn't all that combine to make the Rams, like Los Angeles, exceptional? Because what other city could claim Hollywood?

It's a selective identification, though. It neglects the foul-mouthed genius of a quarterback with a face for radio. Or the devout thinker from outside Pittsburgh, who is black, and who is studying to become a minister. Or the intensely private offensive lineman with bad knees who marries a schoolteacher. Which Los Angeles are they?

When it's there, and when it's fierce, the identification of a city with its professional team is always blind. It's a manufactured illusion, a communal willingness to believe in something that's not real. Yet that fierce belief, that loyalty and identification, is itself a true, verifiable thing. The passions, the enthusiasms, the shared irrationality—they exist. And when that identification is broken, when a team like the Dodgers leave Brooklyn, it can rend hearts.

It's like love that way. Or the movies.

◆

NEVER HAD THE RAMS suffered a losing season in Los Angeles. But here they were, 4–8, the 1956 season over, last place in the Western Division. From top to bottom in twelve months. That they won their final two games seemed not to matter.

Too many fumbles, too many interceptions. Wade threw thirteen; Van Brocklin, playing less often, added twelve. Even the third string quarterback, Rudy Bukich, who once in a panic had tossed the ball to John Hock for a safety, threw three interceptions. That's twenty-eight altogether. Those three quarterbacks combined for only eighteen touchdown passes.

And the absence of Paul and Robustelli? With them in 1955, the Rams defense allowed opponents to score only 231 points. Without them? Opponents scored 307 points—an extra touchdown every game.

Just before the season ended, a reporter from the *Los Angeles Times* visited Gillman's wife, Esther, at the Gillmans' new house on Mulholland Drive in Sherman Oaks, in mountains above the city. The Rams then had lost eight games with one more to play. Esther admitted to the reporter that her husband wasn't accustomed to losing, so neither was his family. "Why, it's his first losing season!" she said. "Losing is something new. It's not pleasant."

But then she looked out the living room's bay windows to the surrounding slopes leading down to the city. Nearby was acreage graded level, ready for foundations and frames, and nearby were frames ready for walls. People were coming, more and more people. Esther's disposition tended toward optimism, and here she was, living in that most forward-looking of cities, in a hopeful country, during what may have been its most optimistic decade.

Losing isn't easy, but this was Los Angeles. It was all so new, each day so full of promise.

"Every morning," she told the reporter, "we wake up to the sound of bulldozers carving new lots out of the mountains. 'It's sounds of progress,' I say to Sid. 'Everything is all right as long as those bulldozers keep moving.'"

PART III

CHAPTER 13

A Special Invocation Honoring the Mothers

THE SEASON NEAR ITS end, there'd be a banquet. There was always an end-of-the-season awards banquet at the Ambassador Hotel's famous Cocoanut Grove or at the Biltmore or other such places, always presented by the Ye Olde Rams club. There'd be white tablecloths and waitstaff in uniforms. There'd be beer and cocktails, cigarettes and ash trays. John and Micki Hock and Duane and Patty Putnam and all the others would sit before plates of chicken ("Got to get all dressed up and eat that chicken again," Patty Putnam recalls saying to her husband). Depending on the year, Jerry Lewis would take the stage, or Bob Hope, or Milton Berle.

The comedian would make a joke at the expense of each player—get the laughs going, comedy as social lubricant. As many as a thousand fans bought seats or tables, and old-timers like Bob Waterfield would present awards for best rookie or best lineman or most inspirational player.

Some banquets proved happier affairs than others. When the team in 1956 finished 4–8? Less happy.

When in 1956 the team finished 4–8 and players selected five veterans to make demands of management? With those veterans insisting on salaries and expenses during preseason games, and threatening a player protest—maybe even a strike?

Less happy, much more tense.

Van Brocklin, who had led the players' committee that met with Rams owners near the end of the 1956 season, also happened to be his team's representative to a new league-wide players' association. Its purpose was to provide a united voice for the guys in helmets and pads as they called for changes similar to those the Rams had made of their own owners. The players' association had even picked Van Brocklin as one of two players to bring the new group's demands to the NFL commissioner, Bert Bell. Rams players had each ponied up twenty-five dollars to pay for the trip.

Yes, at that year's banquet, Milton Berle or Jerry Lewis or whoever better have brought his best material.

◆

WITH THE AWARDS BANQUET and season over, the Rams management would issue to players their final paychecks. These last were larger than the others, because they included the 25 percent that front office folks had held back all season, saying they didn't want players to be broke at the end of the year and asking to borrow money from the team for travel expenses home.

Then the players would head for their off-season lives—jobs, reunions with family, rest, healing. The better players, though, still had a bit of football to go: games like the Hula Bowl in Hawaii, pitting the pros against some college all-stars, or the NFL's Pro Bowl right there in Los Angeles, in which the best from the Western Division played the best from the East. "The sixty greatest football players in the world," promoters called the game.

After that disastrous 1956 season, only a few Rams got picked up for either game. But Duane Putnam was invited to both.

Putnam accepted—Hula and Pro. In particular, he appreciated the invitation to Hawaii, because it would be a way to take Patty home. They'd met as students at the College of the Pacific in Stockton, California, but she'd grown up in the islands (she'd named their cat *Popoki*, Hawaiian for cat) and still had family on Maui.

So, with the promise of a $700 payday and a family reunion, Duane and Patty packed suitcases, took their two kids in hand, and left their tract home in Grenada Hills to board a flight headed even farther west.

◆

A FEW DAYS BEFORE the Hula Bowl, Putnam received a transpacific phone call from Paul Schissler, the Pro Bowl's promoter. Schissler had been an LA sports figure for years, having owned and coached the Hollywood Bears, the team that signed Kenny Washington when the NFL still shunned black players. Before that, he'd coached four losing NFL seasons in the mid-1930s, including with the Chicago Cardinals. He'd run the Pro Bowl since its start after the 1950 season, and he was running it now, a voice from thousands of miles away with a recommendation for Putnam.

"You can take your time coming back," Schissler said.

Practice had begun for the Pro Bowl, and Schissler noted that Putnam wasn't there for it. The game was supposed to include the world's best sixty players, not its best fifty-nine. If Putnam was going to skip practice and assorted publicity, he could just enjoy that vacation in Maui. The word had come down from the commissioner, Bert Bell himself. Schissler was just making the phone call.

Putnam was furious. First, he wanted to talk to Bell directly, "To see what the score is." Other players had participated in both games, he said, including Otto Graham and Crazylegs Hirsch. "I'm the first one to be punished," he told a reporter. "Nothing happened to them." Then, he said he might ask the new players' association to weigh in, take some action against Pro

Bowl officials. "I'm just a lineman," he said. "I don't make much money."

Putnam knew, though, that his complaints would take time to be heard and any actions by the players' association wouldn't get him back on the Pro Bowl roster, not for that game in January 1957. The Pro Bowl would need another offensive guard. So, even though he was steamed, while Putnam had Schissler on the phone he made a suggestion.

"John's right there in town," he said.

◆

WHEN BOB GAIN REMEMBERS playing in Pro Bowls, he recalls the strange looks he got from bellhops in the hotel lobby as he crossed the polished floors carrying so many boxes of Jezebel brassieres.

Gain, the Browns' defensive lineman who had also played for the University of Kentucky against John Hock and Santa Clara, played in five Pro Bowls—all in Los Angeles. The city gave birth to the game, and Los Angeles would hold onto the Pro Bowl for decades. The idea had come from George Preston Marshall, Washington's owner, who had mentioned it to Schissler. Schissler, in turn, brought it to the Los Angeles Newspaper Publishers Association, who agreed that it was a good idea, one they would sponsor if proceeds went to charity.

So each year, coaches voted for the best players, and the commissioner's office tabulated the results. One team represented the Western Division; the other, the Eastern. Fans could tell them apart because the best of the West always wore blue helmets, and the best of the East wore red. A coach from each division was assigned to work with each team. The teams always stayed at either the Biltmore or the Ambassador, and each year they switched locales. For out-of-state players, especially those like Gain from Cleveland, the Pro Bowl was a vacation from grim winter weather.

"A buddy of mine said, 'If you get to the Pro Bowl, you'll love it,'" Gain recalled. "'There's no scrimmages, a little contact.' The Pro Bowls were light, too. If we did something, and the coach didn't like it, we'd tell them, 'Go to hell!' We didn't play for them!"

Gain invited his wife to come along, though she never did. Instead, she'd give him her measurements and send him to Los Angeles's garment factories to buy lingerie for her, wholesale. In particular, she wanted those Jezebel brassieres.

"If you bought them in downtown Cleveland, you'd pay six, seven, eight dollars for a bra," Gain said. Wholesale in LA, he'd pay a buck a piece. He could buy a dozen or more, easy. And he did.

"When I walked through the lobby with all those tied together," he said, "you could see the bellhops looking at me funny."

◆

JOHN HOCK'S PRO BOWL? There's not much to say about it. About the Pro Bowl, there rarely is. The West won, 19–10, behind four field goals kicked by Baltimore's Bert Rechinchar. But, as Gain explained, the results of the Pro Bowl—the game itself—didn't matter so much. In most players lives', certainly in John Hock's, what mattered about the Pro Bowl was, first, its prestige and, second, the payday: $700 for every player on the winning team; $500 each for the losers.

John and Micki took that seven hundred out shopping. They drove through Los Angeles from department store to furniture stores, from Sears to J. C. Penney, and in the end purchased their first bedroom set. The wood was stained a shade or two lighter than mahogany. Micki particularly liked that the headboard came with sliding doors. It cost them about $500 of that Pro Bowl money. Thereafter, they called it their "Pro Bowl Bedroom Set." They never got rid of it. One day, it would still be in use at their daughter's home.

◆

AT WHICH EVENT WOULD John Hock find more to make him smile?

Shoulder-to-shoulder with celebrities at the Cocoanut Grove for a Rams banquet? Jerry Lewis on stage, all knees and elbows and grating voice? Marjorie Merriweather Durant offering cheek pecks for him and Micki?

Or would he find more charm through the doors of a junior high school, on the night of a mother-son banquet?

It was April 12, 1957, a Friday. Micki was pregnant with their second child and having trouble with bleeding, so doctors said she ought not to travel. John kissed her goodbye—kissed Jay, too—then drove east to Highland, which was something like a town, east of Los Angeles and north of Redlands, tucked tight against the mountains. The Parent-Teacher Association there had asked him to serve as the featured speaker for its banquet at which sons honored their mothers, what the *San Bernardino County Sun* said was "always the highlight of the school's program."

The event was scheduled to begin at 7:00 p.m., and those coming early to the school's quiet parking lot arrived with dusk, the dry desert air cool enough to make a man grateful for a jacket. Inside, the aromas of the evening's dinner—Swiss steak, not chicken—had begun to suffuse through the school hallways. Here there were boys wearing their best, shiniest shoes, and mothers with makeup just so.

Jerry Lewis or Jerry Cox? Jerry Cox was the eighth grader who stood bravely in the school's auditorium to give "a special invocation honoring the mothers." One hundred and thirty-six people attended, mothers coming as guests of their sons. Instead of the Harry James Orchestra, the assembled enjoyed the Eighth

Grade Girls Ensemble and the Ninth Grade Girls Sextet, both "under the direction of Mrs. Kathryn Callahan."

Then came the time for John Hock, introduced as a Pro Bowler since last January, now a Ram and once a Cardinal, who had served in the Army and was cocaptain of that Santa Clara team that upset Kentucky in the Orange Bowl. Ladies and gentlemen…

And the polite applause.

John Hock would not have spoken long. Likely, he would have consulted a few notes, reminders of what to say, things he'd thought about on the drive from Los Angeles. It was a mother-son banquet, so likely he thought about Micki and Jay, the mother and son he knew best. And of his own his mother, Elizabeth, that stern Irish woman who in those first months after the move from Pittsburgh kept him dressed in knickers, as Pittsburgh boys dressed, even though the Los Angeles kids found knickers to be hilarious and a great reason to pound the snot out of him. He was nine years old, so he didn't have that much snot to get pounded, and his mother knew that. She knew no kid his age could do him lasting damage. She sent him out in his knickers and let him suffer the little-boy punches, and when he came home she cleaned him up, and sent him out again—still wearing knickers. *Mothers*, he could tell these Highland boys, *if they love you and understand the world the way an Irish woman understands the world, will let you get hurt, because they know pain has limits. They know you can take it.*

After his talk, the mothers and sons and their featured guest ate their Swiss steaks, and probably Mr. Hock signed some autographs, answered questions, and encouraged the boys who professed to play football, too. He raised his glass of iced tea or milk or Kool-Aid, whatever it was he drank that night, when John Kennedy, a ninth-grader, offered his toast to the mothers, and again when Mrs. Floyd Porter, immediate past president of the PTA, offered a toast to the sons.

Later, they all watched a film of highlights from the 1956 Rams season.

Had there been highlights? It's easy to imagine a Van Brocklin quip: "If our fifty-six highlight reel won an Oscar it would be in the category 'best sixteen-second film.'"

Then, it was time to say goodbye, and mothers and sons rose and moved toward the parking lot, lit that night by a moon nearly full. There, if the boy was a young gentleman, he opened the door for his mother, though she, of course, sat behind the wheel. Soon, they'd all be home, except for John Hock, whose drive back to Los Angeles would last a couple of hours through that moon-bright night.

Thank you for coming, the mothers had said. Thank you, said the boys. Out here, he was a celebrity. He wasn't Hollywood, and he didn't need to be glib or fashionable or witty. He didn't need to have big plans or ideas that would change the world or Southern California's landscape—or that would even change football. For the boys of Highland and their mothers, he needed to be polite and to enjoy their company, and he needed to be a Ram. For them—and for him, too—that was enough.

◆

IN THE PHOTOGRAPHS TAKEN at the Rams offices on Beverly Boulevard, a young man shakes Sid Gillman's hand. Gillman is older, thicker, wearing a sport coat with a plaid shirt and no tie. Southern California formal, ca. 1957.

The young man, on the other hand, looks as if he just flew in from Madison Avenue in New York City: suit coat buttoned, white shirt pressed, the pocket handkerchief squared like it was folded with a ruler. The knot in his tie is so small it hides inside his collar. A tie tack finishes the look.

To their right is a large split-leaf philodendron, the only decor. The light from flash bulbs is harsh. It's a conventional grip-and-grin shot, a staple of unimaginative journalism. The men smile at each other. Gillman looks as if he's laughing at his own joke. The young man's smile is polite; it gives little away.

It's April 8, four days before John Hock is to speak to the Highland Junior High mothers and sons. The Rams have just announced the hiring of a new top assistant for Dan Reeves, a position that in years to come will be called a general manager, and the team has invited the press for photographs and questions. If the reporters and photogs have any age on them, they know this young fellow. He's a Southern California native, born in South Gate a few miles south of Los Angeles. A few years back, right out of the University of San Francisco, he worked for the Rams as a publicity guy and later for their scouting operation. He left to become a partner at an up-and-coming West Coast public relations company, where he'd handled—among other clients— the 1956 Olympics in Australia. Now, at age thirty-one, he's back on Beverly Boulevard to take over the Rams day-to-day operations and to make personnel decisions.

His name is Pete Rozelle. One day he'll become the most influential figure in NFL history.

But for now, he's here because Bert Bell, the NFL commissioner, asked him. The Rams have been without an assistant to the president since Tex Schramm—weary of the owners' bickering and Reeves' drinking—quit the job in January to join the sports division of the CBS television network. Not surprisingly, Reeves and his co-owners couldn't decide on a replacement. Anyone Reeves supported, Edwin Pauley spurned. Anyone Pauley wanted, Reeves rejected. Bert Bell, like Schramm, tired of the gridlock. He intervened, suggesting young Rozelle, whom he remembered from his days with the Rams. A few nights later, Rozelle received a phone call from the NFL commissioner.

"We checked around," Bell told him, as Rozelle recalled in an interview conducted in 1991. "You are the first thing the Ram owners have agreed upon since Garfield was shot. So do you want to take the job?"

The Rams were coming off their worst season in Los Angeles. The quarterbacks were unhappy, and the season had ended with no definitive answer to the question of who would call plays each game. Average home attendance had dropped. Players had organized to demand more money and team-funded medical care. Owners feuded, and one drank too much. And LA's mayor had recently led a delegation to spring training in Vero Beach, Florida, to convince the Dodgers that Los Angeles was ready for major league baseball. Who could predict how the arrival of the Dodgers might affect the Rams' bottom line?

All those challenges awaited the man who would be assistant to the Rams' president and none would be easy to solve. But the money the Rams offered was twice the pay Rozelle was making at the public relations agency.

Do you want the job? Bell had asked. Rozelle's answer was yes.

So the Rams called a press conference, photographers took aim, and Rozelle shook Sid Gillman's hand.

CHAPTER 14

Not A Very Nice Thing To Do

"Victory is sweet. It is also bittersweet. The Los Angeles Rams learned this yesterday. Veteran linebacker Larry Morris broke his ankle in the first quarter of Friday's 45–14 conquest of the Washington Redskins and will probably be sidelined for the season… The Ram casualty list also included regular guard John Hock, victim of a ligament strain, which will probably inactivate him for a month…"

—Jack Geyer, *Los Angeles Times*, August 18, 1957

BEFORE, IT HAD BEEN a tendon in the knee. Now, a ligament. Had he heard a pop? Most people hear a pop when a knee ligament sprains, but it's hard to hear anything when you're wearing a helmet and seventy-five thousand fans are shouting and you're grunting and some guy with a burgundy-colored jersey is bringing a shoulder at full-speed. Had he heard a pop? Does it even matter? He *felt* the difference. A knife pain and the joint wobbly, then more stabbing every time he put weight on the leg. Even later, with the knee iced and braced, the whole leg felt so loose.

The way the doc explained it, the ligament stretched too far. Probably some fibers tore. Not a complete rupture. Hard to know, though. X-rays won't show that sort of thing. Exploratory surgery, though, would have allowed a peek inside the knee. Whatever the doctor did, whatever he learned, three or four weeks of rest and rehabilitation was the early and optimistic estimate for John Hock's knee. That would take the team through its exhibition season. He'd be back in time for the games that mattered.

A small consolation. At twenty-nine years old, he knew he didn't have much football left in him. Every game felt like a gift, especially for a guy whose knees sometimes seemed made of driftwood, dry and brittle and hollow. He'd kept them working with surgery and liniment and stretching, with ice and massages and whirlpools, and it was a sort of miracle, really, that for two seasons he'd only had to cope with pain and stiffness.

This sprain was different. For the first time in two seasons, he couldn't just grit his teeth and drag the joint back into service. This would take time. Only a month, true, but football time runs faster than other sorts. Football time rushes by. It can't be stopped or even slowed. The gridiron isn't Disneyland, where a ticket-buyer might find a never-ending century of horse buggies and gas lamps. The gridiron isn't Hollywood, either, where actors and actresses use makeup and lighting and scalpels to stave off the future and stretch their youth. Football time is relentless and overwhelming and quick. Vicious and sudden as an arm bar tackle across the head.

Sit on the bench for even a month, and the game might damn well move on without you.

◆

At age eighty-two, a person has lived so much life that some bits can't be recalled. You might not remember, for example, which of your husband's knees was the one he hurt that season, or in which game (but probably it was the right knee, because that one was always the worst). You might not remember whether he needed crutches. Or how he managed to climb the stairs to your second-floor apartment. You remember a second surgery, maybe that was in 1957. The operation could have been exploratory. What you remember with certainty is that after a second surgery, doctors took you aside for a private talk, but you don't remember if that was in a hospital hallway or in an office, or when exactly. You don't remember which doctors they were, if they worked for the Rams or not. You remember that you were pregnant with your third child, because at that point the children were arriving once a year. You remember that those doctors—at the hospital or the office, who knows?—gave you an instruction about your husband, something other than to massage the knee or to give him these pills twice a day and these others every eight hours. You don't remember all the details—that was more than fifty years ago!—but you remember exactly what the doctors said you had to do.

You have to tell him, they said, *he shouldn't play football anymore, because if he does, he won't walk normally, ever again.*

You remember what you thought: that asking his wife, of all people, to give him that news—it wasn't a very nice thing to do.

◆

IN A HOLLYWOOD STUDIO remade to appear like the small bedroom of an LA apartment, the cameras stand in four or five places to capture the scene from various angles: close-up, distance, John Hock in the bed, Micki at the doorway. The casting department advertised for a pretty young actress to play Micki's role, and the director wanted someone with Audrey Hepburn's spunk, only more maternal and more Irish. A Susan Hayward type, maybe, only younger, with Hayward's reddish hair and round cheeks and the small chin that made a heart of her face.

The director has already decided that this scene won't include any background music. It will be a scene of silences, of quiet. John Hock believed in doing things quietly, never making a fuss. So there will be no fuss in this scene. Later, the sound editors will add the voices of toddler-infant play—Jay and Mary, distant and quiet, as if from another room, another life.

One camera watches Hock lie in bed with his right leg elevated on pillows and the knee wrapped with so much bandage over so much swelling it looks as if he's got a football swaddled there. It's good-sized, this Pro Bowl bed, with its headboard that has sliding doors. Hock's in a white T-shirt, which is tight and shows his Charles Atlas physique, and he's working a newspaper crossword puzzle. It's light duty, the puzzle, you can tell from his expression; it's nothing he's fretting about. Now and then he flips the pencil to erase, and he blows at the eraser shreds, then slaps the newspaper to get rid of the ones that stick. Another camera catches Micki arriving at the doorway. She's pregnant but still several months from delivery. With both hands she holds a tray. On the tray is a plate with a sandwich and beside that a sweating bottle of beer. A small fan whirrs, sitting on a windowsill.

"How's anyone supposed to know Texas's third largest city unless you live in it?" he asks, and he chuckles. "Do you know Texas's third-largest city?"

"Aren't all Texas cities the largest?" She fixes the tray over his lap, making sure the fold-down legs are secure. He scooches back, setting aside the crossword puzzle at the same time, and she adjusts the pillow under his leg. After a thank-you, he tries a bite of the sandwich.

"I brought your pain pill, too," she says.

"I don't need that."

"But the doctor says."

So he reaches for a water glass from the side table and gulps down the pill. A moment later, he sips from the beer bottle.

"Anything else?" she asks, taking his hand. Here, a camera closes on her face, and it's clear that her expression doesn't match the tone of her voice. The voice is full of cheer, but the face is sober. Her eyes dart from his face to his knee, from knee to face.

"A slice of chocolate cake?" he asks, and she nods, then kisses his hand as if her kiss might break him into pieces.

At the doorway she turns back to face him. She folds her arms across her pregnant belly, wrapping herself tightly, as if for protection, as if holding herself together. Is this the time? If it is, she must be fierce and quiet as she tells him. Her husband is a fierce and quiet man, and it will be best if she is, too. The breath she takes in, then, is huge, as if breath is a prayer and gives strength.

This is the time. She speaks his name, and the camera catches him turning to her. He raises his eyebrows in question even as he swallows a mouthful of sandwich.

"The doctors asked me to tell you something," she says. "I don't know why they wouldn't tell you themselves. But they didn't. They asked me."

Then she tells him. Exactly what they said, and no more.

He's not grinning anymore, but the look that's taken hold of his face isn't awful, either. If this news gives him pain, his expression will hardly show it. His brow furrows a bit, his lips purse. For a moment, his jaw expands as if he's clenched his teeth, but just as quickly the muscle relaxes. He seems not to breathe. Then he does.

"Well," he says, "that's the way things go." Then he looks at her. "I'm sorry they asked you to do that. Thank you for telling me. It was important."

She nods. Then she turns to leave the room. "I'll bring you cake," she says.

❖

"I'M SURE EVERY YEAR John was ready to retire," said Duane Putnam, thinking about his old friend. He's certain, because every year he, too, thought about retirement.

Football wasn't so lucrative that a Putnam or Hock could sock away savings for those decades after they and football parted ways. When football ended, they would need another career. Every year in football meant another year away from building their resumés with the sorts of experiences men in their twenties could usually claim.

Also, the work of a football player wore a body down. Injuries played a part, but so did the day-to-day exertion. "It was always running," Putnam said. In preseason, in regular-season practices, in games, if you weren't repeating plays and working on timing, you were running. That's how coaches kept you in shape, and it didn't matter if you were a big guy or a little guy. "You always had to run," Putnam said. "After ten or eleven years, your legs get a little tired of that."

Then, if you are a John Hock or a Duane Putnam, you think about retiring. You hear from doctors that you might not walk normally again, and you have every good reason to retire on the spot.

Why, then, do you come back for more?

◆

FOR DECADES AFTER HIS football career ended, John Hock kept a black and white photo of himself with four other Rams, taken one evening during training camp in Redlands. It's a joy-filled photo, snapped after a day of practices as the players entertained themselves on the quiet campus. The five men crowd together on a dormitory porch—probably Melrose Hall—and behind them a window is open to gather breezes. Each man wears slacks that are probably khaki-colored and T-shirts that look white, and on each T-shirt are iron-on letters across the chest that read "LA RAMS." All five appear to be backed up against a railing, in front of an audience, with Duane Putnam in the middle, the only one seated, his hair in a brush cut, and he holds a small acoustic guitar on his lap. Over his shoulder, a fellow blows harmonica. Putnam is laughing, and the three others, including John Hock, seem to be desperately holding a note, strangling some off-key harmony while trying not to laugh. Hock's arm wraps around the back of the harmonica player, his hand rests on the fellow's shoulder. Hock's head tilts back; he is giving full and jolly voice to whatever he is singing badly.

Here's something to consider about that photo and perhaps why John Hock held on to it for so long, kept it framed and so often in view. It isn't just a photograph of five men goofing around like boys. It isn't just five friends entertaining themselves and others. It's five men who live with an every-day intensity marked by sweat and pain, shared violence, and even this: earned moments of equally intense giddiness.

◆

HERE NEXT IS THE testament of John Houser, a robust man in his seventy-eighth year, broad-faced and tall and slightly stooped, thus giving the impression that he looms over you. A man with the stiff knees of an ex-NFL lineman, a preacher's passion, and a salesman's gift of gab, who joined the Rams as a rookie in 1957:

"I'm John W. Houser, Jr., and God Almighty for years, I was called Joe. If you were to go to my high school, which is a boys school out in Chino, you'll see they knew me as Joe. As a matter of fact, there's a citizenship award out there on a plaque...and it's got my name on it, Joe Houser, which didn't bother me much when I was seventeen going on eighteen. Then at the University of Redlands where I went to school, gee whiz, the coaches and everybody knew me as Joe. So when I finally joined the Los Angeles Rams, the nickname came along with me, but that's when I tried to reverse the process, because I signed a contract with *John*, and that's when I started realizing it wasn't going to get me too far, legally… It's a nickname that came about when I was a very young youngster—actually a baby.

"The Rams conducted their training camp, preseason training camp, at Redlands, and unbeknownst to me at the time, my coach just happened to say to the Rams, who were touching base with him, preparing for training camp, 'Would you be interested in one of our local boys trying out for the team?' The Rams said, 'Bring him on!' They're thinking this would be PR for them using the school, using the facilities. I was walking across the campus quad one day, Coach says, 'Hey Joe, I wanna talk to you.'

"'Yeah, Coach, what do you want?'

"'How would you like to have a try out with the Los Angeles Rams?'"

The big man with the boyish face, the Pride of Redlands, got his opportunity. He tried out at tight end, but the pro quarterbacks threw with such zip he couldn't catch the passes. So then the Rams tried him on the line, put him at guard. Lo and behold, he made the starting lineup.

Houser: "Mainly with the help of John Hock. He got his knee busted. And that's kind of a backdoor way of getting to be a starter."

279

◆

AT REDLANDS, A TINY college with not much of a football team, John Houser played tight end and running back and center and tackle. But he'd never played guard—and that's the position the Rams thought he'd fit. But he was all "fumble feet," he said, stumbling and stuttering around. On the practice field, Duane Putnam helped by showing him the footwork, explaining the timing. Then, at lunch, he'd sit with John Hock, who would give him lessons of an hour or longer about the men Houser would face in the next exhibition game. Hock offered tips about the likes of Leo Nomellini of the 49ers (they called him "The Lion" because he roared when he played), Dick Modzelewski of the Giants (small at six feet tall, but solid as a concrete plug), and Art Donovan of the Colts. Donovan, Hock told him, would line up nearly six yards away from the line and let you rush him, then sidestep you like a matador. Offensive line judo. "You had to be under control," Houser said, "or you'd be brushed aside, and he'd make a fool out of you."

The scouting reports kept Houser on the field and mostly succeeding—but not always. Once that season, against San Francisco when Houser faced Leo "The Lion" Nomellini, Van Brocklin called for a long pass play. That meant Houser had to keep Nomellini occupied for five seconds, the time it would take Elroy Hirsch to run down the field. "You're supposed to pop him," Houser explained, "then, when he comes back, pop him again." Two pops equals about five seconds. But Nomellini feinted inside, and when Houser followed him Nomellini spun around pop-free and sacked Van Brocklin before Dutch could take five steps. "Look, rook!" Van Brocklin roared. "We're paying you ten thousand a year to keep that SOB off my back!"

That confused Houser, who as a rookie was actually making only $5,500. "Yeah, Dutch," he answered anyway, "but they're paying him twenty-five thousand to get you."

After those failures, Houser would find himself on the sidelines standing next to Hock, who would say in his calm, quiet un–Van Brocklin way, "Well, that didn't work."

◆

IN THAT SUMMER OF 1957, John Hock came back after missing three games and began again the burdensome work of a shuttle guard, this time sharing the duties with John Houser. Hock stayed with the team even after Sid Gillman, midway through the season, named Houser as the starter at right guard because, as the newspapers reported, "John Hock has not recovered fully from an earlier injury."

He stayed through all that, and even stayed after Micki gave him the doctors' warning, a warning that placed him at the juncture of two equally difficult truths: his knees could cripple his career, and his career could cripple his legs.

That summer, he tilted toward the career.

It wasn't money that kept him on the field, because the pay was mediocre. It wasn't his meager celebrity, which only troubled his sense of self. It wasn't the thronging bellow of Rams fans on Sundays.

But Hock had seen his father lose his job at US Steel in Pittsburgh, and toil at a service station and for a soap company. He'd seen his wife grading student work. He himself had peeled potatoes in the military and sold rabbit skins door-to-door. He knew about work. He knew that football, like no other job available to him, demanded that he give himself—every iota of mind and soul and body—to his labor.

Perhaps that's why John Hock found it difficult to give up the game—despite pain, despite the mediocre pay, despite the risk to a lifetime of walking. What other job could provide this every-day intensity? What other work could promise—as his hometown, as Los Angeles itself promised—that something spontaneous and thrilling would happen today, if only you stepped outside and gave yourself wholly to the great ongoing game?

John Hock had signed a contract. That meant he could still play.

He would still play.

CHAPTER 15

LA Bums

NEARLY TWO HOURS BEHIND schedule the airplane at last appeared, a promise from the East, delayed but true. When people in this patient, eager crowd saw its flying lights flash out of the night sky they began to cheer. Then the Convair 440 Metropolitan touched down and taxied toward the celebrating crowd, its twin engines winding down and propellers slowing to a *thup-thup-thup*. It was October 23, 1957, so crisp an evening that Roz Wyman wore a long unbuttoned coat over her professional-style city councilwoman dress. And if moments ago she had felt the chill, now she likely felt only exhilaration, because the airplane turned, and on the fuselage, just behind a logo of a giant baseball, were painted the happy words, "Los Angeles Dodgers."

The future she'd dreamed for her city had just landed.

Two bands, including a bunch of fellows in top hats, played welcoming fanfares. A man lifted his son to his shoulders so the boy could see. A woman in glasses and a cardigan gawked as she petted a small dog she clutched to her chest. Nearby, a strange sight: In a wooden chair built several sizes too big, like a movie prop for the film *The Incredible Shrinking Man*, released earlier that year, a grown man sat, dwarfed. The fellow wielded a super-size bat twice his height, grinned, and waved a placard that read, "WELCOME O'MALLEY & LADS TO A BIG TOWN."

Wyman, just twenty-seven years old, and Kenneth Hahn, a county supervisor and political ally, stood ready as the plane parked, waiting for its door to open and its steps to lower. And when those steps came down, the two politicians, each wearing a baseball cap, climbed up to be the first to greet Walter O'Malley, their new neighbor.

There had been times Roz Wyman thought this would never happen. She'd been working to bring major league baseball to Los Angeles for most of four years, with special attention given the last three years to the Dodgers. Some nights she'd arrive home after a day of phone calls and letter writing and wrangling and her husband would ask, *What do you think? Will they come?* and a pit would grow in her stomach, and she'd have the sense, as she once said, "that after I beat my guts out" the Dodgers would decide not to come. Yes, O'Malley's unhappiness with Ebbets Field was legendary, and the failed efforts to find a new home in Brooklyn were well-publicized. But Brooklyn's famed "Bums" had been part of the borough since the nineteenth century. *How do you leave after all that time?* she wondered. How do you leave a place like Brooklyn? How do you leave New York?

Even in the wake of that skepticism and doubt, she gave the long hours. In small moments of apprehension, she might have believed the Dodgers would never leave Brooklyn, but she always believed Los Angeles needed major league baseball. So Wyman kept pushing and pushing, even up to the night of October 7, just three days after her twenty-seventh birthday, when all of her efforts almost fell apart.

That night, the city council was to vote on a binding deal negotiated with O'Malley's representatives and meant to bring the Dodgers west. The council needed ten votes from its fourteen members who were present, and Wyman wasn't at all sure that nine of her peers would vote with her. At City Hall, as the council debated, she paid careful attention to each member's concerns and worked to allay them. Moreover, she was four months pregnant, and she had already lost one pregnancy. "It was terrible," she recalled of the stress that day. "It was hard on me."

Then, the mayor, Norris Poulson, interrupted her work with an urgent message. He wanted her to come to his office but wouldn't say why. She ignored him, believing the situation with the council to be too tenuous. Poulson insisted, sending note after note and, eventually, a Los Angeles police officer. Finally, she slipped away to his office. He told her he wanted to telephone O'Malley.

Poulson was in a tizzy. To that point, the city's negotiators had only been talking with people who worked for O'Malley. Sure, they said he'd like the deal. But they weren't him. Poulson wanted to hear from O'Malley himself that he'd go for it. Politically, a lot was at risk. The deal—a huge land swap, deeding hundreds of acres of city property to the Dodgers—was likely to be controversial among Los Angeles voters. If the council approved the deal and O'Malley rejected it, wouldn't Poulson and the city council look like a bunch of provincial suckers?

But Poulson was too nervous to talk himself with O'Malley. So he handed Wyman the phone. She tried to hand it back. "Oh, no," he told her. "I don't want to talk at all."

Then a voice came on the line. Roz Wyman said hello. "Mrs. Wyman," said Walter O'Malley. For all Wyman's efforts, this was the first she'd ever actually talked to the Dodgers' president and primary owner.

"Mrs. Wyman," he said, "I want to thank you for all you've done. I know it's been difficult."

Not knowing what else to say, Wyman asked about the weather in New York.

She didn't want to ask about the deal, because, unlike Poulson, she didn't want to know what O'Malley thought. Ignorant of that knowledge, she could tell her peers on the council a simple, limited truth: His people say he'll like it. But if she asked and if O'Malley offered no assurance, what would she tell others on the council? She couldn't lie. She could only hope they wouldn't say, "Mrs. Wyman, does Mr. O'Malley agree to this deal?"

"Ask him! Ask him!" said the mayor.

And if some council member put her on the spot that way, and she said, "He offers no assurance," then the votes might go away and all her years of work could vanish the way blue sky disappears on a smoggy day, and Los Angeles would remain a city of the second rank.

"Ask him!" the mayor said.

Wyman breathed and steeled herself. She had to say something; there had to be a reason for the call. "Mr. O'Malley," she said, "I take it if we vote this deal through, you will come?"

He told her that he didn't know.

"I'm certainly giving it serious consideration," he said. "Do you have the votes?" She said she thought she had the votes.

He reminded her, then, that he was after all a New Yorker, and he professed to still believe that New York might be better for the Dodgers than Los Angeles. He told her that baseball had never proven to be a big success in California. He said, "I don't know if we will come."

"That's a pretty disappointing answer," she replied. "We've gone a long way to get here." Nevertheless, she told him, she would go back to the council chambers and "fight this thing through."

And then they said their polite goodbyes.

She took a few moments to gather herself, then returned to the debate, which lasted for a couple more hours. Remarkably, no one straight-out asked her if she knew what O'Malley thought of the deal. At last, exhausted and with some confidence, Wyman called for the vote.

It was 10–4. The council approved the contract with the Los Angeles Dodgers.

The next day, the Dodgers released a statement announcing that the team would move to Los Angeles for the 1958 season.

Wyman, giddy with the news, didn't know why O'Malley had refused to commit in the hours before the vote, but that didn't matter so much. What mattered was that the Dodgers had decided to come to Los Angeles. A New York institution would uproot itself and settle in the nation's opposite corner. The City of Angels was now major league.

Wyman, Mayor Poulson, County Supervisor Hahn, and half a dozen of Wyman's fellow yes-voting council members then held a ceremony to sign the contract with the Dodgers. One councilman brought a bat; Wyman and a few others wore baseball caps with wide pieces of tape affixed across the crown, and on the tape, in thick marker, they'd written, "LA BUMS".

The contract they signed called for Los Angeles to deed more than three hundred acres in Chavez Ravine to the Dodgers; in turn the Dodgers would give to the city an LA minor league ballpark they owned, which amounted to much less acreage. The Dodgers, with all that extra land, would then build a fifty-thousand-seat stadium, and they'd do it with no public funding except the swapped land. The team also agreed to pay about $300,000 a year in property taxes for the site. Other minor aspects of the deal included the Dodgers funding a youth recreation center.

About two weeks later, O'Malley stepped off the Corvair airplane with a baseball in each hand, and he tossed those into the crowd. Wyman shouted into a microphone, "Welcome to Los Angeles!" and Hahn presented O'Malley with a proclamation. Reporters from KTTV and KTLA recorded the speeches, and newspaper photographers snapped away, their flash bulb pops sparkling off the shiny brass of tubas and trombones.

And then another man hurried toward the plane and handed O'Malley an envelope before rushing away.

"What's this?" O'Malley asked Wyman.

She answered quietly. "You have just been served," she said. Then she added, "There may be a few lawsuits."

Out in the crowd, plenty of people waved signs saying, "Hello, Dodgers!" and the like. But there were a few, too, that weren't so cheerful. These signs were held by people who thought the giveaway of Chavez Ravine was too great a price to bring the Dodgers to Los Angeles. The city had acquired the property through a complicated series of events involving eminent domain condemnation, federal money for public housing, and a backlash against such housing by people who believed it would lead to communism. Now land on which various governments had spent millions of dollars, taken from private owners and once intended for poor people specifically and the public good generally, was about to go to a privately owned baseball team. Not everyone liked that. Blared one protester's sign:

"IT'S NOT THE DODGERS WE OPPOSE! IT'S THE DEAL!"

◆

HAVING BEEN BEATEN IN order by San Francisco, Detroit, and Chicago, the Rams arrived home in Los Angeles by plane that same week as the Dodgers. But instead of bringing major league status, the Rams brought with them a record of 1–3. At the airport, no crowds cheered them, no bands played. Some of the players, at least, had wives and kids to greet them.

That Sunday following Dodgers Week was a beautiful afternoon for football. Smog had cleared, sun shone, and the day was warm, reaching to eighty-eight degrees.

Norm Van Brocklin trotted onto the field for pregame introductions before the crowd of more than seventy-seven thousand—and boos welcomed him home.

One victory against three defeats? the boos seemed to say. Why are we buying tickets? Will this season be a repeat of last year? Good heavens, will it be worse?

So far, the 1957 season *was* worse, with old, tired tensions persisting: controversy over who would call plays, over which quarterback—Van Brocklin or Bill Wade—ought to get more field time. Add to that some troublesome injuries, such as to John Hock and Ron Waller, the rookie all-star running back from the season before, and the Rams lacked a spark. Critics had even called the offense—and Van Brocklin—"unimaginative."

Unimaginative? Was there any worse insult in the movie capital of the world, the epicenter of Googie architecture, the home of Disneyland? And to make this accusation of the Rams—the team that had invented the wide receiver, put logos on helmets, had tried three "bull elephant" running backs at once? The team that had first dared to go west?

Unimaginative!

They got boos while every day the biggest headlines proclaimed the Dodgers. Billboards extolling the Dodgers read "Good luck, team!" Everywhere Walter O'Malley appeared people applauded. The Dodgers had yet to play a game in the city, and already Los Angeles swooned for them.

The Rams—and particularly Van Brocklin—felt frustrated, angry. And on this Sunday, the last in October, facing Detroit's Lions, they played that way.

They'd already lost to Detroit that season, 10–7, and John Houser, the rookie from Redlands, remembered it well. Veteran offensive linemen had taken him for dinner to a Detroit restaurant called the Brass Rail, and as they ate their steaks they heard a lot of carrying on coming from a private room, separated from the main dining area by accordion-folding walls. At last they asked their waiter who it was having all that fun, and the waiter told them it was players from the Detroit Lions. When the Lions exited, recognizing the Rams and saying, "We'll see you guys tomorrow," the last bunch of them were two guys carrying out a third who looked to be inebriated. *And who's that?* the Rams asked their waiter. "That's Hunchy Hoernschemeyer," the waiter said. The next day, when the Rams kicked off, Houser looked down field and saw a Lion leaning on the goal post, puking. The Rams kicker sent the ball into the air, and the sick guy staggered under it, then ran it back forty-six yards. "Hunchy Hoernschemeyer," said the public address announcer. Houser turned to one of the veterans. "We should see what kind of booze that guy was drinking," he said.

It had been that kind of season.

But now Detroit was on the Rams' turf, and Los Angeles unloaded its frustrations.

The first time their offense had the football, the Rams needed only nine plays to score a touchdown, finishing the drive when Tank Younger ran into the end zone from three yards out.

On their second drive, they again needed only nine plays—this time to cover fifty-one yards and score a touchdown. Van Brocklin, making the calls, mixed passes with runs, and handed off to different running backs. He ended the drive himself by pushing the ball in from the one-yard line. The score was 14–0.

Then, Rams linebacker Les Richter intercepted a Detroit pass on the Rams' side of the field. The offense again worked its way to Detroit's one-yard line, but on their fourth and final down, the Rams still hadn't scored. From the sidelines, Gillman and his coaches were waving and shouting for a field goal attempt. That was conventional wisdom, after all. If you've got a lead, build on it with the easy three points. Don't risk failing and losing momentum.

It was the boring call. The *unimaginative* call.

Van Brocklin ignored the coaches. He wanted another touchdown, and he wanted it for himself. He took the ball on the snap from the center, then leaned left. Or, as the *Los Angeles Times* put it, he "stuck his helmet in the seat of Guard Duane Putnam's football pants and charged across."

Not only was it a touchdown, it was a touchdown with style. Swashbuckling. And with the extra point kick, the Rams led 21–0. Now, as the offense trotted off the field, thousands of fans rose to their feet to give Dutch and company an ovation.

John Hock watched most of the action from the sideline. He was unaccustomed to this role, backing up another guard. Throughout his career with the Rams, if he was healthy enough to suit up, he had started. Now it was a knockout gorgeous Sunday in Southern California, a Marilyn Monroe of days, and he wore shoulder pads and cleats and a knee brace. Healthy enough to suit up, every muscle, every nerve, every day he'd lived since he'd joined the Rams four years earlier told him he should be playing, but instead he watched. He knew Gillman would eventually call his name, that he'd play a few downs, spell young John Houser when the rookie got winded or had his skull rattled. Until then, he'd stalk the sidelines. Blame it on the knee, sure, yeah—and maybe he *had* come back too soon after the ligament strain. Maybe he *did* need more time to strengthen the joint. Whatever the reason, though, Gillman, by putting Hock on the bench, even if only for a little while, had sent a message that number sixty-three wasn't the player he'd been.

Enough of that. It wasn't the time to contemplate or muse about such things. He still had to pay careful attention, help the kid, Houser. He needed to know what was happening on the field in case the coaches sent him in. Still, this was such a different experience than playing. Then, his body, his head, his heart—every part of him—had been caught up in the game. Now there were moments his mind could dart away from the action—and maybe light upon a thought or two. Maybe it was in one of those moments that he began to understand the growing reality.

Given the knees, the coaches, and the doctors, a decision about retirement might be made for him if he didn't make it himself.

◆

CONSIDER, FOR A MOMENT, the numbers. Consider their context.

Los Angeles was ga-ga for the Dodgers, and the Rams had lost three of their first four games. Yet a crowd of 77,314 showed to watch the football game against Detroit.

The Rams won that day. For their next game— the Chicago Bears at home—80,456 people showed, including former President Harry S. Truman. Rams co-owner Edwin Pauley had served various roles with the Truman administration—among them special assistant to the secretary of state. He'd long been a friend and fundraiser for Truman, and he had invited the president. Truman, in a tie and overcoat, watched from a corner seat in the press box. He munched on a sandwich, and he kept the teams' rosters and a pair of binoculars handy, even as the Rams lost.

Next, San Francisco's 49ers came to town. Though the Rams' win–loss count stood at a lousy 2–4, the crowd size again grew for this in-state rivalry, this time setting an NFL record: 102,368, nearly a full house. Never before had so many people watched an NFL game live.

No other team in the league could boast such astronomic attendance. That the Rams could draw those numbers with a depressing, dismal record meant something more was happening.

What was happening was Pete Rozelle. The calm, quiet man with the Madison Avenue wardrobe had come into his new job in the midst of a player revolt coupled with owner acrimony and peevishness. One of his first accomplishments was to persuade the owners to pay each player fifty dollars per exhibition game and to raise their per diem from six dollars to nine. He even convinced Reeves and the rest to pay part of the players' health insurance premiums.

Then he smoothed relations between the owners. They still weren't talking—especially Reeves and Pauley—but they weren't so much working at cross purposes, either. That made the day-to-day operations more efficient. Rozelle believed patience to be one of his skills, and he figured that if he approached each situation patiently he could ease tensions and find solutions.

Acting on what he'd learned in public relations, he then brought a more professional look to the team, giving attention to small details company wide. For example, he hired a graphic artist to modernize the look of the game-day programs. He also worked to create a retail outlet for Rams merchandise—selling everything from T-shirts to bobblehead dolls of players.

If he couldn't change what happened on the field, the former public relations executive could at least sell Los Angeles something other than a losing team. For the cost of a ticket, Rozelle was selling excitement, thrills—a modern spectacle. Gladiators clashing with Lions and Bears.

And as the crowds grew he was also selling a sense of belonging. For the cost of a T-shirt a fan could join the tribe. For the cost of a ticket, any Los Angeleno could join the crowds, then bear witness on Monday morning, say "I was there."

It's possible that Rozelle and the Rams ownership felt some urgency. After all, the Dodgers brought a shiny new game to provide competition for the Los Angeles sports fan's dollar. It's possible much of Rozelle's efforts were meant to secure a fan base before the Dodgers threw out their first pitch. But Roz Wyman doesn't think so. Years later, she believes the Rams owners likely wanted the Dodgers, too. She knew Ed Pauley better than the others, and to the best of her recall she believes he thought the more sports the better.

"It's like a market in the mall," she explains. "If you have more than one market, it's good."

Los Angeles was prosperous after all; plenty of people carried full wallets. And to each sport there was a season, so it would be rare when baseball and football found themselves in direct competition. If people could become accustomed to two sports, if they came to love two sports, wouldn't they support two sports? Look at New York or Chicago or Pittsburgh or Detroit. Why not Los Angeles?

There could be two of Hollywood's Teams, right?

◆

THERE ARE PEOPLE WHO look forward, imagine how things might be, and act on their imaginings to transform a city, a town, or how things work. Walt Disney was a leader in that club, and Dan Reeves belonged, and so did Roz Wyman and Walter O'Malley and Pete Rozelle.

There are also people who wake every morning and go to work. Though they dream, their focus mostly stays with today. Without this last bunch, everything the visionaries imagine would fall apart. In Los Angeles, in the 1950s, they were carpenters and TV repairmen and maids and grocers and soda jerks. They took visitors' money at Disneyland and belted kids into rides. In Hollywood, they built sets and hauled lights. They drove streetcars until there were no more streetcars. They emptied trash cans at the beach. They cut meat. They picked oranges from trees. While standing at conveyor belts, they connected engine parts. They packed brassieres into boxes for shipping. They taught long division to schoolchildren. They tossed beer kegs into trucks. They bought tickets to football games and brought their children and fed them hot dogs with ketchup. They cut their own lawns, they cooked their own dinners, they enjoyed a cold beer. Innovations begin with the Walt Disneys and Dan Reeves of the world, but their ideas depend on these others who know when to flip a switch or how to lift a crate, and at their best do that job with efficiency and skill. Call them the offensive linemen of the world. Snap a chin strap or punch the clock, these are people who grind through the same work day after day after day until the days behind them rise in a towering uncountable stack.

Eventually, the body becomes weary.

It was mid-November, 1957. When those 102,368 people set an NFL record for attendance, they watched the Rams beat San Francisco, 37–24. It was the third straight game John Hock had not started, though for this one Gillman brought back the shuttle-guard system, so Hock and Houser played about the same number of snaps.

It's likely Hock had been thinking more and more about retirement, about what might come next in his life. In football years, he was growing old. He'd turned twenty-nine in the spring, and if he played another season, he'd be thirty, a year older. That Houser kid would just be a year better. Quite likely, Hock would back him up all year. If the knees let him. There were so many kids like Houser now, and so few old-timers. Even Putnam was talking about retirement. So were Van Brocklin and Tank Younger, and Will Sherman, the defensive back and cocaptain. When

Hock had come to the Rams he was blocking for guys like Skeet Quinlan and Woodley Lewis and Vitamin Smith. Even their names sounded old. They were all gone now, traded or retired. Last year, he'd blocked for Ron Waller, and now there was an even younger kid—Jon Arnett, a rookie from USC, chewing up the gridiron grass with his quick moves.

It wasn't pain from the knees that would have given him thoughts of retirement. Pain he could handle. Pain was irrelevant. But if the knees—one or both—didn't work, couldn't do what he needed them to do, pain or no pain, it was over.

He had always loved that Los Angeles seemed so new, so dynamic. He'd come home from Japan to a city where change was the constant. Young and unmarried, all possibility lay ahead of him, and his city and its football team seemed that way, too. But now the city and team had both become something else—and it was hard to put a finger on what was different. The city had aged, somehow, in just a few years. The Rams had, too. Just like John Hock, now married and with a family, the Rams and Los Angeles had begun to settle down a bit, to grow closer to a definition of themselves. The Rams were an institution, a team that could lose but still draw larger and larger crowds, even as the coaches and front office took more and more control. In the city, plans for highways had led to highways themselves, the culture of cars established. Those highways led to bulldozed fields that were now neighborhoods where people lived, making decisions about life insurance and their kids' teachers, and worrying about the belt that squeaked each time the Chevy started.

Millions of people had moved here over the last twenty years, and now millions were getting on with their lives. The decade was nearing its close. Pretty soon it would be 1958. Soon, Los Angeles would have the Dodgers and the Rams and a new baseball stadium. It was, as the man's sign read, a grown-up town.

John Hock was twenty-nine years old. He had a wife and three kids. Maybe it was time for him to find a different role in this new era, in this grown-up city.

Teaching history at a high school—that appealed to him. Spending days with young men and the long-gone centuries, then changing into a T-shirt and carrying a whistle through the afternoon, instructing many of those same young men at football practice. That life sounded good. It sounded so good there were times a return to the Rams seemed like the fall-back position, what he'd do if he couldn't find a teaching job.

And if that were the case, if the Rams were the fall-back position, then this probably would be his last swing through an NFL season. Having beaten San Francisco on that record-setting day, the Rams were about to embark on a three-game road trip. Then two more back home. Five games to go.

It looked to be the start of John Hock's last weeks as a Ram.

CHAPTER 16

The Most Quiet Part

B Y ALMOST EVERY MEASURE, the last game of 1957 meant nothing to the Rams. The team had played eleven games, and its record was 5–6. The Western Division title lay beyond reach, no matter the result of this final game. Victory or defeat, the season ended on December 15 when the Rams played Johnny Unitas and Baltimore Colts. But Pete Rozelle and the front office staff had learned that even a losing team, marketed properly, could draw record crowds. They just needed to give this last game some meaning.

For their most recent contest, the eleventh of the twelve-game season, the Rams had drawn nearly seventy-one thousand people to the coliseum. And that figure gave Rozelle and his staff an idea. Add all the attendance from exhibition games, away games, and home games, and the total attendance came to 998,546. With some quick research, Rozelle and company realized that with one game to go, the Rams could be the first football team ever—college or professional—to play before a million fans in a single season.

All they needed was 1,454 people to show for the finale against the Colts. That figure was guaranteed, but they could use that "million fans" goal to sell even more tickets. Pitch it as an historic moment for the NFL in particular, and football in general. No other team, not in New York, not in Chicago, could claim this accomplishment. Los Angeles would be the first. And wouldn't fans line up to have a chance at making history?

Bingo. Touchdown. Now the game had meaning.

◆

THE NIGHT OF THE Ye Olde Rams banquet, four days before the season's final kickoff, Sid Gillman added some meaning of his own.

Microphone in hand, he prowled the stage in front of all those celebrities, players, and fans, looking for offensive linemen to call out. He started by inviting Ken Panfil onto the stage. Panfil, six foot six and some 250 pounds hopped up on stage. He was big-chested with a sweet smile and a face that could have belonged to a movie star if he'd had a smaller nose. He regularly started at tackle on John Hock's side of the line.

"Look, folks," said Gillman. "Doesn't he look big enough to stop Gino Marchetti? No one has done it this year, but Ken has been playing good ball for us, and I think he can do it. Don't you?"

Marchetti was widely acknowledged as one of, if not the best defensive tackle in football. When the Rams and Colts met later that week, Panfil would line up across from Gino. Given the Baltimore reporters in the room, odds were certain that Marchetti would hear about Gillman's boast.

Panfil stepped down, and maybe those eating their banquet chicken noticed a little less sweetness in his smile.

But Gillman wasn't done. Next he summoned Duane Putnam, who was going to face his old Rams teammate, Gene "Big Daddy" Lipscomb. As Putnam stood in the glare of the lights, Gillman started on him.

"Here's the top offensive guard in pro football," he said. "He has to spot around eighty pounds Sunday, but we know he can do it. Putnam's target is Big Daddy Lipscomb. Watch Put cut him down. It should be a real battle."

Later, reporters did indeed bring Gillman's boasts back to Marchetti and Lipscomb. Said the latter: "The best thing that happened to me was being traded to Baltimore. They aren't going to scare us, that's for sure." And Marchetti promised Panfil would have a most uncomfortable day. "He won't be picking cherries," he said.

The Colts needed no such chest thumping as Gillman provided. They had beaten the Rams two weeks earlier in Baltimore, 31–14. Given their 7–4 record, a victory at Los Angeles would put them in position to go to the NFL championship game. It was, as *The Baltimore Sun* reported, the most crucial game in the franchise's short history. And though six Colts suffered sore throats from breathing a week's worth of Los Angeles smog, on the day of the game the players were all in top playing shape. Even as the game began, the Colts principal owner, Carroll Rosenbloom, strolled through the press box and said, "Boy, if ever a team is ready, it is the Colts today."

◆

John Hock's credo: do things quietly.

Come Sunday, the morning of the last football game he'd ever play, who would have known it was the end but him? To make an announcement would add noise to the day, people shaking his hand, saying goodbye, making a fuss the way people did over Tank, who'd told the newspapers he was through. Whisper it to even a few, and word would spread.

John Hock would have kept it quiet. He wouldn't have told a soul.

In Los Angeles, where spotlights heralded movies and department store openings and where cameramen gathered as a woman in a sparkling gown stepped from a limousine, John Hock's reticence would have confused a lot of people. In a city where even the mobster Mickey Cohen had once taken a photographer from *Life* magazine on a tour of his home, such self-effacement as John Hock's struck an incongruous note, contradicted Los Angeles's narrative about itself, was so unique it could have drawn attention—if it weren't that everyone's attention was drawn to the spotlights and glitter.

Because it was a Sunday morning, he and Micki would have gone to Mass at Church of the Transfiguration as they always did. They would have dressed in raincoats and likely carried an umbrella or two, because two storm systems had collided over Southern California and the rain fell heavy, more than three inches up in the San Fernando Valley. On the radio were reports of cars stalling in deep water on the valley's west side, and of houses flooding in the Glendale foothills. Telephone cables in west Los Angeles were under water, limiting communication. The coliseum field promised to be muddy and slippery. Maybe there wouldn't be eighty thousand fans, as some had predicted. Maybe a bunch of folks would stay home.

John Hock would want Mass on this morning, because he would want everything to be the way it always was. He'd want Latin and the sign of the cross and hymns and the body and blood. At the stadium, he'd want the weight of shoulder pads, and to rub something into his knees, and for Dutch to say some smart-ass thing, just as he always did. On that road trip, Hock had regained the starting role, so on this day—as on so many before—he would run out onto the field for the Rams' first down, in the company of the Dutchman and Crazylegs and Tank, and he'd line up beside everyone else wearing blue and gold. He'd listen to Van Brocklin's cadence, and at the moment of the snap he'd jump from that three-point stance and smack into old Art Donovan or somebody. Everything just as it always had been.

As it always had been in Mass, too, and after he'd knelt and taken the wafer on his tongue, he'd lift himself and walk past the Christmas poinsettias to the pew where he'd pray. And, maybe, what came then was the only difference for him on this morning, this day.

Maybe then, with hands folded and eyes closed and an organist blowing a hymn through the pipes, somewhere in the quietest part of him, John Hock in his prayer thanked God for the games, every blessed one of them.

CHAPTER 17

Next Time

Nathan: Is there any, uh, particular attraction
in California?

Nella: No, nothing special. Just like everybody else, I'm
looking for the end of the rainbow.
—from *The Tall Men*, Twentieth-Century Fox pictures,
premiered September 22, 1955, in Los Angeles; with Robert
Ryan as Nathan Stark and Jane Russell as Nella Turner

CLOUDS ROLLED AND CHURNED that Sunday morning, and at last let a flash of sun fall on Anaheim, just enough light to convince Monte and Juanita Craig to brave the rain and drive into Los Angeles for the Rams game.

They filled a thermos and bundled up, she in a long plaid overcoat buttoned to the neck, he in a jacket with a cowboy look to it, a material like lamb's wool lining the collar. In fact, with his lean face and pointed nose, Monte, a Texas native, could pass for an older Hank Williams—if Hank had worn eye glasses.

Juanita kept her curly, short hair tucked behind her ears. She and Monte had moved with their two children, Bobby and Charlotte, from the Lone Star State as part of the great Southern California migration in the years around World War II. He found work as a radio and TV repairman, and the family settled on the eastern edge of Greater Los Angeles. Now, Bobby and Charlotte were grown, Monte and Juanita were each forty-six, and they hadn't missed a Rams home game all year.

They arrived early to the ticket window and bought general admission seats, as they usually did, then headed for a gate into the stadium. The odd thing, though, was that all the gates were closed but one. So they joined that line, which moved pretty quickly. Not much of a wait at all. Maybe just enough time to remark on how the clouds had crowded out that earlier, brief sun. Now the skies looked ready to open up and soak everyone.

Just as the Craigs reached the front of the line and stepped through the turnstile, someone grabbed Monte by the arm.

"You!" that someone said. "You're the Rams' millionth fan!"

Next thing you know, Monte and Juanita were grinning and posing for pictures at the gate with Rams president Dan Reeves. Standing behind them, a uniformed ticket taker in a cap and tie raised a yard-long poster that read "Mr. MILLION." Reeves handed Juanita a football, which was autographed by players and marked to commemorate the occasion of the "1,000,000th FAN."

"This is the most thrilling thing that ever happened to us," Juanita said.

Reeves congratulated the couple and delivered the news that they'd won an all-expenses-paid trip for two to the NFL championship game. Then the Craigs were escorted to the press box where President Truman had sat a few weeks earlier, and to seats reserved for them. Person after person shook their hands. Reporters asked them questions. Just like that, they had become celebrities of a moment; just like that, they'd become part of the great Southern California story. As so many others had, they'd followed a rainbow west, and they'd caught a lucky break. It was a story repeated so often it had become myth—the proverbial waitress noticed by a studio exec. But sometimes it was real, say, a football player whose buddy has to drop out of the Pro Bowl and hands off his spot. Sometimes those lucky breaks led to big change. Sometimes the story didn't end so well. Sometimes nothing much changed, except that the busy world took a moment to notice, and a person could later say, as did Monte and Juanita Craig, that you'd been favored with a most thrilling thing.

By definition, the Craigs' moment wouldn't last, not in a city and a decade where change was the constant, where it was all so new. Wasn't there always a prettier actress, a rookie lineman with healthier knees, another movie premiere, a highway opening, a shopping mall ribbon-cutting, another ball team arrived from thousands of miles away? To live that great Los Angeles story—to catch the break and gain your moment—meant also to watch it end.

The Craigs were neither movie stars nor politicians. Sitting in a press box was for them a rare treat. One day next season, they'd probably go to a Rams game and cheer with thousands of others in general admission, as they so often had, and that would be fine, a pleasant afternoon. But for now, from the press box high above the coliseum, Monte and Juanita looked over the whole thing: the sky smudged gray and tucked in to each horizon, a string of Christmas lights affixed to the Olympic torch-holder at the stadium's east end, mountains to the north, and in the west, at field level, the tunnel from which the Rams, in blue and gold, and the Colts, in white trimmed with blue, poured onto the field. Taken together, it was a breathtaking sight.

Imagine how much more impressive the view if the stadium were filled! Today whole sections sat empty. The rain storms had, after all, kept many away. The fifty-three thousand people out there constituted the lowest turnout of the year.

But wasn't that good news for Mr. Million and Mrs. Million-and-One, who might have missed their moment if just one other person had braved the rain, and who now turned their attention to the field as the Rams lined up and kicked off to the waiting Colts.

◆

NOW COME THE END of things. So many that day, and no one knew them all.

Tank Younger had announced his retirement, so even he expected this to be his last game. It wouldn't happen, though, as he'd planned. In another few months, the Rams would trade his contract to Pittsburgh, and he would play his last NFL season for the Steelers.

Likewise, Norm Van Brocklin would soon be traded to the Eagles, putting an end to the Rams quarterback controversy and his play-calling spats with Sid Gillman. Elroy "Crazylegs" Hirsch, probably the most popular Ram in Los Angeles, had insisted he'd be back for another year, but he would retire, too. It was to be the last game for a host of other players, including Bob Boyd and Will Sherman. Come the next season, there'd be only one familiar face left from that Rams team which had won the NFL championship in 1951: Dick Daugherty, a defensive back. He'd stay just that next year, then retire, too.

And, of course, it would be John Hock's last game.

One other finale? The end of football's sole reign at the coliseum. In April, the Dodgers would arrive for their opening day, and they would control the space for months. When next the Rams took the field, their chalk lines would cross dirt base paths. The gridiron, so emblematic of Los Angeles's own grid layout, that predictable and comforting structure that had given rise to such imagination and magic, would exist in the same plane as a cockeyed baseball diamond.

For now, though, the rematch with the Colts and their second-year phenom, quarterback Johnny Unitas. The Rams had nothing to play for but pride. The Colts knew another victory would give them a shot at the NFL championship game.

But this game was to be played in Los Angeles where Hollywood writes the stories. Given all that was ending for the Rams in this last game of the 1957 season, it was a climactic moment in team history. And if it were a movie, wouldn't the script call for the Rams to win?

◆

FOUR PLAYS AFTER THE kickoff. One minute, forty-one seconds. That's all Baltimore and Unitas needed to score their first touchdown. Things looked worse for the Rams soon after, when Big Daddy Lipscomb barreled past Duane Putnam and sacked Van Brocklin. Dutch came up limping with a crumpled toe or two.

It was an exquisitely awful start to a meaningless game played on a dreary day at the end of a mediocre season.

But it was only the beginning, because—for whatever reason—Crazylegs, a football ancient at age thirty-four, and Dutch, who was thirty-one and had probably just broken a toe or two, played as if it were 1951 again—when their younger selves scored almost at will and the Rams had last won the NFL championship.

This day, as on those days' years before, Van Brocklin zipped passes to the sidelines and downfield, and Hirsch, more often than not, was the one to drag them in. When that combination wasn't at work, the Dutchman floated a few to the rookie, Jon Arnett, or he handed off to Ron Waller or some other running back, who—rather than crash through that gargantuan Baltimore defensive line—sprinted to the edges and around.

The Rams kept on that way through the first half. Though Putnam struggled with Lipscomb, the other Rams linemen—Panfil, Bob Fry and the Hock-Houser combo—kept the massive Colts linemen corralled. Then, the rain did indeed fall as the skies had promised, and all through the coliseum umbrellas popped open— gold, blue, orange, and pink bursts, like fireworks in the gloom. Stadium lights burned, though it was still afternoon. On the field, players slipped and splashed, and those pretty white and gold and blue uniforms became a confusion of mud. Wet dirt smeared across jersey numbers, ground into the knees of the pants, and soaked into the seats. In such weather, coaches will tell you, hands get slick and wide receivers can't make sharp cuts in the muck. The best strategy becomes the running game. Give up on the pass. But that would have been like asking Hirsch and Van Brocklin to give up on their best selves. Dutch wasn't about to do that. Not even late in the second quarter, with ten yards to the end zone, when a pass play to Hirsch went awry. In the next huddle, Van Brocklin called the very same play, and this time the ball settled softly into Elroy's arms for a touchdown.

The Rams led, 20–7.

◆

WHEN THE TEAMS RETURNED for the second half, they found the field littered with confetti left behind by a high school band that had entertained the crowd. As a high point to the show, the students had released a flock of pigeons, and a few of those lingered, too, *flup-flup-flupping* across the field.

The Rams received the kickoff. A few plays in, they returned to the huddle, but as they circled to hear the next play, something fell into their midst. Or flew. Who knows whether the players were more startled than the pigeon that landed in a flock of sweaty, muddy men.

"I thought for a moment it was a new kind of secret weapon the boys from Baltimore were trying to spring on us," Dutch joked later.

Van Brocklin's hand darted. *Zzzt!*—and the pigeon was his. Sometimes it's that kind of day—passes on the mark, bird in the palm. Dutch cradled the pigeon—holding it at arm's length—and walked it off the field, its white wings beating. A photographer met him partway and took custody of what the *Los Angeles Examiner* later called "a living forward pass."

◆

THE TEAMS EXCHANGED TOUCHDOWNS—FOR the Colts, a ninety-nine-yard drive that took most of the third quarter; for Los Angeles, another Van Brocklin-to-Crazylegs pass. Then the Rams added a field goal for a 30–14 lead with less than six minutes to play.

From that point, the Colts became desperate, maybe even a little goofy. A trick involving a backwards pass led to a ninety-nine-yard touchdown, but Gillman would later dismiss the play as better suited to a school playground than the gridiron, calling it "intramural."

The Colts then attempted an on-sides kick, perhaps the most desperate maneuver in football. If the high-risk play worked, the Colts would wrest the ball from the Rams and have another opportunity to score. Chances were the play would backfire, though, giving the Rams an easy shot at a field goal, perhaps even a touchdown.

Which is exactly what happened.

So here came Van Brocklin and the Rams. With only a few minutes to go, the polite and courteous thing would have been to run a few plays, let the minutes tick away, maybe kick a field goal. With the Rams defense stifling the Colts again and again, three more points would give Los Angeles an almost-insurmountable lead.

Van Brocklin wasn't interested in being courteous. It's easy to guess why after all the crap he'd heard over the last two seasons from fans, after the arguments with Gillman, and after he'd been made to share his job with Bill Wade. Maybe this was the end of all that, and he was going to take the ball and throw it down the metaphorical throat of everyone who rankled him these last two years—and if the Colts got in the way, well, boohoo for them.

Or maybe he knew that with one more touchdown, he'd break his own team record for touchdown passes in a season, set in 1953 (John Hock's first year), when Van Brocklin had thrown nineteen.

Or maybe it was just Dutch being Dutch.

It could have been all those reasons.

What's verifiable is that with just a few minutes to go and a 30–21 lead, the Dutchman came out gunning for one last touchdown. First, he passed thirty-three yards to Bob Boyd. A pass to a fullback gained another fifteen, and now the Rams needed only eight yards for a fourth touchdown. This time, Van Brocklin lofted the ball to a rookie, Lamar Lundy, who stretched his arms and gave Dutch his fourth touchdown pass of the day, and his record-breaking twentieth of the season. An extra-point kick made the score 37–21, and that's where it would stay.

Soon after, the final gun sounded.

The game ended. The season was over. An era closed.

With mud gritty on their faces and wet in their shoes, with rain dripping from their helmets, Hollywood's team—the lot of them, unglamorous as could be—walked off the field.

◆

LET THE CAMERAS FIND John Hock, one last time.

The scene starts in the locker room, after the Colts' game. A close-up to open. With both hands, Hock slaps his clean face, especially around that rock-outcropping of a jaw. The sound is so crisp you can almost smell the aftershave. Around him is the din of men joking, laughing. The scrape and hiss of a beer can as it's tugged open.

"This one's for Putter," someone says, offscreen. "You get your ass beat by Lipscomb like that, you need a beer." Hock turns from his locker, and those glaring fluorescent lights shine down on him. The camera sits a little low, just enough to remind the viewer of Hock's size. He's just about dressed, and costume has put him in slacks zipped and fastened but the belt not yet buckled, a long-sleeve dark-blue sport shirt—unbuttoned, and T-shirt bright white. A squat, balding guy walks past with a cooler, and Hock grabs a beer can of his own, pulls the tab. At the next locker over, Putnam finishes a long draw of his own suds, looks at the Hooker, and shakes his head.

"Next time," says Hock, lifting his can a smidgen, a quiet toast.

"Next time," says Putter, and clinks his can to Hock's. Then he rubs a big hand over his brush cut. "To heck with next time."

The camera pans the room. Gillman's still gabbing with one or two reporters, and Tank Younger's walking here and there, getting fellows to sign his game ball. There's a glimpse of Ron Waller grimacing as he tries to move a knee that is wrapped and iced, another of the big rookie John Houser, and guys congratulating Ken Panfil for getting the best of Gino Marchetti. Then there's Crazylegs in front of a mirror, putting something in his hair and working it with a comb. Finally, the camera settles on Van Brocklin, sweaty undershirt still clinging to him, still wearing his muddy pants. He's sitting at his locker, legs splayed, barefoot, and with a beer in hand. He's laughing already, like what he's about to say is the funniest thing he ever thought of. "Hey, Lantern Jaw!" he shouts. "Hooker! You keep playing like you did out there against Donovan, you might have a future."

Hock grins. "Is that a thank you, Dutch?"

"Naw," says Van Brocklin. He's grinning, too, showing those gaps in his teeth. "You don't thank a man who does the job he's supposed to."

Now, the director waves a hand, a signal, and Hock leans over to pick up his duffle bag—a prop the director wants to connect back to the opening scene, when the big man in the Army uniform arrived home on a bright January day almost five years before. Hock stuffs the bag with his equipment, his muddy shoes, a few bottles of red liquid magic for his knees. It's slow going. He hesitates now and then. In the background, Van Brocklin's voice barks, "I think Lipscomb broke my goddamn toes."

"I'm ordering the biggest steak Don Paul's place serves," Hock tells Putnam. "Have the kitchen cook it until the fat's crisp."

"Burn it," says Putter.

"Then I'm ordering another."

Next, Hock's making his way through the locker room, duffle bag over his shoulder, shaking hands. Everyone's shaking hands, everyone's saying goodbye.

Outside, in a mist lit by a few sconces along the stadium wall, he meets Micki, gives her a kiss. She's carrying an umbrella big enough for the two of them. Together, they stroll to the parking lot, but even at a stroll he falls behind a half step. "Are you sore?" she asks. "Do you want me to drive?" He answers by opening the driver's side door for her, then stepping around the back of the car.

Off they go, heading north on the freeway, then west, then north again, past palm trees shining with bulbs of Christmas green and red, past neon Santas and reindeer, the car's windshield wipers beating away the mist, drops on the passenger windows gathering and fragmenting the evening light. He leans back, shakes his shoulders into a more comfortable position, ignores the complaints from his knees, and welcomes the drive through this familiar and all-so-new city, on his way to a familiar and all-so-new life.

CHAPTER 18

Epilogue

NOT LONG AFTER HIS four-touchdown game against the Colts ended the 1957 season, **Norm Van Brocklin** was traded to Philadelphia where his new coach deferred to the Dutchman when it came time to choose plays. Van Brocklin in turn led the Eagles to the NFL championship in 1960, a year he was also voted the league's most valuable player. Dutch retired after that season and became a head coach for two teams: the Minnesota Vikings and the Atlanta Falcons. In both cases, he started with bad teams and built them into solid—though never championship—franchises. His coaching record was 66–100–7.

After the Falcons fired Van Brocklin in 1974, he divided his time between commenting on games for television broadcasts and raising pecans at his farm in Social Circle, Georgia. When a reporter asked Dutch's wife, Gloria, if he could be happy on a farm, so far away from the game that had been his life, she answered, "Let me put it this way: pecan trees don't drop touchdown passes."

In 1971, two decades after he won the NFL championship with the Rams, he was inducted into the Professional Football Hall of Fame. He died eight years later, at age fifty-seven.

◆

WITH VAN BROCKLIN TRADED to the Eagles, **Bill Wade** became the Rams' primary quarterback for the 1958–60 seasons, a stint that included his own Hollywood moment: a guest appearance on *The Donna Reed Show*. In that idealized world of after-school milk and cake, in an episode that opened with Donna wearing a seamstress's tape measure around her neck along with pearls, Wade and other Rams helped convince a neighbor boy's mother to let him play football. An actor portrayed a Rams publicity man named Bert Rose, and it's likely the show was a coup for the real Rams publicity man, whose name really was Bert Rose, and his boss, Pete Rozelle. The episode, called "All Mothers Worry," ended with **Jon Arnett, Les Richter, Don Burroughs** and Wade, all decked out in suits and ties, joining Donna and her family for dinner. Wade had the episode's last line, saying politely in his native Tennessee twang, "Mother always told me when you're asked for dinner, be helpful!"

Wade joined the Chicago Bears for the 1960 season, and in 1963 he and the Bears won the NFL championship. He retired in 1966.

❖

JOHN W. HOUSER, JR., who as a rookie was John Hock's fellow shuttle guard, played two more years with the Rams before he was acquired by the Dallas Cowboys for their inaugural season. He ended his playing career as a St. Louis Cardinal, leaving the game when he noticed his speed diminishing. "I got into the league as a big guy who was quick," he recalled in a conversation during the summer of 2013, "and I could get in the way or get out of the way as I pleased. Now, I couldn't get out of the way anymore. I could see myself playing one or two more seasons." He shrugged. "Just had a feeling that this was a time to get out."

He joined the Owens Corning corporation in sales and marketing, learned about fiberglass insulation and commercial roofing, and worked for that company in their Los Angeles and Denver offices. After he retired, he became active in the struggles of NFL old-timers to win compensation from the league and its players' union for lingering brain damage brought on by concussions. With a color-coded map of his brain in hand, Houser can point to the color that shows his trouble spots and quote the doctor who told him he had a better-than-average shot at dementia.

"The owners are waiting for us to die," he said in 2013. "Plain and simple."

◆

IN A 1958 RAMS game day program, a page of photographs shows Rams "on the lighter side," and includes one of **Ron Waller** inspecting a new bowling alley he and a business partner owned. Worried that football would do him some crippling injury, his wife's grandmother, the Post cereal heiress, wanted him to move into business, and the family backed him. The 1958 season, in fact, would be his last as a Ram.

In the spring after the Rams beat the Colts in front of their millionth fan, a misdemeanor drunk-driving charge against Waller's wife, **Marjorie Durant,** led to banner headlines in Los Angeles, especially after she accused the officers who stopped her of making "improper advances." A jury acquitted her of the charges.

Waller, meanwhile, was looking to buy an NFL franchise and bring it to Miami. But the Wallers separated in 1960, thus ending his opportunity to become an NFL owner. That same year, he joined a new team in a new league formed to challenge the NFL. Waller, the first player signed by the American Football League's Los Angeles Chargers, played for them one season. He and Marjorie divorced in 1961.

A decade later, Waller had become an assistant coach with the Chargers, and then, after his boss was fired, he coached the Chargers for the last six games of the 1973 season, going 1–5. He coached one more team in another upstart league that folded quickly. Eventually, he moved back to his native Delaware, settling about seven miles north of his hometown.

◆

WALLER'S COACH IN THAT inaugural Chargers season was **Sid Gillman**. His tenure with the Rams ended after 1959's 2–10 debacle. But less than a month after Pete Rozelle fired him, Gillman had been named head coach of the Los Angeles Chargers in the new AFL.

In that league, Gillman made a great reputation as a football innovator and became, as his biographer Josh Katzowitz calls him, the "father of the passing game." With the San Diego Chargers until 1969, Gillman applied mathematics and precise timing to the design of passing plays, and thereby revolutionized football.

He also never stopped wearing his bow tie.

After his last head coaching job ended in 1974, Gillman still worked occasionally as a special assistant coach, including for the Chicago Bears and Philadelphia Eagles. He was inducted into the Professional Football Hall of Fame in 1983.

◆

PETE ROZELLE FIRED GILLMAN, but the Rams' 2–10 misery in 1959 may well have started with Rozelle himself, and a trade he announced via telegram to the NFL league office on February 28, 1959. The wire revealed that the Rams were trading nine players to the Chicago Cardinals—and getting one in return.

The trade was dramatic, but for the Rams it had a precedent. In 1952, they had traded eleven players for Les Richter, a linebacker from UCLA. But Richter then was at the start of a Hall of Fame career. Rozelle's nine-man trade brought the Rams a twenty-nine-year-old running back.

That running back, Ollie Matson, had been a star for the University of San Francisco when Rozelle was a student there. He'd won bronze and silver medals in track at the 1952 Olympic Games, and, for the Cardinals, he'd had a 924-yard-rushing season in 1956.

Maybe a great running back is worth nine players, but the Rams' fortunes suggest otherwise. Matson didn't disappoint, gaining 863-yards rushing and another 130-yards receiving in his first Rams season, but the team had been decimated. They'd lost valuable linemen, including Ken Panfil, Glenn Holtzman, Frank Fuller, and Art Hauser. The ensuing 2–10 record made a strong case that the Rams had lost more than they'd gained.

A month after Rozelle fired Gillman, he himself left the Rams—elected by the league's owners as a surprising compromise choice to succeed Bert Bell as the new commissioner.

Rozelle remained in the commissioner's chair until his retirement in 1989, becoming perhaps the most successful league commissioner in any sport ever. During his tenure he negotiated the NFL's first nationwide television contract, increased its number of franchises, merged the league with the AFL, and oversaw the birth and growth of the Super Bowl.

He, too, was inducted into the Pro Football Hall of Fame, in 1985.

It would require nearly a decade after Rozelle left the Rams for his old team to again become a playoff contender.

◆

THE OWNERS' SQUABBLES INTENSIFIED after Rozelle left. In 1963, **Daniel Reeves** finally bought out Edwin Pauley and others whose contributions had allowed the Rams to survive their earliest days in Los Angeles.

Reeves continued to work his way through coaches, though, giving the team to Bob Waterfield for two seasons, then to former Rams linebacker Harland Svare for three seasons. Not until George Allen coached the team from 1966–70 did the Rams begin to win again. But Reeves and Allen meshed like gin and milk, two beverages emblematic of their personalities. Reeves fired Allen in 1968, only to rehire him after players rebelled. Two years later, he fired Allen a second time. It was the last time Reeves would ever fire a coach.

Reeves died from throat cancer in the spring of 1971 at age fifty-eight.

He had been inducted into the Pro Football Hall of Fame three years earlier.

◆

OTHER RAMS FROM THE 1950s enshrined in the Hall of Fame are **Tom Fears** (1970), **Elroy "Crazylegs" Hirsch** (1968), **Dick "Night Train" Lane** (1974), **Les Richter** (2011), **Andy Robustelli** (1971), and **Bob Waterfield** (1965). **Tex Schramm**, the general manager for most of those years, was welcomed into the hall in 1991.

◆

FOR THEIR FIRST GAME at the coliseum, the **Los Angeles Dodgers**, in uniform, rode in a motorcade of open convertibles along their new city's Broadway from downtown to the parking lots of Memorial Coliseum, past thousands of cheering fans. Nearly eighty thousand people filled the stadium to watch the Dodgers beat the San Francisco Giants, 6–5.

From the start, the Dodgers excited Hollywood's imagination. Celebrities on hand for opening day included Zsa Zsa Gábor, Jimmy Stewart, Danny Kaye, Edward G. Robinson, Dinah Shore, Groucho Marx, Gene Autry, and a dozen or so others.

That opening day party was tempered somewhat by a looming election. Enough opponents had signed petitions to put the Chavez Ravine deal to a public referendum. Supporters of the land-swap organized a five-hour "Dodgerthon" on KTTV, and, again, Hollywood turned out. Some who appeared on the team's behalf included Jerry Lewis, George Burns, Dean Martin, Jack Benny, Debbie Reynolds, and Ronald Reagan. Clearly, much of Hollywood wanted a major league team.

The vote, held that June, favored the Dodgers by a few percentage points, but didn't end the controversy, especially after some people—mostly Hispanic—refused to leave their homes in the Chavez Ravine. In front of newspaper photographers, law enforcement officers carried a woman out by her arms and legs. Various books, films, and people still refer to the taking of the area from its mostly Hispanic residents as "The Battle of Chavez Ravine." Dodgers Stadium opened on April 10, 1962.

The Los Angeles Dodgers have since given four World Series championships to their adopted city.

◆

THIRTEEN DAYS BEFORE THE Dodgers were to play their first game in Los Angeles, **Roz Wyman** gave birth to her first child. Groggy just after, she reportedly asked three questions. The first was about her husband; the second, whether the child was a boy or girl (it was a girl); and the third: can I go to opening day?

Who would have told her no? So it was that she and her husband, Gene, sat next to Walter O'Malley and his wife on chairs brought down to the field's level.

Her strong stand fighting for the Dodgers and the landswap had cost her much political goodwill across the city. She had received death threats and notes full of vitriol, often focusing on her being Jewish or a woman—or both. Some Democrats said they'd never vote for her again. Allies within the party fell away. But she never stopped believing that helping to bring the Dodgers to Los Angeles was the best thing she'd ever done as a councilwoman. In 1958 the *Los Angeles Times* named her the city's woman of the year.

Later, she played a smaller role in bringing the National Basketball Association's Minneapolis Lakers to Los Angeles in 1960.

When Wyman ran for a fourth term on the council in 1965, she lost, but she and her husband remained powerful forces in state Democratic politics.

And if the Dodgers played at home yesterday, odds are good she was at the game using her season tickets.

◆

DUANE PUTNAM REMAINED A Ram until the new team in Dallas, the Cowboys, acquired him for their inaugural season in 1960. The next season he joined the Cleveland Browns, but the season after that he returned to wear Los Angeles's blue and gold, before retiring. Subsequently, he served as an assistant coach for several teams. He and his wife Patty finally settled in a suburb about halfway between Los Angeles and Redlands. In the same way Putter once regularly attended Mass with John Hock, though he wasn't Roman Catholic, after he retired he would also go with buddies to Christian Reformed church services, though he wasn't Christian Reformed, either.

He and John Hock remained good friends until the Hooker died in 2000. The three time all-Pro Putnam died in March of 2016.

◆

MONTE AND JUANITA CRAIGS memories of a Rams game on a rainy day passed through the generations of their family, so that even decades after they had died, their grown-up granddaughter, Carri, could, at mention of the Rams, exclaim, without prompting, that her grandfather "was Mr. Million."

The game that is part of the Craig's family lore is not much more than a footnote in NFL history, but it had been for Monte and Juanita one of the most exciting days of their lives. Watching from the press box, they kept dry, even as all those colorful umbrellas bloomed beneath their view like flowers popping. Pigeons flew at halftime, and there were hot dogs to eat, and coffee to drink from a thermos, and that autographed football to bring home. On the field, so far below that the players looked like little plastic toys, the Rams' defense proved able to stifle Johnny Unitas when it needed to.

The Craigs watched that, and they watched the Rams' offensive line, entangled with those behemoths for the Colts. And Jon Arnett, nicknamed the "Jaguar," zigging and zagging, and Crazylegs dancing along the sidelines, and the Dutchman—he of the stubby fingers and sharp tongue—*zinging* pass after pass exactly where it needed to be. By watching, by witnessing, the Craigs and every other fan in this stadium had given Los Angeles another reason to brag: the first city with a team to reach a million fans. Fifty-three thousand in the stadium that day, and maybe most weren't movie or television stars or politicians, but they were Angelenos, and they'd done their part to make something happen for their city. By buying a ticket and braving the rain, they—the crowd, the audience—had created this great scene: the concrete stadium with its white lights, the Southern California sky so strangely gray, John Hock blocking to give Van Brocklin time, young Lamar Lundy reaching high to snag the Dutchman's final touchdown spiral, and all the players who endured weather and pain to make this sloppy, messy thing of beauty.

It was Los Angeles Rams football. It must have seemed as though it would last forever.

"HE MISSED IT," MICKI Hock says, quietly. "I'm sure he missed it. He didn't complain, though. But you knew he missed it. How could you not?"

Perhaps to take the sting out leaving the game he loved, **John Hock** spent the spring of 1958 with seven other Rams, including Putnam and Ron Waller, barnstorming as a basketball team. Lamar Lundy, who at six foot seven had once been named the Purdue University basketball team's most valuable player, anchored the Rams at center. Hock and Les Richter, the linebacker, started at guard. "We don't know how good the boys are," said a Rams spokesman, "but it's a cinch they could be rough." The group played charity games, including one in Redlands to benefit high school student scholarships. They played and lost another, 59–46, to a similarly constituted group of San Francisco 49ers.

Hock would teach for a year or so, then take a job as a sales rep with Western Car Loading, a company that moved freight from coast to coast. The Hock family continued to grow with four girls and three boys, and John and Micki bought a house in Anaheim, about five minutes from Disneyland. On Sunday nights, if the kids were well-behaved, they'd allow them to stand on the family station wagon and watch the Enchanted Kingdom's fireworks explode in the distance. Their seventh and final child Jim was born in 1969.

John had worked his way up in the company, which transferred him to New York, residing in a little town called Mahwah ("the meeting place") in northern New Jersey. On the East Coast, he reunited with Andy Robustelli, now an executive with the Giants, who gave him an in to purchase season tickets with the team.

Micki missed California, but John loved the trees of the east coast. To keep Micki happy, John would drive the family back and forth numerous times to Los Angeles, with a wooden box on top of their station wagon specially built to give each of the seven kids the exact same amount of room for their things. John loved being behind the wheel, enjoying country music on the radio and the greasy food served along America's highways and interstates. "My father would always say the best food is truck stop food," recalled his daughter, Anna. Simple and solid as always, just the way he liked it.

In January 2000, the Rams played in their first Super Bowl. They weren't Los Angeles's team anymore—having abandoned Southern California for St. Louis, their last game as the LA Rams falling on Christmas Eve day, 1994—but they still wore blue and gold, still displayed the Rams horns on their helmets. There may have represented a city with which he had no connection, but with those famous horns they remained his one and only team to the very loyal John Hock. So at age seventy-two, with Micki and family around him, he sat in the Georgia Dome in Atlanta to watch his team beat the Tennessee Titans, 23–16.

The following September, John contracted an aggressive form of lung cancer. He had thought the cough was annoying, but nothing more than a nuisance cold. The doctor said he must have had some nearly superhuman pain threshold not to notice the melon-size tumor in his lung. For roughly three months after the initial diagnosis, John Hock fought for life, expiring on December 9, 2000. Draining gallons of fluid from his lungs the days before his death, Micki knew that John did not want to go. The day before he died, he said to Micki, over and over, "too short…too short." But it was now his time. Cancer had won.

Fast forward to August 2016. The Rams are back in Los Angeles for their first preseason game after twenty-two years away. Nearly ninety thousand fans are in attendance for a welcome home celebration. The same tunnel eight, once the wives entrance that Micki used time and again to enter the Coliseum would now see her grandkids pass through it sixty years later. Youngest son Jim Hock and his boys, William and John, named after his grandfather, used that same historic tunnel to say hello to the Coliseum for the first time. To watch the Rams return to their longtime home. Between the chills and the tears, the young boys feel their grandfather's powerful presence in the place he loved so much.

John Hock is smiling. Smiling down from above watching Hollywood's team take the field once again.

ACKNOWLEDGMENTS

HOLLYWOOD'S TEAM WOULD NOT have been possible without the boundless support and love of my wife Kellie Meiman Hock. Thank you for the hours upon hours helping commiserate, edit, humor, research, and listen to far too many stories about the Rams.

Micki Hock, for your faith, love, tireless storytelling, and fact-checking about your time with Dad and the team he loved.

My brothers, sisters and family are owed a special thank you for everything else, ranging from finding photos, to sparking memories, and hanging me over the bannister.

To my fantastic in-laws, Patricia and Gary O'Connor, for more support than anyone could ever ask for.

To the numerous former NFL players and their families who we interviewed, both living and deceased, including Duane Putnam, Frank Gifford, Art Donovan, Raymond Berry, Sam Huff, Charlie Trippi, Bill Wade, Walt Michaels, Don Paul, and Harry Thompson. This book and the game of football itself has, at its core, your passion and aspiration for greatness.

Roz Wyman, former Los Angeles City Councilwoman, who provided an incredible first person account of bringing the Dodgers to Los Angeles.

To Doug Hensch, for decades of helping with brainstorming, editing, fact-checking, traveling to the Pro Football Hall of Fame, and for being the world's best best friend.

To Kevin Grzanka, Dave Wisotsky, Joe Nazzari, Randy Nukk, John Gunther, Mike Klaschka, Ken O'Donnell, Kam Kuwata, Stephanie Cutter, Christine Thornton, Sissy Estes, Catherine Baker, Steve Benza, and Mark Nevins for all your support along the way.

To the many people of 463, VRGE, and Next15 companies—especially Tom Galvin, Sean Garrett, and Tim Dyson.

To Dan Gerstein, for your steadfast counsel and key prodding at the perfect times.

To Michael Downs, for your incredible partnership and friendship. May your mom rest in peace.

To Jason Taylor and Athina Koulatsos, graduate students in Towson University's professional writing program, thank you for assisting with early research for this book and compilation of the endnotes. To Rick Davis of Towson University's Cook Library who pointed us toward several valuable databases and books about Southern California. To military researchers Katherine Rasdorf and Jaclyn Ostrowski who helped with details of John Hock's military service, and Matt Burke and Norio Muroi in the Japan bureau of Stars and Stripes for providing articles about Camp Drake football.

BIBLIOGRAPHY AND FURTHER READING

READERS INTERESTED IN LEARNING more about Los Angeles, the National Football League, and the Rams in the 1950s might consult the following books, all of which we relied on while writing this book.

Braudy, Leo. *The Hollywood sign: fantasy and reality of an American icon.* New Haven, CT.: Yale University Press, 2011.

An excellent short book about the Hollywood sign and Hollywood's history and culture. Accompanied by an impressive bibliography.

D'Antonio, Michael. *Forever Blue: The True Story of Walter O'Malley, Baseball's Most Controversial Owner, and the Dodgers of Brooklyn and Los Angeles.* New York: Riverhead Books, 2009

Herskowitz, Mickey. *The golden age of pro football: a remembrance of pro football in the 1950s.* New York: Macmillan, 1974.

Emphasizing the barnstorming culture of the NFL in the 1950s, Herskowitz's book is a fun mishmash of interviews, anecdotes, and photographs.

Katzowitz, Josh, and Dick Vermeil. *Sid Gillman: father of the passing game*. Cincinnati, OH.: Clerisy Press, 2012.

Though occassionally incorrect in its details and its assumptions, this overview of Gillman's life—written with the cooperation of his family—offers a convincing portrait. It includes two chapters that focus on Gillman's tenure with the Rams.

MacCambridge, Michael. *America's game: the epic story of how pro football captured a nation*. New York: Random House, 2004.

The definitive history of the NFL beginning with the Rams' move west through 2005. A work of astonishing breadth and detail that argues for the NFL's significance in American culture.

Maxymuk, John. *NFL Head Coaches: A Biographical Dictionary, 1920-2011*. Jefferson, N.C.: McFarland & Co., Inc., Publishers, 2012.

An excellent resource regarding NFL coaches, their histories, and their relationships.

Russell, Jane. *My Paths and Detours*. New York, N.Y.: Franklin Watts, Inc., 1985.

Russell's autobiography includes details of her marriage to and divorce from Rams quarterback Bob Waterfield. She also writes about Hollywood and Southern California in the 1940s and 1950s.

Smith, Rick. *Stadium stories: St. Louis Rams.* Guilford, Conn.: Insiders' Guide, 2005.

Smith, a former public relations official with the Rams, offers an easy-to-read survey of Rams' history from the team's founding through its Super Bowl XXXIV victory on January 30, 2000, with special attention to Tank Younger's role as a Rams player and executive. Though the book includes no documentation, much of its information is verifiable through other sources.

Starr, Kevin. *Golden dreams: California in an age of abundance, 1950–1963.* Oxford: Oxford University Press, 2009.

Starr's book, nearly six hundred pages long, provides excellent context for California in the 1950s. Of particular interest to those focusing on Los Angeles are the chapters "The Cardinal, the Chief, Walter O'Malley, and Buff Chandler: Redefining the City of Angels" and "Freeways to the Future: An Epic of Construction on Behalf of the Automobile."

Waldie, D. J. *Holy land: a suburban memoir.* New York: W. W. Norton, 1996.

Waldie's elegiac, poetic memoir evokes day-to-day life in the Lakewood suburb during the early 1950s, even as it explores the history of land development in Southern California.

ENDNOTES

ALL TEAM RECORDS, ATTENDANCE figures, player draft orders, training camp locations, and many player statistics can be found through these sources:

The Pro Football Archives at profootballarchives.com, copyright Maher Sports Media.

Pro Football Reference at pro-football-reference.com, copyright Sports Reference, LLC.

Weather reports come from *Weather Underground's* historical weather almanac, copyright The Weather Channel, LLC.

Several documents pertaining to the Dodgers' move to Los Angeles are available as PDFs on walteromalley.com, the official web site of the former Dodgers owner, controlled by O'Malley Seidler Partners, P.O. Box 861623, Los Angeles, CA 90086.

CHAPTER 1: THE RABBIT SKINNER COMES HOME

It's warm, this January day: According to John Hock's Army personnel records held at the National Archives in St. Louis, Hock was discharged at Fort Ord on January 21, 1953. We imagine him arriving at home a day or so later.

The Hocks were part of that migration: For more on the migration from the southwestern states, see Gregory, James N. "Dust Bowl Legacies: The Okie Impact on California, 1939-89." *California History* (Fall 1989), 75-85. The Hock family history comes from John Hock's children.

to offset that season's reported $50,000 loss: see Smith, *Stadium Stories,* p. 27.

"And you call this a national league?": see MacCambridge, *America's Game,* p. 16.

The population estimate for 1953: For population figures comparing 1930 to 1953, we used figures compiled by the research department of the Los Angeles Chamber of Commerce and published in 1953 as *Population of the Cities and Communities in Los Angeles County For the Census Years, 1930, 1940 and 1950 with Estimates for 1953*. According to the document: "The 1930, 1940, and 1950 population figures are based on official reports from the Bureau of the Census, US Department of Commerce. The 1953 estimates are by the Research Department of the Los Angeles Chamber of Commerce, based largely on dwelling unit estimates provided by the Los Angeles Regional Planning Commission, together with Special Census reports availalbe from a few of the cities." The original pamphlet is available in the special collections of the library at UCLA.

one continuous boom: from Carey McWilliams's book, *Southern California: An Island on the Land.* Layton, Utah: Gibbs Smith, (1946, 1973). p. 114.

Ernie Pyle called them "Aviation Okies": see Starr, *Golden Dreams*, p. 26

no down payment: see Waldie, *Holy Land*, p. 33-34; ... **added 17,500 of these houses in three years**: ibid, p. 1; **"With a Waste King electric garbage disposal"**: ibid, p. 70; **"We sell happiness in homes"**: ibid, p. 93.

and a deal with Paramount Pictures: from William Robert Faith's book, *Bob Hope: A Life in Comedy.* Cambridge, MA: DaCapo Press (1982, 2003), p. 85.

That's what he told a reporter: Venzor, Cpl. Tino. "Chotto Matte," *Pacific Stars and Stripes,* Oct. 26, 1952, p. 12.

and falling on a dropped lateral in the end zone: "Drake Rips TQMD, 74-0; HSC Clobbers Yoko, 61-0," *Pacific Stars and Stripes,* Oct. 20, 1952, p. 14.

for a rookie linebacker from Tennessee and a tackle out of Texas Tech: The Rams traded Texas Tech's Jerrell Price and Tennessee's Gordon Polofsky. See "Rams Acquire John Hock from Cards," *Los Angeles Times.* July 16, 1952, p. C2. According to profootballreference.com, Polofsky played three seasons with the Cardinals, though he never started a game. Price played in no NFL games.

In fact, answering the census worker: 1940 United State Census, Los Angeles, California, Assembly District 65, Ward 6, 1738 W. 52nd Street; Sheet #7B, lines 65-68; April 11, 1940; Ancestry.com.

Chapter 2: Training Camp

"READY-SET-*HUT*-TWO-THREE-FOUR!": Finch, Frank. "Tobacco Auctioneers: Ram Quarterbacks Speed Up Count to Insure Quicker-Starting Plays." *Los Angeles Times,* July 15, 1953, p.C3.

he'd signed a contract with the Rams: "Hock, Carter Sign Pacts With Rams," *Los Angeles Times,* **May 6, 1953, p.** 35.

coaches wanted him to report early with the rookies: Finch, Frank. "Ram Rookies Begin Training Grind Today at Redlands." *Los Angeles Times,* July 13, 1953, p. 33.

rookies who'd come from as far and wide: Los Angeles Rams souvenir program, *Ninth Annual Charity Football Game: Los Angeles Rams vs. Washington Redskins.* August 19, 1953, p. 21.

a Negro All-American at Wilberforce University: "New Rams, Redskins," *Los Angeles Times,* August 12, 1953, p. C3. Also, "Drake Rips TQMD, 74–0; HSC Clobbers Yoko, 61–0" *Pacific Stars& Stripes,* Oct. 20, 1952, p. 14.

what the military had called the Rice Bowl: *Associated Press, Milwaukee Sentinel,* "Camp Drake '11' Beats Sea Hawks in Rice Bowl," January 2, 1953, part 2, p. 4.

That first day was a get-to-know-you affair: see Finch, "Ram Rookies Begin Training Grind Today at Redlands."

every scoring record in the NFL belonged to the Los Angeles Rams: see Finch, "Tobacco Auctioneers: Ram Quarterbacks Speed Up Count to Insure Quicker-Starting Plays."

Take, for example, night golf: see "Framework," *Los Angeles Times* photography online, posted January 8, 2014 by Scott Harrison. Original reporting by Curtis, Charles. *Los Angeles Times,* Feb. 3, 1952 and Feb. 5, 1952.

the humongous four-level stacked freeway: Masters, Nathan. "LA's Famous Four-Level Freeway Interchange, 'The Stack,' Turns 58," KCET.org, Sept. 22, 2011.

released the Vincent Price film, *House of Wax*: Parnum, John E. "House of Wax (1953)." *Midnight Marquee Actors Series: Vincent Price,* ed. Svehla, Gary J. and Susan; Baltimore, MD: Midnight Marquee Press, Inc. (October 1998). p. 88-99.

"… I'm moving downtown.": see Finch, "Tobacco Auctioneers: Ram Quarterbacks Speed Up Count to Insure Quicker-Starting Plays."

he was the Rams' fifth "boss coach" in eight seasons: for context and details about Poole's tenure, see Maxymuk, *NFL Head Coaches: A Biographical Dictionary, 1920-2011.* p. 237-39.

in a game played in snow with a temperature around zero: Many sources report on this game, but we used in particular Smith's *Stadium Stories,* p. 23-25 and MacCambridge's *America's Game,* p. 3-7

became known as the "Wow Boys": for a thorough history of the T-formation and Shaughnessy's coaching at Stanford University, see Johnson, James. W. *The Wow Boys: A Coach, a Team, and a Turning Point in College Football.* Lincoln, Neb., Bison Books, The University of Nebraska Press, 2006.

the wide receiver and the modern passing game: see Maxymuk, *NFL Head Coaches,* p. 278, MacCambridge, *America's Game,* p. 64 and many other sources.

Shaughnessy scoffed: "Tackle Eligible Play Gets Okay," *Los Angeles Times,* Jan. 19, 1950. p. C2

"internal friction": Finch, Frank. "Stydahar To Style Rams After Bears" *Los Angeles Times,* Feb. 20, 1950, p. C1.

"a milk shake drinker who neither drank nor smoke," and "aloof with a superior attitude and a penchant for cutting, sarcastic comments": see Maxymuk, *NFL Head Coaches.* p. 278.

Shaughnessy sued the Rams: "Shaughnessy Files Back Salary Suit." *Long Beach Press-Telegram,* Aug. 29, 1950. p. 16.

"When Stydahar gets through coaching the Rams…": see Maxymuk, *NFL Head Coaches,* **p.** 278.

chewing tobacco, all at the same time: see Maxymuk, *NFL Head Coaches,* **p.** 308-9.

he accused Pool of betrayal: ibid, p. 238; also, Herskowitz, *The Golden Age of Pro Football,* p. 60.

a master's degree in education from Stanford: see Everett, Hap. "Quick Peek at Record Shows Pool Really Backfield Man." *Los Angeles Times,* March 12, 1950. p. B16.

The first photo of him as a Ram: ibid.

worked his butt off: see Herskowitz, *The Golden Age of Pro Football,* **p.** 59.

"I'm glad I got out": *Associated Press,* "Joe Stydahar Out As Coach Of Rams," *Sarasota Herald-Tribune,* Oct. 1, 1952, p. 6.

she had become the youngest person ever elected: see Meyer, Richard E. "When JFK accepted the Democratic nomination in LA, he had Roz Wyman to thank for the crowd that showed up." *Los Angeles Magazine,* July 2010. Accessed via website archive.

"You talk so much, why don't you run?": Interview with Rosalind Wiener Wyman, July 16, 2013.

went to pieces: ibid.

I Love Lucy **episodes**: see Meyer, "When JFK accepted…"

in a photo published that year: Interview, Wyman.

she put check marks next to her goals: see Meyer, "When JFK accepted…"

Fortune 500 companies and a major opera house: Interview, Wyman.

For her first act as a city councilwoman: Walter O'Malley: The Official Web Site: "This Month in Walter O'Malley History: July 7, 1953." Retrieved Oct. 2, 2016.

Norm Van Brocklin nicknamed him "Lantern Jaw": Interview with Duane Putnam, July 14, 2013.

Coaches worshipped at the Church of Running: ibid.

Sun glared off windows: The physical descriptions of Redlands training camp come from on-site visits to the University of Redlands coupled with photographs from the *Los*

Angeles Herald-Examiner Collection of photographs housed in the archives of the University of Southern California Digital Library.

Van Brocklin and the veterans arrived: Finch, Frank. "'Youthful' Ram Veterans Begin Practice at Redlands Tomorrow." *Los Angeles Times*, July 19, 1953. p. B10.

"carbonated remarks": Durslag, Melvin. "Pro Football's Brat." *Collier's Magazine*, Sept 4, 1953, p. 99

"Duane is a deadly blocker": Finch, Frank. "LeBaron's COP Mate Seeks Rams Guard Post." *Los Angeles Times*, Aug. 1, 1952. p. C3.

"… he wants to be the best man at his position in the league": ibid.

"Van Brocklin would always sit down by the far door": Interview, Harry Pattison, Aug. 22, 2013.

room for a half dozen circle-tables: The building that housed Ed and Mary's still sat on the southeast corner of Mentone Boulevard and Opal Avenue in the summer of 2013. The basic layout of the place hadn't changed since 1953, a bartender said, and the bar itself had definitely not moved.

"… the pitcher would end up with frost around it": Interview, Putnam.

Jane Russell recalls him doing one-armed handstands: see Russell, *My Paths and Detours,* p. 52.

"There wasn't anyplace he couldn't do a one-arm handstand," Russell wrote. "I remember seeing him poised on the corner of a three-story building at Muscle Beach in Santa Monica. I was terrified."

He used to say to me just five words all day: Haddad, Dana. "Ram's Quarterback a Man of Few Words." *Los Angeles Times*, June 18, 1997. Accessed via online archives at latimes.com.

"bottled his emotions perfectly": see Durslag, "Pro Football's Brat." *Colliers*, p. 98

"He took the responsibility for the team's success too personally": see Russell, *My Paths and Detours*, p. 139-40.

"Afoot, he was very inept," recalls Durslag: Interview, Melvin Durslag, July 13, 2013.

"Van Brocklin can throw. Period.": see Herskowitz, *The Golden Age of Pro Football*, p. 49.

"floating bubbles": see Durslag, "Pro Football's Brat," p. 99.

passes that "belong in a museum.": ibid. Durslag attributes the quotation to Bill Howton of the Green Bay Packers, who said it after catching a Van Brocklin pass in the 1953 Pro Bowl game.

"the man most likely to be babied by an airline hostess": ibid, p. 97.

"from his asshole?": Interview, Harry Thompson, Sept. 20, 2002.

"if some lineman doesn't break his neck first": see Durslag, "Pro Football's Brat," p. 97.

Stydahar knew … [h]e needed Van Brocklin's arm: see Herskowitz, *The Golden Age of Pro Football*, **p.** 40.

with the idea of asking for more in 1954: see Durslag, "Pro Football's Brat." p. 98.

threw kegs in trucks: Interview, Putnam.

Lewis worked with juvenile delinquents: Webster, William. "Woodley Lewis—The Forgotten Ram." *The Pittsburgh Courier*, Nov. 13, 1954, p. SM3

Robustelli owned a sporting goods store: Goldstein, Richard. "Andy Robustelli, 85, Who Helped Weave 'DEE-Fense' Into Giants' Fabric, Is Dead." New York Times, June 1, 2011. p. A25. Accessed online.

Hirsch even starred in a couple: see Smith, *Stadium Stories*, p. 54, 59. More information on Hirsch as a film star and on the film *Unchained* can be found on the Internet Movie Database.

to paint sleek yellow Rams' horns on the players' helmets: This story is treated in many sources, but we primarily used these: MacCambridge, *America's Game*, p. 61; Smith, *Stadium Stories*, p. 36-7; and "Historic Horns," from the *1958 Rams Yearbook*, p. 49.

No pay until you play: Interviews, Putnam.

Frank James at Redlands Community Hospital: Zimmerman, Paul. "Rams, Redskins Collide Tonight." *Los Angeles Times*, Aug. 19, 1953, p. C1.

The Rams would face Fort Ord's football squad: Finch, Frank. "Rams Open '53 Season With Ft. Ord." *Los Angeles Times*, Aug. 1, 1953, p. B1.

the Rams offense performed as if cockeyed: Finch, Frank. "Rams Beat Rugged Soldiers, 24 to 0." *Los Angeles Times*, Aug. 2, 1953, p. B9.

In the previous year's match-up … suffered a broken arm: see Morton, Hugh. "Charlie Justice Injured in Stands," caption for digital photograph. Sept. 27, 1952. Hugh Morton Collection of Photographs and Films, University of North Carolina's Wilson library. Accessed online.

with celebrities on hand… and a five-ring circus: see "Five-Ring Circus Planned at Halftime of Charity Tilt." *Los Angeles Times*, Aug. 9, 1953. p B7.

CHAPTER 3: "GIT-GAT-GIDDLE WITH A GEET-GA-ZAY"

$3.90 for a reserved seat, a quarter for a game program: To create a sense of the run-up to the *Times* Charities Game, we relied on a variety of sources including: *Times* Charity game advertisement, *Los Angeles Times*, Aug. 2, 1953, p. B13; Game program, *Los Angeles Times Ninth Annual Charity Football Game*, Aug. 19, 1953; Zimmerman, Paul. "Rams, Redskins Collide Tonight." *Los Angeles Times*, Aug. 19, 1953, p. C1; "Five-Ring Circus Planned at Halftime of Charity Tilt." *Los Angeles Times*, Aug. 9, 1953. p B7; Hyland, Dick. "Hyland Fling." *Los Angeles Times*, Aug. 10, 1953, p. C2;

Finch, Frank. "Entire Squad of Rams Set for Redskins." *Los Angeles Times*, Aug. 11, 1953, p. C3; Finch, Frank. "Younger and Davis Ready for Action." *Los Angeles Times*, Aug. 15, 1953, p. B3; Zimmerman, Paul. "Rams Rally for 20-7 Win Over 'Skins." *Los Angeles Times*, Aug. 20, 1953, p. 1; Geyer, Jack. "Everyone a Winner: Color, Thrills Mark Ram, Redskin Classic," *Los Angeles Times*, Aug. 20, 1953, p. C1.

the Russians have, for the first time, detonated a hydrogen bomb: "Russ Claim H-Bomb Explosion; U.S. Says Reds Set Blast Aug. 12." *Los Angeles Examiner,* Aug. 19, 1953, p. A1.

"Your number is on the front of the program": Game program, *Los Angeles Times Ninth Annual Charity Football Game,* **Aug.** 19, 1953, p. 37.

and it cost Ben four toes on his kicking foot: The story of the Toeless Wonder can be found via many sources, but we relied primarily on Dwyre, Bill. "Kicking pioneer makes his case," *Los Angeles Times,* Oct. 27, 2007, accessed online. NB: At least one other source say Agajanian's shoe sizes were 10 and 7.

The other two are: For starting lineups, we use the rosters published by the *Los Angeles Times* on game day. For who played in a game, we rely on the *Times'* game stories, which usually included a complete list of who played and at what position.

John Hock wears Santa Clara's ring: Photos of John Hock show him wearing his college ring as early as his senior year at Santa Clara University when he posed for a photo with his fellow team captain, Hall Haynes. He wore the ring until his death in 2000.

The Santa Clara Broncos were almost midway through Hock's senior season: For details about the UCLA game and Hock's senior season at Santa Clara, we relied heavily on the Santa Clara *Redwood* Yearbook, 1950, published by the Associated Students of the University of Santa Clara, p. 90-107, which include game-by-game reports and photographs.

it had cancelled its football program during World War II: McKevitt, Gerald. *The University of Santa Clara: A History, 1851-1977.* Stanford, CA.: Stanford University Press, 1979. p. 261.

with nearly twenty cars, bound for Miami: Coonan, Dan and Sam Scott. "The Bronco Orange Bowl trophy turns sixty." *Santa Clara Magazine,* Spring 2010, accessed online.

dogs fared better in the gauzy, steamy heat when he limited their workouts before a race: ibid.

"You ate like a bunch of pigs. You better run it off": Interview, Bob Gain, July 26, 2014.

"Jimmy The Greek," bet $265,000 on Kentucky: see Coonan and Scott, "The Bronco Orange Bowl trophy turns sixty." NB: *The Washington Post,* in a 1971 story about Snyder, gave the figure as "as high as $250,000." Whatever the number, The Greek lost a lot of money betting on Kentucky.

Kentucky's advantages were obvious: see Coonan and Scott, "The Bronco Orange Bowl trophy turns sixty."

An AP reporter later described them as "iron": Grimsley, Will. *Associated Press* college football roundup, as published in *The Lowell Sun*, Lowell, MA., and elsewhere, January 3, 1950.

hopping in celebration and clapping twice to punctuate the play: "Football Bowls Games 1950," YouTube video, 3:10, posted by "historycomestolife," May 10, 2011.

kept his coat buttoned and wore a tie with a tight knot: Hock family photo.

Because here was Curly Lambeau propped on the edge of Hock's neatly made bed: story from John Hock, as told to Jim Hock.

they live in a closed world: Whitehead, James T. "Good Linemen Live in a Closed World." *Local Men,* Urbana: University of Illinois Press, 1979, p. 23.

and a 7–0 lead, just that fast: See in particular: Zimmerman, Paul. "Rams Rally for 20-7 Win Over 'Skins." *Los Angeles Times*, Aug. 20, 1953, p. 1l; Oates, Bob. "Lewis Returns Punt 79-Yards for Tally." *Los Angeles Examiner,* Aug. 20, 1953; Durslag, Melvin. "Redskins Technical Blunders Disastrous." *Los Angeles Examiner,* Aug. 20, 1953.

with jerseys that would tear away rather than rip: see Geyer, "Everyone a Winner: Color, Thrills Mark Ram, Redskin Classic."

More than 2,500 boys have enjoyed: see Times-Charities advertisement,Times-Charities gameday program, p. 4.

a city shaped by an oligarchy: see Starr, *Golden Dreams: California in an Age of Abundance, 1950-1963.* p. 154.

a taint kept alive by scandal sheets: for a larger discussion of the tensions between scandalous Hollywood and oligarchical Los Angeles, see: Braudy, *The Hollywood Sign*, especially Chapter 2, "Hollywood Becomes Hollywood."

an upstart league called the All-America Football Conference: The San Francisco 49ers also played in the AAFC. When the league failed, the NFL absorbed the 49ers, giving the NFL its second California franchise.

Harry James and Betty Grable. Jerry Lewis and Bob Hope: Interview with Patty Putnam, July 14, 2013.

earned off-season money working as extras in films: see "Ramblings," Times-Charities gameday program, p. 16.

"—only in football, I get paid for it!": movie poster, *Easy Living,* RKO pictures, 1949.

she never put on airs: Interview, Patty Putnam.

"Boy, there's a break," Pool said: see Durslag, "Redskins Technical Blunders Disastrous."

CHAPTER 4: "GRIDS AND GRIDIRONS"

he's really two inches shorter: Garber, Greg. "Stature didn't deter 'Littlest General.'" *ESPN. com,* Jan. 9, 2009.

an unconventional throwing style called the "jump pass": Whittingham, Richard. *Rites of Autumn: The Story of College Football.* New York: The Free Press, 2001. p. 273.

he can hardly bend over to take the ball on the snap: see Oates, Bob. "Lewis Returns Punt 79-Yards for Tally."

"you'll stay on the same grid of streets": see Waldie, *Holy Land*, p. 46. **"the common grid of fifty-by-one-hundred-foot lots…"**: ibid, p. 33. **"The streets do not curve or offer vistas"**: ibid, p. 44. **"The sidewalk is four feet wide"**: ibid, p. 48. **"as regular as any thought of God's…"**: ibid. **"The necessary illusion is predictability"**: ibid, p. 2.

no Negro players on the field: because the NFL's ban on African-American players was informal, multiple sources make note of it but none we found offers definitive details. We relied on MacCambridge, *America's Game*, p. 17; Smith, Thomas G. "Outside the Pale: The Exclusion of Blacks from the National Football League, 1934-1946." *The Coffin Corner,* Vol. 11, No. 4, 1989; and other sources.

change the course of professional football history: for details of the meeting at the coliseum, the ways African-American journalists pressed the Rams to integrate, and the introduction of the Rams and the NFL, we relied primarily on these sources, especially those written by African-American reporters working in Los Angeles at the time: Fentress, J. Cullen. "Los Angeles '11' Interested in Young and Kenny: Grid Aces May Get Chances." *Pittsburgh Courier,* February 2, 1946, p. 26; Robinson, Edward "Abie." "Rams Sign Kenny Washington: 1st Negro in Pro League." *Los Angeles Sentinel,* March 28, 1946, p. 22; Young, A.S. "Doc". "Dedicated writers and editors paved way for integration of major sports." *Ebony,* Vol. XXV, No. 12, Oct. 1970, p. 56; Strode, Woody and Sam Young. *Goal Dust: The Warm and Candid Memoirs of a Pioneer Black Athlete and Actor.* Lanham, MD: Madison Books, June 4, 1990; Smith, Thomas G. "Outside the Pale: The Exclusion of Blacks from the National Football League, 1934-1946." *The Coffin Corner,* Vol. 11, No. 4, 1989; Ross, Charles K. *Outside the Lines: African-Americans and the Integration of the National Football League.* New York: New York University Press, January 2000; MacCambridge, *America's Game.*

Built of reinforced concrete…could hold more than one hundred thousand people: Charleton, James H., *National Register of Historic Places Inventory–Nomination Form: The Los Angeles Memorial Coliseum,* written June 21, 1984, filed with the United States Department of the Interior, National Parks Service.

Harry Chandler's influential role in the coliseum's financing and construction: ibid.

a letter to *Ebony* magazine: see Young, "Dedicated writers and editors paved way for integration of major sports."

meeting with them at the Last Word Club: see Entress, "Los Angeles '11' Interested in Young and Kenny: Grid Aces May Get Chances."

downtown's elegant Alexandria Hotel: see Ross, *Outside the Lines,* p. 82.

Strode himself watched from the sidelines: see Strode, Woody and Sam Young, *Goal Dust.* p. 153.

"If I have to integrate heaven, I don't want to go.": ibid, p. 155

"I doubt we would have been interested in Washington" The quote is attributed to Bob Snyder, who later became the Rams head coach. See Smith, Thomas G., "Outside the Pale."

but somehow stayed on the roster: White, Lonnie. "Harry Thompson, 78; Key Blocker for Rams in 1950s." *Los Angeles Times*, Nov. 29, 2003, accessed online.

less integrated even than the Rams locker room: Ethington, Philip J., William H. Frey and Dowell Myers. Chart, "Overall Population Figures: Total and Proportional Racial Population of Los Angeles County, 1940–2000" from "The Racial Resegregation of Los Angeles County, 1940–2000." *Race Contours 2000 Study: A University of Southern California and University of Michigan Collaborative Project,* May 12, 2001. p. 10.

by selling her house to a "non-caucasian" family: Barrows v. Jackson, 346 U.S. 249 (1953).

chanting "protect our children.": Straus, Emily E. "The Making of the American School Crisis: Compton, California and the Death of the Suburban Dream." (dissertation, Brandeis University, 2006). p. 93-94

black players stayed with people who opened their homes: This practice lasted for well into the Civil Rights era. John Houser, a rookie lineman with the Rams in 1957, recalled flying into Mobile, Alabama that season for an exhibition game. As soon as the plane landed, Houser said, black players stepped one way and whites another. Tank Younger, Lamar Lundy, Bob Boyd and other African-American Rams met men who drove sedans—Cadillacs and Buicks and such—who took the players to stay in the homes of lawyers and doctors and other pillars of Mobile's black community. White players stayed at a rundown hotel, Houser said, where the elevator was so rickety it wouldn't rise when three linemen tried to ride it at the same time. Interview, John Houser, Aug. 25, 2014.

smiling up toward the camera: photograph, courtesy of John Hock family.

John Hock's knee had gotten wonky: "14 Rams on Injured List, 11 Hurt Against Giants." *Redlands Daily Facts,* Sept. 29, 1953. p. 6.

no grabbing, no shoving, no nothing: Interview, Duane Putnam.

CHAPTER 5: SAFETY

"struggling through the worst slump of his pro career.": "Rams 7-Point Choice Over Bears in TV Feature Today," *Long Beach Press-Telegram,* Nov. 29, 1953.

Hamp Pool's job was in jeopardy: ibid.

having lost nearly a quarter million dollars: see MacCambridge, *America's Game*, p. 78

Their starting quarterback had suffered a season-ending shoulder injury: "Colts Battle Rams Eleven," *The Baltimore Sun,* Dec. 5, 1953, p. 13.

scheduled for a national television broadcast.: ibid.

those fans saw was Dutch Van Brocklin…throwing fifty yards to Skeet Quinlan: "Los Angeles Rams Trim Colts By 45-2 Score." *The Baltimore Sun,* Dec. 6, 1953, p. S1.

tossed what one report called a "throw-away.": "Rams Blast Colts 45-2," *Kalispell Daily Interlake,* Dec. 6, 1953.

"lift a twenty-four-ounce can of Schlitz": Interview, Art Donovan, Sept. 24, 2002.

the *Associated Press* named its All-Pro team: Playoff Foes Dominate All-Pro," *The Alton* (Ill.) *Evening Telegraph,* Dec. 24, 1953.

had become for him a personal crusade: see D'Antonio, *Forever Blue,* p. 177-78.

author Michael D'Antonio describes Flaherty: ibid, p. 177.

Howard Hughes sent a $1 million check: ibid, p. 178.

Chapter 6: The Weights

Build their own magic kingdom: Details of John and Micki Hock's wedding come from interviews with Micki Hock (April 1, 2013; Jan. 18, 2014), family photographs, and visits to the Costellos' former home and the Church of Transfiguration (July 2013).

A Chinese temple rising along Hollywood Boulevard: This is a reference to the famous Grauman's Chinese Theater, which celebrated its grand opening in 1927.

Sergeant Joe Friday…interview police academy applicants: see Starr, *Golden Dreams,* p. 142.

$17 million 160-acre fantasy land: for the size of Disneyland, see Hill, Gladwin, "Hollywood is Shifting Her Civic Scenery," *New York Times,* May 8, 1955, p. 37. For the cost, see Hill, Gladwin, "Disneyland Gets Its Last Touches," *New York Times,* July 9, 1955, p. 32.

agreed to a blind date with a friend's cousin for St. Patrick's Day: Interview, Micki Hock, April 1, 2013.

medium rare is growing on me: ibid.

They became beach people: ibid.

Adonis. *Greek God*: Interview, Duane Putnam.

Charles Atlas made a fortune: for an excellent treatment of Atlas and his cultural impact, see Black, Jonathan, "Charles Atlas: Muscle Man," *Smithsonian Magazine,* August 2009, accessed online.

had dropped to a skinny 207: Finch, Frank. "Rams' Duane Putnam Adds Pounds by Lifting Weights," *Los Angeles Times,* July 25, 1955, p. C3.

Putnam met a familiar face on campus: ibid.

the first game she ever watched him play: Interview, Micki Hock, Jan. 18, 2014.

likely the patellar: The authors are grateful to Dr. Michael Higgins, chair of Towson University's Department of Kinesiology, for his expertise in helping us to understand John Hock's injuries.

Hauser…won the Hooker's spot: Interview, Art Hauser, Nov. 13, 2014.

"Ramanian Empire": Finch, Frank. "Rams Ran Fourth, but '54 Wasn't Total Bust," *Los Angeles Times*, Dec. 14, 1954, p. C2.

Pool changed the offense every week: see Herskowitz, *The Golden Age of Pro Football*, **p.** 61.

several assistant coaches pledged to quit: Finch, Frank. "Hamp Pool Resigns as Coach of Rams," *Los Angeles Times*, Dec. 18, 1954, p. B1.

"Happy Warrior": Finch, Frank. "Pool Flare-Up Riles Players," *Los Angeles Times*, Dec. 3, 1954, p. C1.

Norman Vincent Peale's *The Power of Positive Thinking*: Olderman, Murray, "Winner of a Key Pro Game Leaves Everything on the Field," *The Telegraph*, Dec. 14, 1961, p. 24.

"We're going to play this my way, again": see Finch, "Pool Flare-Up Riles Players."

Reeves insisted Pool would be his coach again: ibid.

Football should be a simple game: see Herskowitz, *The Golden Age of Pro Football*, p. 61.

the two-headed quarterback: see Finch, Frank. "Wade to Start Saturday in Van Brocklin's Spot," *Los Angeles Times*, Dec. 2, 1954, p. B1. Also see Maxymuk, *NFL Head Coaches*, p. 238.

He lifted books, too: Interview, Micki Hock, May 30, 2014.

suffered a fractured skull—in practice. "LA Rams, Chicards Clash in Portland," *San Bernardino County Sun,* Sept. 4, 1954, p. 17.

had his leg snapped for his troubles: Finch, Frank. "Rams' Carey Out With Broken Leg," *Los Angeles Times,* Oct. 5, 1954, p. C1.

his front teeth drove straight through his lip: see Herskowitz, *The Golden Age of Pro Football*, p. 11.

"deserting the bachelor ranks": Zimmerman, Paul. "Sportscripts," *Los Angeles Times,* May 21, 1955, p. B1.

John planned to report early: Finch, Frank. "Gillman Enthusiastic About Larry Morris," *Los Angeles Times,* July 13, 1955, p. 29.

a fellow who played jazz piano: see Katzowitz, *Sid Gillman: Father of the Passing Game*, **p.** 27.

wore a bow tie on the sidelines: see photographs in Katzowitz, *Sid Gillman*.

new ways of studying game films: see Katzowitz, *Sid Gillman*. p. 77-79.

Chapter 7: Tomorrowland

appointed by her colleagues to pursue the New York's Giants or Brooklyn's Dodgers: "Los Angeles Gets in Bid," *New York Times*, Aug. 23, 1955, p. 25.

Louise Brough of Beverly Hills won Wimbledon: Tupper, Fred. "Fame in the Center Court," *Sports Illustrated* (reprinted with permission from *The New York Times*), July 11, 1955, p. 18.

"22,000 Guests Attend Disneyland Premiere": "22,000 Guests Attend Disneyland Premiere," *Washington Post*, July 18, 1955, p. 25.

"Crowds Jam Disneyland Opening Day": "Crowds Jam Disneyland Opening Day," *The Baltimore Sun*, July 19, 1955, p. 3.

"Disneyland Is a Child's World of Fantasy Come True": Hill, Gladwin. "Disneyland Is a Child's World of Fantasy Come True," *The New York Times,* July 9, 1955, p. 32.

"… the wonders of this playground": Hopper, Hedda. "Walt Disneys Fete 250 at Fabulous Disneyland," *Chicago Daily Tribune*, July 16, 1955, p. 17.

groundbreaking to grand opening took one year and a day: "Disneyland, Multimillion Dollar Magic Kingdom, to Open Tomorrow," *Los Angeles Times*, July 17, 1955, p. A1.

$17 million to build and, with parking, covered 160 acres: "TWA Offering 'Flight to the Moon' feature," *Chicago Daily Tribune*, July 10, 1955, p. J3.

more than seventy horses: "Disneyland, Multimillion Dollar Magic Kingdom, to Open Tomorrow," *Los Angeles Times*, July 17, 1955, p. A1. **trees of 30 to 50 years old to be shipped**: ibid. **3 million square feet, all paved**: ibid. **3.5 million board feet of lumber**: ibid.

Fifteen thousand people stood in line: "Disneyland Opens Gate to Thousands," *Los Angeles Times,* July 19, 1955, p. 2.

Thirty thousand visited that day: see "Crowds Jam Disney Opening Day," *The Baltimore Sun*. **jammed for five miles**: ibid. **50 cents for children**: ibid.

both repairs were made in a short time: see "Disneyland Opens Gate to Thousands," *Los Angeles Times*.

flying by helicopter from his offices in Burbank: "Disney (Nightmare) Land," *Daily Boston Globe*, July 8, 1955, p. 21.

the loss of construction workers: ibid.

dominating that night's ratings: Kirkley, Donald D. "Walt Disney's Big Day," *The Baltimore Sun,* July 17, 1955, p. SF11.

"world's fair of fantasy": Hill, Gladwin. "Disneyland Gets Its Last Touches," *New York Times,* July 9, 1955, p. 32.

"A juvenile fairyland": see "Disney (Nightmare) Land" *Daily Boston Globe*.

the future with a sentimental past: see Braudy, *The Hollywood Sign*, p. 89.

theorizing what the decades would bring: "Disneyland, Multimillion Dollar Magic Kingdom, to Open Tomorrow," *Los Angeles Times*, July 17, 1955, p. A1.

a photograph of Gillman sitting beside a film projector: wire service photograph, accompanying Finch, Frank. "Sid Gillman Named New Coach of Rams," *Los Angeles Times*, Jan. 26, 1955, p. C1.

David Gillman, Sid's father: see Katzowitz, *Sid Gillman: Father of the Passing Game*, p. 25.

Films allowed him to "grade" his college players: ibid, p. 77-79.

The nickname Van Brocklin gave his new coach: Interview, Durslag.

an assistant coach at Ohio State University under Francis Schmidt: *see Katzowitz, Sid Gillman*, p. 62.

a friend asked him to play for a fledgling team: ibid, p. 57.

Everyone was so nice: Interview, Joanie Hauser, May 30, 1954.

he'd starred as himself: *Crazylegs*, film, directed by Francis D. Lyon (1955; USA: Hall Bartlett Productions).

"It seems some of the Rams will never mature": *Associated Press*, "Ram Coach Pool Gets Support of Owner in Tiff with Squad," *The Lawrence* (Kansas) *Journal-World*, Dec. 4, 1954, p. 9.

Kelley kept having to pull to the side of the road to throw up: see Russell, *My Paths and Detours*, p. 165-66. Russell in her book describes the friendship of her husband, Hamp Pool, Don Paul, Bob Kelley, and their wives as involving a needling, acerbic sense of humor often fueled by alcohol. "We played jokes on each other right and left," she writes. "No holds were barred." One such joke involved putting a drunk Hamp Pool to bed with a bloody, raw steak under his arm pit in the hope that he'd wake in the morning, hungover and nauseated, and vomit.

a passing game that a Hollywood critic would call melodramatic: Murray, James. "Cleveland Won the Title Again but not Before the Whole NFL had Come To Appreciate Coach Sid Gillman and his LA Rams," *Sports Illustrated*, Jan. 2, 1956. Accessed online.

Throw to the sidelines. Throw shorter: ibid.

defense's shock absorber: ibid.

Gillman put Waterfield in a dark room: Finch, Frank. "Richter's Toe to be Checked by Waterfield," *Los Angeles Times*, Aug. 3, 1955, p. C1.

he ran a different sort of training camp: Zimmerman, Paul. "Sportscripts," *Los Angeles Times*, Dec. 10, 1955, p. B1.

An exhibition game was a learning tool, a classroom exercise: see Murray, "Cleveland Won the Title Again but not Before the Whole NFL had Come To Appreciate Coach Sid Gillman and his LA Rams."

"But what about December?": ibid.

Roz Wyman had written to Walter O'Malley: Rosalind Wiener Wyman to Walter O'Malley, Sept. 1, 1955. Retrieved from "Historic Documents: June 3, 1955 - December 5, 1955," Walter O'Malley Official website, walteromalley.com.

a telegram…wired at Wyman's urging: Special to *The New York Times*, "Los Angeles Gets in Bid," *New York Times*, Aug. 23, 1955, p. 25.

"…and 'look-see' at our facilities": Walter C. Peterson to Walter O'Malley, Aug. 22, 1955. Retrieved from "Historic Documents: June 3, 1955–December 5, 1955," Walter O'Malley Official website, walteromalley.com.

the council agreed with her that it should empower Wyman and Roybal: see Special to *The New York Times*, "Los Angeles Gets in Bid," *The New York Times*, Aug. 23, 1955, p. 25. Also, *Associated Press*, "Los Angeles Wants Giants or Dodgers," *The Washington Post*, Aug. 24, 1955, p. 20.

"I assumed it was part of a publicity stunt": Walter O'Malley to Rosalind Wiener Wyman, September 7, 1955. Retrieved from "Historic Documents: June 3, 1955–December 5, 1955," Walter O'Malley Official website, walteromalley.com.

"O'Malley had dealt too long with New York politicians": Shyer, Brent. "Wyman's Historic Effort Brings Dodgers to Los Angeles," www.walteromalley.com, p. 6.

western aspirations against eastern eminence: see Tower, Whitney. "Nashua and Arcaro: First All the Way," *Sports Illustrated*, Sept. 12, 1955, p. 23-27. Also see Christine, Bill, "A Day that was Hard to Match," *Los Angeles Times,* Aug. 31, 2005.

into a muddy path where the run was troublesome: "Swaps vs. Nashua—1955 Match Race," YouTube video, 3:01, posted by "Vintage North American Horse Racing," Feb. 2, 2008.

Nashua won by 6.5 lengths: Shevlin, Maurice. "Nashau Defeats Swaps by 6½ Lengths," *Chicago Daily Tribune,* Sept. 1, 1955, Part 6, p. 1.

as if the bird flies from the heart of the sun: onsite visit to Baltimore's basilica, July 8, 2014.

"How many times is that coming around?": Interview, Duane Putnam.

"we're getting up and down so many times": ibid.

"John's knees … were *so* bad.": ibid.

"real good whippings": Zimmerman, Paul. "Sportscripts," *Los Angeles Times,* Dec. 4, 1955, p. B7.

CHAPTER 8: THE SWEEP

His new restaurant the Ram's Horn: Finch, Frank, "Rams to Start Team that Beat 49ers" *Los Angeles Times*, Nov. 11, 1955, p. C1.

***Vipers*, he called them**: Durslag, Melvin. "Pro Football is Plenty Rough," *Sports Illustrated*, Nov. 28, 1955, p. 32-33, 59-61.

nobody in football played dirtier than Don: ibid.

"Don't go messing up Hollywood like that": ibid.

"Bumstead": ibid.

Connor was penalized again: ibid.

suffered a concussion against the Giants: Smith, Wendell. "Wendell Smith's Sportsbeat: Graham's Squawk Raises a Question," *Pittsburgh Courier,* Nov. 19, 1955, p. A20.

"They're chiefly interested in protecting themselves": United Press, "Walker of Lions Backs Graham Charges of 'Dirty Football' in National League," *New York Times*, Nov. 16, 1955, p. 46.

the 49ers' coach publicly accused the Rams: Finch, Frank. "Rams's Carey Out with Broken Leg," *Los Angeles Times,* Oct. 5, 1954, p. C1.

"nothing but a crybaby": "Pool Nothing But a 'Crybaby,' says Wolfner," *Los Angeles Times,* Nov. 18, 1954, p. C3.

the NFL would make that technique illegal: In 1956, the NFL made grabbing a facemask illegal, except in the case of the ball carrier. Grabbing the facemask of the ball carrier became illegal in 1962. See Nelson, David, *The Anatomy of a Game: Football, the Rules, and the Men who Made the Game*, Cranbury, NJ: Associated University Presses, 1994, p. 478. Also, see *Associated Press*, "National Football League's First Rule Change in 4 years," *New York Times*, Jan. 10, 1962, p. 26.

"I don't believe there is dirty football": "I Don't Believe There is Dirty Football" *Sports Illustrated*, Jan. 21, 1957, p. 27.

with a broken bone in his throwing hand: Zimmerman, Paul. "Sportscripts," *Los Angeles Times,* Dec. 4, 1955, p. B7

sprained his neck: Finch, Frank. "Rams Whip Lions, 17-10, Stay in Lead," *Los Angeles Times,* Oct. 10, 1955, p. C1.

Deacon Dan Towler, Bob Boyd, and Crazylegs Hirsch: The injuries to these players were reported in the *Los Angeles Times* throughout the 1955 season.

"…that player comes through": Zimmerman, Paul. "Sportscripts," *Los Angeles Times,* Dec. 4, 1955, p. B7.

"They were great guards, man": Interview, Ron Waller, July 10, 2014.

"I didn't ask any questions": ibid.

a blight in the 1940s: Quinn, Judith A. and Bernard L. Herman, *National Register of Historic Places Inventory–Nomination Form: Sweet Potato Houses of Sussex County Delaware,* prepared January 1988, filed with the United States Department of the Interior, National Parks Service.

The Rat's high school graduating class numbered forty-four: Interview, Waller.

"Shit, I'll never make this team": ibid.

offered him an $8,000 salary with a $1,000 bonus: ibid.

"one of the most graceful runners in Rams' annals." Finch, Frank. "Rams Whip Lions, 17-10—Stay in Lead," *Los Angeles Times,* Oct. 10, 1955, p. C1.

"He minces, he drives, he sprints…": Finch, Frank. "Rams Tame Lions, 24-13, Take Loop Lead," *Los Angeles Times,* Oct. 24, 1955, p. C1.

"John … was more mild-mannered": Interview, Waller.

"Lions were flying all over the joint": see Finch, "Rams Tame Lions, 24-13, Take Loop Lead."

"Tacklers never get a square shot at him": Cronin, Ned. "Cronin's Corner," *Los Angeles Times,* Dec. 9, 1955, p. C3.

"squirted around the Colts' flank": Snyder, Cameron. "Rams Defeat Colts, 20-14, to Keep Lead," *The Baltimore Sun,* Dec. 5, 1955, p. 17.

rain and mud and fifty-degree misery: Finch, Frank. "Rams Lose in Last 24 Seconds, 30-28," *Los Angeles Times,* Oct. 17, 1955, p. C1.

in a single game managed only thirty-four: ibid.

Dutch kept mum about it then: Zimmerman, Paul. "Sportscripts," *Los Angeles Times,* Dec. 4, 1955, p. B7.

"The only time you weren't hurt": Interview, Waller.

benched him for the second-string quarterback, Bill Wade: Finch, Frank. "Rams Lose in Last 24 Seconds, 30-28," *Los Angeles Times,* p. C1.

he was accustomed to hearing a sound—*zzt!*: see Herskowitz, *The Golden Age of Pro Football,* p. 62.

Oddsmakers gave the advantage to the Rams … for the 2:05 p.m. kickoff: Finch, Frank. "Rams Battle Packers Today with League Title at Stake," *Los Angeles Times,* Dec. 11, 1955, p. B7.

fans still waited to buy their way into the stadium: *The Baltimore Sun*'s correspondent reported that the crowd "arrived late, with hundreds streaming in long after the kick-off" (see *Associated Press,* "Rams Whip Packers, 31-17, To Win Western Title," *The Baltimore Sun,* Dec. 12, 1955, p. 17). Also, Ron Waller recalls "Sixty-thousand walked in the day of the game and bought tickets." Given that the pregame ticket sales led to a predicted crowd of about fifty thousand, the final attendance of more than ninety thousand does suggest a large walk-up crowd and long, slow lines to get into the stadium.

about as many people as lived in Burbank: Burbank's estimated population in 1953, based on United States Census reports, was 86,500. See the pamphlet, *Population of the Cities and Communities in Los Angeles County For the Census Years, 1930, 1940 and 1950 with Estimates for 1953*, compiled by the Research Department, Los Angeles Chamber of Commerce. The original pamphlet is available in the special collections of the library at UCLA.

"With gold and glory within their grasp...": Finch, Frank. "Rams Battle Packers Today with League Title at Stake," *Los Angeles Times*, Dec. 11, 1955, p. B7.

CHAPTER 9: GAME BALL

"a certain amount of entertainment sophistication": Interview, Durslag.

never ... deafened a visiting quarterback with their roar: ibid.

children and adults waited outside the locker room: Interview with John Houser, July 9, 2013. Houser, a Rams' rookie lineman in 1957, described the scrum that greeted Rams when they entered the tunnel outside the locker room. "When you come out all these kids come around," Houser said, "'Can I have your autograph? Who are you?' They're shoving (and) Elroy (Crazylegs Hirsch) would always have 'em line up. He says, 'All right!' He called 'em, like, Little Rams. 'I want you Little Rams to line up.' They'd all line up."

more fans than had ever witnessed a single game: *St. Louis Rams Media Guide, 2014*, St. Louis, Mo: St. Louis Rams, owner E. Stanley Kroenke, p. 529. Accessed online via stlouisrams.com.

"Free Football for Kids": see Smith, *Stadium Stories*, p. 36. See also Dyer, Braven. "Sports Parade," *Los Angeles Times*, Dec. 9, 1955, p. C1.

that number grew to three million two years later: see "Total TV Set Production," Television Receiving Set Production, 1947-53, compiled by Radio-Electronics-Television Manufacturers Association, PDF image accessed through tvihistory.tv.

Admiral Television Company offered to sponsor broadcasts: see MacCambridge, *America's Game*, p. 69.

Admiral would subsidize ticket revenue: ibid.

"Ye Old Rams" fan club offered weekly luncheons: Ye Olde Rams fan club. November 1955. Advertisement. *Official Program: Los Angeles Rams vs. San Francisco 49ers.*

"the finest book on professional football": The Los Angeles Rams by Bob Oates. December 1955. Advertisement. *Official Program: Los Angeles Rams vs. Green Bay Packers.*

$21.50 for a Rams blanket: Rams Xmas Gift Suggestions. December 1955. Advertisement. *Official Program: Los Angeles Rams vs. Green Bay Packers.*

regularly broadcast on KABC-TV: Los Angeles Rams 1955 roster. December 1955. *Official Program: Los Angeles Rams vs. Green Bay Packers.* p. 10.

George Halas … wore sunglasses: Condon, David. "Rams Rout Packers, 31 to 17; Gain Title," *Chicago Daily Tribune,* Dec. 12, 1955, p. E1. **he'd brought the Bears to Chicago in 1921:** ibid. **Newspaper photographers stalked Halas:** ibid. **gathered at the Edgewater Beach Hotel:** ibid.

drive out to the valley for dinner at the Ram's Horn: Interview, Micki Hock, May 30, 2014; also interview, Joanie Hauser.

they'll wear their gold jerseys: *Associated Press,* "Rams Whip Packers, 31-17, To Win Western Title," *The Baltimore Sun,* Dec. 12, 1955, p. 17.

Six days ago he met: *Associated Press,* "Reeves' Rams Partners Seek Policy Change," *Chicago Daily Tribune,* Dec. 6, 1955, p. C4.

had sold stakes in the team for a dollar: see MacCambridge, *America's Game,* p. 59.

with a stake in the team of 33 1/3 percent: *Associated Press,* "Three Partners Move to Oust Reeves as President of Rams," *The Washington Post,* Dec. 6, 1955, p. 31.

if he couldn't give himself fully to the job: ibid.

purchased the Rams with Levy in 1941: see Smith, *Stadium Stories,* p. 14.

a New York-area grocery store chain: ibid, p. 13.

Daniel Reeves & Company: Reeves' company name is given in his obituary. United Press International, "Los Angeles Rams' Owner Dan Reeves Dies of Cancer," *Palm Beach Post,* April 16, 1971, p. C1. See also United Press International. "Ram Owner Reeves Dies of Cancer," Chicago Tribune, April 16, 1971, Section 3, p. 1.

he'd been an athlete at Georgetown University: ibid, p. 14.

"I have no intention of stepping out": see *Associated Press,* "Reeves' Rams Partners Seek Policy Change."

"… he may continue as president": ibid.

Reeves had probably been drunk: see MacCambridge, *America's Game,* p. 82.

"… the guy had a drinking habit": Interview, Durslag.

"Crushing," the *Times* would call that block: Finch, Frank. "Rams Beat Packers; Win Division Crown," *Los Angeles Times,* Dec. 12, 1955, p. C1.

covering fifty-five yards to the end zone: ibid.

even Rams fans applauded Green Bay: ibid.

Breezy Reid, who fumbled: see *Associated Press,* "Rams Whip Packers, 31-17, To Win Western Title."

Art Hauser of the Rams fell on the ball at the one-yard line: Hauser held onto that ball on the sidelines and never gave it up. "I still have that ball!" he said in an interview nearly sixty years later. Interview, Art Hauser, Nov. 13, 2014.

"We knew they were going to fumble": Whorton, Cal. "Gillman Lauded, Game Ball Saved," *Los Angeles Times,* Dec. 12, 1955, p. C1.

"Is that what it is?": see Condon, "Rams Rout Packers, 31 to 17; Gain Title."

Thousands spilled over the stadium walls: see *Associated Press*, "Rams Whip Packers, 31-17, To Win Western Title."

thumped drums: Whorton, Cal. "Gillman Lauded, Game Ball Saved," *Los Angeles Times,* Dec. 12, 1955, p. C1.

his pants legs rode up to his knees: Bath, Phil. Photograph, *Los Angeles Times,* Dec. 12, 1955. Accessed online at framework.latimes.com.

shaking this player's hand: see Whorton, Cal. "Gillman Lauded, Game Ball Saved."

shouting their triumph as one: Bath, Phil, Larry Sharkey and Dan McCormack. Photographs. "Camera Records Rams' Victory Over Packers," *Los Angeles Times,* Dec. 12, 1955, p. C4.

ran nearly fifty-five yards to break a 17–17 fourth-quarter tie: see MacCambridge, *America's Game*, p. 73.

Then, he'd improved the defense with a trade: see Murray, "Cleveland Won the Title Again but not Before the Whole NFL had Come To Appreciate Coach Sid Gillman and his LA Rams," *Sports Illustrated.*

using the run more often and the shorter pass: ibid.

every player off the bench could contribute equally: Zimmerman, Paul. "Sportscripts," *Los Angeles Times,* Dec. 4, 1955, p. B7. Van Brocklin told Zimmerman, "We've had more injuries this year than I can remember, maybe twice as many as last year. And yet we've thought less about it. Coach Sid Gillman never moans about them to us like some other coaches I've known. Maybe that's part of his psychology. He just keeps putting someone else in there to fill the gap and that player comes through."

"...there's an even more important game coming up": see Whorton, "Gillman Lauded, Game Ball Saved."

"...for his fine play in the line": ibid.

"Game Ball," it said, "to John J. Hock": John Hock's game ball from the victory over Green Bay remains on display in the Hock family home.

had pulled a cuff link from his pocket: Waldman, Frank. "Frankly Speaking," *Christian Science Monitor,* Dec. 16, 1955, p. 18.

"Let's wait until we get over the Cleveland Browns": ibid.

Practice, he added, would start again on Thursday: see Whorton, "Gillman Lauded, Game Ball Saved."

CHAPTER 10: THE LOSER'S PURSE

"…but what about December?" see Murray, "Cleveland Won the Title Again but not Before the Whole NFL had Come To Appreciate Coach Sid Gillman and his LA Rams."

touched down at Burbank's airport: Finch, Frank. "Browns Picked to Whip Rams," *Los Angeles Times,* Dec. 25, 1955, p. A6. **a new $16,000 tarp:** ibid. **where icy fields made practice hazardous:** ibid. **looked up into the dreary sky and deadpanned:** ibid.

He wore a dark intensity like a mask: Photographs of Graham are easy to find, and a quick survey of them shows that off the field Graham had an easy, friendly smile. With a helmet on, and especially in action, his intensity was plain.

he announced his retirement: see MacCambridge, *America's Game,* p. 81.

Brown telephoned Graham: United Press, "Brown Pays Tribute to Graham as Cleveland Star Ends Career," *New York Times,* Dec. 27, 1955, p. 32.

the highest pay in the NFL: Goldstein, Richard. "Otto Graham, 82, Dies; Cleveland Dynasty's Quarterback," *New York Times,* Dec. 18, 2003.

the line running as high as six points: Finch, Frank. "Browns Picked to Whip Rams," *Los Angeles Times,* Dec. 25, 1955, p. A6.

straight to a field nearby for practice: ibid.

The day after Christmas, they'd meet the Rams: Recalling this Christmas away from his wife and children, Cleveland's Bob Gain said he kept telling his wife, "The only reason I'm doing this is to pay off the bills for Christmas for you and the kids." Interview, Bob Gain, July 26, 2014.

Otto Graham planned to retire: ibid.

Lou "The Toe" Groza, kicked a field goal: *Associated Press,* "Browns Are Favored to Overcome Rams," *Corpus Christi Caller Times,* Dec. 25, 1955.

but NBC had paid the league $100,000: Finch, Frank. "Browns Picked to Whip Rams," *Los Angeles Times,* Dec. 25, 1955, p. A6.

sixty thousand tickets had been sold: "Sunshine Forecast for Ram-Brown Tiff," *San Bernardino Sun-Telegram,* Dec. 25, 1955, p. 37.

the previous best was 58,346: *Associated Press,* "Browns Win Pro Crown From Rams," *The Baltimore Sun,* Dec. 27, 1955, p. 1.

a hairline fracture: *Associated Press,* "Younger Lost to Rams for Browns Battle," *Chicago Daily Tribune,* Dec. 20, 1955, p. B5.

as he finished his medical degree: "Hall of Famers—Dan Fortmann." Pro Football Hall of Fame. www.profootballhof.com. Accessed online, May 2014. Fortmann was inducted into the Hall of Fame with the class of 1965.

"… not deemed advisable to permit Younger to play": *Associated Press*, "Younger Lost to Rams for Browns Battle," *Chicago Daily Tribune*, Dec. 20, 1955, p. B5.

on the sidelines in street clothes: Heaton, Chuck. "87,695 See Browns Keep Title," *Cleveland Plain-Dealer*, Dec. 26, 1955. Accessed via Cleveland Browns History, www. cleveland.com, May 2014.

already bearing the nickname, "Tank": see Smith, *Stadium Storie*s, p. 41-43.

an agriculture and industry school for black students: "Grambling University/About Us/ History." Grambling University. www.gram.edu. Accessed online, May 2014.

the first player from an all-black college: Young, A.C. (Doc). "Pro Football Discovers The Black College," *Ebony*, Sept. 1970, p. 116.

no other team would want Younger: see MacCambridge, *America's Game*, p. 57.

the first in NFL history: ibid, p. 56-57.

"Have you ever considered playing pro football?": ibid.

bushy-browed and dapper: photograph accompanying "Pro Football Discovers The Black College," *Ebony*, Sept. 1970, p. 118.

happy to play a hand of gin rummy: Interview, Jack Teale, Rams public relations director, July 10, 2013. "I used to watch Eddie Kotal and our business manager playing gin rummy after work," Teale said.

Reeves had a network … hung a wall map in his office: see MacCambridge, *America's Game*, p. 58.

Dan Reeves and Eddie Kotal deserve a lot of credit: Finch, Frank. "Scouting the Pros," *Los Angeles Times*, Dec. 21, 1955, p. C3.

The Rams paid his $1,000 bail: International News Service. "Tank Younger Freed on Bail," *Atlanta Daily World*, Oct. 11, 1952, p. 5.

custody of a keeshound puppy named Jolie: "Tank Younger: Grid Star Divorced." *Pittsburgh Courier*, April 17, 1954, p. 1.

he studied at USC toward a graduate degree in theology: Goldstein, Richard. "Dan Towler, 73, All-Pro Back Who Studied for the Ministry," *New York Times*, August 3, 2001.

Deacon suffered a leg injury: *Associated Press*, "Younger Lost to Rams for Browns Battle," *Chicago Daily Tribune*, Dec. 20, 1955, p. B5.

the first year-round assistant coaches: see MacCambridge, *America's Game*, p. 35.

first to add a single-bar face mask: ibid, p. 86.

to draft African-American players: ibid, 29-31.

"I didn't really head slap. I punched." Interview, Gain.

He's got huge hands: Whalen, James D. "Bob Gain: Cleveland Tackle," *The Coffin Corner: The Official Magazine of the Pro Football Researchers Association,* Volume 17, No. 6, 1995.

might be vulnerable to a passing game: *Associated Press,* "Browns Win Pro Crown From Rams," *The Baltimore Sun,* Dec. 27, 1955, p. 1.

"We got our butts kicked": Interview, Waller.

"We ended up winning it pretty good": Interview, Gain.

an NFL record no quarterback would ever want: Finch, Frank. "Graham Great in Browns' 38-14 victory," *Los Angeles Times,* Dec. 27, 1955, p. C1.

offered a loud and long ovation: ibid.

congratulated each of the winning players: *Associated Press,* "Browns Win Pro Crown From Rams," *The Baltimore Sun,* Dec. 27, 1955, p. 1.

they had staked the NFL to its largest net profit: *Associated Press.* "Browns' Players Get $3,508.21 Slice Each," *The Baltimore Sun,* Dec. 27, 1955, p. 16.

"but—like—a Chevy": Interview, Gain.

CHAPTER 11: THOSE STRANGE THINGS YET TO COME

First circular office building in the world: The Capital Records Tower is easily visible to anyone driving Highway 101. The building, which calls to mind a stack of records, was completed in 1956. See "Capitol Records Tower," at *Capital Records Tower | Los Angeles Conservancy,* Los Angeles Conservancy website, retrieved July 28, 2014.

massive new church the Mormons built: Durham, G. Homer, "A New Horizon in Southern California," *The Improvement Era: The Voice of the Church,* Volume 58, No. 11, November 1955, p. 790.

with a giant donut on its roof: The building is Randy's Donuts, which was completed in 1953 on West Manchester Boulevard in Inglewood. See "Randy's Donuts," at *Randy's Donuts | Los Angeles Conservancy,* Los Angeles Conservancy website, retrieved July 28, 2014.

a coffee shop that looked like it had been built on Venus: The building is Pann's Coffee Shop, completed in 1958 on La Tijara Boulevard, Los Angeles. See "Pann's Coffee Shop," at *Pann's Coffee Shop | Los Angeles Conservancy,* Los Angeles Conservancy website, retrieved July 28, 2014.

a drive-in diner with enough angles to confuse a billiards whiz: This building is Bob's Big Boy Broiler, completed in 1958 at Firestone Boulevard in Downey, California. See "Bob's Big Boy Broiler," at *Bob's Big Boy Broiler | Los Angeles Conservancy,* Los Angeles Conservancy website, retrieved July 28, 2014.

a bowling alley … straight out of Egypt by way of Polynesia: The building is the Covina Bowl, completed in 1956 on San Bernardino Road in Covina. See "Covina Bowl," at *Covina Bowl | Los Angeles Conservancy*, Los Angeles Conservancy website, retrieved July 28, 2014.

"It was all so new": John Hock's children recall him often using this phrase to describe Los Angeles in the 1950s.

"We call it Googie architecture": Haskell, Douglas. "Googie Architecture," *House and Home,* February 1952, Volume 1, No. 2. p. 86-88.

"almost beyond parody": Novak, Matt. "Googie: Architecture of the Space Age," *Smithsonian Magazine,* June 15, 2012, retrieved from Smithsonian.com, July 28, 2014.

"which will truly make good sense": see Haskell, "Googie Architecture."

Micki was pregnant: Interview, Micki Hock, Aug. 14, 2014.

had been voted to the Pro Bowl: Finch, Frank. "Seven Rams Chosen for Pro Bowl," *Los Angeles Times,* Dec. 15, 1955, p. C1.

a 'toughest guy' poll among the [Rams]": Finch, Frank. "Rams' Duane Putnam Adds Pounds by Lifting Weights," *Los Angeles Times,* July 25, 1955, p. C3.

Lipscomb was putty in Putter's hands: Interview, John Houser, July 9, 2013.

"his blocking has been terrific": Zimmerman, Paul. "Sportscripts," *Los Angeles Times,* Dec. 10, 1955, p. B1.

"the perfect guard": Finch, Frank. "Little Similarity Between '55 Rams and Powerhouse Elevens of the Past," *The Daily Boston Globe,* Dec. 25, 1955, p. C18.

by offering resolutions to the council: Soliz, Barbara K. "Rosalind Wiener Wyman and the Transformation of Jewish Liberalism in Cold War Los Angeles," *Beyond Alliances, The Jewish Role in Reshaping the Racial Landscape of Southern California,* George J. Sanchez, editor, West Lafayette, Indiana: Purdue University Press, 2012, p. 81

before you make fifteen thousand": Interview, Waller.

one of the country's wealthiest women: Special to *The New York Times*, "Marjorie Durant Bride in Capital," *New York Times,* April 20, 1956, p. 19.

"Won't you marry me": *Friendly Persuasion,* directed by William Wyler (1956; Allied Artists Pictures, California: Warner Home Video, 2000), DVD.

"Wanna drink?": ibid.

Filming took place over autumn in 1955: Internet Movie Database, "Friendly Persuasion (1956)—IMDb," IMDb.com, Inc., April 20, 2015.

married Ronald Bowles Waller at St. Thomas Episcopal Church: see Special to *The New York Times*, "Marjorie Durant Bride in Capital".

near where the bride's mother raised thoroughbreds: Rasmussen, Frederick N., "Adelaide Close Riggs, 90, supported horse industry," *The Baltimore Sun,* Jan. 7, 1999.

Among them was Mrs. Bud McFadin: see Special to *The New York Times*, "Marjorie Durant Bride in Capital."

a personal assistant to Charlie Chaplin: see the father of the bride, Thomas W. Durant, mentioned in "Marjorie Durant Bride in Capital." See also Milton, Joyce. *Tramp: The Life of Charlie Chaplin,* Da Capo Press, 1998, p. 361.

She was represented by Allied Artists: see Special to *The New York Times*, "Marjorie Durant Bride in Capital."

player could mingle with Hollywood actors: Interview, John Houser, July 9, 2013.

"Why the heck aren't you coming to my party?": Inteview, Micki Hock, Jan. 18, 2014.

"Old man, if I'm kicking you…": Interview, Micki Hock, May 30, 2014.

"It was different, the Hollywood part": Interview, Joanie Hauser.

and 2,200 black and white marble floor blocks: Beinke, Nancy K. and Samuel Proctor. "Part I: Mar-a-Lago" Historic American Buildings Survey, No. FLA-195, National Parks Service, Department of the Interior, 1967 and 1972.

"It was a big jump": Interview, Waller.

once Walt Disney joined them: Interview, Micki Hock, Jan. 18, 2014.

babysat for Walt Disney's grandchildren: Jim Hock recalls hearing about this from his parents.

Disney demanded his son-in-law: email interview with Dale Pollock, entertainment writer for the *Los Angeles Times*, April 24, 2015.

bring the families … anytime, gratis: Interview, Joanie Hauser.

"you're the greatest bunch of men": see Whorton, "Gillman Lauded, Game Ball Saved."

Ma Robustelli's spaghetti: Interview, Putnam.

Robustelli … had all signed new contracts: United Press International, "Rams Sign Van Brocklin," *New York Times*, Feb. 12, 1956, p. 52.

pregnant with the couple's fourth child: Anderson, Dave. "Robustelli's Family Came First, and Giants Reaped the Benefits," *New York Times,* June 4, 2011.

"Make the deal": ibid.

The announcement came on July 27: "Football Giants Obtain Robustelli from Rams," *The New York Times*, July 28, 1956, p. 54.

a player lost zip after age thirty: Izenberg, Jerry. "Izenberg: Andy Robustelli Almost Never Made It Here, But He Became the Perfect Giant," NJ.com (*The Newark Star-Ledger*), June 2, 2011.

CHAPTER 12: SHUTTLE GUARD

Brown who'd pioneered it: Bechtel, Mark. "The First Helmet Radio: Paul Brown and Football's Forgotten Dynasty," *Sports Illustrated: MMQB*, June 11, 2014, retrieved electronically from *mmqb.si.com*, July 24, 2014.

Hit the lineman right between the eyes: Interview, Harry Thompson, Sept. 20, 2002. "I remember one time Van thought that (defensive lineman) Ed Sprinkle of the Bears had hit him too late so he told us guys on the line to let him through the next time. He then threw the ball so hard it hit Sprinkle right between the eyes and knocked him backwards. He did that just to hold him up a little bit and make him think. That was Van."

head coach at the Coast Guard Academy: Oates, Bob. "Otto Graham: He's Calling New Signals–This Time Against Particularly Threatening Foe," *Los Angeles Times,* April 10, 1985.

"he was calling plays": see Herskowitz, *The Golden Age of Pro Football*, p. 49.

because his quarterback chose the wrong plays: see Katzowitz, *Sid Gillman: Father of the Passing Game*, p. 133-134. Katzowitz tells of Gillman answering a challenge from a booster who said Van Brocklin's job was jeopardized by Gillman's play calling. "Lady," Gillman said, "if he calls the signals, he's jeopardizing mine."

"read quotes from the Bible": Interview, Art Hauser.

"…elements in Los Angeles that did not want me to be the quarterback": Interview, Bill Wade, Sept. 23, 2002.

Gillman benched him for Wade: *Associated Press*, "Rams Turn Back Eagles, 27 To 7," *The Baltimore Sun,* Oct. 1, 1956, p. S17.

more interceptions than touchdown passes: According to statistics from profootballarchives.com, Van Brocklin finished the 1956 season with 12 interception but only seven touchdowns. Wade threw 13 interceptions against 10 touchdowns. Even third-string quarterback Rudy Bukich threw three interceptions against one touchdown.

sometimes snapped back his answers: see Katzowitz, *Sid Gillman*, p. 133-134.

"Sid wanted to be in control": Interview, Duane and Patty Putnam.

retired to run his restaurant: *Associated Press*, "Don Paul, Rams' Defensive Star, Quits Football," *Ellensburg* (Washington) *Record*, July 25, 1956, p. 3.

Frank Fuller … had suffered a broken leg: "Rams In First Hard-Contact Scrimmage," *Redlands Daily Facts*, July 31, 1957, p. 8.

"He didn't like to take any extra steps": Interview, Duane Putnam.

'If it hurts, don't play': Interview, Micki Hock, Jan. 18, 2014.

an undisclosed price "in seven figures": Stern, Walter H. "Ebbets Field Sold for Housing; Dodgers Can Stay Five Seasons," *New York Times,* Oct. 31, 1956, p. 1.

"outmoded, dirty, and inadequate": ibid.

"to keep the Dodgers from playing in Brooklyn": ibid.

Dodgers home games in Jersey City, New Jersey: ibid.

"a move to Los Angeles with a stop in Jersey City": "Dodgers Endorse Sports Authority," *New York Times*, Feb. 7, 1956, p. 33.

"free hot dogs": Conklin, William R. "Boos and Catcalls Fill Night Air When Brooks Play in Jersey City," *New York Times,* June 26, 1956, p. 46.

"Would it still be Brooklyn?": Lardner, John. "Would It Still Be Brooklyn?" *The New York Times*, Feb. 26, 1956, p. SM110.

"He had LA in his fist": Interview, Duane Putnam.

"It's not pleasant": Hoffman, Jeane. "Sid's Wife Speaks: 'Gillman Proved He Can Take it,'" *Los Angeles Times*, Dec. 14, 1956, Part 5, p. 2. Katzowitz also treats this scene in his Gillman biography, p. 146.

" ... 'as long as those bulldozers keep moving.'": ibid.

Chapter 13: A Special Invocation Honoring the Mothers

"...get all dressed up and eat that chicken": Interview, Patty Putnam.

threatening a player protest: *Associated Press*, "Ram Owners And Players Discuss Exhibition Game Pay," *The Baltimore Sun*, Dec. 12, 1956, p. S23.

a new league-wide players' association: Strauss, Michael. "Football Pros Form Player Association," *New York Times,* Dec. 30, 1956, p. S1.

to pay for the trip: Interview, Art Hauser. At a team meeting in the summer of 1956, Hauser recalled, Gillman ripped into the players for their labor activities. "I remember Gillman using cuss words," Hauser said, "and saying, 'If I find out who's organizing this thing, I'll get rid of him right away.' He showed his true colors. Went against the players."

25 percent that front office folks had held back: Interview, Waller.

"The sixty greatest football players in the world": Schissler, Paul. Advertorial, "Pro Bowl Game," *1958 Rams Yearbook*, p. 51.

Hula and Pro: "Pro Bowl Group May Face Action By Ram Player," *Eureka* **(Calif.)** *Times Standard,* Jan. 8, 1957.

Popoki, **Hawaiian for cat**: Interview, Patty Putnam.

promise of a $700 payday: see "Pro Bowl Group May Face Action By Ram Player."

their tract home in Grenada Hills: Interview, Patty Putnam.

Paul Schissler, the Pro Bowl's promoter: see Maxymuk, *NFL Head Coaches*, p. 268-269.

"…take your time coming back": see "Pro Bowl Group May Face Action By Ram Player."

"I'm just a lineman": ibid.

"John's right there in town": Interview, Duane Putnam.

boxes of Jezebel brassieres: Interview, Bob Gain.

brought it to the Los Angeles Newspaper Publishers Association: Schissler, Paul. Advertorial, "Pro Bowl Game," *1958 Rams Yearbook*, p. 51.

in LA, he'd pay a buck a piece: Interview, Bob Gain.

West won … field goals kicked by Baltimore's Bert Rechinchar: The Baltimore Colts, though obviously located on the East Coast, did indeed compete in the NFL's Western Conference in the 1950s and later. The team, when it had been the Dallas Texans, played in the Western Conference, and a change of locale didn't change the NFL's need for six teams in each division. Geographic titles have never been a literal matter for the NFL. The New York Yanks played in the Western Conference in 1951, and the Rams—after relocating to St. Louis—still played in the AFC-West.

$500 each for the losers: Schissler, Paul. Advertorial, "Pro Bowl Game," *1958 Rams Yearbook*, p. 51.

"Pro Bowl Bedroom Set": Interviews, Micki Hock, Jan. 18 and Aug. 4, 2014.

"always the highlight of the school's program": "Football Player to Speak at Highland Mother-Son Banquet," *San Bernardino County Sun*, March 29, 1957, p. 18.

"a special invocation": "Highland Area News: Two Churches Join for Good Friday Services," *San Bernardino County Sun*, April 19, 1957, p. 18.

Los Angeles kids found knickers to be hilarious: Interview, Micki Hock (Jan. 14, 2014) and Hock children.

offered a toast to the sons: see "Highland Area News: Two Churches Join for Good Friday Services."

It's a conventional grip-and-grin shot: Mack, Lou. *New General Manager of the Rams, 1957*. Digital. Los Angeles: University of Southern California Libraries, April 8, 1957. *Los Angeles Examiner* Negatives Collections, 1950-1961. Black and White, negative. 10x13 centimeters.

He's a Southern California native: see MacCambridge, *America's Game*, p. 138-144.

"So do you want to take the job?" ibid.

a delegation to spring training in Vero Beach: "Walter O'Malley Official Web Site: 195758 Timeline." Walter O'Malley: The Official Web Site. Retrieved July 31, 2014.

CHAPTER 14: NOT A VERY NICE THING TO DO

Guard John Hock, victim of a ligament strain: Geyer, Jack. "Morris Breaks Ankle, May Be Out for Year: Rams' Hock and Waller Also Injured," *Los Angeles Times,* Aug. 18, 1957, p. C1.

it wasn't a very nice thing to do: Interview, Micki Hock, May 30, 2014.

"…your legs get a little tired of that": Interview, Duane Putnam.

photo of himself with four other Rams: Micki Hock still keeps this photo on a shelf in the house she shared with her husband.

"I'm John W. Houser, Jr.": Interview, John Houser, July 8, 2013.

"…a backdoor way of getting to be a starter": ibid.

he was all "fumble feet": ibid.

you'd be brushed aside: Interview, John Houser, July 9, 2013.

the starter at right guard: "Houser to Start for Rams," *The Redlands Daily Facts*, Oct. 26, 1957.

CHAPTER 15: LA BUMS

Nearly two hours behind schedule … the Convair 440 Metropolitan touched down: "Walter O'Malley Official Web Site: 1957-58 Timeline: Oct. 23." Walter O'Malley: The Official Web Site. Retrieved Aug. 16, 2014.

The fellow wielded a super-size bat: Several details mentioned in the scene of O'Malley's arrival in Los Angeles are drawn from thirty-one photographs found in the digital archives of the USC libraries. See in particular: Monteverde, Snow. *Dodgers Arrival, 1957.* Digital. Los Angeles: University of Southern California Libraries, Oct. 23, 1957. *Los Angeles Examiner* Negatives Collections, 1950-1961. Black and White, negative. 10x13 centimeters.

"that after I beat my guts out": Shyer, Brent. "Wyman's Historic Effort Brings Dodgers to Los Angeles," www.walteromalley.com, p. 8.

How do you leave a place like Brooklyn?: ibid and interview, Wyman.

"It was hard on me": Interview, Wyman.

wanted to hear from O'Malley himself: Shyer, Brent. "Wyman's Historic Effort Brings Dodgers to Los Angeles," www.walteromalley.com, p. 9.

"I don't want to talk at all": ibid.

"I know it's been difficult" ibid, p. 10.

And then they said their polite goodbyes: ibid.

the team would move to Los Angeles: "Walter O'Malley Official Web Site: 1957-58 Timeline: Oct. 7 and Oct. 8." Walter O'Malley: The Official Web Site. Retrieved Aug. 16, 2014.

they'd written, "LA BUMS": Five images. *Dodgers Sign Contract with Los Angeles, 1957.* Digital. Los Angeles: University of Southern California Libraries, Oct. 8, 1957. *Los Angeles Examiner* Negatives Collections, 1950-1961. Black and White, negative. 10x13 centimeters.

The contract they signed ... funding a youth recreation center: The details in this paragraph come from the Walter O'Malley timeline, September 16, Oct. 4, and Oct. 7. "Walter O'Malley Official Web Site: 1957-58 Timeline." Walter O'Malley: The Official Web Site. Retrieved Aug. 16, 2014.

a baseball in each hand: Monteverde, Snow. *Dodgers Arrival, 1957.* Digital. Los Angeles: University of Southern California Libraries, Oct. 23, 1957. *Los Angeles Examiner* Negatives Collections, 1950-1961. Black and White, negative. 10x13 centimeters.

"Welcome to Los Angeles!": "Walter O'Malley Official Web Site: 1957-58 Timeline, Oct. 23" Walter O'Malley: The Official Web Site. Retrieved Aug. 16, 2014.

Reporters from KTTV and KTLA: Monteverde, Snow. *Dodgers Arrival, 1957.* Digital. Los Angeles: University of Southern California Libraries, Oct. 23, 1957. *Los Angeles Examiner* Negatives Collections, 1950-1961. Black and White, negative. 10x13 centimeters.

"There may be a few lawsuits": Shyer, Brent. "Wyman's Historic Effort Brings Dodgers to Los Angeles," www.walteromalley.com, p. 6.

The city had acquired the property: What has often been called "The Battle of Chavez Ravine" is well documented. See among other sources PBS's Independent Lens program *Chavez Ravine: A Los Angeles Story*, and its web site at http://www.pbs.org/independentlens/chavezravine/film.html. See also, see Starr, *Golden Dreams*, p. 150.

IT'S THE DEAL!: Monteverde, Snow. *Dodgers Arrival, 1957.* Digital. Los Angeles: University of Southern California Libraries, Oct. 23, 1957. *Los Angeles Examiner* Negatives Collections, 1950-1961. Black and White, negative. 10x13 centimeters.

boos welcomed him home: Geyer, Jack. "Rams Beat Lions, 35-17, Before 77,314." *Los Angeles Times*, Oct. 28, 1957, p. C1.

some troublesome injuries: Waller hurt a toe, and that injury was well documented through the season. See particularly, Geyer, Jack. "Morris Breaks Ankle, May Be Out For Year: Rams' Hock and Waller Also Injured," *Los Angeles Times*, Aug. 18, 1957, p. C1.

"unimaginative": see Geyer, "Rams Beat Lions, 35-17, Before 77,314."

Billboards extolling the Dodgers: uncredited photograph, "Water and Power Associates: Baseball in Early Los Angeles," Water and Power Associates, http://waterandpower.org.

"We should see what kind of booze that guy was drinking": Interview, Houser, July 9, 2013.

"in the seat of Guard Duane Putnam's football pants": see Geyer, "Rams Beat Lions, 35-17, Before 77,314."

thousands of fans rose to their feet: ibid.

special assistant to the secretary of state: Devine, Michael, director of the Harry S. Truman and Museum in Independence. "Devine: Harry S. Truman and professional football." *The (Independence, MO) Examiner*, online, www.examiner.net, Aug. 6, 2011. Retrieved Jan. 28, 2014.

he kept the teams' rosters and a pair of binoculars handy: Monteverde. *Football—Chicago Bears and Los Angeles Rams, 1957*. Nov. 3, 1957. Digital. Los Angeles: University of Southern California Libraries, *Los Angeles Examiner* Negatives Collections, 1950-1961. Black and White, negative. 10x13 centimeters.

Never before had so many people watched an NFL game: Miller, Bill. "Record Crowd, 102,368, See Rams Top S.F." *Pasadena Independent*, Nov. 11, 1957, p. 9.

What was happening was Pete Rozelle: see MacCambridge, *America's Game*, p. 144. That Rozelle won a little extra money for Rams players didn't necessarily mean he was beloved by them. "He was probably the most disliked guy anywhere," recalled lineman Art Hauser. "Guys would just come out of his office cussing and mad as all get-out. He was a smart guy but was not warm and close to the players. The players basically detested him. ... They'd call him Greasy Pete because his hair was always slicked down." Interview, Art Hauser.

believed patience to be one of his skills: Academy of Achievement. "Pete Rozelle Interview—Academy of Achievement." Last modified April 11, 2009. http://www.achievement.org/

T-shirts to bobblehead dolls: see MacCambridge, *America's Game*, p. 144-45.

"It's like a market in the mall": Interview, Wyman.

brought back the shuttle-guard system: Shafer, Bob. "Dutchman Hot, Says Gillman," *Pasadena Independent*, Nov. 11, 1957, p. 9.

Teaching history at a high school: Interview, Micki Hock, Jan. 13, 2013.

a return to the Rams seemed like the fall-back position: Geyer, Jack. "Van Brocklin May Retire After Colt Game," *Los Angeles Times*, Dec. 12, 1957, p. C1.

CHAPTER 16: THE MOST QUIET PART

play before a million fans: *Associated Press*, "Rams Headed For Record Gate," *The Baltimore Sun*, Dec. 12, 1957, p. S25.

"big enough to stop Gino Marchetti?": Snyder, Cameron C. "Gillman Fires Up Rams For Colt Game Sunday," *The Baltimore Sun*, Dec. 12, 1957, p. S25.

"Watch Put cut him down": ibid.

"He won't be picking cherries": ibid.

the most crucial game: Snyder, Cameron C. "Colts 'Ready' For Crucial Game with Rams Today," *Baltimore Sun,* Dec. 15, 1957, p. 39.

six Colts suffered sore throats: Snyder, Cameron C. "Moore, 5 Other Colts Suffer Sore Throats," *The Baltimore Sun,* Dec. 12, 1957, p. S29.

"...if ever a team is ready": Snyder, Cameron C. "Colts Were 'Ready,' But Foe Too Good," *The Baltimore Sun,* Dec. 17, 1957, p. S21.

Tank, who'd told the newspapers he was through: "Will Tank Younger Really Retire?" *Los Angeles Sentinel,* Dec. 12, 1957, p. B3.

a photographer from *Life* magazine: see photographs at life.time.com, "Mickey Cohen: Gangster in the Sun." Several of Ed Clark's 1949 photographs of Cohen at home are published on this site, though they were not published with the original 1950 Life magazine story about Cohen, titled "Trouble in the Sun."

two storm systems had collided: "2 Storms Collide, Drench Southland: Rains Flood Homes; More Due Today," *Los Angeles Examiner,* Dec. 14, 1957, p. 1

houses flooding in the Glendale foothills: "Rain Stalls Autos; Three-Inch Fall in Valley: Showers Forecast for Today," *Los Angeles Examiner,* Dec. 16, 1957, p. 1.

Hock had regained the starting role: Geyer, Jack. "Relaxed Rams Smash Packers, 42-17," *Los Angeles Times,* Dec. 9, 1957, p. C1.

CHAPTER 17: NEXT TIME

I'm looking for the end of the rainbow: *The Tall Men*, directed by Raoul Walsh (1955; Twentieth Century Fox Film Corporation, USA: 20th Century Fox Home Entertainment, 2006), DVD.

drive into Los Angeles for the Rams game: "Sun 'Shines' for Millionth Fan," *Los Angeles Examiner,* Dec. 16, 1957, Sports, Section 4, p. 1.

with their two children: 1940 United States Census, Precinct 6, Amherst City, Texas; Sheet #4A, Household No. 76, lines 11-14; April 9, 1940; Ancestry.com.

as a radio and TV repairman: see caption description for "23 images. Football—Los Angles Rams versus Colts. 15 December 1957," written by *Los Angeles Examiner* photographer Monteverde and found at Los Angeles: University of Southern California Libraries, *Los Angeles Examiner* Negatives Collections, 1950-1961. Black and White, negative. 10x13 centimeters.

they hadn't missed a Rams home game all year: see "Sun 'Shines' for Millionth fan," *Los Angeles Examiner.*

the "1,000,000th FAN": Monteverde. *Football—Los Angeles Rams versus Colts, 1957.* Digital. Los Angeles: University of Southern California Libraries, Dec. 15, 1957.

Los Angeles Examiner Negatives Collections, 1950-1961. Black and White, negative. 10x13 centimeters.

"the most thrilling thing": see "Sun 'Shines' for Millionth fan," *Los Angeles Examiner.*

Younger had announced his retirement: see "Will Tank Younger Really Retire?" *Los Angeles Sentinel.*

had insisted he'd be back for another year: When asked by the *Los Angeles Times* whether he planned to retire, Hirsch answered, "Me retire? Heck no." Geyer Jack, "Van Brocklin May Retire After Colt Game," *Los Angeles Times,* Dec. 12, 1957, p. C1.

a meaningless game played on a dreary day: for the narrative on John Hock's last game as a Ram, we relied on coverage by Los Angeles newspapers and *The Baltimore Sun,* including:

- Geyer, Jack. "Rams Ruin Colts Bid, 37-21," *Los Angeles Times,* Dec. 16, 1957, p. C1

- Shafer, Rob. "Van Wants to Fish, Then Talk Retirement," *Pasadena Independent,* Dec. 16, 1957, p. 15

- Snyder, Cameron C. "Baltimore Pros Score in First 4 Plays, then Fail in Coast Contest," *The Baltimore Sun,* Dec. 16, 1957, p. S19

- "Van Brocklin Snags—Yes, A Pigeon!" *Los Angeles Examiner,* Dec. 16, 1957, p. A1.

- Oates, Bob. "Van Brocklin Passes Do It," *Los Angeles Examiner,* Dec. 16, 1957, Sports, Section 4, p. 1.

- Hafner, Dan. "Rams Better than 6-6 Mark—Gillman," *Los Angeles Examiner,* Dec. 16, 1957, Sports, Section 4, p. 2.

getting fellows to sign his game ball: Younger received a game ball as a retirement gift. Other game balls went to Sid Gillman and Norm Van Brocklin. See Hafner, Dan, "Rams Better than 6-6 Mark—Gillman."

a knee that is wrapped and iced: Waller suffered a painful knee injury in the game, according to Hafner. Ibid.

"I think Lipscomb broke my goddamn toes": Though this is an imagined scene, in the locker room after the game Van Brocklin did indeed finger his big toe and tell a reporter from the *Pasadena Independent,* "I think the thing's broken. Yep. Did it in the first quarter. Big Daddy Lipscomb crunched me on the play." See Shafer, Rob. "Van Wants to Fish, Then Talk Retirement."

CHAPTER 18: EPILOGUE

deferred to the Dutchman: Maule, Tex. "The Dutchman Had a Feeling," *Sports Illustrated,* Nov. 28, 1960.

"…pecan trees don't drop touchdown passes": Grizzard, Lewis. *If I Ever Get Back to Georgia, I'm Gonna Nail My Feet to the Ground.* New York: Ballantine Books, 1990. p. 230.

"…when you're asked for dinner, be helpful!": The Donna Reed Show. "All Mothers Worry." 25:50. Nov. 26, 1959.

"Just had a feeling that this was a time to get out": Interview, Houser. July 9, 2013.

owners are waiting for us to die: ibid.

inspecting a new bowling alley: "On the Ligher Side," *1958 Rams Yearbook.*

"improper advances": "Detectives Guarding Home of Ron Waller: Heiress in Court Dispute," *Los Angeles Times*, March 3, 1958, p. A1.

A jury acquitted her of the charges: *Associated Press*, "Waller's Wife Cleared in Drunk Driving Case," *The Baltimore Sun*, March 15, 1958, p. 11.

buy an NFL franchise and bring it to Miami: Brandt, Edwin H. "Waller Eyes Miami Pro Grid Link," *The Baltimore Sun,* April 14, 1958, p. 17.

first player signed by the American Football League's Los Angeles Chargers: *Associated Press*, "Harland Svare Resigns As Coach Of Chargers," *Washington (Pa.) Observer-Reporter,* Nov. 6, 1973, p. C4.

divorced in 1961: *Associated Press*, "Ron Waller Accused of Cruelty in Divorce Suit," *The Lewiston Evening Journal*, June 23, 1961.

"father of the passing game": see Katzowitz, *Sid Gillman: Father of the Passing Game.*

trading nine players: Klemko, Robert. "The History of the NFL in 95 Objects: The Telegram Detailing the Ollie Matson Trade from Chicago to LA," MMQB: Sports Illustrated. com, June 25, 2014. The article includes a photograph of the telegram taken by John DePetro.

as the new commissioner: see MacCambridge, *America's Game*, p. 148-150.

meshed like gin and milk: Rogin, Gilbert. "A Marriage That Was Doomed," *Sports Illustrated,* Jan. 6, 1969. See also, Allen, Jennifer. "Best Wishes, George Allen's Daughter," *New York Times Magazine,* Sept. 24, 2000.

Reeves died from throat cancer: United Press International. "Ram Owner Reeves Dies of Cancer," *Chicago Tribune,* April 16, 1971, Section 3, p. 1. Also see MacCambridge, *America's Game,* p. 296.

enshrined in the Hall of Fame: see The Pro Football Hall of Fame website at profootballhallof.com.

a motorcade of open convertibles: "Walter O'Malley Official Web Site: 1957-58 Timeline: April 18, 1958" Walter O'Malley: The Official Web Site. Retrieved Aug. 16, 2014.

Celebrities on hand: Shyer, Brent. "History in the Making: First Major League Game in Los Angeles" Walter O'Malley: The Official Web Site. Retrieved Aug. 17, 2014. p. 5

a five-hour "Dodgerthon": "Walter O'Malley Official Web Site: 1957-58 Timeline: June 1, 1958" Walter O'Malley: The Official Web Site. Retrieved Aug. 16, 2014.

gave birth to her first child: Shyer, Brent. "History in the Making: First Major League Game in Los Angeles" Walter O'Malley: The Official Web Site. Retrieved Aug. 17, 2014. p. 5

Can I go to opening day?: see Soliz, "Rosalind Wiener Wyman and the Transformation of Jewish Liberalism in Cold War Los Angeles." p. 92.

chairs brought down to the field's level: Shyer, Brent. "History in the Making: First Major League Game in Los Angeles" Walter O'Malley: The Official Web Site. Retrieved Aug. 17, 2014. p. 5

notes full of vitriol: see Soliz, "Rosalind Wiener Wyman and the Transformation of Jewish Liberalism in Cold War Los Angeles," p. 90-91.

bringing the National Basketball Association's Minneapolis Lakers: interview, Wyman.

Christian Reformed: Interview, Putnam.

"He missed it": Interview, Micki Hock, Jan. 18, 2014.

Purdue University basketball team's Most Valuable Player: Noland, Claire. "Lamar Lundy, 71; Part of Feared Rams Line." *Los Angeles Times,* Feb. 25, 2007.

"it's a cinch they could be rough": United Press International. "8 Ram Gridders Form Cage Team; Open Play Tonight," *Oxnard Press-Courier,* Feb. 8, 1958.

if the kids were well-behaved: Interview, Anna Maria Hock, Jan. 18, 2014.

"… the best food is truck stop food": ibid.

her grandfather "was Mr. Million.": Interview, Carri Gunn, Jan. 21, 2014.

SEX, LIES AND QUESTION TIME

SEX, LIES AND QUESTION TIME

KATE ELLIS

Hardie Grant

B O O K S

To Sophie, Charlotte and Milla and their generation
of girls who are going to run the world

Published in 2021 by Hardie Grant Books, an imprint of Hardie Grant Publishing

Hardie Grant Books (Melbourne)

Wurundjeri Country
Building 1, 658 Church Street
Richmond, Victoria 3121

Hardie Grant Books (London)
5th & 6th Floors
52–54 Southwark Street London SE1 1UN

hardiegrantbooks.com

 A catalogue record for this
book is available from the
National Library of Australia

Sex, Lies and Question Time
ISBN 978 1 74379 639 9

10 9 8 7 6 5 4 3 2 1

Cover design by Ella Egidy
Typeset in 12.5/18 pt Minion Pro by Post Pre-press Group, Brisbane
Printed in Australia by Griffin Press, part of Ovato, an Accredited ISO AS/NZS 14001 Environmental Management System printer.

 The paper this book is printed on is certified against the Forest Stewardship Council® Standards. Griffin Press holds FSC® chain of custody certification SGS-COC-005088. FSC® promotes environmentally responsible, socially beneficial and economically viable management of the world's forests.

Hardie Grant acknowledges the Traditional Owners of the country on which we work, the Wurundjeri people of the Kulin nation and the Gadigal people of the Eora nation, and recognises their continuing connection to the land, waters and culture. We pay our respects to their Elders past, present and emerging.

CONTENTS

Introduction: Time for change   1

Chapter 1: Where have we come from?   11
Chapter 2: Weaponising sexual gossip   27
Chapter 3: Slut shaming   41
Chapter 4: She's wearing what?   57
Chapter 5: Social media madness   79
Chapter 6: The 'sisterhood'   99
Chapter 7: First to the top   121
Chapter 8: The politics of motherhood   135
Chapter 9: Choosing to make it work   149
Chapter 10: Giving it all away   165
Chapter 11: Shaking up the parliament   183
Chapter 12: Why it's worth it   203
Chapter 13: Women changing the nation   221
Chapter 14: Where to from here?   235

Sources   251
Index   265
Acknowledgements   275

INTRODUCTION
TIME FOR CHANGE

THERE AREN'T MANY times when you get to witness the world changing before your very eyes. I clearly remember the difference it made when Julia Gillard became the nation's first female prime minister. As a member of parliament, I used to regularly visit the schools in my electorate and ask students to put up their hand if they thought they might be prime minister one day. As soon as Julia became prime minister, an army of girls would enthusiastically raise their arms. At community meetings parents would bring along their young daughters and explain how they were interested in running for parliament one day. An inspired generation of girls was emerging and seeing the world of possibilities available to them. It was such an obvious and palpable change that tears of joy welled in my eyes whenever I witnessed this wave of young women who were going to stand up and change the world.

This is how it should be.

But it didn't last. Attention soon turned to the overtly sexist and misogynistic treatment Gillard received as prime minister. In the years that followed the headlines were full of controversies that raised new questions about why on earth any woman would want to go into politics.

Sarah Hanson-Young spoke out about being 'slut shamed' in the federal parliament after she was told to 'stop shagging men'; Julia Banks and Lucy Gichuhi both publicly alleged that bullying of women was commonplace in our political institutions; Emma Husar's career as an MP ended following unsubstantiated sexual allegations; and Julie Bishop was overlooked by her colleagues as a leadership candidate in favour of men who were far less popular with the general public. These are the stories that reached the public and dampened the mood of optimism and inspiration that had emerged all too briefly with Gillard's ascension in 2010.

By 2017 a Plan International Australia survey showed that zero per cent of the young women aged eighteen to twenty-five surveyed would consider entering politics as a future career. Zero. The most recent follow-up survey in 2019 showed that 90 per cent of young women still believed Australian female politicians were treated unfairly.

One of the things I find most jarring about this is that the almost fifteen years I spent as a member of Australia's House of Representatives were easily one of the most amazing experiences and greatest privileges of my life. I will never again hold a job that is as rewarding, interesting and inspiring as being a federal MP. I don't want a generation of women turned away from that opportunity. And I don't know that we are necessarily giving these young women a clear and full picture on which to base this decision.

The key question, though, is how will we ever get enough women into our parliament if the perception remains that politics is hostile to women's interests, women's needs and women's lives? And how does that impact the nation more broadly? A parliament that is not representative of our wider community is never going to be best able to select, address and prioritise the issues important to us all.

Since I retired from federal politics at the 2019 election my belief has only strengthened that we need more women fighting in our parliament to ensure that issues affecting all women in Australia are at centre stage. We continue to see women and children killed with devastating regularity across Australian cities and towns. We see women disproportionately shouldering the burden of the impacts of COVID-19 and facing a lifetime of disadvantage as a result. After an all too brief experiment with free and accessible childcare we have now returned to the outdated and fragmented childcare funding model, despite overwhelming evidence of the constraints this places on women's economic participation. Women make up over half of our population and we need their voices to be heard on issues across the board, from economic decision-making to policies on climate change and immigration. And it's not just about hearing their voices but also ensuring that their attitudes, their management and leadership styles and their interests are fairly represented.

At a time when we have a critical need for strong women fighting for reform on the issues that matter, we have thousands of young Australian women turning away and not even considering entering politics.

When I was an MP, my press secretary would sheepishly approach me with a request to speak about my experience as a woman in politics, already knowing full well what my answer would be. It was always no. Many of my female colleagues say the same thing.

I always felt very strongly that my job was to speak about the community that I was elected to represent. Not myself. We fight elections on issues and policy solutions and values, not so that we can be commentators on our own profession. It just seemed self-indulgent.

An even bigger reason I turned those offers down was that I am aware of my privilege. Mine is not a sob story. The issues faced by women in Australian politics are first world problems. We are women who are highly paid, who have access to power and who have a voice and a platform from which we can wield that power. If we want to focus on women's issues there are many other matters that are a far greater priority. Our job is surely to fight for those living in crippling poverty or sliding into homelessness, those facing sexual assault, domestic violence and being killed each week at the hands of men, those who are unsafe and helpless without any avenue to a fair and just existence. Of course we want our elected MPs focusing on these issues, and not on themselves.

So, in breaking the habit of a lifetime, in the pages that follow I write about the real-life experience of being a woman in Australian politics. This is not an academic thesis. It is an insider's account of what I experienced in the years I had the privilege of serving in the parliament, and a reflection on the fact that while I am grateful for every second that I served, there are some things that happen to women that just should not occur, there are some things that we face disproportionately compared to the men we work alongside and there are some things that we need a broader public discussion about.

It is also a collection of firsthand insights from women who have served in our parliament. Over the past year, I interviewed a number of women from different political backgrounds about key issues women face in parliament. Some interviews were much longer and more personal than I had expected. Some were short and over the phone. Despite having worked alongside many of these women for years, I wanted to understand more of their lived experience: the good, the complicated and the hard parts of their daily realities. I am tremendously grateful to all the women who spoke so openly and honestly with me about their experiences and insights. I am also very aware of the number of amazing women who have made remarkable contributions who I did not speak to in this process. Those achievements are not unnoted.

Politics is a tough game for both men and women, but the obstacles and attacks that women often face are different. As Penny Wong told me, 'What is different for women in politics? Any woman who has achieved a position of significance has been subjected to different standards of behaviour to those which would be expected of men. Sometimes that has been more and sometimes it has been less. That disparity has been greater for some women than others. But there is still always a difference.'

Different methods are used to undermine women. Different standards are set for women. Different attention is paid to the appearance and private lives of women. Different levels of respect and recognition are paid to the achievements of women.

Ever since I first contemplated writing this book I have struggled constantly with the sense that I am breaking the unspoken code of not acknowledging the sexist and unfair treatment that has long bubbled away in the background of parliament. It's a bit like that silly old view that you only share the full and gory details of childbirth with women who have already been through it, as though no woman would ever choose to have a child if they knew the truth. There are some who believe we shouldn't acknowledge the ugly stuff that occurs, out of some sense of fear that we will turn others off. In my view that horse has long since bolted.

The public has already seen the brutal side and have read the headlines. Former Prime Minister Malcolm Turnbull said, in a speech at Oxford University in 2019, 'I am a very, very strong critic of the culture in Australian politics ... the culture with respect to women and with respect for women and attitudes to women in Australian politics is more like the corporate world in the 1980s, maybe a bit earlier. It's far, far too blokey.'

Staying silent, hoping behaviours will change, showing that we are strong enough to brush things off really isn't helping anyone. Pretending that everything is sunshine and lollipops is not only disingenuous, it is also counterproductive. I often wonder, if we had been more forthright in calling the culture out earlier, would the appalling misogynistic attacks on Julia Gillard still have occurred? Could we have stopped things before they exploded so dramatically? Of course we will never know – but we should do all we can to stop this behaviour now.

I will not sugar-coat some of the examples of women's poor treatment, because I want it to be called out. I want it to stop. At the very least I want the next generation of women to go in with their eyes open, fully aware of the obstacles that they might face. Of how the culture in parliament has yet to catch up with the rest of Australian society, which has become better at calling this behaviour out more often. The next group of women do not need to start with a blank page. They can learn from the successes and struggles of those who have preceded them.

As Julia Gillard told me, 'Women starting in the parliament now have got the fantastic benefit that they've seen this movie before. And when you've seen the movie before, your ability to think in advance about how you will react and what you will do if these moments come in your political career is far better than it's ever been. That is such a huge advantage.'

I have tried to explore more than just the shocking stories that made headlines. I spoke to women about some of the silent challenges they have faced. There are some genuinely inter-esting issues in the support women provide to each other, and the relationships that women have within their own parties and across the chamber. I was surprised by how many women spoke of the role that fertility choices, pregnancy and balancing work and family had played in their careers.

My favourite were the genuinely uplifting stories of what makes it all worthwhile. Tanya Plibersek summarised this most bluntly: 'It's utterly worth it. I would put up with ten times as much shit if I had to.'

Strangely, this is the part of the story that has largely been left untold – why it is worth every second. Almost every woman I spoke to had zero regrets about entering politics. Every woman spoke of how rewarding their work had been. We've seen how women can change the nation firsthand. It is so important that we highlight and celebrate the issues that have been acted upon because women worked in the parliament to champion them. There are many programs that have been funded and rolled out because a woman stood up and fought for them, many policies that deliver daily improvements to the lives of millions of Australians, and which only exist because a woman spoke up at the cabinet table. These are the achievements that we should highlight and celebrate. These are the reasons I believe with every inch of my being that being an MP is good for the women who do it, good for the parliament and absolutely good for the nation.

Of course, the under-representation of women in our parliaments isn't just about a lack of interest. It's about the male-dominated structures of power that still control our political parties and our preselections. As Labor's example with ambitious affirmative action rules shows, you need women involved to advocate and achieve reform. The Labor Party now benefits from the decades-long campaign by many women and some men to adopt rigid rules around increasing the number of women in parliament. This doesn't just benefit those women, it begins to erode the male-dominated power structures and brings different voices into the decision-making process – something that is proven to improve outcomes in all industries.

I want to see more women in politics and I also want politics to be better for them. But not just for those women, for everybody. Our federal parliament sets the tone for the nation. It determines what the future of Australia looks like. I suspect many women in parliament would say, 'It's a tough job and it's not everyone's cup of tea but we will just get on with it.' That is exactly what I would have said a few years ago. You become acclimatised to it. I now think differently. I've seen how much the culture in parliament is behind the rest of society. It is outdated, toxic and often unfair, particularly for women. That cannot be the right environment in which to set the laws that impact us all, and nor does it reflect our values.

A better parliament would mean a better Australia. That's why it should matter to all of us.

CHAPTER 1
WHERE HAVE WE COME FROM?

AUSTRALIAN PARLIAMENT WASN'T always lagging behind the rest of the nation and in need of urgent change. Australia was once a trailblazer throughout the world for ensuring a place for women in our political system. Our nation has been home to some of the biggest achievements of women throughout the years. In 1902 we became the first country to give women the right to vote and also to run for and serve in federal parliament, following on from New Zealand, which was the first nation to let women vote in 1893. This was a major breakthrough, and a huge credit to the legacy of the suffragettes and others who had agitated for change. By comparison, the United States took a further eighteen years before allowing women the vote in 1920.

From here though, progress was slow. The time lag between women being allowed to run for federal parliament and the first women actually being elected was a staggering forty years.

The first female state MP was Edith Cowan, elected to the WA Parliament in 1921, but it wasn't until 1943 that federal parliament had its first female MPs with the election of two trailblazers, Dame Enid Lyons for the United Australia Party and Dorothy Tangney for Labor. And we had to wait until 1976 before Senator Margaret Guilfoyle became our first female cabinet minister, serving in the Fraser Government.

In 1990, Carmen Lawrence became premier of WA, in the same year that Joan Kirner became premier of Victoria. Rosemary Follett had been chief minister of the ACT in 1989 and was again from 1991 to 1995. It felt like change was afoot, with a number of women in key leadership positions for the first time.

In 2010, a full 107 years after women won the right to run for public office, Australia finally had its first female prime minister in Julia Gillard. And there are firsts that still remain. Of the forty federal treasurers since Federation, not one has been a woman, with the nation's supreme economic decision-making role having been deemed a men-only affair throughout the entire history of our nation.

I suspect those women who fought so hard for the right to vote in 1902 hoped we would have come a bit further since then. In 2019, 51 per cent of Australia's population was female. After the May 2019 election, forty-six of the 151 seats in the House of Representatives were filled by women. That's 30 per cent. In better news, after the 2019 election, thirty-nine of the seventy-six senators are women, meaning the Senate has finally reached equal representation.

It is worth noting though that this representation is not evenly spread across the major parties. As of December 2020 the number of ALP MPs who are female is 47.9 per cent, for the Liberals this figure is 26.1 per cent and for the Nationals 25 per cent.

For most of its history, parliament has been a boys' club, and boys' clubs are not in the business of going into voluntary liquidation. History shows us that the gains women have made have only ever been achieved as a result of protest and agitation, pressure and persuasion.

The role of Victoria's first female premier, the late Joan Kirner, in smashing down these barriers cannot be underestimated. As a prime mover behind the Emily's List organisation, which works to elect and support Labor women, Kirner argued that without set affirmative action targets, Labor's ability to do something meaningful about gender inequality would remain well-meaning talk with no real action.

The Labor Party's historical roots are in the union movement, whose leadership over the years has been almost exclusively male. And within the Australian Labor Party there are factions – highly influential groups with ideologies on either the right or left of politics – which have equally been male dominated. While the Labor Party operates as one party, most elected members align themselves with either the right or the left faction for ideological and organisational purposes. Kirner realised that, without the forced discipline of hard-and-fast rules, the Labor Party, like the Liberals today, could continue to see gender equality as something nice to aim for, instead of a non-negotiable.

The hard-fought advocacy that followed the formation of Emily's List in 1996 culminated at the Australian Labor Party's national conference in 2015 when the party adopted binding rules that commit it to achieving equal gender representation by 2025.

The Liberal Party has yet to adopt this course of action. In 2019, the Coalition Morrison Government had six women of the twenty-three cabinet ministers, just one woman serving in the seven-member outer ministry, and only three women of the twelve assistant ministers – an embarrassing and inexcusable female participation rate of 23 per cent.

There was something sadly predictable about the October 2020 report by the Menzies Centre, the Liberal Party's research arm, into their poor performance in boosting female participation in our parliaments. For the first time, the party admitted that it had a problem, with the proportion of female MPs in the federal Liberal Party languishing at around 25 per cent. It felt like progress to read such an honest admission, but yet again, the party baulked at the idea of quotas, still claiming that natural attrition, the targeting of seats for female candidates and the innate goodwill of sitting male MPs to vanish into the night could somehow boost female participation through a process of evolution. It hasn't worked so far, so on what basis do they think it will suddenly work now?

It will likely take dedicated advocates within the Liberal Party to start speaking up before real change will happen. Minister Sussan Ley has become one of the first to go on the record saying the Liberal Party should, in the first instance, adopt targets and then consider quotas.

She explained to me, 'I was sitting in the last few months of the last parliament, and someone said to me, "I've been looking down at your party. Do you realise how few women there are and how unrepresentative of broader society that suggests that your party is?" I thought, I want more women in our party.' She remains ambivalent about quotas though. 'I feel like it is the outcome not the mechanism that is important. Should it be a quota? As soon as you say that, the next question is, how will it work? To that I would say, it's actually a matter for my party. And I would like my party at divisional level in New South Wales to consider it.'

Some baby steps, maybe.

Getting to Canberra is only part of the challenge for women. As almost every woman I have spoken to for this book attests, the next obstacle is being taken seriously, being heard, being promoted and being respected. Unfortunately women in politics don't always enjoy these rights as a matter of course. At its worst, to co-opt that infamous line from former right-wing shock jock Alan Jones, there is a view that letting women into politics simply results in them 'destroying the joint'.

Clearly, the problems female politicians have in the workplace are not unique to parliament, or indeed the Australian Public Service (where the 'marriage bar' still forced women to give up their jobs after marriage until 1966). Any woman who has worked in a male-dominated industry knows what sexism looks like. But while corporate Australia has made big strides in favour of equality on many fronts – like new policies promoting work–life balance, robust anti-bullying and sexual harassment policies, and an embrace of more flexible work – parliament remains stubbornly stuck in the past. Former foreign minister and deputy Liberal leader Julie Bishop believes there is something innately sexist about parliament and that this can be traced back to its origins. 'It's the whole culture of the place,' she told me. 'The way it developed, the environment of parliament, the adversarial nature that was developed and devised at a time when there were only male parliamentarians and no, or very few, women. It was a male domain, and I think that culture remains. While men are in the majority, and women are in the minority, it will be harder to effect change.'

The sense that parliament is a male domain infects its processes, too. Politics is all about conversation. At the electoral level it is an ongoing conversation with your constituents about the issues that affect them, but at the policy level it is about your ability to champion and critique ideas. This can be when you are on the floor in the chamber of the House of Representatives when MPs gather during question time, or within caucus or your party room (where members of your political party hold meetings). And, if you are among the lucky female few who becomes a minister in charge of a particular department, like Defence, then this can happen around the cabinet table when you are meeting with other senior ministers.

The nature of male networking and male behaviour can mean that, at times, women's contributions fall on deaf ears. One current sitting MP describes a world in which women's ideas are invisible and unheard, only to be hailed as visionary when repeated by a male colleague. 'It is all of the classic stuff, sitting in a meeting with six or eight people around the table and a woman saying an idea and nobody really acknowledging it,' she said. 'Then a bloke will say it five minutes later and everyone will respond: "Great idea. Let's do that." That happens to me a minimum of once a week. They just cannot hear a woman's voice. It manifests itself in people taking credit for your work, for your ideas. People are really confronted if you challenge them on it directly.'

Double standards apply to the conduct of male and female MPs, which see men who become forceful or fiery as passionate advocates, while women who behave that way are viewed as typical irrational females flying off the handle.

Equally, men who make rare familial sacrifices are hailed as heroes, while women are dismissed as distracted or unfocused if they must adjust their work commitments to care for or accommodate a child. Perhaps it explains why, after Ros Kelly gave birth while serving in the House of Representatives in 1983, it took until 1999 for Anna Burke to become the second woman to do so. A male politician who puts family first is a role model, whereas a woman who does so is conflicted, unreliable, and probably suffering from baby brain. These stereotypes are not unique to parliament but are arguably more ingrained within a culture that is out of step with mainstream Australia on gender roles.

'Men's anger is treated in different ways to women's anger,' Tanya Plibersek said. 'I can never lose my temper. Blokes do it all the time. And that's just completely par for the course. And it's forgiven. It's acceptable behaviour. If a woman did it she'd be a hysterical bitch. I think I have to be better at my job than the equivalent bloke. I think if I say I can't come to a meeting because of family stuff, people mark that against you as proof that you're not up to the job. If a bloke says that they say, "What a great bloke, what a fantastic guy." If you're a bloke and you say you can't or won't because of family reasons you are commended for having got the balance right.'

True diversity, and even gender diversity, must run much deeper than just an even spread of men and women. In so many ways, our parliament is far from being representative of our community.

In the early years of my career, my experiences were shaped by my relative youth and all the stereotyped scrutiny that came with that. I was twenty-seven. The current average age of Australian MPs is fifty-one, and the average age of the Australian population is thirty-seven. So perhaps it's time for more young voices to be heard as well.

Then there are women who face the double, or even triple, whammy of being excluded or regarded differently (or unfavourably) on the basis of not only their gender but also their race, disability or sexuality.

While people with a disability make up a whopping 18 per cent of the Australian population they represented just 1 per cent of major party candidates at the 2019 election. Indigenous Australians represent 3.3 per cent of the Australian population, but fewer than 2 per cent of candidates in 2019 were First Nations people. Australia is one of the greatest multicultural success stories on earth, its development and growth made possible by successive waves of immigration, but less than 10 per cent of 2019 candidates were regarded as having a multicultural background.

Recent analysis showed that in 2019 our federal parliament was no more diverse than it was in 1988.

My fellow South Australian Labor MP Penny Wong finds herself in the unique and sometimes unenviable position of being an outsider across several key criteria, and has a hilariously awkward moment from a commercial television appearance to prove the point. 'I did this breakfast TV show once and one of the hosts said to me: "You're Asian, gay and a woman, that's the holy trinity!" And I was like, oh no.'

Penny admitted she has struggled with the burden of being someone who appears to be staging a one-woman exercise in smashing simultaneous barriers. But she's learnt to live with the role. After all, there is nothing she can do to change it. She has also accepted that her progress is meaningful to others in the same position as her.

'I used to resist notions of "trailblazer" or "role model" or those sorts of labels because I felt the weight of them,' Penny told me. 'But I remember early on in my career giving a speech at a university, where all these young women were coming up to me. A lot of them were kids of Asian heritage who had come to see me and they were really excited. I realised it had changed their perception of their own aspirations and their own possibilities. And I thought, well, that's actually why this does matter, because it's not about you, it's not about self-aggrandising, or thinking of yourself as a role model because you're great. It changes how

people perceive their own possibilities and that is really important to social change. Thinking about it like that helps. But I
found it hard at times, the personal weight of it all.'

It has been easier for Penny to deal with issues of prejudice
and discrimination on the basis of gender than it has with the
challenges brought by race and sexuality. 'The gender stuff is
shared,' she said. 'We know what that is, we know that patriarchy
exists, we see that every day. It's something shared and understood by other women.'

As the highest profile lesbian woman in parliament, Penny
faced the 'traumatising experience' of carrying the expectations
of the LGBTIQ+ community in the years leading up to the
Marriage Equality Law Postal Survey in 2017. For someone
who is portrayed as tough and tenacious – and sometimes,
wrongly, as unemotional – she admits that the pressure came
with an emotional toll, which only became obvious at the joyful
moment the yes vote prevailed. Iconic footage shows Penny
breaking down in tears of relief.

'When we look back now there was lots that was
wonderful – the win itself and the fact that the country was so
affirming – but for many people it evoked a lot of pain, a lot of
fear and a lot of their own grief over their own challenges about
coming out,' she said. 'I remember at one point going to a pub in
Brisbane and giving a speech, and people were really stressed.
It was a pretty difficult point in the campaign. There'd been a
lot of aggro. There were grown men and women crying. And
I thought, I don't know how to keep doing this. I have to keep
projecting optimism and positive energy and empowerment

and strength. But actually, I just felt overwhelmed. But I decided that I couldn't let anyone see that. They needed to see me saying that we could do this.'

Penny had earlier become a target of critics who were blind to her long-term internal advocacy to change the party position on marriage equality and her work to achieve change from within.

'There were times when people became personally aggressive. I remember one gay man accusing me of homophobia, and there were some pretty awful things written about me by the very group of people I was trying to represent. That was hard. But that's life.'

There was another exchange Penny recalls that underscores a great hypocrisy in the expectations placed on women in senior political roles. While our parliaments have been filled since the dawn of democracy with male ministers who have no direct life experience of their portfolio, with female MPs the question is often asked: what would she possibly know about that? In Penny's case, this once again became an issue not just of gender but of race and sexuality.

'When I was first on the frontbench and was given employment services, a journalist asked me, "How can an Asian lesbian talk with any authority about the northern suburbs of Adelaide?" And I thought, wow, you would never say that John Howard as a white, wealthy man couldn't represent certain people.'

There is further evidence of how slow parliament has been to be truly representative of the Australian community. It remains extraordinary to me that we did not elect our first Aboriginal woman to the House of Representatives until Linda Burney became the Member for Barton in 2016. It was the same election that brought our first Muslim woman to federal parliament in Anne Aly.

For Linda, being the sole representative of Aboriginal women was nothing new. 'By the time I got into mainstream politics, I was used to being very often the only Aboriginal person in the room, and also very often the only woman in the room.'

Linda is passionate about her background, her purpose and ensuring that her perspective is heard. She acknowledges the role that her experiences as an Aboriginal woman have played in making her a successful trailblazer. 'I also was in the Aboriginal movement. I was an activist, I had dealt with Aboriginal politics, which are complex and extremely difficult. That was a great grounding for me being a mainstream politician. I really felt that my Aboriginality was an enormous positive for me going into the political arena as a woman. I just saw it as a real strength, a real grounding. I knew where I came from. I knew what I stood for, and I didn't have any of that angst.'

It also means that she carries more weight than most. She balances cultural issues and considerations with policy analysis and has extra work that is barely seen by the rest of us – meeting with Elders wherever she travels, showing respect and consulting on issues far broader than her own portfolios. She also helps her community far outside the borders of her own electorate.

'They ring me when things get really hard. There's not only the expectation within the parliament, but there's the expectation within the community as well that I don't think the parliament really sees. There are things that I had a responsibility for that probably other people wouldn't have responsibility for.'

The weight of the Indigenous communities' views and hopes continues to fall on the shoulders of a disproportionately low number of elected Indigenous MPs and senators, and our parliament is poorer for it.

We have to travel further afield than Canberra to find the story of another truly remarkable trailblazer who represented yet another desperately under-represented group of Australians. In 2010, Kelly Vincent was elected to the South Australian Parliament at the age of twenty-one, making her the youngest woman ever elected to any parliament in Australian political history. The Dignity Party MP is a pioneering campaigner for the rights of people with disabilities. Kelly had been second on the upper house ticket for the Dignity Party, which secured 1.2 per cent of the vote. Tragically, the party's number one candidate, Paul Collier, died of a brain haemorrhage eleven days before election day, meaning Kelly won the seat.

For Kelly, entering politics wasn't so much about overcoming the obstacles that had historically troubled women trying to enter parliament. It wasn't even about her youth, at least not at first. It was a much more literal battle with the physical obstacles preventing her from even getting into the building. She has spastic cerebral palsy which affects both her legs and her left arm. Upon her election, works needed to be carried out to the South Australian Parliament House to modify the toilets and even the parliamentary chamber to ensure she could access it in her wheelchair. She, too, faced questions about whether as a

21-year-old woman she had the required experience to serve as an MP. In an interview after her election she answered that she had 'twenty-one years of life experience with a disability which, let me tell you, is twenty-one years more than anyone else in this building'.

Parliament is the highest office in the country, the place where decisions for the benefit of all Australians are made, ones that will affect everyone from an Indigenous person from rural Western Australia to a second-generation migrant from Brisbane to a woman with a disability in Adelaide. Our parliament must be reflective of our community, but right now the statistics, and our own eyes, show us that it is not. There are consequences of this: the disconnect between parliament and the people it should benefit, and a parliamentary culture that is not reflective of Australian society.

In November 2020 the ABC's *Four Corners* aired a program titled 'Inside the Canberra Bubble' that pointed to deep cultural issues in parliament. The program centred around the revelation that married Morrison Government Minister Alan Tudge had engaged in a consensual affair with one of his staff members, Rachelle Miller, and that following its conclusion she was basically blacklisted, moved on, and eventually moved out of her job entirely. Further sexual allegations were also raised about fellow married minister Attorney-General Christian Porter.

The program received an explosive reaction. The Morrison Government declared it an outrage and an intrusion on the male ministers' privacy and sent off complaints to the Chair of the ABC. But it also elicited a huge private reaction from current and former female staff who found it deeply triggering. It was all too familiar.

I remember how I felt when I was hit on by a fellow MP. It was a crude approach rather than a romantic one; from his bombastic tone, it was clear he did not value me as an equal. I was shocked and offended but also scared. Though I awkwardly laughed it off and pretended it wasn't a big deal, I wondered if there would be professional repercussions. Had I just made a powerful enemy? I was a federal government minister at the time, so I can't imagine how it must feel for female staff who are subjected to this kind of behaviour much more frequently. The power imbalance is so much greater. MPs have the ability to hire and fire at will. They determine which staff will be promoted and whose careers will be left to languish. In many cases they determine who to mentor and support to be preselected. In other words, they choose the people who can become our future members of parliament.

One of the things that I found most concerning about the *Four Corners* episode was the reaction to the story from members of Canberra's press gallery. Opinions on the merit and importance of the story were divided largely along gender lines. Many were asking, what is the public interest in this stuff? On what basis is the invasion of privacy justified? I would have thought the cultural issues presented provided a pretty obvious answer to this question.

Parliament should set the standard for the nation, showing us who we are and who we want to be. The laws made there affect every single one of us, and the visibility of our parliamentarians makes them role models, for better or worse. Their behaviour sets the tone for our national discourse. Yet it's clear our national parliament – its members, its processes and its norms – is seriously out of step with Australian culture. And it isn't going to change by itself. Cultural change will only happen if we demand that it does. So let's start talking about what needs to change, and why.

CHAPTER 2
WEAPONISING SEXUAL GOSSIP

I HAD ONLY been a politician for a few weeks when I was approached in a Canberra bar and told, 'The only thing anyone really wants to know about you, Kate, is how many blokes you had to fuck to get into parliament.'

This statement was made to me by a then Liberal staffer who went on to be a senior MP, who interrupted a conversation I was having at the pub during one of my first sitting weeks. I had won a marginal seat from a popular, long-term incumbent Liberal MP in an election when my party was largely annihilated. But, sure, if that's how he thinks elections work. I had never spoken to him before and subsequently tried to limit our interactions over the next decade.

It was the kind of run-of-the-mill sleaze and innuendo which is so common it is almost unremarkable in the culture of federal politics.

I was interested to speak to other women about their experiences to try to determine exactly how often this was occurring in our parliament. Why does it happen? What impact does it have and is there a way we can prevent it?

In parliament, sexual rumours are often weaponised to destabilise a politician. When this happens it is often the culmination of months or years of sexual gossip that has explicitly been circulated through parliament. It's not exclusively aimed at women, but the cases that I heard about men seemed to often involve allegations of secret same-sex encounters. Perhaps this demonstrates that sexism has a friend in homophobia in the parliament, and that sexual rumours are only really damaging to men if they involve other men. It is only when men reach the very top job that they seem to become common targets of gossip, and in the case of Tony Abbott I suspect that was driven by an attempt to undermine the authority and influence of his chief of staff, Peta Credlin, more than being aimed at him. In the majority of cases sexual gossip is saved for use on women, I suspect because that's who it inflicts the most damage upon.

As Natasha Stott Despoja, former leader of the Democrats, said to me, '[Male parliamentarians'] relationships are considered private – even if there are issues in those relationships.'

Until the *Four Corners* report in 2020 very little had ever been reported or published about male parliamentarians' sex lives. What is it that makes women the target of sexualised rumours? And why is it that some women cop it while others dodge it entirely? I certainly copped my fair share in the fifteen years I was in parliament. Perhaps I just exude an air of insatiable sexual animalism, but I suspect there is more at play.

Soon after my arrival in parliament, a rumour started that Labor Member for Watson Tony Burke and I were sleeping together. It was a rumour that would become widespread and persist on and off for most of the next decade. Years later when my husband told one of his mates that we were dating his mate responded, 'Is she still having sex with Tony Burke though?' For what it's worth, we never were.

Rumours would follow about my alleged sexual liaisons with other MPs, ministers, countless staff members, sporting administrators when I was sports minister (the allegations seemed to peak in the years when I was a minister) and who knows who else. While interviewing women for this book I learnt of rumours that had been spread about my sex life that I was completely unaware of until this point. When I was heavily pregnant with my first child I hired a new and amazing press secretary, Joanne Cleary; she only recently told me that when she took the job she was warned by others that I was quite the 'party girl' and she'd need to work hard to keep my sex life out of the papers. People apparently believed I was really, really busy.

Not that it matters, or is actually any of your business, but I had two long-term monogamous relationships that lasted my entire parliamentary career. Beyond that, I wasn't sleeping with half of Australia's politicians or Australia's political staff members or Australia's men – in fact, none of them at all. But none of this is really about facts.

As Penny Wong noted, 'Women's sexuality has been used against us as a well-documented tool of control through much of human history.' And it seems that our parliament hasn't shown many signs of breaking this long-term tradition or indeed even wanting to address it.

If anything surprised me when researching this book it was actually that many of the female MPs that I spoke to stated that they had heard sexual rumours and smears spread about another woman, which were used to undermine her confidence or credibility, but had never been on the receiving end themselves. Yet, regardless of their personal exposure, nobody seemed to view it as surprising or uncommon when these acts occurred.

Liberal Cabinet Minister Karen Andrews mused, 'I think women can be quite vulnerable to the shaming and rumours about who were they sleeping with. They can just be seen having a cup of coffee with someone and then all of a sudden, a rumour starts. That's just nonsense. I think it's immature but it happens and it is unacceptable.'

Youth seems to be an obvious factor in determining the likelihood you'll be on the receiving end of these rumours. I was twenty-seven years old when I became an MP. Natasha Stott Despoja, who was twenty-six years old when she entered parliament, told me, 'No one else's marriage or relationships or partnerships were anyone else's business ... I just found that there was a salacious interest in my personal life.'

Marital status is another factor. As an unmarried woman, Julia Gillard said that 'because your personal life wasn't seen as settled, it was easy for rumours to fill that space'. But the former prime minister also pointed out that it is not as simple as just our relationship status. 'I'm not one hundred per cent sure if married–unmarried is the line. Because I can think of women who came into parliament when I did who are very attractive women. And even though they were married or partnered, that didn't stop a series of what in high school would be the sort of "pretty girl" rumours. You know, "She uses her looks to get along," "She uses sex appeal to get along." So there's certainly that.'

Sarah Hanson-Young entered the parliament as a married woman but became single after two years in the job. 'There was a very quick change from the moment people discovered I wasn't married anymore,' she told me. And it wasn't long before she saw the result of this new interest in her personal life.

'Bob Brown was still leader at the time … Bob is my political mentor. And he's much older – I don't know, sixty-something, close to seventy at this point. And he calls me into his office because someone upstairs in the *Herald Sun,* I think it was, was going to print a story about me being busted having sex in the prayer room.

'They had gone to Bob for comment. And of course I'd never even put foot in that prayer room. I don't even fucking know where it is.'

I don't imagine many male backbenchers have experienced the joy of having to have these conversations with their boss.

This specific claim wasn't one that Sarah was unique in facing. Apparently I have also been known to use the prayer room for impromptu sexual liaisons. As Sarah said, sexual gossip plays out almost like a meme on social media: 'They refresh it and just put other people's faces in.'

For the record, I, too, have never been to the prayer room. It does seem to be one of the first go-to rumours that gets spread about you though. Being caught having sex with a Comcar driver is another popular one.

Having your sex life – or rumours about your sex life – used against you serves a few different purposes. It can be used to try to put you off your game in the parliament, it can be used to undermine your credibility among your colleagues, or it can just be gossip for people's entertainment.

Labor MP for Kingston Amanda Rishworth told me, 'I think that it is something that is used as a weapon. I had one experience where it was yelled across the House of Representatives chamber, "We all know that you effed such and such". It was deliberately done to make me feel uncomfortable and to undermine me in front of my colleagues.'

Sarah Hanson-Young agreed. 'Yeah, I think it's designed to play with your head. Peta Credlin said [to me], "It's like mind warfare." It is, isn't it? It's meant to get in your head and fuck with you.'

It's a tactic to which even Penny Wong was not immune. 'I think once [Liberal Senator Eric] Abetz made a comment about Jay [former South Australian Premier Jay Weatherill]. I went nuts, like, how dare you? And I think they were all a bit freaked out and it didn't happen again.'

I wish I had sent a few people to Penny so she could have gone nuts on my behalf.

I never experienced these jibes across the parliament from political opponents myself, possibly because, for much of my career, I was already so visibly uncomfortable in the chamber that it wasn't seen as necessary! Parliament, and particularly question time, was never my strong point as an MP. Standing up and pretending to be surprised to be asked a question, or a 'Dorothy Dixer', by one of your colleagues when you had written the question yourself felt so inauthentic to me that I never confidently embraced the theatre of it all. And it showed.

The motivation for the attacks on me was different. The rumours weren't always sexual in nature, but almost always undermined my worth. In politics, people often 'background' you, which means they speak to journalists and spread rumours but do so 'off the record' so that it is never traced back to them. One of my colleagues backgrounded the media that I was known as 'The Pot Plant'. The suggestion was that I looked nice but didn't add any value.

When Tanya Plibersek and I were discussing some of the various rumours that had been spread about us, she brought a new one to my attention. 'You had that whole vajazzling thing to deal with.'

I had no idea what she was talking about. Absolutely none.

She went on to explain that there had been a little piece in one of the papers about how one female minister had taken preparations for the annual Midwinter Ball so seriously that she had been seen earlier that day checking in to a local beauty clinic to be vajazzled. For the uninitiated – and the unvajaz-zled – the practice of vajazzling apparently involves having pretty gemstones and sparkly rhinestones adorned to your pubic mound, to jazz yourself up downstairs.

'The whole parliament was talking about how it was you!' Tanya informed me.

Um, no, that would be drastically overstating my commitment to personal grooming. Even after googling the topic I still have so many unanswered questions – mainly, why?

But I'm sure the rumour did little to boost my credibility or gravitas.

It's tempting to see this sexual weaponisation as just another manifestation of inter-party politics: the same-old Liberal versus Labor but with a sexual twist. That's part of the story, but it's not the whole picture. If it were, surely we'd hear a lot more about men's dodgy sexual encounters. The reality is that there are also plenty of examples of the weaponisation coming from inside your own party.

Ben Smee wrote an explosive report for *The Guardian* in July 2020. He outlined how nine women who sought preselection for the Queensland LNP were asked intensely sexual, explicit questions by the male officials who interviewed them as part of the vetting process. One claimed that she was given a piece of paper and asked to write the names of every man she had ever had sex with. Another said she was questioned about her favourite sexual position. My mind is actually still boggling about what the most 'electable' answer to that question is, and of course the very gall of it being asked.

I was just thirty years old when Kevin Rudd appointed me as the Minister for Youth and Sport and I became Australia's youngest ever federal minister. Why is my age relevant? I think it helps explain in part why I was a target. My elevation to the ministry was not supported by even my own state faction after we had agreed on another candidate but had been overruled by the prime minister. I was as surprised as anyone by my appointment and suspect there were many others who felt stronger emotions than surprise about it. But this is why you get into politics, for the ability to make real change and improve people's lives. Though it was unexpected, of course I was going to grab the opportunity with both hands.

We had just had a huge win in the 2007 election. We had a backbench brimming with talented and ambitious caucus members. Many would have seen themselves as much more suitable and deserving potential ministers than me.

Of course, in politics, you can't be promoted until there is a position open and available. You can wait it out, or you can try to hurry things along. Proving that I was frivolous, unprofessional, stupid or lacking commitment would go a long way towards delivering a vacancy in the ministry for those who felt more deserving of it. Outlandish sexual rumours would be a great way to start.

It is not only vulnerable junior women who receive this treatment either. One of my former colleagues who was promoted to a senior position told me of a conversation two of our male colleagues had regarding her promotion. When one asked why she got the position, the other replied that it was 'because she gives good blow jobs'.

As she pointed out to me, 'That's a lot of blow jobs!'

'I find it unsurprising in our workplace,' she continued somewhat wearily. 'I find it completely unsurprising. I think it's a really easy way of belittling women. It's very easy to dismiss someone as lightweight or, you know, using her feminine wiles. If a bloke is good company, if a bloke knows how to mix it with the fellows, then he's a good bloke. If you want to put down a woman who's doing that, then it very quickly turns to a sexual putdown.'

Clearly, not every bloke in the parliament is an arsehole out to undermine women. There are incredibly good, decent and supportive men on all sides of politics. But we need to be aware of what women may face, where it might originate, and actually make some choices about how we will approach it ... while working towards a time when women won't have to make those choices.

Like many industries, networking and building personal relationships play a vital role in getting ahead in politics, and the power of the boys' club is in what happens away from the workplace. But being seen out and about also hugely increases the amount of gossip spread about you.

Sarah Hanson-Young talked about how the rumours about her started. She believed that the most ridiculous was that she was sleeping with journalist Tony Wright, who she said was 'old enough to be my grandfather'. It was a rumour I had myself heard many times, in the parliament, in media circles and back in South Australia.

'It came from being seen at Aussies [a cafe in Parliament House] having coffee or at the pub having a beer when we were talking about asylum-seeker stuff. He'd been to Manus Island and Nauru before and I hadn't been there. Just being seen, a young female politician talking to an older man in the gallery, people thought, oh, they must be fucking.'

I have no doubt that the rumours about me and Tony Burke started because we were friends and would often be seen talking or having a meal or a drink.

Julia Gillard also noted, 'You know what federal parliament is like. You work hard, but people go out and have a few drinks and stuff too, particularly on Wednesday night, letting off steam. People misconstrue a nice night out with a group of people having a few drinks and a few laughs as having another agenda.'

Sarah Hanson-Young explained the professional consequences of feeling that, as a woman, you weren't free to go out for a drink with other politicians and journalists. 'It cut us out of that conversation and that ability to have influence. Like that's where the real conversations happen. They don't happen in the chamber and mostly don't even happen in people's offices. You work out who's talking to who and about what, if there's any alliances on issues.'

Eventually Sarah decided that being exposed to rumours was a risk she had to take in order to be part of those conversations. But many women raised with me their lack of socialising and networking in comparison to their male colleagues. The potential to be implicated in sexualised rumours if seen out and about adds to the existing power imbalance.

It means that women are left with an impossible choice: do we vacate the sites of information sharing and network building or do we face the reputational consequences of playing the same game as men? Or can we find a third way?

Another issue facing female MPs is how they socialise and deal with the media. For a variety of reasons, female MPs reported having much less inclination to seek out journalists and those with influence without a specific and compelling reason to do so. Julia Gillard noted the ease with which men managed to glide into this parliamentary environment which for women remained confronting.

'Looking back on it now, I realise that a lot of the young men coming into parliament just felt a breezy, easy confidence to take up more space in the world.' She recounted frequently running into male MPs who had been to see the CEOs of major Australian brands just to introduce themselves. 'It always used to rock me back on my heels, like, why would the CEO of a business as big as that make time to see an incoming MP? And what sort of a degree of confidence would you need to have to think that they would reorganise their diary to see you?'

Boys' clubs are far from exclusive to the parliament. Women in many industries still note the informal work and networking done by their colleagues on the golf course, at the pub or in a strip club. I do think this is improving in the broader business community. In politics, however, the exclusive nature of the boys' club is increased due to the possibility that if a woman does venture out into networking territory, she opens herself up to a new range of slurs.

One relatively simple way of attempting to address this would just be to cease participating in the resulting gossip. I have heard so many stories of alleged sexual exploits by one current female government MP that I would be impressed with her time management if even half were true. Each time I was told a rumour I would respond, 'Yeah, right. Do you know how many similar things were said about me?'

And it is certainly not always men spreading this gossip.

Former federal Labor MP Emma Husar has her views on this. 'What I've learnt about slut shaming is that it actually starts with women and then men weaponise it. Women talk about it. Gossip about it. Then it's the men who actually weaponise it in an employment setting and use it to prevent women from getting promotions, women from climbing any further than where the men get. Keeping them constrained.'

For the most part, the sexual gossip stays in the shadows as persistent and undermining rumours. It may seem pretty harmless at times, it may be annoying at others but it can also be something much larger – significant and life-altering lies. Weaponising sexual gossip can be much more dangerous than just rumours. It can end women's careers.

CHAPTER 3
SLUT SHAMING

FOR THOSE UNFAMILIAR with the expression, the Oxford dictionary defines slut shaming as 'the action or fact of stigmatising a woman for engaging in behaviour judged to be promiscuous or sexually provocative'. In 2018 we saw the term linked to our national parliament when two huge stories broke almost concurrently. The attention on these stories drew the spotlight to the treatment of women in Australian politics once more and left many debating why women are having to deal with this in our federal parliament – and why any woman would want to subject herself to a career in parliament.

In July 2018 Greens Senator Sarah Hanson-Young made national headlines when she called out then Senator David Leyonhjelm for what she described as his 'slut shaming' of her in the parliament. During a debate about women's safety he yelled at her to 'stop shagging men'.

The warped implication, we assume, was that if men were so bad then she should not have sex with them, with the added suggestion that it was something she did a lot of. When she approached him to question what he had said he told her to 'fuck off'.

Sarah told Radio National at the time, 'I decided at that moment I'd had enough of men in that place using sexism and sexist slurs, sexual innuendo as part of their intimidation and bullying on the floor of the parliament.'

In contrast, David Leyonhjelm doubled down on his comments, making further slurs and accusations about her in follow-up media interviews on Sky News, 3AW, ABC's *7.30* program and in a media statement posted online.

What many people don't realise is that Sarah had been dealing with comments like this for quite a long time – this was just the moment when she finally decided to do something about it.

Despite the fact that there are only a few metres between the Senate and House of Representatives chambers, politicians in the different chambers don't have a huge amount to do with each other regularly. Although I was in parliament at the time, I don't remember having any awareness of what Sarah had been facing on a regular basis. I assumed that she had an opportunity to call out an awful man on his bad behaviour and publicly shame him for it and that she had taken that opportunity. When I spoke to her about her experience it rapidly became obvious that her actions were motivated by something else too – desperation. She had reached her limit and could no longer brush off the distressing sexist comments she copped with alarming regularity.

Sarah had tears in her eyes as we went through the events that led up to that famous exchange. I was taken by surprise at her reaction and felt guilty that I had been so unaware of the extent of what she had been going through. It shows how hardened those of us in parliament have become.

'For six to twelve months it had just been getting worse and worse,' she told me. 'There had been a number of incidents where I had been on my feet asking questions in question time and the yelling would start. People shouting rumours of who I've done this or that with. People yelling men's names across the chamber. Men they are alleging that I had slept with … It was like a game these blokes were playing with just the most intense level of scorn. And I hated it.'

She started despising being in the parliament – a place where she had previously felt both confident and comfortable. 'I became increasingly anxious about even walking into the chamber. Every time I stood up, this became the sport. It's just really demeaning. Even if people aren't participating in it, they're sitting there watching it. I just thought, oh my god, how humiliating.'

She also found it utterly exhausting. 'It's also the energy that I was spending, trying to put up this kind of force field around me to continue to be standing up every day and taking on the fight and being able to roll with the punches … I even think how I would sit in the chamber was different. I did not want to make eye contact with anybody. I hated question time. I'd rock up late or I wouldn't rock up at all some days. I just hated it.'

This 'game' and the effects it was having on the increasingly fragile senator were not unnoticed by others in the Senate. One of the government's most senior members, Finance Minister Simon Birmingham, noticed and checked in to see if she was okay. 'He said, "Sarah, you really don't seem to be in question time much during this week." And I said, "I can't do it, Birmo. I just can't do it this week." So it was enough for other people to notice.'

The yelling, slurs and accusations continued to grow louder, and their impact started to become more widespread.

'It started affecting me outside of the chamber as well. I'd be sitting in the party room and my portfolio would be the day's front-page story and I'm not wanting to pitch for a question. I don't want to have to stand up in question time. It was having a flow-on effect on my ability to do my job.'

One day, after a particularly bad question time, Sarah returned to her office visibly upset. A friend was waiting for her and was shocked at her appearance. Sarah had so 'normalised' the behaviour that she was now constantly subjected to that she was taken aback when her friend declared that she had to stand up and make it stop.

There are many reasons why women have chosen not to call out this kind of treatment in the past. We don't want to become the issue of the day, we don't want to give the people insulting us the satisfaction of seeing us react and, frankly, it can be really personally embarrassing to draw attention to these sorts of slurs. Sarah Hanson-Young had her own reasons. She didn't think it was either possible or advisable.

'I'd kind of thought, oh, I've just got to deal with it, and I don't want to make a thing of it. I thought, if I stand up now, it's going to make it bigger. And I didn't want to call it out then because I was too afraid that people would go, "Well, what is she hiding? Why is she so upset about this? She can't handle it."'

Although she didn't have a plan, the idea of calling the poor behaviour out, asking for intervention or finding a way to make it stop remained with her – until things came to a head in the Senate in July 2018 with Leyonhjelm's comments.

'I didn't think I was going to stand up publicly, but I thought, I'm just going to go over to him and ask if that's what he said. Surely that will be enough to put this to bed. And when he told me to fuck off, I thought, oh my god, he now knows that it upsets me. He's not going to stop now. I felt totally cornered.'

It is extremely rare for a politician to sue another sitting member, but Sarah decided it was worth it. The court found in her favour, and she was awarded $120,000 in the defamation case, which she donated to women's charities. The judge found that Leyonhjelm's claims about her were 'actuated by malice' and voiced to a 'mass audience with the intention of publicly shaming her'.

The court case was groundbreaking for a couple of reasons. First, it gave a rare and fascinating insight into some of the worst parliamentary behaviour, which usually happens off camera and out of the parliamentary record Hansard. Second, Sarah's response suggested a new way of dealing with this treatment. Rather than the dignified silence that others had employed previously to deal with similar incidents, she was calling it out and literally making him pay. Her strength and courage were commended widely by those from across the political spectrum and even by some media commentators who would probably not classify themselves as fans of hers.

Sarah felt like the whole process made her stronger, and that she'd made progress by calling out the behaviour. I have no doubt that is true. By publicly drawing attention to the issue, she brought this dirty tactic out of the background and showed Australia what sort of behaviour still lurked in our parliament. She contributed to an increasing debate about women's treatment in politics. In doing so, she added to the case for the need for change.

Just a few weeks later, the 'slut shaming' of a female MP would again be one of the biggest news stories in the country.

On 2 August 2018 the online news site BuzzFeed ran one of the most salacious stories ever written about an Australian politician. It was also total garbage.

The story leaked claims about the behaviour of Labor MP for Lindsay Emma Husar, alleging, as she put it in later defamation proceedings, that she was 'a slut who boasts about who she has had sex with, which includes other members of parliament and members of her staff'. Most shockingly it included an allegation that she had performed a 'Sharon Stone move' as per the movie *Basic Instinct* and uncrossed her legs to reveal her vagina to fellow MP Jason Clare as he was sitting on his office floor playing with his toddler son.

The story was immediately denied by both Emma Husar and Jason Clare but it was already out there. BuzzFeed subsequently confirmed that it had made no attempt to contact Emma and put these allegations to her before publishing them.

Emma told me about the moment the story came out. 'I was in my car and my phone just started to light up. And I just thought, what the fuck? I didn't even read the article. I just skimmed it because the headline and photo told me everything that I needed to know. I just fell apart. I don't even remember driving home. I just lost any sort of consciousness of the next three or four days.

'That level of trauma, stress and disbelief and just being completely vulnerable and exposed was like nothing I had ever, ever experienced.'

The contrast between the story and the usually dry content coming out of Parliament House meant that, of course, it spread like wildfire. It was picked up and republished by other websites and took on a life of its own on social media. Husar remembers that 'the worst part about it was how dehumanising that entire experience was. Like they were talking about me, they were writing about me, they were making cartoons about me and there were lots of memes going around the internet about me, as if I wasn't a person.'

Just days after the publication Emma Husar announced that she would not be recontesting her seat. She told Leigh Sales on ABC's *7.30*, 'that's actually what brought my career in politics to an end, was being slut shamed so viciously, with no ability to come back and stand up for myself.'

This is how Emma's story differs from Sarah's. It ended her career. At the time, she was facing a range of other allegations that were being internally investigated. They included bullying and misuse of entitlements. But she believed she would never be able to shake the salacious sexual allegation. The damage was done.

Her ordeal wasn't over though. Emma Husar sued BuzzFeed and journalist Alice Workman for defamation. The organisation argued a truth defence to allegations that Ms Husar was 'sexually perverted' and 'engaged in inappropriate sexualised behaviour toward her staff'. Unbelievably, Husar effectively had to go through a court case to determine whether or not she was a sexually perverted slut.

The case was eventually settled for an undisclosed amount, and BuzzFeed took down the story and acknowledged they should have contacted Emma prior to printing the allegations.

It seems almost unthinkable that such damaging and sexualised stories could be published without first checking with the person involved. But it wasn't without precedent in the world of Australian politics.

Imagine waking one morning, casually opening the newspaper and finding nude or semi-nude pornographic photos of yourself splashed across the front page claiming to be long-lost images from a secret R-rated photo shoot. This is exactly what happened to Pauline Hanson in 2009.

Pauline Hanson is a deeply controversial figure, and not someone I've ever agreed with. Yet no matter what you think of her, what happened to her in 2009 was humiliating. No male politician has ever been subjected to a similar experience. I wanted to speak to Hanson about how this unfolded and how she looks back on it now. I sent off an interview request with no idea how she would respond. I had never spoken to her before and never really expected to. I was nervous as the time of our interview grew near. Then her media adviser emailed me to say Pauline was stuck in the parliament for some votes and she'd call me later. As it turned out, she was happy to talk. She was exactly like the Pauline Hanson I had seen in the media over all of these years.

When I asked about her faux porn exposé she told me, 'I had no idea at all that it was coming.' She had immediately and publicly responded that the pictures were absolutely not her. The paper that had published the photographs, *The Sunday Telegraph*, dug in, with editor Neil Breen stating in *The Daily Telegraph* at the time, 'I have to say that I can't look at those pictures without wondering how someone else could look at them and think it was anyone but Pauline Hanson.'

It was an explosive story that went everywhere. Breakfast TV shows filled slots with forensic analysts, professors and facial anatomists who dissected the photos, talkback radio was ablaze with opinion and debate about the controversy, and across the country people joked or argued about the identity of the provocatively posed redhead. It even made international headlines from South Africa to Asia, Britain to New Zealand.

It got to the unimaginable point where Pauline was offering to publicly reveal her belly button as proof of her innocence.

She was mortified by the experience. 'I have always acted like a lady and to see that photo was humiliating. It was wonderful that my ex-husband came to my defence, along with my family, to assure that it wasn't me.'

After six days of national debate *The Sunday Telegraph* conceded that the pictures were not in fact of Pauline Hanson at all. It is now widely believed that they were instead an unidentified European porn star who may to this day have no idea that she was front-page news in Australia for millions of people.

There are many possible motivations behind media running stories like this. They may honestly believe the stories to be true and somehow in the public interest. They may just think that it's a way to sell lots of newspapers and give little thought to the people involved. Pauline Hanson seemed convinced about the motives behind the publication of the images. She noted the timing, which was just before the Queensland election in which she was running as an independent candidate. 'It was just the low-life media trying to destroy my chances at the election, which was six days away. They ran that story that whole week, and it was just before 6 pm on election day I received a phone call from Neil Breen to say the photo wasn't me. I answered, "I know!" But by then the damage had been done.'

Fortunately for Hanson, it is easier to prove a photograph is a hoax than it is to disprove other sexual allegations, which you can often never completely shake. Hanson successfully sued *The Sunday Telegraph* for defamation and has continued her political career as a federal senator. The newspaper's public apology to Hanson concluded with the line, 'We have learnt a valuable lesson.'

If the lesson was that media outlets should check before running explosive allegations, it is a lesson that Emma Husar no doubt wished all media had learnt. Unlike Hanson, her political career is finished and she remains deeply scarred. She even continues to have recurring nightmares about the incident.

'When they pull you apart like that, limb by limb, and when they make you not human and they invade you like that, it really impacts your ability to live your life day to day, even two years later. You've got no credibility, you've got no dignity anymore.'

I still struggle to find the words to adequately explain the absurdity of the day it nearly happened to me.

It was early on in my time as a minister and I was working in Sydney for the day. I came out of a meeting and the look on my chief of staff's face immediately told me that something very bad was happening.

My chief of staff at the time was Shannon Rees. She was smart, hardworking and completely dedicated. After shepherding my guests out the door I asked her what had happened.

She took a deep breath and then explained that she had just found out a newspaper article about me was going to run on the weekend. My former fiancé had received a call from the national political editor for News Corp Sundays, Glenn Milne, who was writing a piece for the Sunday papers. Milne has vanished from journalism now but at the time wielded significant clout writing for the nation's highest selling newspapers. He apparently asked if my ex would like to comment on the sordid office love triangle that I was involved in, which was supposedly the reason we were no longer getting married.

The story went that I was apparently sleeping with one of my advisers but didn't realise that my chief of staff, Shannon, was sleeping with him too. When we discovered that we were sharing a sexual partner we sat him down and gave him an ultimatum: he had to choose one of us and immediately end things with the other. The justification for this even *being* a story was that the sexual activity and tension within my office was such a distraction that it was destabilising Prime Minister Rudd and the government, which presumably had to work out how to get us all to put our pants back on and get back to work.

If it's not already completely clear, there was not a single element of truth in any of this. But I knew that it didn't matter. In that moment I believed with every ounce of my being that my credibility would never survive this story being printed. I was a new minister. Australians outside of my electorate didn't know me and this was the basis on which they would form their view as to my competence and appropriateness for the role. It would be career ending. I continue to believe that today.

I called the prime minister's press secretary, Lachlan Harris, and explained what was happening. He tried to reassure me that it could never be printed as fact and Milne could only write about it as a rumour that was doing the rounds.

I knew that didn't matter. It wasn't long before this that articles had run claiming that entertainer Tania Zaetta had been allegedly having sex with troops while visiting Afghanistan with the Australian Defence Force. The story was big. The retractions and apology were barely noticed; the damage had been done. I argued that the same would happen to me. You get labelled an unprofessional slut, and it sticks.

Lachlan agreed to do what he could and said he would seek further advice and get back to me. He also warned me that we had to act quickly otherwise it would be on the news list that was circulated nationally. If that happened we wouldn't just have to convince one paper not to run it but instead each of the News Corp Sunday papers across the country.

I tried to go about my day. I had a jam-packed schedule of meetings and events to get through, there were phone calls back and forth and I was also worried about Shannon. As horrible as all of this was for me, I felt desperately protective of her. She was a staff member who had done nothing but work loyally yet she was in the firing line, about to be publicly named and shamed. She would end up being collateral damage. I was concerned for my adviser as he was about to be publicly named too, but he was far less likely to be shamed

I was also booked in that afternoon to do an event discussing – what else? – women in leadership. One of the women's magazines had organised a roundtable discussion to be recorded and photographed for an upcoming feature. As we were being asked to share our insights into the obstacles women continue to face, any barriers women routinely run into and advice we had for other women, I was constantly ducking in and out to take calls and try to save my own career from this very gendered scandal.

By this stage several of these calls were with the prime minister's chief of staff, Alister Jordan, whom Lachlan had enlisted to my cause. Alister quite reasonably asked me to outline to him what truth lay behind this story. If they were going to redirect their efforts from running the country to trying to save me, they wanted to know that it wasn't in vain. I explained that there was none. I had not slept with my adviser, Shannon had not slept with the adviser, there was no conflict or love triangle, the whole thing was pure fantasy. Alister agreed that he would step in and go above Milne to his editor to try to stop the story from appearing.

He later called back, optimistic that they could find a better story to give the paper so they would drop the one about me. But only if I spoke directly to the editor to give him my personal assurance that there was no truth to this story.

So there I was, an Australian federal minister, pleading on the phone to an editor I had never met or spoken to before, and I will always cringe as I remember the exact words I said: 'Honestly, I promise. I've never even kissed him.' How pathetic.

Lachlan and Alister saved me that day. That Sunday an article instead ran about how Malcolm Turnbull had once sought to join the Labor Party. I had dodged the bullet – this time.

I later learnt how widespread this particular rumour about me was. Every single colleague I talked to about my experience confessed that they had heard this gossip, often from several sources. We even discovered a 'Chinese whispers'-style distortion where those in Victoria had heard the adviser chose me after the ultimatum, and those in New South Wales believed he chose Shannon. These weren't just members of parliament; the story was so widespread even people loosely associated with the Labor Party had heard it. And no one had told me about it.

There is no suggestion that Glenn Milne fabricated this story, although he did pursue it without ever once contacting me or my office. The media did not make up this story. It didn't come from my opponents in the Liberal Party. This was not a misunderstanding or an incorrect assumption. There is only one way a story so elaborate and with such knowledge of the composition of my office could be devised and so widely circulated.

It came from my internal colleagues.

CHAPTER 4

SHE'S WEARING WHAT?

KAMALA HARRIS HAD just been elected the first female vice-president of the United States and the first woman of colour to hold that role. Britain's *The Telegraph* chose to celebrate this momentous occasion with the following headline: 'Why Kamala Harris is the modern beauty icon the world needs'.

The article was posted less than an hour after Harris's remarkable victory speech with her running mate, President Joe Biden, in which she drew on her own story as both a woman and an American of joint Indian–Jamaican ancestry to send a message to the US and the entire world that change was possible.

The best *The Telegraph* could do over several hundred words of infantile non-analysis was to talk about how pretty she looked. 'Liner, lashes, lip gloss: beauty tricks behind Kamala,' this penetrating article promised. What a bunch of nonsense. I did not see any such coverage of Joe Biden's beauty regime, although that's not really the issue.

When I was first preselected to run for parliament a male Labor Party elder took me aside and quietly gave me what he thought was helpful advice. It was about my appearance. He was genuinely trying to help me win my seat, and his comments were sincere. But the nature of his advice was a pretty remarkable demonstration of the different expectations faced by an aspiring female MP versus the army of blokes who have dominated all our parliaments without ever thinking about their clothes, their shoes, their hair or their make-up, and the apparent insights all these earth-shattering things provide into our abilities and ideas.

My male colleague told me that, as a newly endorsed candidate, I should cut my long hair short and head into a well-known Adelaide boutique which catered for conservative older ladies. He told me that I should also wear flat shoes, and even suggested that I could start wearing glasses. When I informed him that my eyesight was perfect, he pondered whether we could perhaps get some with plain glass in. He appeared to want to mould me after Margaret Thatcher.

I was a bit flummoxed. Why had they supported me to run for the seat if they wanted someone who looked completely different? How was I meant to go out and make authentic connections with voters if I was pretending to be someone I was not? And more importantly, what is the point of electing young women if we are just going to do our best impersonations of middle-aged men? All of this was reinforcing to me: 'You don't look like a politician. You're different.'

There is nothing new about this kind of treatment. I am sure that if you went back to an earlier political generation, Joan Kirner, Cheryl Kernot and Carmen Lawrence would have many stories to tell showing that the focus on the physical appearance of women in parliament is nothing new. The treatment of Cheryl Kernot provides one depressingly powerful example – when she defected from the Democrats to the ALP, *The Australian Women's Weekly* asked her for a profile piece but insisted that she also take part in a photo shoot and dressed her up wearing an outfit decorated with red feathers. The entire discussion around the article went to her outfit, not her ideas, her motivation for joining the ALP or her ministerial ambitions.

This kind of scrutiny still affects female MPs every day. And it can be truly distracting and destabilising when, no matter what you do or say, there is a focus every day not on how you think and perform, but how you look. When I was interviewing female MPs for this book, the focus on their appearance was the biggest single issue that women spoke to me about. Everybody had a story.

Blair Williams is an Associate Lecturer in the School of Politics and International Relations at the Australian National University. As part of her PhD she studied the manner in which sexist and demeaning comments about female MPs and their physical appearance and outfits have actually become significantly worse since Margaret Thatcher allegedly smashed through the glass ceiling as Britain's first female prime minister in the late 1970s. Williams found there was much more gendered discussion of Theresa May in 2016 than there was of Thatcher in 1979. In an Australian context, Williams also found the same was true of Julia Gillard when she became Australia's first female prime minister in 2010.

'It's getting worse not better,' Williams told the ABC's Triple J in 2020. 'This negatively impacts women in politics as they always have to consider how their appearance, gender and personal life might be portrayed ... When the media present the most privileged and powerful women in our society in this kind of way, then what messages is that sending to women in our country, who are not nearly as privileged or have that same extent of power?'

Julia Gillard told me that Blair Williams's research showed the extent to which women could be trivialised on the basis of their appearance even when they were involved in momentous policy work. If we're focused on what they're wearing then we are missing out on more important things they have to say.

'Some of the stuff printed about Theresa May was unbeliev-able,' she said. 'I mean, things like that photo of her next to the Scottish leader, Nicola Sturgeon, where they were both in skirts with their legs crossed. And it's like, "Forget Brexit – who won Legs-it?"'

As a trailblazing youthful MP, former Australian Democrats Leader Natasha Stott Despoja found herself in the unwinnable position of being asked constantly about her outfits – principally her signature Doc Martens – and then being attacked for being trivial. It got to the point where it was even the stuff of casual conversation within the parliament itself.

'There certainly wasn't a week that went by in the Senate where someone in the parliament didn't comment on how I looked,' Natasha said.

Amanda Rishworth told me about the online feedback she received about her 'messy' hair. Karen Andrews spoke of being told that she looked like she was wearing 'Michael Jackson's jacket'. Sarah Hanson-Young cringed while remembering a magazine running a story about her cleavage being on display. 'It was unbelievable,' she told me. 'I was actually asking a question during question time. It was put to me that, how could I be serious about asking my question when I had my boobs hanging out?'

In Julia Gillard's memoir, *My Story*, she recounts the media coverage of her first day as Australia's first female prime minister. It was largely focused on the coat that she was wearing. The elevation of our first female PM received the sort of vacuous coverage normally reserved for Melbourne Cup Day.

Tanya Plibersek told me there is no doubt there is a massive double standard between the treatment of women and men when it comes to appearance. 'For women, be it consciously or subconsciously, what you look like counts for or against you much more than it does for the blokes. It doesn't matter how old or ugly men are, they are fine in politics. But women will be overlooked or put down if they are too pretty or too young. And then they can also be overlooked if they are too old and not pretty.'

It often seems like we cannot win.

You might think that after decades of women in parliament, female MPs and their physical appearance might no longer be regarded as such a source of fascination, as though we were a novelty. Although perhaps it is not surprising when you consider that, other than some variations in facial hair, male politicians have looked pretty much the same for hundreds of years now: middle-aged blokes in suits and ties. To this day I am still not sure what the mould for female politicians is meant to be. I am not the only woman who tried unsuccessfully to fit myself in it, aided by my older Labor Party friend who wanted to take me to the frumpiest frock shop he could find.

Julie Bishop told me a similar story of 'helpful' advice. 'When I became aged care minister, one of the senior advisers in Prime Minister Howard's office rang me with a specific request that I not dress like a corporate lawyer anymore, but to dress like an aged care minister. I said, "I have no idea what you're getting at." He said, "Less Armani, more cardigans."

'I laughed, until I realised they were serious. I did it for a while, and tried to change my style of dressing, more like what I thought was expected of me. But that changed, as it was ridiculous; it had to be me.'

One after another it seems that women in politics have tried to fit in with some unspecified set of rules about how we look and what we wear.

Sarah Hanson-Young told me how she overhauled her entire wardrobe on arriving in Canberra. 'When I first came in, I bought a suit. I never wear suits. And I remember the first few weeks I was just so uncomfortable. I was pretending, and I wasn't me, so eventually I said to myself, I'm not going to dress like all these blokes here, just ditch it.'

Hanson-Young said the pressure to wear suits is part of the parliament's way of flattening out women's identities and reinforcing the male personality of the place.

'There is something about dressing like the men in that building and taking on the persona of the men. It's taken me a long time to realise that's actually what I'm trying to resist, as much as just being myself and trying to be comfortable. I need to concentrate on what it is that I'm saying and what I'm working on, as opposed to the other bits.'

When I arrived in Canberra in 2004, I tried to ensure that people's preoccupation with the physical appearance of female MPs wasn't an issue I had to face. I had put some thought into what I would wear on the day I arrived. Like many twentysomethings who needed a new professional-looking outfit, I had gone to Cue to buy something sensible and unremarkable. I'd settled on a nondescript blue-grey pinstripe pantsuit. Professional, but not too 'look at me, look at me'. I teamed it with a simple black camisole and some standard black heels. I pulled my long hair off my face in a neat low ponytail that could never be described as glamorous. I entered the chamber excited to be sworn in as a real-life politician.

I was surprised the following day to see that I had been mentioned in two different newspapers even though I had done nothing more than been sworn in along with every other member of the House of Representatives. I hadn't even spoken in parliament yet! *The Age* ran a piece which stated, 'Kate Ellis – who seems a lot younger than her 27 years – looked like she was on a day out to the cricket'. *The Daily Telegraph* wrote that, 'new girl Kate Ellis donned impossibly tight pants'. Shit. This was actually my best effort at dressing the way I thought a politician was supposed to. What the hell was I meant to wear?

As she so often does, Tanya Plibersek bluntly summarised what women need to aim for to best avoid attention. 'It's sort of blandness that you're going for. It's not too pretty. Not too ugly. Somewhere in the middle. Unremarkable. That's the sweet spot for women.'

Do we all then aim to be unremarkable women? Is that what we want in parliament? And does trying to be unremarkable actually undermine women's ability to do their jobs? It is here that women seem to take two starkly different approaches.

Julia Gillard has considered, spoken and written about this issue at length.

'You can know it's going to happen and deliberately step up your appearance,' she told me, 'and therefore try to turn the inevitable commentary into positive commentary. Or you can try to minimise the commentary cycle by effectively adopting a uniform. And this is the great benefit that men have basically day after day. You just wear the same uniform: shirt, tie, suit, job done. So I went that route of increasingly trying to get a more and more standard look, in the hope that it would take appearance issues out of the question.'

Julia pointed to German Chancellor Angela Merkel as the standout for 'having adopted the uniform'. Merkel always wears black pants and a coloured jacket in the same style. It seems she made a conscious choice early on to take her clothes out of the equation.

In the past women were able to get ahead in traditionally male spheres by trying to 'out-male' the men. This meant doing things like ensuring they remained unemotional, taking on assumed male traits – and adopting power dressing. It does lead me to wonder though, what is the point of including women if we are going to spend our time trying to imitate men? Shouldn't we be celebrating the things that make us different? Shouldn't we all be able to express our own style?

The former US secretary of state and presidential candidate Hillary Clinton described female political dress as a form of male mimicry. 'When Hillary Clinton was first coming up in the world as a female lawyer,' Julia Gillard told me, 'she noticed there was a very structured dress code for female lawyers. And it was absolutely the female version of the male suit. You'd have the jacket, the skirt and you'd have a shirt with a little pussy bow. It's almost like a fake tie.'

Julie Bishop decided to go the other way.

'I have always loved fashion, ever since I was a little girl, and I had a professional career before going into parliament. I had worked in law firms for twenty years. I had developed a certain professional style and had adopted dress standards that I thought appropriate for a career professional.

'So when I went into politics, it was natural for me to combine what I thought was a professional standard of dress with my love of fashion. Over time, I did find that it was used as a supposed weapon against me, suggesting that if I were interested in fashion,

I could not be interested in serious political issues – as if they were mutually exclusive. The more that it was raised, the more determined I was to not let others define who I was or how I dressed or what I could achieve. Being authentic was far more important than playing to the rules that were being set for me by others.

'It almost became a badge of honour to be ridiculed for your fashion sense. It said a lot more about the people who were focusing on it. They sought to criticise me because I loved fashion? Guilty as charged.

'The funny thing is that the young women who followed me on social media gave me heart – it was clear that they appreciated that I was in a serious career but that I was open about my interest in Australian fashion.'

This is an important point. Many people outside the parliament appreciated seeing someone who was more human, showed actual personality, and was therefore someone they could better relate to.

Julie Bishop was definitely not going to be confined to a certain look.

'I remember my last budget night before I left parliament. I was looking through my wardrobe and I thought, okay, I'm sitting up on the backbench but there's no reason to hide away. I think this blue sequin number will do for tonight.'

Julia Gillard hopes that fashion standards and expectations will change for both women and men.

'I think it's going to be interesting to watch. The optimist in me says it's a fantastic direction that things are loosening up. Maybe over time we'll see men going into the parliament without a tie on.

'The pessimist in me says the greater the variety, the greater the space for this to be an issue. I'm genuinely conflicted about it. I don't know which is the best thing to strive for. A hundred per cent taking it out of the equation, which many women would experience as a stifling of their own personal creativity, or trying to get the world to accept that women are going to be more creative about their dress, but don't expect it to be commented on. So it's a difficult line.'

Maybe men see wearing a suit and tie as stifling. I suspect that most would see it as convenient. It's one less thing to have to think about. Regardless of what we wear, the conversation often goes beyond women's clothes anyway. Our hair, our noses, our boobs, our 'arses' have all become popular talking points at times.

No matter how you choose to address the challenge, the reality is that there are consequences of this fascination with women's looks and appearance. For me, there is no question that I suffered from imposter syndrome in the first years of my political career. The American Psychological Association characterises imposter syndrome as occurring 'among high achievers who are unable to internalize and accept their success. They often attribute their accomplishments to luck rather than to ability, and fear that others will eventually unmask them as a fraud.' I didn't have to fear being unmasked as a fraud. It happened daily. I didn't look like a politician, I didn't dress appropriately for a politician, I didn't fit the mould of a politician. And all of this was constantly reinforced.

Like me, Sussan Ley's seat in the parliament was the seat directly behind the despatch box where people like the prime minister or leader of the opposition would stand to speak. This is a pretty common and transparent political tactic – the overwhelmingly male-run parliament stick a few women behind the PM to create the illusion of gender balance for those watching on television. The consequence is that you are in the television shot whenever anybody on your side is speaking. Sussan told me how every single day she would return to her office and get public feedback on her physical appearance. Someone didn't like the colour she was wearing, someone didn't like her hairstyle, her lipstick, her jacket.

She said the attention was constant but that she chose not to let it bother her. Instead, she drew on her own efforts in obtaining a pilot's licence to remind herself of her own achievements, and that the hard work she put in to achieve this was far more important than what others thought of how she looked. 'My sense of self-worth has never been connected to my personal appearance,' she explained.

But why should women have to find strategies to cope with this attention? Why is the onus on women to solve the problem, to become resilient, rather than trying to change the focus on their appearance in the first place?

And of course, there are also other consequences of this attention on women's appearance. Julia Gillard noted that one of the biggest of these was less time in her diary.

'It's measured in hours of lost time,' she said. 'Before I was prime minister, all those years, I did the *Today* show debate with Tony Abbott on a Friday. So I'd come out of Canberra after a spirit-crushing, mind-numbingly huge parliamentary week. You'd dash on a flight to Sydney, get up ridiculously early Friday morning to be across all of the newspapers and media. And I used to get to Channel Nine at six thirty in the morning for make-up and hair. And we used to go to air about ten past seven. Tony would meander in at about three minutes past seven. I always bloody resented that half hour.'

Natasha Stott Despoja shared her experience of this assumption that women would put the time in to keep themselves looking nice.

'I remember going back to work after having my son Conrad. And I thought, you know, by then I'm in my thirties. I'm older, wiser, in theory. And I dressed up for work. I'd colour-coordinated. I was ready to take on the world.

'And I remember *The Australian* did a piece saying, "Well, we know she's just had a baby, but you think she could make a bit more effort with her outfits." I just thought at the time, are you kidding me? I'm juggling a baby in the parliament, and working around the clock, and you're worried about how stylish my outfit is?'

Sarah Hanson-Young said this focus on appearance has the extraordinary ability to overshadow every other aspect of a female MP's working life.

'You have to put in all this effort because the last thing you want is somebody seeing you on the television in question time asking a question and if you look like shit, that's all people are going to talk about. They're not going to hear what you've said. I can have the most brilliant question and it doesn't mean anything.

'We really can't win either way. If you're attractive, you're too attractive. If you dress too nicely, that's all you care about. You don't care about substance. But if you don't [dress well], you're a fugly bitch. There's no nice balance. Some days you're a bimbo, other days you're a bitch. Sometimes both things happen on the same day – you're a bimbo in the morning and you're a bitch by the afternoon. That's just the way it is.'

All this attention on appearance comes with a financial cost. Julia Gillard said it was also one more thing women in politics have to think about, unlike the blokes who are set up with three navy and two black suits.

'It's just another track in your head,' she said. 'You've got television cameras following you around because you're going to a school, because you want to make a point about school funding and the government's reform agenda. You're relating to the people around you. You want to get the message out there. You're conscious of the television cameras and you've got to be conscious of how you're going to look on those television cameras, rather than just relating to the people around you and focusing on the message. So it's another track.'

One of the most important objectives for any member of parliament is to be able to effectively communicate your message to the Australian public. This is the very bread and butter of our profession. Your measure of success is being able to get coverage on the issue, policy or announcement that you are trying to convey. But there are limits on how much newspaper column space or TV news coverage will be dedicated to any MP. It's hard enough to get the message out; knowing that any airtime focused on your appearance is time lost on your political message is even more frustrating. So it does harm you. It limits the effectiveness of female MPs getting their message out, and for politicians that is a huge price to pay.

Most women I spoke to had several stories about times when their message was overshadowed by their outfit or looks on the day. Like them, I have experienced many of these moments, but there are two that stand out.

I don't just groan aloud about revisiting the *Grazia* magazine story about me. I actively avoid it. This whole book was almost completed with a line saying 'Insert *Grazia* story here' before I could finally bring myself to revisit the whole absurd affair. I don't want to think about it, I don't want to talk about it, and I really don't want to write about it. But it's often still the story that many people associate with me, my little version of the photo of Alexander Downer in fishnet stockings. It would seem an odd omission if I didn't mention it.

After the 2007 election I entered the Rudd Government's first ministry as the Minister for Youth and Sport. There had not been a Minister for Youth for some time after the position was abolished by the Howard Government. I took the opportunity seriously. I wanted to represent young Australians on the issues that mattered to them and make sure their voice was being heard.

The 2007 Mission Australia Survey of Young Australians revealed that body image was the number one issue concerning our youth. I thought it was important to listen and act on the issues they identified and not just the issues we thought should be of concern to them. So we created a Body Image Taskforce to develop concrete recommendations on how to address the issue and produce a media code of conduct. The research showed that we had a generation growing up being bombarded by unprecedented levels of unrealistic imagery. Digital technology was ensuring that 'perfection' was displayed in every featured body shape, skin tone and appearance and that girls in particular were suffering enhanced anxiety and going to extreme lengths to try to meet these 'ideals'.

I wanted to speak directly to the young women most affected. *Grazia* was a leading fashion magazine at the time, and they contacted me to be part of a body image story that would cover how big the issue was and let their readers know how unrealistic the images that they portrayed were, how much photoshopping and digital altering they did and why the ideal that they portrayed was in fact completely unattainable. I thought it was a brilliant idea.

So far so good, right? I sat down with *Grazia* and did an interview highlighting the extent of the body image issue. Still good. We did a photo shoot where I got to wear the most amazing suit and shoes. I would never afford or be likely to wear anything as luxurious ever again. We made it clear that we were leaving the pictures untouched to make a point about photoshopping and re-touching images. Still good. This was a fine idea. Until the very last bit. The stylist suggested we just take a couple more photos in a different outfit. She picked out a tight leather dress. She teamed it with a pair of studded black

Gucci heels. Uh-oh. At the time I thought, well, it's not really my style, but it is their magazine. I'll go with it if it means getting my message out there. You can probably guess which picture they ran.

The article was published in the very slow news cycle just before the Easter break. The photos were picked up by everyone. Newspapers ran them, TV news stories featured them, talk-back radio and chat shows dissected them, mass outrage and controversy ensued. Did I get my message out to the target audience of *Grazia* readers? Maybe. I was naive and foolish to not realise that I would also be sending out a different message to the broader public, who had no idea of the context. That message was that I was a vacuous show pony, allegedly unfit to be a government minister. The images completely eclipsed any message I was trying to deliver.

Yet the truth is that sometimes it doesn't actually matter what you do, or how careful you are about what you wear; your message can still be overshadowed.

In June 2011 Fairfax's *Sunday Life* magazine ran an interview with me about women in leadership roles. I was the Minister for the Status of Women at the time and proud to be working on the establishment of the Workplace Gender Equality Agency. It was a contentious proposal as we were going to mandate compulsory reporting by companies on the gender composition in their organisations and on their boards. They would have to report on their employment conditions and on their employees' access to flexible work practices. This would be publicly reported annually. There would be consequences for non-compliance, including the loss of all government contracts. Though we were also providing funding and support to help companies improve their performance in these regards, business groups and the opposition were up in arms. The Business Council of Australia's stated position was that it did 'not support any additional business reporting on workplace gender equity issues'.

We had a fight on our hands. I was passionate about the policy and convinced that shining a public spotlight on gender equality in the workplace would encourage real and lasting progress. When I was approached by *Sunday Life* to speak on the issue of women in leadership roles as their cover story, I jumped at the suggestion. Having learnt from the *Grazia* ordeal, I also insisted that the photo shoot would only be done in appropriate office wear. So that's what we did. A high-neck, long-sleeved pink pussy-bow blouse, a knee-length pencil skirt and some gorgeous aqua heels. Again, I thought, what could possibly go wrong?

A few weeks after the story, *Sunday Life* ran a follow-up. It featured the same photograph but this time under the headline, 'What's wrong with this picture?' The article explained that the criticism they received following the original publication was 'relentless'. As the journalist wrote at the time, '*Sunday Life* received a sizeable spike in reader mail after the Minister for the Status of Women, Kate Ellis, appeared on our cover ... Ellis was interviewed for our story on why women were still not breaking through the glass ceiling in business and politics. But the responses were not about the story. More than a few of our readers (almost all of them women) viewed Ellis's make-up, clothes and, in particular, her shoes as inappropriate.'

Specific comments included: 'If you are railing against discrimination, why intentionally dress somebody up like a model to illustrate the article, which has the result of demeaning Ellis and all those other women who try to be taken seriously in a discriminatory world?'

Another wrote, 'The wearing of super high stiletto heels represents women as vain, attention-seeking, foolish and potential victims'.

But it wouldn't have mattered if I was in different shoes; one woman wrote to me complaining of the pink shirt as if I were trying to 'look like Barbie'. Another thought my long hair made me look more like the secretary than a minister.

The only conclusion that those hundreds of women who were outraged enough to put pen to paper took out of that article was that they really, really did not like the way I looked. Well, I suspect it was also that they didn't like me. Didn't like me then, won't like me now and probably won't like this book either. A lot of people feel a real tension between women espousing views on gender equality while also adhering to what they see as stereotypical views on women's presentation. I understand that. I also believe that women can make choices, can be creative, can wear what they think suits their style.

For what it is worth, the Workplace Gender Equality Agency was established in 2012 with mandatory reporting requirements for business. It has become an important organisation and its annual reports shine a spotlight on the progress being made for women at work. The organisation also offers vital support to encourage businesses to establish best practice and to receive public recognition when they do.

The circumstances don't have to be so extreme to damage women politicians though. Polling has shown that any focus on a female MP's appearance damages her credibility.

In 2013 a study was released by 'Name It. Change It', a US project run by the Women's Media Center and She Should Run. It surveyed voters across America on their views about the appearance of female political candidates. It found that any time a woman's physical appearance was mentioned, whether in a positive or negative sense, it made voters less likely to vote for her. Specifically, it found that every mention of that woman's looks led voters to believe that she was less qualified, less effective, less likeable and less confident. Every single key trait that determined a candidate's electability was damaged. Despite the fact that the physical appearance of male politicians received much less attention, this study also found that when it was mentioned it did no damage to that male candidate's standing. It was only women who received this level of focus and it was only women who were hurt by it.

If we are to believe this research, it's hard not to conclude that this issue is an ongoing problem that almost solely affects female MPs, and one that is harming their electability and career progression.

So, what do we do about it?

The Name It. Change It. survey concluded that the only way a female MP or candidate can regain the ground that they lose through this focus on their looks or appearance is by calling out the coverage as unacceptable. We saw this in Australian politics when South Australian Liberal MP Nicolle Flint called out a local newspaper columnist who detailed in great length her clothing and footwear choices. She filmed a video that was spread widely on social media, where she ended by taking off her trench coat to reveal that she was wearing a garbage bag, while asking the question, 'What would you like me to wear? A garbage bag?'

By late 2020, the video had been watched 277,000 times, and had spread around the world. I have no doubt it was effective in ensuring that the newspaper columnist will think twice before writing similar articles. It may also discourage others from doing the same. What I am not yet sure of is what it does for Nicolle Flint, or any other woman calling it out, when they receive more coverage for talking about themselves and standing up against this ongoing problem than they get for their work in the community or fighting for the electorate. It is the catch-22 that takes us back to the struggles of getting your message out.

The answer must surely be for others to stand up and call it out too: not just the women affected but their colleagues, from all sides of the political divide, the media and the general public. Only a broad pushback will ever see this treatment stop.

This is a long way from where we are today, not just in Australia but around the world. That piece on Kamala Harris's physical appearance at her acceptance speech was followed by another, written by Rebecca Reid for *The Huffington Post*: 'Don't call me a bad feminist for wanting to know about Kamala Harris' makeup'. I don't know if Reid would like to also acknowledge that her article means yet more column inches not dedicated to Harris's policies, aspirations or achievements.

CHAPTER 5

SOCIAL MEDIA MADNESS

THE MEDIA HAS always had its role to play in how Australian women in politics are portrayed, with its ever-shortening news cycles, its ability to twist and turn public opinion, and its willingness to spill private details or pass comment when it comes to female politicians in particular. But now there is a whole new category of media to deal with: social media.

Everyone gets abused on social media. When you're in public life the abuse is worse, whether you're in politics, sport, an actor or a celebrity. Both men and women cop the flak, but as is always the case, women cop it differently and cop more in sheer volume. After a while sexualised threats and attacks on our appearance start to feel standard. Beyond that there is a disturbing sense of indignation bordering on hatred demonstrated by some at the very fact that as women we have dared to enter public life at all. It manifests in the ease with which so many people will openly throw around terms like 'bitch' and 'slut' in their social media attacks on women.

Amanda Rishworth had a story that demonstrated how different the experiences with social media are for male and female MPs. A male colleague of hers had just checked his Twitter messages and exclaimed in outrage: 'I can't believe I've been accused of being inconsistent.' She laughed and responded, 'Hang on a second, let's have a look at my latest messages. Here we go, I've just been told that I am no better than that red-headed slut.'

Current female MPs benefit every day from the trailblazing work of women who went before them and who paved the way for my generation and those that lie ahead. The emerging and often confronting frontier of social media is probably the only area where we now find ourselves the pioneers, grappling with a phenomenon that is both new and changing all the time.

Study after study shows the disproportionate levels of abuse, threats and trolling that women receive online. Australia Institute research commissioned by Ginger Gorman for her 2019 book *Troll Hunting* showed that women were more likely than men not only to be harassed online, but also to receive harassment in the form of abusive language, unwanted sexual messages, and threats of sexual abuse, rape, violence and death. Thousands of people know what trolling feels like and how it differs from a real-life argument that is more likely to escalate gradually. It's also heightened by people's ability to remain anonymous. Even if they aren't anonymous, people seem to feel like social media puts them at a comfortable enough distance to disregard the rules of civility that people generally follow face to face. You can be cuddling your children when you are suddenly exposed to sexualised slurs, relaxing on the couch when you get bombarded by vile insults, or peacefully raising a glass with your partner when the moment is interrupted by horrific threats. This affects all women but is amplified if you have a public profile. It happens a lot. All the time, day and night.

The thing about being a politician is that whatever your political party there is a substantial element of the population who passionately dislike you, no matter what you say or do. Members of parliament are seen as 'being on the public purse' and as such are regarded as fair game. We are not alone in this regard – a quick run through the social media feedback that the ABC's Leigh Sales, and to a lesser extent David Speers, receives indicates that being taxpayer-funded gives trolls a sense of ownership over you. In my opinion, Sales and Speers are among Australia's best journalists. I couldn't guess which way either of them voted. This is probably the reason that they attract incoming fire from both ends; they are not cheerleaders for either extreme. In politics, though, you have to listen and it's expected you will answer, no matter the tone of critique you are receiving. Social media allows people to say things they would never dream of saying to someone's face. It can be ugly, even violent, and it is regularly abusive.

For the purposes of research I took a charming little stroll down memory lane and did a search of my incoming Twitter messages. Most common among the abuse I received were messages along the lines of, 'Kate Ellis is nothing but a hair flicking bimbo. Deliberately mendacious and duplicitous'. Occasionally I got gems that ticked every box, like this one: 'I hate this f@cking bitch commo pinko slut Adelaide bitch'. That bloke seemed nice.

The magnitude of incoming venom was shown in a 2018 study of 778 female journalists and MPs from the US and UK conducted by Element AI and Amnesty International. It found over 1.1 million abusive tweets were sent to these women. That averages one sent every thirty seconds.

The problem for everyone in politics is that we have to take part in public life, which means there's an expectation that we will be accountable and available to both the public and the media. My question is, on what terms? When you team the level and nature of the abuse with the fact that it is an important part of your job to be accessible and listen to feedback, this makes for a dangerous combination. Usually the advice on trolling is to just get off social media, but when it is a major part of your job to communicate and have a public profile it is not so simple. It builds and builds, an avalanche of ugly feedback. What often happens is you either begin to have a skewed idea of the community's view on whatever issue it is, or you have a much more negative view about yourself. It is so worrying that the most senior women I spoke to in Australian politics all expressed their deep concerns about these social media attacks, and the impact they could have on newly elected women still finding their feet.

I remember the moment when I realised that social media wasn't the place where normal, rational conversations and debates took place. Twitter was still pretty new and I was single and living on my own at the time. One night I heard my phone make the notification ding, and was a bit bemused to see that I had been included in a Twitter conversation between two men that was along the lines of 'How many cocks do you reckon @KateEllisMP sucked to get her preselection?!' (original line, boys). I would normally just ignore such rubbish but I'd had a hard week, was finally home relaxing and just thought, I don't need to be disturbed by this in my rare downtime. I didn't want to have to be part of the responses and conversation that followed, so I blocked these two men, the first people that I ever blocked.

Pretty soon my phone was singing ding, ding, ding, ding – my notifications had gone bananas. When I looked I was surprised to see that I had become the subject of my first Twitter 'pile-on', where an angry mob of people came from all corners to join in the abuse. One of the blokes had tweeted how disgusting it was that, as his local member, I had blocked him on Twitter. He said that I clearly couldn't handle hearing anyone's opinions that didn't line up with my own. Bizarrely, a local woman who worked in PR and had a social media following had also tweeted about this disgusting behaviour of mine and, soon after, I was being widely condemned.

I felt disbelief. This was madness. How on earth was I the bad guy? I politely sent the PR woman a direct message suggesting she go back and have a look at the offending tweet they had sent me. She responded, 'He's saying u r blocking many though'.

Over a decade has now passed since that experience and

I don't think it would happen today. The general awareness of social media abuse is higher and the fact that there are a number of legitimate ways to deal with trolls is now understood. That certainly doesn't mean that there aren't still issues and unanswered questions for women, particularly high-profile women, to grapple with.

Julia Gillard explained to me that she saw herself as part of the 'transition generation'. She was already well established when social media entered political life. She had proven her credibility and done all of the big and scary high stakes TV interviews more than once. She was also already senior enough to have enough staff to manage her social media. She remains deeply concerned about the women who come after her though.

'When you're starting to do your first few TV interviews, the first time you go on *Insiders*, the first time you go on *7.30*, the first time you get asked to do an AM interview, these are all big moments. For each of those first engagements when you're starting in parliament, imagine that what looms in your mind is vile stuff about whether you're fat, thin, tall, short, blonde, brunette, pretty, ugly, good jacket, bad jacket, all of the stuff that happens to women all the time now. I think it would be so spirit crushing when you're already so tense about those big milestone media engagements.'

Penny Wong felt a similar concern for women starting their parliamentary careers. 'I suspect for someone like me who's got a reasonable number of staff, you can put in place systems that protect you just by virtue of the staff dealing with it. But if you're a backbencher and you're new and you still like doing a lot of your own Facebook and Twitter and engaging with people, that can expose you to this abuse.'

I was elected later than both Julia Gillard and Penny Wong. Social media was not as big as it is today when I first entered parliament in 2004 – Twitter, YouTube and Instagram hadn't even been invented then – but by the time I became a minister it was starting to take off and its impact was being felt.

I thought back to the first time that I was a guest on *Q&A*. It was back in 2009 at the peak of its popularity when hundreds of thousands of people tuned in each week. I was up against Tony Abbott on the panel. I was nervous and full of adrenaline. We debated the alcopops tax that was currently before the parliament. I felt like the host, Tony Jones, had forgotten that there were others on the panel and was trying to trip me up on the detail, but I was well across it. Bettina Arndt was also on the panel, leading to an unusual conversation on our different views on women and gender politics. I remember when I got off the stage seeing that I had received hundreds and hundreds of messages and emails. I eagerly delved into them, keen to see how people thought I went. About half of them thought I was amazing, an inspiration! I should be prime minister one day! I was brilliant! The other half thought I was a bimbo, an airhead, a dumb slut, an embarrassment to my electorate and to the Australian parliament, someone who should be locked away and not allowed to do media ever again.

It seems silly now that I didn't instantly recognise that many of the responders were probably heavily invested in one party or another and would have already made up their minds.

They were politically engaged enough to spend their spare time watching politicians talk, and many came to the table with their already firmly formed partisan views. Instead I did what I suspect too many people are prone to do: I took the negative to heart while glossing over the positive feedback. I would just have to do better next time. I'd have to work harder to win them over. I was setting myself an impossible task.

It's pretty natural for people to want feedback or a performance indicator of how they are going in their job. Workers in other professions know how they are going because they often get results-based feedback – they won the case, they landed the contract, they sold lots of product. Politicians don't get any of that feedback. We get an election every few years but that is not necessarily decided on whether an individual is doing a good job but rather which party people like, the demographics of the seat and the key policy issues at election time. So when it comes to your individual performance, you're actively looking for feedback. It's human nature, and it is also human nature to dwell on the worst of it.

Of course the big picture here is that nobody should have to cop this kind of abuse online or elsewhere. Everyone on social media has a responsibility to remember that the people on the other end are actually human and not some abstract being to be used for target practice. We need to have a debate about how we can get social media companies to meet their responsibilities and reduce the widespread bullying on their platforms. In the meantime, female MPs need to make a decision on how we treat this incoming feedback. Is this yet another space that we have to vacate, or should we stay and be accessible and remain part of the conversation? The female MPs that I spoke to had vastly different views on this.

Amanda Rishworth would, I suspect, be regarded by all sides of politics as a workhorse of a local member. She won a marginal seat in South Australia off the other side of politics in 2007 and then worked harder than many would find humanly possible to turn it into one of the safest seats in South Australia. She attributes part of that success to a commitment to staying engaged, while carefully sorting through the abuse to find the feedback that is meaningful.

'One of the things that you've got to be really careful about is being willing to listen to constructive feedback. It can be really important. You don't want to get to the point where you get all this negative feedback so you block everything and develop a tin ear by not actually listening to people who are offering constructive feedback. It is hard, though, when you have to wade through so much incoming personal criticism and then sort through what is legitimate criticism of my party, about my behaviour, about my performance and what are just personal attacks that aren't true.'

Karen Andrews shared that view. 'I've always handled negative criticism by really assessing whether or not there's any truth in what's being said. And sometimes they've got a point. Sometimes they don't. Often if we get unpleasant emails into the office, I will ring the person myself and they'll calm down because basically they want to be heard. As soon as you indicate that you are prepared to listen to what they have to say, they are pretty reasonable. So that's the way that I've dealt with it.'

Of course, Karen's approach really only works with legitimate criticism, not abuse, anonymous or otherwise. Like many female MPs, Karen has now decided that Twitter is not for her and deleted the app from her personal devices. 'I think Twitter's gone beyond what is acceptable. You're not actually getting a clear view of what the community wants. You're getting a very discrete feedback. And it's just not worth it. It can give you a very incorrect view of what people are thinking because it really is a place for keyboard warriors to say and do things that they would not normally say and do. But they do it under cover of a Twitter handle or another fake name on Facebook.'

She has no regrets about the move.

Several other female MPs told me they've now abandoned the platform altogether. Some said they dictate messages which their staff post on their behalf so they can still get their message out but not be exposed to the return fire. Many are of the view that social media causes more problems than it solves and gives you such a slanted view of public opinion as to be completely counterproductive. I can certainly attest that the opinions I received on Twitter were frequently at total odds to the ones I heard at my local community street corner meetings with residents.

Sometimes social media can be so absurd as to actually be helpful. I was set free from the power of negative feedback by one simple tweet during a much later *Q&A* appearance. Someone wrote, 'Who does she think she is kidding with all the botox and the hair extensions?' Yet another person who vastly overestimated my commitment to personal grooming. It was a light bulb moment for me: *These people don't actually know anything about me. They are just trying to get a rise.* Just like that, their power over me evaporated.

━━

I was a marginal seat MP so I felt it was critical that I stayed in touch and heard directly from my community. Throughout my career every email to my public email account, every tweet, every Facebook message came directly to my personal phone. I wanted to see it all. It is part of our job to be in touch with public sentiment. One of the benefits of being on social media is that it does give you a real-time account of how public sentiment is tracking. I can remember that whenever there were developments on an issue like live animal exports, or when there had been a tragedy involving livestock at sea, my phone would literally light up with negative feedback. These weren't people who had an axe to grind or were ideologically obsessed, they were just casual voters who were expressing their disgust about something, as is their right. The issue is when the abuse is personalised and aggressive, or just mindless and based not around policy but about the fact that you exist at all.

I have never had to deal with the full force of social media in a way that too many women and several of my colleagues have. Inevitably, there is of course an intersectional impact here too. Amnesty International UK did an analysis of the online abuse directed at 177 MPs in the United Kingdom in 2017. They found that although only a tiny percentage of the women were Black, Asian and Minority Ethnic (BAME), those women received a vastly disproportionate number of abusive tweets.

Shockingly, they found that almost half of the 25,688 abusive tweets that they tracked were directed at just one woman, Diane Abbott, the first black woman ever elected to the House of Commons. As Julia Gillard said when we spoke about the analysis, 'She was getting 158 vile, sexist and racist social media posts a day. And she actually took a bit of leave towards the end of that campaign [the 2017 UK election campaign]. How much pressure would you have to be feeling under to take the last week of a campaign away from campaigning? I mean, astronomical. But that's how ugly it is. I really don't know how I would have coped with it.'

It's clear that receiving 158 vile posts a day would have an impact on anyone. What we can also predict is the impact it has on every woman of colour watching this unfold online and making decisions about their own ambitions for public life. It's not much of an advertisement.

Anne Aly spoke in her 2018 memoir, *Finding My Place*, of the Islamophobia she regularly faces. Graphic hate mail, threatening phone calls. I shudder to think what her social media inboxes would look like.

Penny Wong told me the story of how she announced the birth of her second child with a photo of her older daughter sitting on the couch holding her newborn sister. 'It was beautiful,' Penny recalled. *The Advertiser* ran the story online along with the picture, and presented the story as it was, a happy and joyful family moment. What happened next was horribly predictable. Comments flowed in focused on Penny's sexuality, her race, and speculation about the child's father. 'They actually had to shut down the comments because they got so much negative stuff,' Penny explained. 'That made me sad.' This was not a political story. It was the announcement of the birth of a healthy baby.

I think back to the excitement, pure joy and pride I had after my children's birth and how I wanted to share the news far and wide, as if no one had ever had a baby before. I actually can't even begin to comprehend what it must have felt like to have that news met with such hate. You wouldn't even have to read the comments; just knowing of their existence would hurt.

———

This is the power that social media has handed to a bunch of screwed-up numbnuts sitting in their bedrooms spewing hate. It makes me angry. But it's not limited to crazies; there are a vast variety of people generating vicious comments, from people who enjoy getting a rise out of posting the most offensive thing possible to people who are genuinely aggrieved about a particular issue and lash out in ways they probably wouldn't in person.

It has also unleashed another dangerous power, that of 'fake news'. Courtesy of Donald Trump, most people know what this is – untrue information presented as actual news. Why does it exist? It's usually there to damage the reputation of a person or organisation. In the past, a piece of inaccurate reporting was limited by the sheer physicality of print media, but now thanks to social media fake news spreads like wildfire.

The use of online groups and social media to spread mis-information is not an issue solely faced by women, of course. I bet Bill Shorten would have something to say about it after the

'Death Taxes' scare campaign run at the 2019 election. It does particularly impact women, though, because the response to fake news is far more likely to be gendered and sexualised when directed at us. As I found out myself, through one of the most innocuous things imaginable.

Each year I sent out a Christmas card to my electorate. I would run a competition among the primary school students in the electorate to draw a picture of what Christmas meant to them. The best picture was meant to form the front cover of my annual Christmas card but, being a pushover and not wanting to pick a favourite, I ended up choosing twelve or so which would all feature alongside each other as the front page. This wasn't something that occupied a huge amount of my time and attention, but it was one of many processes we went through to try to remain connected to the local community, particularly those who may not otherwise get much Christmas correspondence. We picked the winning pictures, got the card designed and out they went to 65,000 households yearly.

In 2016, not long after the cards had been sent out, emails and social media messages started coming in. I was a disgrace. I was a 'leftard bimbo' selling out Australia's history and culture. The messages escalated. I should just go and join ISIS, or even get raped by ISIS, and leave the country better off. Since I took no pride in the nation's history and the sacrifices that had been made for me, someone should come and sacrifice me and send an example to all the other 'Muslim apologists'. The messages were hate-filled, they often included death threats and they were seemingly never-ending.

It wasn't just a few, it wasn't just hundreds – I received thousands of these emails and messages. I received more correspondence about my 2016 Christmas card than I did about any other single issue during my fifteen years in politics. Easily.

My crime was that although four of the pictures on the front page featured the words 'Merry Christmas' and one of the drawings was actually of baby Jesus, the card also featured the words 'Happy Holidays'. Yes, that's it. My critics believed that I was being politically correct and trying to deny the Christian meaning of Christmas with these words.

Most of these critics hadn't actually seen the card. The incoming abuse was largely from interstate after people had been alerted to my sins through social media campaigns and emails among a Queensland veterans' group and some right-wing online groups.

The other problem when garbage like this takes off on social media is that the mainstream media will often respond, and the story gets kicked to an even wider audience. Journalists are always looking for a story, but these days most media outlets have fewer staff and a greater need to feed news websites with stories that will generate traffic. So they also need stories that will get good traffic online. It doesn't take many people on social media piling on to generate a perception that an MP is in crisis or under siege or on the defensive, which is when you see stories saying 'MP X at centre of Twitter storm'. Usually it just means a handful of angry or organised people are having a go at them.

The Christmas card story was picked up by talkback radio in Adelaide. What started with partisan abuse and unhinged rantings against multiculturalism resulted in teary elderly people ringing their local talkback station saying they couldn't believe that Kate Ellis had killed Christmas.

At the time I was already contemplating my future. I knew it would be the final parliamentary term before my son started school, and I was newly pregnant with my second child. My reasons for leaving parliament were complex, but I do remember on Christmas Eve receiving yet another death threat from someone with a very warped view on how best to protect the importance of Christian teachings and I just thought, do I really need this shit for just trying to wish people a Merry Christmas?

—

The real issue with the abuse spewed forth on social media is not just that it is annoying or hurtful or confidence sapping. It is dangerous. We know that the internet isn't a separate universe with no real-life consequences. Violence online can develop into violence in our community. That is the real concern for female MPs, and women generally.

I will never forget how shaken I was when UK MP Jo Cox was brutally murdered in 2016 while doing her job. Jo was meeting with her constituents in a local park when she was shot three times before being stabbed repeatedly. Her murderer, Thomas Mair, was linked to Neo-Nazi and far-right hate groups. She was about my age, a politician going about her business in the same manner as me almost every weekend. This is a tragic and extreme example. But there are many ways women can be put in danger by social media abuse, such as being physically stalked based on their public posts.

Even if it doesn't lead to tragedy like this, online hate directed at female MPs now has the potential to change the way people do their jobs. The danger is that women will not feel safely able to go about their business, which includes doing things like being accessible, meeting total strangers, and inviting the general public to gatherings. How do you do that if you are simultaneously receiving multiple death threats and outbursts of rage? How do you do that if you are traumatised by the level of abuse that you're receiving?

The answer to all of this is largely outside our hands. As Julia Gillard argued, 'There is a big responsibility for the social media companies here that they just haven't stepped up to yet.'

It is such a huge problem for female MPs that it is one of the few things that unites women on all sides of Australian politics. Penny Wong has been approached by women in the Liberal Party about working together on social media strategies and protections.

Clare O'Neil, the Labor Member for Hotham, wants to go further, arguing that if the social media giants don't step up to the plate and address this then the Australian parliament should throw everything it has at them to make them do so. 'I think it would not be that hard for the social media company to work out who the serial abusers are and take them off the platform. When a social media company emerges that actually is willing to have a genuine crack at this problem, I will be on their platform in milliseconds.'

Like everyone else watching this space though, Clare didn't express much optimism that voluntary action is likely to occur anytime soon.

'There have got to be better laws here ... [the social media companies] have got to recognise that they've got massive social obligations and, through various processes of competition policy and regulation, be forced to meet them.'

We may have reached a tipping point with the social media bans imposed on Trump in the wake of the US Capitol violence in January 2021. Twitter permanently suspended Trump's accounts, citing the risk of further violence, and Instagram and Facebook followed with temporary suspensions. But there is still far to go.

By denying that they are publishers, social media companies have presented themselves as neutral, taking no responsibility for what people write. They're just providing the digital chalkboard on which people can express their views. This is patently false, which becomes apparent as soon as you factor in the algorithms that drive certain content to the top. And the content that rises fastest is that which drives the most engagement, which, funnily enough, is often the most inflammatory. As journalist Andrew Marantz wrote in *The New Yorker* in 2020, Facebook's 'content-moderation priorities won't change until its algorithms stop amplifying whatever content is most enthralling or emotionally manipulative.' There's a fundamental conflict between Facebook and other social media giants' profitability – which is based on boosting clicks, likes, comments – and the moral obligation they have to restrain hate speech, which often drives that engagement and profitability.

The only course of action people currently have is to stand up and call out bad behaviour online, to respond to a pile-on with a pile-on of support towards the person being targeted. It is not enough. Australian laws around social media abuse at the moment mean that it's extremely difficult to go to the police about online abuse or trolling – they just don't know how to prosecute it or what support to offer. More needs to be done. Not just for women in politics or those in the public eye, but for all Australians who are increasingly dealing with this scourge on a regular basis. Action needs to be taken both against the companies but also the trolls themselves, with better enforceable penalties for social media abuse; not to limit free speech but to cut out violent abuse and hate speech. And there needs to be a framework for police to implement these penalties. So it's not just, can we force the companies to do the right thing? It's also, can we punish those individuals or groups that don't do the right thing?

In the meantime it remains an issue that women in parliament will have to find a way to deal with, and new women elected will have to work out how to face. The next generation of women, who were born into this world of social media, might have more innovative ways of dealing with it. Although, as always, it shouldn't be an issue that they alone have to solve.

We can also heed the words of Penny Wong, who told me, 'The idea that we are not defined by other people's hatred is something I really try to live by. And you have to try. You really have to try to remember who you love, who loves you, who you are in the world. You can never completely inoculate yourself, you can never completely protect yourself, but you have to be resilient about it and you have to diminish its power.'

This is something we can all take on board as we try and connect through social media without being affected by those trying to circulate abuse or hate speech. As well as inoculating ourselves we can combine our positive power to call out hate speech together, publicly support others who are on the receiving end of abuse, and start pushing back against the hate.

CHAPTER 6
THE 'SISTERHOOD'

FOR PARLIAMENTARY OUTSIDERS there is a seemingly simple solution for women working in a male-dominated culture. I can't count the number of times it has been put to me that women in parliament should just join forces, work together and support each other more. It's a worthy sentiment. It's also one that grossly underestimates the complexities of the inter-relationships of women and the culture of a system which is based around exploiting differences rather than finding common ground. At times this leads more to women feeling like they are competing with one another rather than offering support.

This is true of women across the parliament, and it's true even of some women's relationships within their own parties.

Sarah Hanson-Young explained it by arguing, 'I think the whole structure in general terms sets us up to compete against each other. Even though there's not an official quota for women in parliament, culturally there is. In order to get there, you have to displace somebody else. Because we're not putting more seats at the table. And so, it naturally creates a competition against the women that are there. Inside parties, outside parties, in the media ...'

I was surprised to hear this because it is not at all reflective of my own experience. I have no doubt that there were women in my party who didn't like me, and I know that some actively undermined me, but I have no reason to suspect that this was structural. For Sarah, it explains the specifics of her experience. '[Greens Senator] Christine Milne and I did not get along in the end. And a big part of that was the culture that sets women against each other and particularly a young woman against an older woman.'

She is not alone. Natasha Stott Despoja had a similar view. 'I was surprised early, and I was naive at how, within my own party, women were played off against each other. People tried to play up adversity between Cheryl [Kernot] and I. And I'm not being disingenuous but, at the time, I genuinely didn't understand it. And I felt like I just couldn't do anything to prove to her, or to the public at large, that there wasn't an issue. It got to the point where she did believe there was an issue.'

I suspect that numbers matter here. In a major party, you are surrounded by dozens of women. There is no immediate impetus for anyone to particularly pit one woman against the other. In a minor party like the Greens or for Natasha in the Democrats at that time, there may only be two or three other women beside them. Comparisons are much easier to make. It struck me when speaking to Sarah and Natasha how lonely I would have found that reality, and it reminded me how much I appreciated my amazing female colleagues in the Labor Party.

This isn't just about culture within parties though, it's also about the media's great love of a 'catfight', that lovely term reserved for when women disagree. There's no male equivalent term. Even while I was writing this book, it was impossible not to notice the delight the media took in highlighting differences in views between Queensland Premier Annastacia Palaszczuk and NSW Premier Gladys Berejiklian. The coverage wasn't just about political differences but contained a weird fascination with their personal relationship and interactions. Political stoushes between blokes are a dime a dozen, but two women going head to head? Bitch brawl! Great fodder.

Both Sarah and Natasha noted this additional pressure. Sarah believed that the media was almost willing her and Christine Milne to have a public blow-up because that was the story they wanted to write. 'I could see it happening. And I'm sure she could see it happening. The media tried so hard – they really did. And we didn't give it to them, but it did mean that our relationship was not a functional one and it should have been.'

For Natasha, the media did get the story they were after: a leadership ballot between herself and Meg Lees, who had replaced Cheryl Kernot as leader. In terms of leadership contests I cannot think of any that were so directly driven by a policy difference. Meg Lees as Leader of the Democrats had done a deal with the Howard Government which enabled the GST to be passed as legislation in 1999. Natasha Stott Despoja had vigorously opposed the policy and crossed the floor to vote against her leader and the proposal. They were completely divided on the issue, as were their grassroots party members. It had to come to a head. When it did, it was not portrayed as a question of GST policy. In fact, the GST and indeed all policy questions were largely sidelined. The media presented it as a vacuous physical appearance and caricatured personality contest: the popular, attractive young blonde versus the matronly, serious older woman.

Natasha explained just how ludicrous the contest and its coverage became. 'I know it's easy for many people to forget it because it's a long time ago now, twenty years almost. But for fruit sake, I mean *The Advertiser* quoted [South Australian Democrat] Sandra Kanck saying that my support base [within the party] were "middle-aged men who had sexual fantasies about me and wanted to vote for me because I had pert breasts". Literally "pert breasts" got to run in the paper. That was brutal. Apart from the fact that it actually wasn't true, and it was as negative a reflection on the men in my party as it was on me. But the fact that the media printed it, the fact that another woman in politics would say it – that was a low point.'

Most people in politics will tell you that leadership ballots are one of the most brutal parts of the job. You get elected to be part of your team, to work together and fight for your shared vision. When your team turns upon itself it is unspeakably awful. Friend against friend, colleague against colleague. It's horrible, even when you are not the candidate. You still have to pick a side. But for it to be played out in public like the Democrats ballot was … I cannot begin to imagine how stressful and grotesque that experience must have been for either woman. It's impossible to imagine similar coverage of John Howard and Peter Costello, or Bob Hawke and Paul Keating.

Natasha spoke frankly about how the coverage impacted her; it's clear it left a scar. 'That contest was seen as a catfight. The way it was portrayed was extraordinary to me, to this day. This is the one thing I can't even, I can't even write about. It was so far, so different from what I thought the contest was going to be about, which was a policy ground. Everyone knew about the GST, it's not like it was a secret. Obviously I'll one day grapple with it. But it was so hurtful and actually quite humiliating.'

When picturing how hard that must have been to go through, it is completely unthinkable for me to picture doing it without supportive female colleagues. Obviously there are women in minor parties who form friendships with one another, but it is clear that, as a result of numbers, there are fewer women, more competition and more comparisons made between them. They also may not have the same support structures that the major parties do, both formally and informally.

To this day, I wonder whether I would have made it through my hardest slog – the unrelenting toxicity of the minority government and our divided party after the 2010 election – without the friendship of Tanya Plibersek. We never cried on each other's shoulder or even spoke that much about work, but each sitting week we would go for a walk around the lake together. It gave me just enough of a sense of normality and time out to be able to get back and deal with the barrage of shit that we were facing each day. It was real and so very valuable to me.

Another woman who looked out for me was Jenny Macklin, who was Deputy Leader of the Labor Party when I was elected in 2004. It was a pretty miserable time; we had just lost the 2004 election badly. Mark Latham was still the leader but he had little remaining support. Jenny was getting backgrounded against; her internal political opponents were briefing media that it was time for her to move on. She was yet to receive mass public recognition for the hard work that she had put in, not least in policy development. (Her work would later become obvious when we won government in 2007 and implemented many of the considered policies that she had worked so hard on.) Despite this, I immediately noted how tuned in to the party she was. It was Jenny who would notice when someone was struggling and take them aside for a chat. It was Jenny who would check in and make sure that everybody was doing okay. It was Jenny who would notice rifts forming or conflict building. The role she took on was so incredibly important.

Starting a new job is hard anywhere, but perhaps even more so when it means working 950 kilometres from your home, friends and family. Sharon Bird, the Member for Cunningham, and Justine Elliot, the Member for Richmond, were both elected at the same time as I was, and we instantly formed friendships and supported each other as we tried to learn the ropes. They are both still sitting members and their friendship endures as they often live together in Canberra, riding the ups and downs in tandem. This is despite the fact that they have picked opposite sides on every single one of the leadership ballots they have experienced since their election in 2004.

It's not only the informal networks either. In the Labor Party we have the extraordinary Emily's List organisation, which not only aims to support women to be elected but also advocates for cultural and organisational change to bring parliament in line with best practice in the rest of Australia. Notably, it pushed successfully for the Labor Party to commit to affirmative action policies designed to ensure equal gender representation by 2025. There is also the Labor Status of Women Caucus Committee, the Labor Women's Network, and the Elizabeth Reid Network, which was formed to support current and former Labor staff.

That's not to say it is all sweetness and light. Several Labor women, from both factions, believed the culture is more support- ive in the left faction than the right. Perhaps not coincidentally, the right faction continues to have an under-representation of women, and particularly of women on the frontbench. I recall after one conversation about the gender disparity among the right's frontbenchers, some bloke floated a harebrained idea that after each of the states picked their candidates for the frontbench there should be a remaining spot that all the women could compete for. You know, so we had a way to even things up a bit. Wouldn't that do wonders for the sisterhood – give all the blokes their spots and then watch the women fight it out for the 'women's spot'. I and several others made it pretty clear what we thought about that idea.

The Liberal Party has far fewer formal networks, nor do they have any sort of meaningful plan to increase the number of women in parliament. They do have a long established Federal Women's Committee, and there were moves in 2018 to establish a fighting fund to support female candidates. Despite their ongoing under-representation, female Liberal MPs also spoke of a support network of sorts and a view that women aided each other within the party.

As Sussan Ley put it, 'I'm not saying it wasn't supportive of women before, I've always had one or two close women friends in the parliament. But I would say now it's the most supportive environment I've experienced, and I would credit [Minister for Foreign Affairs] Marise Payne with this. During the [2019] campaign she brought the women candidates together in several different forms, often by phone from all over the country. And then once parliament came, she started to bring them together again. I've actually really enjoyed that supportive network, though it would be good to have a bit more critical mass of women in the parliament.'

It doesn't take a genius to see that the more women, the more supportive the environment, and the better the culture in supporting women to do their job.

The situation for women's relationships *across* the parliament appears vastly more complex. For several years MPs like Sarah Hanson-Young have advocated for a cross-party women's caucus to be formed. A place where women can come together and discuss their common experiences, and perhaps map out some ways to work together towards solutions.

There have been attempts over the years to create something like this. When Natasha Stott Despoja first arrived in parliament, former Labor Senator Rosemary Crowley held cross-party lunches for women at a time when barely 15 per cent of parliament was female. 'I remember going to my first lunch, and they put me next to two Coalition MPs,' Natasha said, 'but I was just honestly so excited because I thought, this is it. My whole life, I've been a product of the women's movement. Sisterhood is powerful! This is going to be the network. And Rosemary Crowley said, you know, "Welcome, sisters." And one of them said to me, "They're not sisters." And yet we went on to have a really great discussion, but that was short-lived – the government changed; there weren't parliamentary networks for women [after that].'

In explaining why she sees a need for a women's caucus, Sarah Hanson-Young said, 'I think it's part of the generational shift in politics that is underway and needs to be underway across the board. You know, I think the way women are treated and the way we respond as a political class to this issue is the signifier for how we then deal with difficult issues.'

When Sarah Hanson-Young and Karen Andrews appeared together on a *Q&A* panel, Karen agreed with Sarah. Karen sees a women's caucus as an important next step in addressing the cultural problems in parliament around sexism and stereotyping.

'I think it would just open up communication. The reality is, as the parliament, we should be doing our best by the Australian people. There are fewer women than there are men. And I think a more collegiate environment would be well perceived by the population and would be quite useful for solving problems. I mean, the reality is, if you know someone you're more likely to sit down and work through a solution to some of the issues than if it's a really adversarial environment where you don't know the other person particularly well. Politics, I think, will always be adversarial, always combative, but there should be a level of consideration and cooperation that cuts across all political parties, because the reality is that we've all been elected to represent the Australian people.'

There is no doubt that these are admirable sentiments. Parliament should certainly be more civil, but when it comes to questions of culture, men are undoubtedly part of the picture. Arguably the standards of behaviour and norms of engagement in Canberra were established by men and continue to be dominated by men, and men are generally the worst perpetrators of poor conduct. How effective would a women's support network be in achieving any real and meaningful change, without men on side too?

As Julia Gillard stated, 'I don't think we're going to get to gender equality through cups of tea and cocktail parties. I'm happy to drink the occasional glass of wine, I'm happy to have a cup of tea. But that is not going to be what ends this for us and gets us to win through.'

Julie Bishop also questioned the effectiveness of such a solution in the parliament. 'I think its very structure is inherently adversarial and so party dominated, it would be very difficult to have a cross-party group.'

The biggest problem with the concept by far though is some women feel their political differences with women from other parties are far greater than their similarities. There's also an argument that the issues each parliamentarian is elected to advocate for are far more important than the narrower issue of women's treatment in politics.

Tanya Plibersek put it pretty bluntly. 'Well, what are we going to be bipartisan about?

'You know, the Liberals support Pauline Hanson's inquiry into the family law [Hanson has long argued that the Family Court is unfair towards fathers and pushed the government to set up an inquiry to study reforms to address this perceived problem]. There's a whole lot of stuff they actively do that is bad for women. They tried to cut funding to family violence prevention, legal services. They cut emergency accommodation. They are sucking up to Pauline Hanson on the Family Court, the family law. They're doing things that are manifestly not in women's interests. Why would we pretend that we can all be girls in this together? What are we going to do? Braid each other's hair? Talk about boys?'

The reality is that you don't go into parliament to make friends. The stakes are high. We are not just fighting for the sake of it, we are fighting over the future direction of the whole nation. Do I care more about ensuring every child goes to a great school regardless of where they live or how wealthy their parents are than if a female political opponent has a hard day? Yes, I do. Do I care more about protecting our public health system or lifting people out of poverty or tackling racism and discrimination? Yes, I do. We aren't just observers of what is happening in parliament but active participants in it. Unless you drastically change the very nature of the way our parliament works – and particularly the way the 'winner' of question time is the team that best scores a hit and humiliates the other side – that is what women are going to do, at times to each other.

So where do we go from here?

Women don't need to change. The system does.

In many ways the system actually creates more distance and animosity between women across the chamber, ironically as the focus on the treatment of women in politics increases. The system is changing in the wrong way.

There is no question that one consequence of Julia Gillard's prime ministership, or more specifically Tony Abbott's opposition leadership, was that women were sent in to do direct battle with one another. As coverage of sexism in politics grew, and women politicians were increasingly singled out for particular abuse, Tony Abbott and many blokes who followed him realised that it wasn't a good look for them to be seen as bullying female MPs. The solution? Get your women to do the dirty work.

Julia herself told me, 'Anybody looking at the parliamentary engagements when I was there in politics would have seen that there were a series of things that Tony Abbott clearly thought he ought not to do himself because he and his team knew he had a polling difficulty with women. And to be seen to be muscling up to me would not have run well for him. There were clearly some things he thought would be seen as unfair or too brutal, that he did get women to do.'

It was largely Liberal women who came out calling Labor women 'the handbag hit squad' for suggesting that, god forbid, Julia Gillard was subjected to sexism in her time as prime minister. It was Liberal women who spoke publicly of their disgust that Prime Minister Gillard was 'playing the gender card'. And it was Liberal women who often fronted up at the despatch box to ask the most personal questions regarding Julia Gillard's private life in question time. In many cases that woman was Julie Bishop. She led the charge on public questioning about Julia's role as a solicitor at Slater and Gordon and a personal relationship she had twenty years earlier with an official from the Australian Worker's Union. Tony Abbott vacated the field on these issues so obviously that Julia told parliament at the end of one particularly murky question time in 2012, 'For the benefit of those following proceedings by radio, I confirm that the leader of the opposition was present at question time today.'

Julie Bishop didn't want to speak on the record about how these parliamentary tactics were decided upon and allocated, or where this line of attack came from. Tony Abbott and his office were likely much more involved than his participation in the parliamentary questioning would otherwise indicate, given that his chief of staff Peta Credlin's favourite accessory for a while appeared to be a large folder titled 'Gillard/AWU'. It was very unusual for these attacks, which were the opposition's main approach over several days, to not have been handled between the leader of the opposition and the prime minister directly. It is noteworthy how much Abbott chose to stay silent on this particular topic.

It is also safe to assume that, whatever forces were at play in setting the tone of the attacks on Julia Gillard, Julie Bishop was also probably regularly facing them herself within the Liberal Party. She was not just the leading woman in the party, but one of very few senior women at the time. She may have faced her own sort of pressure – was she up to the job? Or would she 'wimp out' of it? Was she tough enough to get her hands dirty?

Whatever occurred behind the scenes, it is clear that Julie has reflected on it since. 'I look back at question time and blush at some of the things that we used to do in trying to attack our opponents,' she said. 'It doesn't mean you can't fiercely debate and disagree and advocate your cause, but you don't have to be personally abusive. And that's where question time lost its gloss for me. It really did, if it ever had any.'

The practice of sending women out to attack other women seems to have created its own legacy. Arguably, it's become entrenched in parliamentary culture, at least for now. Naturally, women should be able to question each other's decisions in their portfolios – it's part of the job. But it does seem counterproductive that the effect of an increased awareness of women's treatment in politics is to now send women out to do men's dirty work.

Tanya Plibersek acknowledged, 'I think men have worked out that it does look bad to do it. And if we've got one of the female ministers on the run, it is much more likely that it will be the women asking the questions.'

Sarah Hanson-Young suggested that things have actually now gone a step further. Far from just questioning opposing women on their own portfolios, she argued that we now find a reason to blame women for any and all cultural issues their party may have on gender issues.

'One of the things that I felt really uncomfortable about was sitting in the chamber and watching people stand up and grill

Liberal women over the Liberal Party's women's issue. It came from women in Labor, and it came from one woman in our party. I said, "This is not helping. If you want to hold a woman to account for her job, then do that. But it's not Linda Reynolds's fault that her party has a problem with women." Actually making her stand up and having to answer questions about that is just even more humiliating. And I felt really, really uncomfortable with that. I raised it in our party room and nobody had even thought about it. Right, so every time you stand up and ask Linda Reynolds that, you think you're helping? Do you actually give a shit about the issue? Or is this just blood sport and you are participating in the same stuff?'

According to Sarah, her comments were taken on board. But she felt it shouldn't have taken someone in the party room to point it out.

I asked the women I spoke to how they saw this getting better and it became obvious that there was not any easy answer. Personally, I'm not sure that there is a clear solution, and I suspect many will do what is best for their party. But I have seen both women and men refuse to ask questions in parliament that they don't feel comfortable with. I'm confident the more women there are sitting around the tactics table, the easier it will be to refuse those questions.

The dynamics of the parliamentary tactics used in the Abbott vs Gillard era have had another long-lasting impact which further dampens any hope of a bipartisan women-led push for closer relations and a more supportive culture. The bad blood it created, particularly between Labor and Liberal women who lived through it each day, is enduring. Much of the personal animosity created between women who fought in hand-to-hand combat remains.

I can attest that the scars run deep. Kelly O'Dwyer and I had our first children around the same time, and we had so many media requests wanting interviews or photo shoots with the two of us and our new babies. Nup. No thank you. I wasn't interested. It wasn't anything to do with policy differences. Partly it was because I thought the whole thing was absurdly indulgent and out of touch. Don't hold us up as some sort of heroes for being working mums; perhaps go and do a feature on the thousands of single mums out there doing shiftwork, working for minimum wage and yet somehow ensuring that their children were safe, fed and looked after. But it was also because I didn't want to smile and play happy families with someone who I believed had enthusiastically attacked me and other Labor women in the 'the handbag hit squad' when we had tried to call out the most unforgivable treatment of our nation's first ever female prime minister.

I know that I am not offering the hope or easy solutions that many women (and men) long to hear. All is not lost though. The women elected since 2013, who didn't directly experience the years of attack on the Gillard Government, do appear to have much more collegiate relationships across the chamber, no doubt because they didn't have to live through or participate in the daily warring with one another during that time.

Clare O'Neil articulated well the difference in attitudes now. 'I wasn't there for the Gillard days so I don't carry that sort of memory with me. I personally feel a great sense of shared community with Liberal women. I just have more in common with them than I do with Liberal men. I understand next gen feminist issues around criticising women for how they look, which some of our male MPs will do to Liberal women. And I get defensive when that happens. Across the parliament, I think there's no structural reason why the women shouldn't get along.'

Interestingly, the sense of common ground has been strengthened for Clare by the issues she sees Liberal women facing. 'We [in Labor] can have a really open, great discussion about gender issues with every man in the Labor Party, whereas only a handful of male Liberal MPs would be tolerant and interested in that conversation. Liberal women are having a very difficult time. They are in what's like the Labor Party of the 1970s in terms of how their male MPs think about them. Strength to their arm, because we want Liberal governments, as there inevitably will be, to have strong female ministers. It is actually a very important thing for the country, for them to be successful – people like Kelly O'Dwyer, Jane Hume or Karen Andrews. In my experience, they don't play their politics as nasty and personal as some of their male colleagues and I respect them for that.'

Whenever women are elected there is no doubt that there is common ground to build on. Women supporting women is, and will continue to be, important. I do note that while more women being elected brings more support for many, the remaining shortfall in diverse backgrounds means that many are still walking a solo path. Anne Aly remains the only Muslim woman in the parliament at a time when we see increases in Islamophobia and discrimination against Muslim Australians. Linda Burney noted, 'I'd have a lot to do with the mainstream women's movement, but it never felt like there was a place for everyday Aboriginal women in that.'

On the issues that matter to us all, there is a rich history of women from across the political spectrum joining forces to fight for the common good.

Jenny Macklin found support from Liberal women on the issue of family planning. 'There was a terrible circumstance very early on in my time when Howard decided that they were removing foreign aid to those organisations that provided family planning advice. That was pretty much done to get Brian Harradine's vote, and there were people on our side who agreed with that policy. [Former Labor Senator] Margaret Reynolds was a great support to me on that occasion, but there were Labor and Liberal women quietly working with each other to try to figure out how we could take this issue forward.'

Julie Bishop found consensus in 2006 at the time of the debate around legalisation of the so-called abortion pill, the drug RU486. 'That was an example of the women of the parliament being at one over the issue of whether the health minister should have the say over access to RU486 and not the doctor or the woman. I found that was quite a positive experience, that women were talking about the policy as it applied to women, which had seemingly escaped the understanding of some of the men who were promoting the legislation. There was an expectation at the time that there would be more of this.'

Natasha Stott Despoja has similar memories of the RU486 debate: '2006 was my favourite year in the parliament for women's policy. The Democrats put forward amendments to the RU486 Bill, and the [Coalition] Government did a deal with us that if we withdrew the amendments, but got a cross-party private member's bill, they would put it to the parliament. I was cynical about that, but the person who promised that delivered it. That person was Peta Credlin. We came up with a private member's bill, and it passed. It was so exciting. And I thought, this is the future. I honestly thought the whole parliament had changed. It was going to be great.'

That brief moment of bipartisan accord didn't last. The election of the Rudd Government soon after in 2007 meant that these issues became government policy and no longer required cross-party women's alliances to agitate for them.

Of course, it's wildly unrealistic to expect that women will come together consistently, even on the most basic issues that affect us. Women are not a homogenous bloc but a hugely varied group of humans from different backgrounds. There will always be differences of opinion, informed by the diversity of each individual's experiences. But there will also be differences informed by an internalisation of patriarchal norms or deeply seated conservative views. As Julie Bishop explained it, 'There were women on both sides who actually used [these issues] to align themselves with the very conservative side, to show that they were one of them, and that they weren't one of those "feminist lefty women". Some women will deliberately align themselves with very extreme views because they are looking to their own advancement. That's life, it happens.'

Indeed, it does. Perhaps it is too much to ask for all women to agree on a topic where there is debate? I can't think of any examples where we ask the same of men.

There is no question that women can work more collaboratively together in parliament. In fact, there is arguably fertile ground for greater cooperation of women across the political divide. Julia Gillard put forward one such idea.

'I think there would be merit in women across the parliament getting together to discuss some of the hard-headed research that's available about how women leaders are seen. And a scan around the world about the best possible practice. They could use it to develop a shared reform agenda.'

The opportunity for that shared learning is ample. The parliament could even fund it – a women's leadership development program, in recognition of the cultural issues that exist. I'd argue it could be extended further too. Women coming together and agreeing on appropriate standards and rules of engagement more broadly would be a start. Ensuring accountability around these standards and rules would be essential. It's about creating an environment in which anyone can call out unacceptable behaviour without repercussion.

It would only work if there was a willingness and desire across all parties to pursue this.

As I write this book, in 2020, the Coalition Government voted to abolish the Family Court despite expert evidence that this could endanger the lives of women and children in Australia. Every government member who was present voted for it, both men and women. As Tanya Plibersek told me, 'I think the assumption that we're all going to get along because we're all girls has always been a stupid one.'

CHAPTER 7

FIRST TO THE TOP

'DITCH THE WITCH', 'Ju-Liar', 'Bob Brown's Bitch' – Opposition Leader Tony Abbott and his senior colleagues proudly stood in front of people holding signs with these words deriding Australia's first female prime minister.

The almost daily sexist attacks Julia Gillard faced are well known and have been documented effectively in many places, but it's worth recapping a few. There was the menu at an LNP fundraiser with 'Julia Gillard' quail listed and described as 'small breasts, huge thighs and a big red box'. This wasn't some unofficial party function. It was a fundraiser for former Howard Government Minister Mal Brough with then Treasurer Joe Hockey as the guest speaker. David Farley, CEO of Australian Agricultural Company, called her an 'non-productive old cow'. This was of course after Senator Bill Heffernan's comments labelling her as 'deliberately barren'. Tony Abbott told her she should 'make an honest woman of herself'. The cartoonist Larry Pickering distributed daily offensive and pornographic cartoons ridiculing her. On different occasions, radio host and shock jock Alan Jones argued that she should be put in a chaff bag and dumped out at sea, and commented on the death of Julia's beloved father by stating that he must have 'died of shame'. She became known simply as 'that lying bitch' and worse.

It was like an unstoppable ugliness had been set free. It had probably always existed but had never before had cause to rear its head in such a manner. The elevation of Julia Gillard seemed to unleash this underbelly of misogyny that was bigger than most of us had dared imagine. I asked Julia if there were any events that had been overlooked in the long list of crimes against her. She reminded me that, during her term as prime minister, the ABC showed a supposed comedy about her, *At Home with Julia*. 'Why didn't they make one about Abbott? Why didn't they make one about Turnbull? Why haven't they made one about Morrison? It's because, apparently, having a woman in the job is inherently comedic.'

If anyone wants to revisit the full horror of what was thrown at Julia I would recommend looking up Anne Summers' 'Her Rights at Work: The political persecution of Australia's first female prime minister' speech. Though I warn that it is not pretty. So sexually explicit and violent were the attacks on Prime Minister Gillard that Summers thought it necessary to release two different versions, the 'vanilla' version and the far more graphic 'R-Rated' version.

Marielle Smith is now a labor senator for South Australia. Her most recent employment before that was working with Julia. She told me how one of her first tasks was to compile a list of the most misogynistic things Julia faced. Marielle expands, 'You start the list and you go through the kind of typical stuff which Tony Abbott said, some of the things said about her partner in a past life and things said about her appearance. But as you started getting further into the list and just seeing how far the tentacles of this octopus spread and how nasty and personal it was, by the end of the job I was in tears. I remember feeling like, how is it possible that our public discourse allowed it to get this bad?'

How indeed? There is no greater example of the differential treatment given to women and the brutal sexism that lurks beneath Australian politics than Julia Gillard's experience as Australia's first female prime minister. The focus on her private life and 'slut shaming' was relentless. A royal commission was held into a relationship she'd had with a man twenty years earlier, for god's sake. The focus on her appearance was constant – the size of her 'arse', the shape of her nose, the colour of her hair, her choices in outfits. It continued day after day. The online and social media attacks were pornographic, vicious and frequently threatening. The hatred and misogyny was brutal, violent and constant. Yes, I still hold a grudge about this. But the important thing now is surely to reflect with the benefit of hindsight: how could we have prevented it? What should we have done differently and how do we stop it from ever happening again?

I have frequently pondered, if we had all called out the frequent sexism that we experienced daily in politics before Julia had even become prime minister, would there have been such a fertile environment for this ugly misogyny to emerge from?

It is a question that all the Labor women I spoke to who served at the time had clearly also spent much time reflecting on. Did we let Julia down by not calling this stuff out forcefully enough, or was it right to focus on the job we were elected to do?

Julia herself acknowledged, 'I actually think the uglier it got, the more determined we all got to keep going in the face of it. I think we really gritted our teeth and said, "We're not going to repay this by falling apart – we're going to answer this by getting big things done." So people brought a new determination to doing things in the face of it.'

Tanya Plibersek reflected, 'I still feel like we let Julia down by not calling out the misogynist stuff earlier. You and I, in particular, because we both went in quite young, we were toughened to it because we had gone through it ourselves. It was our view, and it was Julia's view as well, that you just get on with doing a good job. We thought you could fix this stuff by just swamping it out by doing a good job. I didn't call it out in the way I should have.'

Working hard and doing a good job didn't make it better. This method actually just doesn't work. The treatment Julia received grew and became more and more grotesque. The goal posts of acceptable behaviour continued to move in the wrong direction.

Penny Wong also questioned, 'By not raising things earlier,

did we actually not confront norms which then enabled it to go so far in the national abuse of the prime minister?'

She captured the idea in an intellectual context when she went on, 'It reminded me of the sociologist Max Weber who talked about norms of behaviour and how rigid norms are the hardest to shift. And I thought about the way in which Abbott and the Coalition enabled the norms of behaviour to be so denigrated and so low. By standing in front of signs that said "ditch the witch", by not saying that Alan Jones couldn't actually talk about drowning the PM in a chaff bag, by not chiding [MP Steve] Ciobo for talking about her throat being cut … it was an implicit endorsement of abusive language in a way that was very bad for democracy. And it's a reminder that you have to keep reinforcing better behaviour, because if you don't, or you condone language and behaviours that are essentially abusive, that's where we will end up. It was such a degrading experience for the country.'

There is no question that the norms of behaviour shifted.

Julia described it as, 'There was an environment of disrespect that fed on itself. And you never get to run the control test in politics. So, how much was gender? How much was how I became prime minister? How much was minority government? How much was the very vitriolic politics around the emissions trading scheme? It's hard to separate them out. But there was an environment of continuing, just constant low-level disrespect.

'All of those things sent a message that it was okay to show that level of disrespect. Would school kids have thrown sandwiches? Would I have driven past a man in Brisbane who was visibly pointing at me, and making a sign of a noose, you know, like "you should be strung up". Would that have happened anyway? I don't know, but I think the day-to-day disrespect did influence a lot.'

We saw it in the treatment of our prime minister, but also in the way the public, political opponents and media engaged with the government. The culture of disrespect flowed through to all of us.

One of thousands of little examples that I could cite happened on a Friday night as I was enjoying a relaxing night on the couch with my husband. I checked my phone and casually remarked, 'Some poor guy isn't as happy as we are. This real estate agent bloke has just emailed me from his work account suggesting that everyone would be so much better off if I would just go and kill myself.' My husband asked to see the message, then we went back to our evening and I didn't think about it again. I'd grown used to this sort of tone and was more amused by the contrast in how happy and content we were on our Friday night compared to this angry man. It wasn't unusual to me anymore.

Three days later, while back in Canberra, I received a call from my husband who had a confession to make. He was quitting smoking at the time and had gone into what I refer to as 'Protective Papa Bear mode'; he had been thinking about that email all weekend and decided to contact the bloke's boss to let him know what his employee was sending out under the company name. The employer said he would look into it. He eventually came back to my husband saying that he had taken a look at the correspondence and thought it was a perfectly valid expression of political debate, 'in the style of Larry Pickering'.

This was the acceptable standard. I learnt a couple of things that day. One, not to share all incoming abuse with my husband. And two, more importantly, that it was really hard to challenge or change this behaviour. It was the new, apparently totally respectable norm. Even in a high-profile business.

Though Labor women like Penny, Tanya and myself reflect, agonise and feel guilt over the treatment of Prime Minister Gillard to this day, the truth is we did try to call it out. Labor women were named 'the handbag hit squad', predominantly by the women who sat opposite us. Penny Wong recalls, 'I mean, you remember every time we did do something, there was the handbag hit squad line. I used to say to my staff, "I don't even have a handbag. I have a briefcase."'

We were also criticised for 'playing the gender card' by our political opponents, the media and the community. If anyone actually knows what this magical gender card is and where you can get one I would love to know. I didn't see many women gaining advantage by virtue of their gender in my time in parliament. In fact, it seems to be a term that is weaponised against women who try to talk about anything to do with women or particularly women's treatment. It is used to try and silence women.

Regardless, we did call the treatment of Julia out as we saw it and it failed to help. There's an argument that if we had continued to do so, it would have just caused more focus, more criticism, more distraction.

Of course, famously, Julia herself stood up and called it out in the clearest and most public way possible.

To let you in on a badly kept secret, parliament isn't always that interesting. It can be incredibly tedious at times. When something big happens though, you cannot adequately capture the electricity that crackles through the chamber. You can get a sense of the moment through television or radio broadcast but it is within the chamber that you feel something truly electrifying. I had the privilege of experiencing several such events. One was the day that Julia delivered the now famous misogyny speech.

There was nothing to especially indicate that what was about to come was going to be anything different to the fierce back and forth that had become commonplace – except of course the audacity of Tony Abbott having a crack at Julia Gillard for sexism, of all things, after all she had endured. From the moment she began, it was clear that this was going to be massive.

'I will not be lectured about sexism and misogyny by this man. I will not.'

I remember promptly putting down my papers and my phone and sitting up. She had my full attention. I was excited and instantly energised. You could tell from both her tone and the determined look in her eye that she was going to do it. She was going to call it all out.

'The leader of the opposition says that people who hold sexist views and who are misogynists are not appropriate for high office. Well, I hope the leader of the opposition has got a piece of paper and he is writing out his resignation because if he wants to know what misogyny looks like in modern Australia, he doesn't need a motion in the House of Representatives, he needs a mirror.'

And she continued. It felt like we were witnessing years of frustration come bursting out. Her frustrations, but ours too, and those of thousands of women across the country.

Marielle Smith described it. 'I think the misogyny speech was a massive turning point in that it showed through all the shit she went through and the shit that, as a woman with your own career you go through, there was an alternative path to challenging it. I was going through my own shit at the time in the private sector and in terms of the way I was being treated in the business, and I saw that you could actually stand up and fight back and not take it. To see that was really important modelling.'

Around Australia, and indeed the world, her words resonated with women who had experienced the same thing, who had been made to feel the same way, who were similarly fed up and wanted this treatment gone.

The Australian media response was very different. Journalist after journalist lined up to slam her. Peter van Onselen labelled the speech 'hypocrisy writ large', Michelle Grattan called it 'desperate'. Peter Hartcher wrote a piece titled, 'We expected more of Gillard', Dennis Shanahan called her speech 'grubby'. She was variously accused of playing the 'gender card', unfairly 'demonising' or 'vilifying' Tony Abbott. This is to say nothing of the usual media attack dogs' hysterical rants.

As Tory Shepherd wrote eight years later when reflecting on the speech, 'so many in political circles saw her laser-focused anger as nothing more than a ploy'.

It was infuriating and deflating. Had all of the treatment she'd received been invisible, or did the press gallery just not believe it mattered? I felt gutted that even when the behaviour was explicitly called out, it was only regarded as the argy-bargy and politics of the day. This was the prime minister outlining a series of prolonged attacks based around her gender, and journalists thought it was a ploy?

Julia faced fire from multiple fronts. Sexism in the parliament, sexism in the community and sexism from the media. The task of tackling and overturning these attitudes in all three arenas seems mammoth. I recently asked Julia: if we could change just one of the three, which one would have the greatest impact? She didn't hesitate in nominating the media.

She was adamant that the media taking a hard line against this type of treatment would encourage enormous change. 'I actually think if we could fix the media, that would have the bigger impact. Partly because the community's understanding of what's happening in parliament still tends to be moderated through the lens of the media. If they were better, I think the community understanding would be different. If there was clearly a price to be paid for sexist conduct in the parliament, in the media, so a man who did X or Y was going to get pilloried in the media, then at the end, you know, politicians are learning creatures and they would learn not to do it. The media could send almost a price signal that there will be hell to pay if you step over this line.'

There is a cost beyond the personal toll on an individual. There is a political cost.

'It certainly cost, though, in ability to get messages out – political acceptance of the government, of me and of our change agenda to the community. No doubt about that. It's like an old-fashioned radio with plenty of static. You know, the gendered stuff was the static. And it's just harder for the true voice to be heard.'

When politicians don't get their message out clearly, they fail. Having such distraction, such off-message commentary, such debate about sexism and misogyny created an enormous obstacle to try to overcome.

The Gillard Government has a remarkable record of achievement, passing 570 bills through a minority parliament. Julia achieved nation-changing reform, established the National Disability Insurance Scheme, introduced paid parental leave, put a price on carbon, passed the 'Gonski' school reforms and provided the substantial increase in school funding that was required. She overcame fierce opposition to set up the Royal Commission into Institutional Responses to Child Sexual Abuse.

It is these achievements which will be the legacy of Julia Gillard's prime ministership, along with making it easier for the next female prime minister and, if we learn from the experience, ensuring that we never again see such a nationwide display of sexism and misogyny.

Julia wasn't just an exceptional politician. She is an incredible human being, far more balanced and well-adjusted than many who have held the same office. I asked her how she managed to put it all behind her, move on and not carry grudges. How does she not have a huge list of names in her freezer?

'I'd happily buy a very big freezer if I thought that was going to change anything. But what it would end up changing wouldn't be life for the people whose names were in the freezer. It would end up changing me, and my life,' she replied.

I agree with her entirely, but I still have a list of names on her behalf.

It's hard when you know someone. It's hard when you like them, when you believe in them, when you see firsthand how hard they work. It's hard when day in, day out you see what is being thrown at them. The little things that don't make the media, the stuff they are already dealing with behind the scenes, doing undoubtably one of the toughest jobs in the land. It's hard, and the burn lasts.

When you are in politics you put up a wall. You have to. To concentrate on what you have to do next, to focus on the job at hand. Julia showed extraordinary resilience and put up her wall. Your family don't though. I cannot even imagine what it felt like for Julia's partner Tim, or for her mother to hear that her husband, Julia's father, had 'died of shame'. For her sister, her niece, her life-long friends. I am still not okay with what they were subjected to.

Most of all though, it's those girls who lined the streets to Government House to wave at Australia's first female prime minister. The ones who stuck their hands up and said, 'I want to be prime minister one day too.' To all the women who took a moment and thought that perhaps there were other possibilities available to them. I can't stop being angry for them.

Taking a step back, I have tried to assess through a different lens the example of Kamala Harris. Her election as US vice-president has similarly smashed the glass ceiling. She will inspire generations of women. She has given renewed hope of what is possible. What would I want her to do when (not if) she gets subjected to similar treatment? I would want her, as Julia did, to get on with the job and silence critics with her achievements. I would also expect every other leader in Congress and in the community to call it out and make it stop.

Marielle Smith argued, 'I think the best thing that could happen next time is those people who stood quietly and thought it might go away cannot make that assumption again. And I think it's really important that when we see a woman subjected to that kind of sexism that everyone who has the ability to make a public contribution about it does. It's not okay to just let it go by because it's not happening to you.'

There were good people, men and women, who called out what they saw happening to Julia. There were good organisations speaking up, like the amazing Victorian Women's Trust. Next time, there needs to be more, a broad echo chamber of voices saying that it will not be tolerated. Every commentator, every business leader, everybody with a voice in the community, a broad cross-section of strong and diverse individuals prepared to declare that these are not standards that will be accepted. That has to be the answer.

CHAPTER 8
THE POLITICS OF MOTHERHOOD

IN ALL THE interviews that I conducted for this book, with all of the women, on all the different topics, there is one moment that stands out above all others as capturing how brutal and sick the culture that women in politics face can be. It was when I was discussing attitudes to motherhood with Julia Gillard. I put to her that women without children were criticised and judged harshly for what that allegedly said about them, while women with young children were criticised and judged for choosing to spend time working away from their family. Are we stuck between a rock and a hard place?

'If you are in the young kids stage, that's damned if you do. And if you've never had children, that's damned if you don't. I think the slight nuance on the "never had children" side is if it was clear you wanted to have children but some health-related condition meant that you couldn't. I think people would be quite sympathetic to that.'

What sort of sickness lies at the heart of a culture where, politically speaking, the only way a woman can win is if she has fertility issues?

There are few areas where gender stereotyping is more entrenched than in the area of motherhood. This is true not just in the parliament but in the broader community. Motherhood is also yet another tool in the arsenal of weapons that is cynically used against women in politics. Do we want women in politics to have children or not? It seems that, in many cases, motherhood is used as an excuse to limit women's power and authority in political life. Paradoxically, childlessness is used to do exactly the same thing.

On this issue we simply cannot win. The female politician who has children risks being labelled a self-centred 'career woman'; the woman who chooses not to is an offence to maternal instincts.

Julia Gillard was famously slammed as being 'deliberately barren' for not having children. She was subtly judged for it regularly, with the implication being that a woman who chose not to have children must be cold and calculating, couldn't possibly understand the pressures of family life, must be out of touch and held different values to the rest of society. She believes the message was clear: 'What sort of woman doesn't want to have and care for children?' In many cases these judgements stemmed from the belief that eschewing motherhood is contrary to what women 'should' do, what society has traditionally valued most in women. In other cases it was just another political weapon reserved for women. Julie Bishop received similar judgement and criticism, though she said herself it was 'nowhere near the same extent that Julia experienced'.

I remember being surprised when a Channel 7 news story I was watching concluded by saying that perhaps the most surprising appointment in a minor cabinet reshuffle was Kate Ellis as Minister for Childcare when she didn't have any children. I found it particularly odd, and not just because the Minister for Veterans' Affairs had never served in the defence force, the education minister was not a former teacher and the health minister had no background in medicine. But mainly because I was already the childcare minister before the reshuffle and had been for some time. It wasn't new, and the story should have had nothing to do with me. I assume it was an easy go-to angle, playing off gender stereotypes in an attempt to create some interest in otherwise unremarkable news. Or perhaps the journalist never thought to question the assumption that a woman must have firsthand experience of childcare to be able to talk about it in any way.

The message is consistently reinforced that childless women, and particularly childless women in parliament, are different, undesirable, devoid of empathy and understanding. So do we want mums in the parliament then? For many it seems the answer is no.

Court transcripts from early 2020 show that Queensland Liberal National Party Director Michael O'Dwyer is alleged to have told former Brisbane councillor Kate Richards that she should withdraw from preselection because she 'was not capable of doing her job'. The rationale was reportedly that as a mother she would need to be available to pick up her children from school. It made news headlines, but would not have come as a surprise to many of the women I spoke to who had very similar stories to tell.

These double standards around parenting are reflected in the statistics when it comes to the family make-up of male and female MPs. Labor MP Andrew Leigh conducted some illuminating research to which he gave the suitably depressing title 'The Motherhood Tax' to describe why female MPs were less likely to have children than their male counterparts.

Andrew found that in the 2013–2016 parliament the average male politician had 2.09 children while the average female had 1.22 children. Across the parliament, 19 per cent of male politicians had no children; for female politicians this figure was 37 per cent.

Being a parent is not viewed as an impediment to male politicians. In fact, it is often lauded – if it is even noticed. As Annabel Crabb pointed out in her 2019 Quarterly Essay 'Men at Work', hardly anyone batted an eyelid when Scott Morrison and Josh Frydenberg became the first prime minister and treasurer since the 1970s to work together while both bringing up young children. Male MPs are rarely questioned over the arrangements their family has put in place to manage their absence, or how they have come up with a plan to juggle their work and family. That interrogation is saved solely for women. Karen Andrews, Sussan Ley and Justine Elliot all put their hands up to run for parliament as mothers of young children. They all told stories of it being used against them.

Karen Andrews ran for preselection when her children were five, nine and twelve years old. She told me that people questioning her choice to combine motherhood and politics was a constant issue during her preselection. 'So many of the questions during the preselection process were, "How are you going to manage your family?" "How are you going to have the children looked after?" And I think that's fundamentally wrong unless the same questions are going to be put to men.'

Spoiler alert – they aren't.

She went on to recall a particularly charming email that she received from one of her preselectors. A man wrote to her saying that she should not run, she would not win anyway, but also that he would 'never allow his wife to leave their children' in such a way. She received such regular questioning that she began to wonder how many others shared the sentiment, even if they didn't openly say so. The numbers suggest quite a few. Karen's seat is in Queensland and the Queensland Liberal National Party is currently represented in federal parliament by three women and twenty men.

Beyond the appalling numbers, it also means that those women are subject to more judgement, scrutiny and criticism than their male counterparts. As Karen points out, 'There's still a lot of stereotyping. And because of that, the community pressure on women is high, particularly women with families and women with young children. They face a lot more criticism. It is hard to be away from your children, and I don't doubt for a second that it's hard for men. What they don't get is the added pressure of it. "It must be hard. What about your children?"

I would really like to know how many male politicians get asked that question.'

I think we all know the answer to that question. It's a number very close to zero.

Sussan Ley had similar experiences when she nominated for preselection to represent the regional NSW seat of Farrer. She identified that there were two separate motivations for the questioning that she received. The first was pure politics. 'It wasn't because people actually cared about that, it was because people were using that as one of the questions in a preselection. They would think of any reason that they could to make you less attractive than the other person. I put it down to the cut and thrust of how they find a weakness in you as a candidate.'

Being a mother. What a weakness. You can also be sure that every male candidate flashes around their baby pictures, gaining praise and showing what good and doting dads they are.

The other reason is less sinister but can be equally problematic for women's aspirations. As Sussan said, 'The other issue we have in the Liberal Party stems from older women who came from that era; they genuinely wanted to know the answer to that question.' She was talking about elderly women honestly being unsure if women could be both mothers and members of parliament.

I have often heard this view too. Many community members continue to be perplexed by the very notion that a woman should seek professional advancement if it comes at the expense of spending time with her children. A job outside the home may now be commonplace for women, though people still seem to be more accepting of part-time than full-time work. A career that is often on the other side of the country still seems to blow people's minds.

While Karen Andrews and Sussan Ley spoke about questioning from within their own party during preselection, Labor MP Justine Elliot believes that similar issues were used against her by her political opponents. Her children were six and four when she ran for one of the most marginal seats in the country, Richmond, which was held by Nationals Minister Larry Anthony. 'Politicking about kids was always an issue,' she told me. She believes it was in part due to a whispering campaign against her by the National Party. But there has been progress. As Justine observed, 'Communities' perception of women in parliament has changed so much since I was first elected. Back then [in 2004] everything was through the prism of being a woman and being a mum'.

I think she is right. The increase in the number of women in parliament since then and their various parenthood journeys have certainly begun to change community perceptions of what is achievable and acceptable. In fact, as Amanda Rishworth has discovered after having two children since being elected in 2007, many people actually like and respect it.

'The majority of my community has been really, really supportive. I think they feel like they've been able to connect with me on it. A lot of working women connect with you, a lot of women that are juggling family connect with you. And I have had the positives of people often saying, "Good on you. Well done."'

As with other issues, parliament has long lagged behind the rest of the community, where it is generally seen as normal to work while being a mother to young children. The response from Amanda's community shows how much people value seeing their experiences, and their family situations, represented in parliament.

It's possible that as the number of double-income families and parents juggling work and family continues to increase, the judgement of women who choose to work in the parliament while they have young families will decline. As community perceptions continue to evolve, we can hope that the power of the attacks on these women start to wane. Hopefully we will get to a stage where if opponents attack a woman politically over motherhood the community will just shrug and say, 'Get with the times, Grandpa.'

———

You get so acclimatised to the relentless toxicity in parliament, and you are so busy or so caught up in the day-to-day madness that you tend to just accept it all and move on. It wasn't until writing this book that I reflected on how one of the most horrible examples of this putrid culture, where pregnancy and motherhood are just another tool for political gain, actually happened to me.

At the time I felt confusion and some bemusement about what transpired. As I write these words almost ten years later I feel seething rage.

In 2012 I received a call from the journalist Latika Bourke. 'Hi Kate, I know that everybody knows about it, but I'm just calling to see whether you have confirmed your pregnancy yet?'

Hmmm, that's awkward, I thought. 'I'm not pregnant,' I replied.

'Yes, you are!' she informed me.

I assured her that I would know if I was pregnant, and that I was happy to state absolutely that I was not.

A few days later I received a call from Joel Fitzgibbon, who was the chief government whip at the time. He wanted to give me a heads-up that he had received a call from a journalist at *The Australian*. Joel had heard from the journalist that I had severe pregnancy complications and would be unable to travel so was applying for a long-term pair. A pair is when both parties agree to each sit a member out when the House votes so that one or both members can be absent from parliament. In other words, Joel was wondering whether he needed to arrange for me to have leave from parliament.

I was a member of a minority government at the time. When parliament is sitting, there can be a vote called at almost any time. It may be to decide the fate of key legislation, it might be to silence a speaker and force them to sit down, it might be to declare that the parliament no longer has confidence in the prime minister or government. When that vote is called bells ring throughout the building for four minutes, and no matter where you are or what you are doing you must be seated in the chamber at the end of that four minutes, when the bells stop ringing and the chamber doors are locked. The consequences of missing that vote can be massive, particularly if your side does not have a large majority to comfortably win votes without you. If the pair request had not been granted the government would have been down one vote and would lose control of the parliament, potentially leading to a change of government or an early election.

I never saw politics played harder than during that term of the Gillard minority government. One resignation could bring down the government, one heart attack, one prison sentence, one nervous breakdown. This created the political impetus for the opposition to search for any weak link in the chain. One MP gone was all they needed. Even the suggestion that one might go was all it took to fuel speculation about the stability of the government, to ensure the focus remained on the politics of the day and the precarious nature of the government as opposed to policy achievements and debates. It highlighted the ongoing vulnerability of the Gillard Government.

I thanked Joel for letting me know and reassured him that there was no need to put in a request for me to have long-term leave from the parliament. There were no pregnancy complications, nor indeed any pregnancy at all. There was no threat to the government's stability. It was all a bit odd, to say the least.

Where was this coming from? It may have been my imagination but I became really self-conscious entering question time. I felt as if people were examining me differently, talking about me.

I know that this is a grave disappointment to many of my Twitter followers, but my then partner and now husband Dave is a long-term News Corp employee. Going about his business in *The Advertiser* building one day, he was pulled aside by a colleague and friend who wanted to give him a heads up. A then SA Liberal MP had apparently been doing the rounds briefing journos on an explosive story that the government was at risk as a result of my high-risk pregnancy and inability to make it to parliament.

Dave later received a call from Dennis Shanahan at *The Australian*. 'As a mate, I wanted to come to you first,' he began, before putting the story to Dave. I had told Dave about my conversation with Joel, so he suspected that Shanahan hadn't come to him first at all. What followed could, I think, best be described as a relationship-ending exchange between Dave and Dennis Shanahan by both phone and email. Dave emphatically insisted that there was no truth to this rumour, and I suspect made it pretty clear what he thought of the nature of the inquiry.

Instead of focusing on the kind of culture that would allow these sorts of inquiries to be considered in any way normal or acceptable, I immediately just wondered what I had done to create this crazed idea.

I was going through a hard time personally. My closest family friend had recently taken his own life. We had grown up together in our small country town where our parents were best friends. Along with my brother and my friend's sister, we spent most weekends playing, had regular sleepovers, got up to all sorts of crazy adventures exploring the countryside or playing aboard vacant boats left in the Murray River. He had been my first boyfriend and we both got told off in Year 2 when we were caught kissing in class. We smoked our first cigarettes together after stealing them from his mother. We grew up together.

When he finished high school he moved down from the country and came to live with my family, who were now living in Adelaide, so he could attend uni. Though by this time he was battling serious mental health issues, he supported me above all expectations as I ran for parliament, climbing up and down ladders putting hundreds of election posters up. Whenever he saw me in the media he would call with a lengthy precis of all that had been said and how I was depicted. He had become like my own personal media monitoring service. The last time he called me, I looked down and saw the incoming call but decided that whatever I was busy doing at the time was far more important; I didn't answer. I cannot count the number of times that I have reflected on that decision.

Anyone who has lost someone to suicide knows that it is a particularly savage and guilt-ridden form of grief. So when these rumours of pregnancy started in 2012, I was not in a very good place. I probably wasn't living my healthiest life and maybe I'd put on some weight, I don't know. I was just trying to get through each day and had stopped doing extra activities like getting up early to play in the parliamentary netball team. I got leave from parliament to attend my friend's funeral once the inquest was over.

Maybe someone could view these things from the outside and suspect that I was pregnant. Yet I cannot see where the high-risk pregnancy requiring long-term leave from the parliament could come from, except someone's imagination. How nice it would be to work in an environment where people noticed that you were not yourself and asked if you were okay, instead of spreading rumours about you.

I reflected upon the total lack of regard shown for how much extra stress it would have placed on me and my unborn child if this story were true. I was dealing with opposition MPs trying to gain political advantage from it and journalists trying to pursue the story. There was no evidence that my wellbeing or that of my hypothetical baby featured in any of these conversations. It was all about the politics associated with it. I still don't actually know what's worse: if they thought it was true and decided to try to exploit it, or if they knew the whole thing was made up. It's deeply disturbing either way.

The reason for my rage now is simple. There is only one thing that would have made this story remotely worth either spreading or investigating, and that is if there was a chance that the request for leave was not going to be granted. Any MP pushing this story was clearly also implying that this leave might not be granted. Any journalist seeking to write the story would surely only do so if they thought that this was the case.

This entire theory was framed around the presumption that we would make a woman choose between risking the health of herself or her unborn child or potentially bringing down her own government. How could any MP or journalist ever think that was a likely enough outcome to make this worth spreading or pursuing?

I am sickened to think that our parliament could ever operate in a culture where the immediate response to hearing that a woman needed leave due to a high-risk pregnancy wouldn't just be, 'Well of course it will be granted.' In what kind of modern workplace would it even be contemplated that a permanent female employee might not be given an exemption from travel as per her doctor's recommendation for her or her unborn child's health? What kind of workplace? The one that is meant to set the standard and the tone for our community and make the laws for all Australians: federal parliament.

CHAPTER 9

CHOOSING TO MAKE IT WORK

IN JULIA BAIRD'S 2004 book *Media Tarts* she reveals a truth about the optics of parenting and politics that I unfortunately think still stands: 'It has long been assumed that the families of male politicians make sacrifices; the families of female politicians suffer.'

In March 2017 I announced one of the biggest decisions of my life: that I would be resigning from parliament due to family reasons. Later during the same parliamentary term Minister Kelly O'Dwyer made a similar announcement. It created much public debate. Did this prove that you couldn't be a mother to young children and a member of parliament? It is noteworthy that we never have such public debates and scrutinise the decisions of men in exactly the same situations. Where is the discussion on what arrangement they put in place, on how hard it is to juggle it all, or the judgement on the decisions they've made?

What was also missing then, and is still often missing, is the airtime for the stories of the women who have made a different choice and succeeded at balancing work as a politician and a mother. You don't have to look far to see example after example of women who are both wonderful mothers and successful MPs. The parliament is brimming with them.

Clare O'Neil's story is unique and fascinating. Her newborn son, her first child, was just eight weeks old and she had just begun maternity leave from her job as a management consultant when she received an unexpected phone call. It was three weeks away from the 2013 election and the Labor Party were going to replace the candidate who was set to take over from Simon Crean in one of Labor's safest seats, Hotham. They needed to find an inspiring local Labor Party member to do the job. Clare had a hugely impressive background and had previously served as a very young and popular mayor in the area. She was politically engaged and a member of the Labor Party. Did she want to do it? Out of the blue, an offer of a guaranteed safe seat in the federal parliament. She had to make a decision, fast.

You can imagine how bizarre that day must have been for Clare. 'I was just learning how to be a mother, and when you've got an eight-week-old baby you are still in that crazy time where you're only sleeping for three hours at a time and you've got all the hormones and stuff going. But I had to make a decision, and I had to make it within a couple of hours of getting that phone call out of nowhere. I mean out of absolutely nowhere.'

When I was speaking to Clare over the phone I could hear the emotion in her voice. I don't know if she was crying, but I was wiping away tears as I listened to her talk about how stressful it was to navigate that choice. I cannot even begin to imagine how she made the decision to throw herself into politics at a time of such personal change.

She explained that while she loved politics, loved the Labor Party and loved public policy, her partner Brendan had no background in politics; she first had to make it very clear to him what the job would mean for the family. Many MPs are already politicians when they meet and fall in love with their partners (like I was), and as a couple have never known any different. Clare and Brendan were looking at the unknown – an added challenge for them as a couple. They had to sit down and try to reconcile how her head and her heart were pulling in different directions.

'I knew in my rational mind I had to do it,' Clare said. 'My values are my values. To say no would have been to totally go against that. But in my heart of hearts I knew that I didn't want to do it because I had this baby. A lot of children of politicians don't actually have a very good life sometimes. It can do bad things to family. I said that to Brendan and he said, "Well, which do you trust most, your head or your heart?" I said that I trusted my head. And he said, "There is our answer."'

For Clare and Brendan the decision was made. I can't help but wonder how many men in that situation would have gone to bed thinking, 'Shit yeah, I'm getting a safe seat in the federal parliament!' instead of enduring the kind of conflict and guilt that Clare grappled with that night. 'It was very difficult,' she explained. 'That night I went to bed and I literally did not sleep one second. I am getting myself emotional even just talking about it again now. I just lay awake all night thinking, what am I doing? My child! I've just got this tiny little baby that I have to protect. Why am I doing this thing that is going to hurt him? I know it's right. I knew it was the right decision. It wasn't obvious and easy though. But it was what my values inevitably led me to.'

Just three weeks later Clare found herself both a new mum to her then eleven-week-old son and a new member of parliament.

Looking back at my own life, the two biggest learning curves I ever faced were becoming a member of parliament and becoming a mother. Clare did it simultaneously.

'The timing could not have been worse,' she said. 'Well, maybe if it was five or six weeks earlier that would have been worse, but probably not any other way. It was horrible. I didn't feel comfortable and confident to set things up as I needed them to be set up as a new mum. If I had been in parliament for five years and knew the lay of the land, I'd have known what mattered and what didn't matter. I could have structured things differently. Being new, I felt like I had to go to every event. I had a full staff of new people working together in my office, none of whom had ever had a child before. They just did not understand what it means to have to breastfeed every three hours. It was almost like it was regarded as an indulgence. So yeah, in short the timing was crap.'

Clare did it the hard way but she also learnt from it. In the following parliamentary term she had her second child and did things very differently.

'The reality is that you've got to structure everything around you and the baby,' Clare said. 'By the time I had my second child,

I just knew certain things mattered and certain things didn't. And the things that didn't matter, I would not do them. I didn't do unnecessary media performances that no one would ever want to watch or read, unlike the first time around. I didn't go to every single event. I had more of a sense of humour about the chaos of it all. And I was more comfortable that people wouldn't judge me and that I could have my baby with me and even be noticeably kind of not on top of everything at times.'

Clare said that one technique political parents can use is to declare that certain family commitments are off-limits and cannot be adjusted or cancelled for work reasons. She conceded that this is easier to achieve the more senior you become.

'In my own career I have seen MPs who've been around for a long time and who have found a way to meet their family obligations creatively,' she said. 'One good thing about the job is that it brings some flexibility. I know one really senior Labor person who every single Friday picks up his children from school without fail. It wouldn't matter what happened on that Friday and how important it was to his portfolio. He's going to get his kids from school. It's locked in his diary and everything's organised around that.'

For many people, having the ability to collect your child from school once a week may not sound like amazing flexibility, but in politics it's pretty normal for everything else in your life to centre around your work diary, which is jam-packed and irregular in hours.

Another feature of the job Clare identified is that, with the exception of parliamentary sitting weeks, where the schedule of caucus, question time, late sittings and estimates hearings rules your day, electoral work brings with it greater freedom to pick and choose your hours.

Make no mistake, electoral work is daunting, and if you are doing your job properly as an MP, there is rarely such a thing as a day off, but the reality is that when you are required to work weekends as well as weekdays, there is no expectation that every second of every day is devoted to work.

'We have a level of flexibility in our job that most working mums would die for,' Clare said. 'We have to work really long hours but we can structure it in many different ways. It feels like I'm always working on a Saturday or Sunday because I choose to take the time off during the week for school pick-ups. We have this unbelievable flexibility to choose our hours and our priorities. So I actually think it's doable. It's very doable.'

Of course, many women had also found a way to make it work before Clare. It doesn't mean it was always easy. It doesn't mean they don't still at times reflect on that decision. But they all found a way to also make it 'doable'. In all of my conversations for this book there was no topic where women were more frank and unguarded than talking about balancing work with motherhood. Several women teared up when telling their stories. I cried while listening to many of them. All of it highlights what every working mother knows: it can be really difficult to juggle work and family. But how lucky are we to have such choices and opportunities? I feel so grateful to the women who spoke to me honestly about such personal decisions. I hope that the insights they offered will assist others to see the pathway through. I suspect the lessons are relevant to working parents far beyond the realms of parliament too. All of us are juggling ways to make it work.

When I met with Karen Andrews she was polite and professional. She was incredibly generous in making time for me, not least because I had previously been her shadow minister in the Skills and Vocational Education portfolio and, I would imagine, far from her favourite person. She was careful and on message in our opening discussions. Her entire persona changed when I turned the topic to motherhood. It was immediately obvious how much the issue had weighed on her.

'I can even feel my stomach knotting as we're talking about it now, because it is really difficult,' Karen said.

As we were talking I thought to myself, how amazing that you can work across the chamber from someone for years without ever feeling any connection, and then completely empathise the moment you start having an honest and heartfelt discussion about your kids. She went on to say, 'There's no easy answer here. I don't have a magic solution for it. We all just do the best that we can.'

Karen's daughters were still young when she was elected. 'They understood even from an early age when I was going to Canberra,' she said. 'What they didn't understand is why I wasn't home if I wasn't in Canberra. For a federal politician, it's that extra travel. Here I am in Adelaide. I was in Sydney yesterday. I'm in Adelaide tomorrow. I then go home for one day before I go back to Sydney.' This was during her one week 'off', in the middle of four sitting weeks.

Karen told me about the good bits. She noted the incredibly close and precious relationship that her daughters have with their grandmother as a result of her travel, the events they had been able to take part in that few teenagers would ever experience: hanging out at The Lodge with the prime minister, seeing Barack Obama's address to the parliament. She broke my heart, though, when she wondered, 'Does that make up for what they've missed? My biggest concern is that I'll be sitting in a rocking chair on a balcony in my eighties, disappointed at how much I missed of their lives.'

Many women expressed how they worried about the impact their political roles would have on their children, and how they worked to find ways to minimise this. When Pauline Hanson was first elected her controversial and extreme views, particularly on race, caused outrage and protest throughout the community. The Australian Federal Police thought it was necessary to provide her with a constant security detail. She explained, 'I found it very hard to get used to having security around me. The kids, I tried to keep them protected from it. Actually when that did happen, I put the kids into boarding school. They were away and didn't see all this going on with security with me all the time. It's only when I went to visit them, they saw the security people. It's how you talk to them, and if I was to get around and say, "Look, I'm scared of where I'm going, I need these people," of course the kids are going to get worried about it.'

Naturally you find ways to protect your children. That is an extreme example but all women have to find ways to make the juggle work for their families.

Tanya Plibersek seems like she has got it sorted and has found a way to excel in the areas of both motherhood and politics. Since being elected at the age of twenty-eight, Tanya has had three children, one of them while serving as a minister. She did this while her husband was also working as the chief executive of a NSW government department. Tanya did not sugar-coat the effort required to make it work. 'I think any job that takes you literally away from your home for a third of the year is going to be hard on your family life. I think you do have to accept that it's going to be difficult and disruptive for family and make your choices with that clearly in mind.'

Amanda Rishworth has had two children while serving in the House of Representatives. Amanda and I were pregnant with our first children at the same time. She makes the important point that, of course, members of parliament are not Robinson Crusoe in facing this challenge.

'There are so many professions where it's not easy,' Amanda said. 'I do not find it easy. It's hard. I miss my children. But I don't think that's a really unique situation that many other professions don't also feel. During the last term I had the defence personnel portfolio. To put our situation in context, there are women in the ADF that actually get deployed for nine months at a time. So it's not the only occupation that's not easy with kids. But if you have the passion for it and you want to do it, it's absolutely worth doing.'

Amanda has made it work, with her husband Tim taking a year of unpaid paternity leave to be the primary carer of each of their children. She is well aware of the importance of broader family support beyond that first year too.

'I'd be lying to say you could do it without support,' she said. 'You just couldn't. And if it's not your partner, it's other family members or other people; you do need that support. I think you have to have an honest conversation with your partner or whoever is supporting you about what the job might entail. You've got to be in it together. That's not completely different from other professions, but it is something that you've got to do. I think that's true for men as well. Going into politics or other demanding jobs, you need that support, as a family unit, as a wider group of people, to do the job.'

I never imagined what combining politics with motherhood might look like prior to my election. I was twenty-six and unmarried when I was preselected. I didn't know if I would win. In fact, winning was more unlikely than not. I also didn't know if I would hold the seat for more than a term, as the seat of Adelaide had a history of being marginal. I didn't know if I would ever have children.

I passionately want to see more women enter politics, and have felt racked with guilt that my decision to leave and my announcement could be a deterrent. I never wanted to suggest that you couldn't be a mum and an MP. It was simply my own choice. With that in the back of my mind, there were two interviews I conducted which were more important to me personally than any others. I spoke to two women with small children who made a decision to run at the election in 2019. They made their decision after Kelly O'Dwyer and I had chosen to leave politics for family reasons. I needed to know how our announcements had affected the thinking of these women, and how they had weighed up the challenges to which their eyes were wide open. The stories told by Marielle Smith and Anika Wells are both inspiring and uplifting, as they show that it can be done. They show that it is worth doing. That working to build a better country is a really important thing to do for their children.

Marielle Smith was elected as a South Australian senator at the 2019 election; she had a small toddler son and hopes of more children. We had worked together in government and have remained very close friends ever since. She saw my deliberations, heard about the good and the bad of mixing politics and family life. As she explains, she took a particularly methodical approach to assessing her work and family balance before making the decision to run.

'I always knew there was a way through. But I was also very, very aware that the way through required sacrifices. And that I had to interrogate those sacrifices before I put my hand up to do it. I could not put my hand up without thinking through the implications for me and my family and how I would manage it.

'I had to line up those sacrifices against what I thought I could realistically achieve in terms of the things I believed in. I wanted to see change in my community. So it was always a very conscious process for me. I spent more time on interrogating my purpose. Why I wanted to put my hand up to run, because that really had to be very, very clear and very stark to me.

'I knew I would need to be able to hold on to that in times where I found it really tough for my family. And I also needed to think through how I would talk to my children and how I would explain it to them as they grew up. I constantly ask myself, do I think my children will think this was worth it and that this was a meaningful and worthwhile thing to do on behalf of our family? At each point of the process, I ultimately came to the decision that, yes, I could. The balance of those two considerations worked. But I think it's a continual process and a work in progress. If I get to the point where I feel like the contribution I'm making is no longer worthy of the sacrifice, I will make a different decision.'

Anika Wells was elected as the Labor Member for Lilley at the 2019 election. She had a two-year-old daughter, Celeste, at the time she won the seat. When I spoke to Anika in October 2020, she was breastfeeding her ten-day-old twin sons. There were two important things that struck me about Anika. One was the thought and research she had put into assessing the impact of parliamentary life on MPs' children, and the second was her inspiring outlook that she wasn't an MP despite being a mother, but because she *was* a mother. She was an MP because of her love for her daughter. I cried when I talked to her, but more importantly I also felt excited and optimistic about the next generation of women we are going to see in our parliaments.

When she was first thinking of running for parliament, Anika took the innovative approach of seeking out adults who had grown up with an MP for a parent. She spoke to members of many different political families. She wanted to know their thoughts and reflections on how the experience had affected them and their childhood.

She spoke to a woman whose father had been an MP for her entire childhood. Anika told me of the response she got when she asked how the woman felt about that.

'She told me that was just how it was,' Anika said. 'It's a bit like being born a royal. You don't know any different. She said she never knew any different from her dad being away all the time. And she was really proud of what her father achieved.'

'And all these kids are very happy, they've all grown up, and they even ended up joining the Labor Party, being progressive and working for social justice if not specifically in politics.'

She told me of a conversation with another daughter of an MP, who said: 'We loved it. We're proud of it. It was something that I liked at school, that he did something that we had to take notice of in the classroom, that we learnt about as being important to democracy.'

Anika took much heart from a conversation with an MP who had a son exactly the same age as her daughter was when she entered the parliament. 'She told me that not once had her son fought with her or thrown it back at her. Instead she said he'd told her, for all the times we didn't get to see you because you were working, we got to meet U2 or we got to come backstage with you at the Olympics or whatever. The payoff of all the things that we got to do because you were an MP, which were incredible, are what we actually remember most fondly from our childhood.'

Perhaps most significantly, Anika said, 'Nobody that I spoke to said that they wished that it had been any other way or that they resented their parents for their decision. So that was very comforting.'

There is no doubt that this was an important process and good feedback for Anika's own thoughts on her future career and its impact on her children. Especially because her first child was her ultimate motivation for entering politics.

In 2016, when Anika was pregnant with Celeste, she was watching the US election. 'I remember that when I sort of dozed off for a nap in the morning, it all looked fine. Hillary was on track to win. I woke up from my nap and she had lost Florida. And all of a sudden the world changed. I didn't then know if I was having a boy or a girl but I knew that the world had changed.'

Trump's election was proof once more that while women will have any perceived sexual indiscretion held against them forevermore, for men it is often casually disregarded and rarely an impediment to their success in public life. Donald Trump had not just regularly espoused offensive, anti-women sentiments but the whole world had actually seen him on videotape bragging about committing sexual assault. And he was elected to the most powerful position in the world. It was the response of women worldwide that inspired Anika though. Millions of women stood up to be counted as women's marches around the world made clear that we would stand up and fight to protect women's rights. The message and the images were an inspiring reminder of the power of collective action.

'[My daughter] was actually born just a couple of days after inauguration. So we were in the hospital. I was holding her in my arms and we were watching coverage of the week, which included the inauguration and the women's marches. I'm holding her and watching the women's marches and watching these women, many of whom were being active for the first time almost as an apology for just assuming that things were going to work out how they thought it would. I was just horror struck by the fact that [Trump] was now in the White House and Celeste was going to grow up spending the first four years of her life under a Trump presidency. So in that moment I really identified with the women in the women's marches and thought, well, I can't be complacent here either. And I'm going to take the opportunities as they come. So I put my hand up to run for Lilley. To me, it was so intertwined with Celeste's future that it was always clear that, yes, I will have to spend time away from her. But it's also very specifically that moment that was like a lightning bolt; it sort of crystallised for me that I would do it, that I would run.'

What better motivation is there than to change the world than for your children?

CHAPTER 10
GIVING IT ALL AWAY

I AGONISED FOR a long time over my decision to leave parliament in 2017. I wholeheartedly believed – and still do – that I had the best job in the world. I was also completely aware of the message that my announcement – as a 39-year-old woman with a young child – might send to other women. I tried as hard as I could to manage that. I fear that I did not succeed.

In a letter to my local community, I wrote honestly, 'In the end it is a decision that I have made for only one simple reason. Whilst my son could travel with me as a baby, during the next term of parliament he will start school and need to stay in Adelaide. The simple truth is that I just cannot bear the thought of spending at least twenty weeks of every year in Canberra away from him and the rest of my family. When I think about having to regularly miss things like his first day at school, his presentations at school assembly, a first sporting match or even just being there for him when he is sick and wants his mum, I know that it would make me absolutely miserable.'

I explicitly pointed out that this was my personal choice and one that I made knowing that I was surrounded in the parliament by people who were both excellent parents and excellent MPs.

I never intended to send the message that being an MP is not compatible with being a mother. But I knew that this would be the message some heard – despite the fact that, not long after my announcement, WA Labor MP Tim Hammond also made the difficult decision to leave politics to spend more time with his three children. Almost immediately after I announced my resignation it was met with responses like:

'I am seething with anger. The painful truth is that motherhood and politics don't mix' – Jamila Rizvi, News.com.au

'It's another sign of how stacked in favour of men with wives the political system is' – Stephanie Peatling, Twitter

'More than anything, I wonder how disheartening it will be for other women out there to have it reiterated to them, once again, that being a working mother is still just as hard it as ever was' – Katy Hall, Mamamia

I felt that some of the commentary was dismissing all of the experiences of the women who had already successfully combined motherhood and a career in politics, of the women who were doing it at that very time or the ones who would do it in the future. As Julia Baird wrote in *Media Tarts*, over a decade earlier than my experience, 'Anxieties about working women are still lived out in public disputes about the life decisions of female politicians'. It felt like my decision was being held up as the sole example that could prove what was possible. There were many opinions, much debate and discussion about what it all meant, leaving me feeling exhausted and guilty. Leaving parliament was an extraordinarily hard choice and one I felt like I had to justify on behalf of all women. I still do feel a bit like that.

It's hard for me to write this chapter. I feel uncomfortable and vulnerable about opening up publicly about something so personal. But I think it's important to outline the thinking behind my decision to hopefully show that this was about me and my circumstances. It was not illustrative of what works for women or even women in politics, more generally.

Firstly, this was not a decision I ever imagined making. In fact, when I first started pondering it my husband said to me, 'You're talking crazy. You will never leave by choice. That job is who you are.'

The reality is that I am actually so far removed from the mother that I thought I would be before I had children that I suspect younger me would be mortified.

A couple of years before I fell pregnant some close friends of ours had their first child. He was seven weeks old when my husband and I invited them to spend a night at our shack with us. I assured them that our bedroom was at the other end of the house so a screaming baby would not disturb us and maybe we could indulge my friend with some of the luxuries that she had missed out on during her pregnancy.

When their car pulled in we quickly noticed something missing. The baby. 'We decided to have a night off and left him with Mum,' my beaming friend announced upon arrival. The four of us went on to enjoy an amazing night filled with much laughter, oysters, soft cheeses and probably too much champagne. When they left the next morning I declared to my husband, 'That is exactly the kind of mother I will be. Any children will fit in around our life, not dictate what we do and when.'

I was stupidly naive about the realities of parenthood. At the time that I fell pregnant with my firstborn I had not one but two mischievous puppies. How much harder could a human be, right? I actually seriously believed that a baby would be somewhere in the same realm of work as two cavoodles. I was totally clueless. I had no idea about the sleep deprivation, no idea about the anxiety over doing right by the tiny human I was besotted with, no idea about how my sense of identity would instantly be turned on its head. I arrogantly scoffed at the saying that 'there is no harder job than the job of being a mum'. Yeah, I was different, I thought. I had already conquered a really hard job.

Having my son Sam in the world is one of the greatest things that has ever happened, certainly to me, but as a very biased and lovestruck mother I would also suggest maybe for the entire universe. Yet, with the possible exception of my father's death, giving birth to Sam was the worst thing that has ever happened to me. It wasn't a pleasant birthing experience. I will spare you the gory details except to say that I wasn't just in more pain than I had imagined I would be, I was in more pain than I had ever imagined anyone could be. I felt powerless, invisible and completely unheard, and I was deeply traumatised by the experience. Less than a day after the ordeal, and only hours after I finished haemorrhaging, I discharged myself and took my darling baby home. I wanted to get as far away from the scene of the crime as possible.

For the first six weeks of Sam's life he screamed. Constantly. I'm not talking about normal baby cries but pained, piercing roars for help. He wouldn't sleep for longer than forty minutes before he would wake again, screaming. Near constant breast-feeding was his only comfort. It was devastating to me that I was so happy that he was in the world but that he clearly wished he wasn't. I immediately lost myself in a desperate effort to comfort this poor child. I spent literally weeks not even bothering to go to bed but instead just napping on the couch next to his bassinet in between his cries. I was on automatic, more tired than I'd thought humanly possible.

The home visit nurse was concerned and suggested he should immediately go to the doctor for examination. He was just eight days old when I first took him to the emergency department for testing. Nothing obvious emerged. I was constantly calling Health Direct, visiting doctors, making appointments with baby-settling experts and searching for answers to try to help my troubled darling child. All agreed that there was something wrong but nobody could pinpoint what it was. We tried different things, he was put on silent reflux medication, but nothing seemed to make any difference. He screamed, he breastfed so constantly that he became almost comically big, and he screamed some more. At this point, I wasn't even thinking about going back to work; I felt like a robot just trying to get through each day.

This may sound like the start of a story on postnatal depression or motherhood disappointment. If anything, it is the opposite. I know what I am about to say makes me sound a bit bonkers and is not backed up by any medical or scientific evidence, but Sam's screaming actually meant I bonded with him strongly, convinced that he too was traumatised by the horrific manner of his birth. I had been induced unnecessarily, as it turned out, and I don't think that my body or indeed his was ready for his entrance into the world. My beautiful husband had been there supporting me through every moment, but I felt that Sam and I were the only two people who completely understood what had happened to us and how awful it had been. If I as an adult was still grieving the experience, I could only imagine what he was going through. I knew that I would stop at nothing and not leave my innocent newborn child's side until he was comforted.

It took all of a week for my foolish notion that my child would not dictate my life and would learn to work around me to be thrown out the window. Within days I had already surrendered the notion of having a bed or even attempting a night's sleep. I was entirely his.

And then for whatever reason, just before he was six weeks old, Sam suddenly stopped screaming. That was lucky, because we were back to work the following week.

Members of parliament find all sorts of different ways to balance their work and family. For my family though, what worked best was Sam travelling with me. My husband Dave works on breakfast radio, which meant if Sam was to stay home we would need to find a nanny available to start each day just after 4.30 am. There weren't many takers. Added to this, shortly after Sam's birth one of Dave's best mates was diagnosed with cancer. We didn't want the friend living on his own while going through chemo and radiotherapy, so invited him to move in with us while he was undergoing his treatment. We had the two of us, my two stepchildren Sophie and Jim, a newborn baby, a cancer patient and two energetic cavoodles all living under our roof. We decided that the inn was too full to contemplate an au pair or any sort of live-in arrangement. Sam would be my travelling sidekick. And so it was.

Sam was eight weeks old when he took his first flight. He was like an angel; fellow passengers questioned whether I was actually holding a doll. It was the first of hundreds of flights that he would embark on over the next year and then again in the years that followed. He was less than three months old when he attended his first ALP national conference, where I spent much of the time crying in corridors after failing to find a quiet, secluded place to breastfeed my constantly hungry child. I hadn't really thought about the logistics, I hadn't asked for help and I was travelling alone with him, still getting used to his constant breastfeeding. He travelled back and forth to Canberra with me for each parliamentary sitting week but also visited every state and territory as I travelled for my work as Shadow Minister for Education and Early Childhood. He visited schools, factories and childcare centres. He sat on

SEX, LIES AND QUESTION TIME

my lap for meetings with stakeholders, policy discussions and factional caucus meetings.

Of course there were some logistical issues. Getting a child out of his cot while it is still dark to take him on the first flight out in the morning wasn't always fun. Mid-air nappy issues were never fun. Bathing your child in a baby bath on your office floor in between having to run to the chamber to vote had its moments.

People often say how much babies crave consistency and routine. My darling Sam had none of that. He had only one thing that was constant in his life: me. Every night, no matter where we were or what craziness had unfolded during the day, we would snuggle up to sleep. Together. We slept in exactly the same position each night, me lying on my back and him lying on his back on top of me. We were like a mother and baby otter. Don't try this at home: I know it's very contrary to safe sleep recommendations, but I cannot count the number of different locations we went to sleep like this. We were each other's stability.

In the lead-up to the 2016 election, I was seriously stressed. I was incredibly proud that we were making education the centre-piece of our campaign. We were pledging billions of dollars more than the Coalition to adequately fund our schools and keep the original Gonski vision alive. As Labor's education spokesperson I was asked to spend the first two weeks of the campaign travelling with Labor leader Bill Shorten and promoting our schools policies. Awesome. Except, despite now being fifteen months old, Sam was still breastfeeding. Regularly. I hated the thought of having to completely wean him so suddenly, but how could I take him on the road where he would no doubt be a distraction to Bill Shorten, who was working on the most stressful and important task of his working life – trying to win government and become prime minister. After many sleepless nights I finally raised the issue with Bill. He didn't hesitate in responding, 'Don't be silly, we'll bring him with us.' And so Sam spent much of his first election campaign zipping around regional Queensland and New South Wales in the opposition leader's private plane.

In early 2017 when I made my announcement to leave, I had still never had a single night apart from Sam. I just never learnt how to be away from him.

I was so close to Sam that we were essentially co-dependent, and I didn't want it any other way. The thought of having to leave him once he started school was unbearable. How could we go from being inseparable partners in crime to spending a minimum of twenty weeks a year apart and probably much more? The very thought of it tore my heart out, and in the end made my decision a pretty straightforward one.

The other big factor was that I had my eyes wide open to what I could be about to experience. My entire political career was spent as a marginal seat MP, which means that the twenty weeks a year in Canberra is far from the only challenge to family life. My role meant working every weekend, and attending dinners, awards nights and other community events several nights every week.

I also thought there was a better than likely chance that Labor would be in government after the next election. (I was wrong, as it turned out.) I had previously served as a minister, and I knew how much additional time that also meant away from home. That is true of all ministers, but even more so if you are not from the eastern states. Restrictive flight schedules to and from Adelaide make daytrips far less possible and result in extra nights away from home. The fact that most stakeholders and major conferences are still on the eastern seaboard means that additional trips are required. The twenty weeks away from home in Canberra can rapidly become thirty or more when ministerial responsibilities are included. Add the overseas travel of an international conference or delegation you are required to lead maybe once a year, and you can easily find yourself away from home much more than you are there.

On top of all of this, I was also mindful of my experience serving in a minority parliament. Every sitting, every vote, every day needed to be attended by every member. Getting leave was extraordinarily difficult and flexibility almost entirely non-existent. I had to decide whether this was the environment I wanted to be in when I had a small child. But at least I had a choice. Unlike many, I have an amazing and supportive husband who does more than his fair share on the home front. I have family support. I had remarkable staff who always found a way to help me make it work.

There is another factor that probably played a role in my decision. It's a big part of who I am, and has shaped my attitude to life since I was fifteen.

I am so remarkably privileged to have grown up in a loving, stable, happy family. We weren't rich by any stretch, but as a kid I had everything that I needed and still cherish my wonderful childhood as the foundation of the person I grew up to be. I also learnt how quickly it can all disappear.

I was in Year 11 when, out of the blue, we learnt one day that not only did my dad have cancer, but he had less than six months to live. When he died a few months later it shook my perfect upbringing and left me with a very concrete understanding of just how precious our time with our loved ones can be.

My father was forty-five when he died. His own father had also died young. In fact my dad never got to meet his own father, who got sick and died while my nanna was still pregnant with Dad. There is absolutely nothing to suggest that I will die at the same age as my dad. But if it were to happen, it would be in less than three years' time. My children would be eight and six.

I can't count the number of times I reflect upon something I wished I had asked my own dad about. Things I will never get the chance to learn his views on or experiences of. I suspect that my own life experience has played a significant role in my own priorities and choices regarding my family. I will always be so grateful and proud of my fifteen years in parliament, but my family is my number one priority now. I want to take every opportunity to be there for my children. To teach them my values, to make sure they know who I am, what I believe in, and what I hope for in their lives.

———

I enjoyed circumstances in my workplace that most parents could only dream of: the chance to do a rewarding, exciting job that I loved while also having the kind of flexibility that allowed me to have my child with me throughout my working day. I had the most amazing, helpful, talented and kind staff helping me. I had an onsite quality childcare centre in Parliament House, allowing me to visit Sam or peer through the windows at him playing at any opportunity between meetings. I had the kind of understanding work colleagues who would not only help me to juggle my family and professional responsibilities but who also valued the impact of Sam's presence on our often sterile work environment. In Chris Hayes, I had a compassionate chief whip who would pull me aside if there were no votes expected on a sitting night and give me permission to leave early and get Sam into bed at a reasonable time. In Bill Shorten as leader, I had a boss who knew the importance of family and wasn't just tolerant of my juggling act but I think was even appreciative of it.

All of the struggles and logistical issues actually had an unexpected and huge benefit. There's nothing like being beholden to the needs of a small person to put things in perspective. I was never better at my job, more confident at work or more grounded than when I was doing it as a working mum. So much of the bullshit that had consumed me earlier in my career and eaten away at my confidence was now irrelevant. I just didn't have the time or energy for it anymore. It meant I was able to get on with the job that I was elected to do.

I also noticed the difference it made to civility in the building to have a baby around. People I would normally regard as political enemies or who I would never normally exchange a word with would pass me in the corridor as I was walking Sam in his pram. They would stop to admire him and ask how it was going. At the time of Sam's birth Scott Morrison was the minister with responsibility for childcare and I was his direct shadow minister, whose job it was to constantly point out everything that he was doing wrong. Upon news of Sam's birth he sent me a generous flower arrangement adorned with dummies and bibs. It was kind. Having a baby or children in the building changed the atmosphere. It made it feel less combative, even a bit normal.

Once I had made my decision to leave, it was important to me to communicate it as soon as possible. Although it was only a few months after the 2016 election and years before the next election was due, there were a number of reasons I wanted to move quickly. I wanted to give the most notice and the greatest opportunity to find excellent candidates to run in my place. My local community had been amazing and loyal and supportive, electing me five times, and they deserved the best quality representative available to them.

South Australia was about to lose a seat in the federal parliament. It meant the state would go from having eleven members of the House of Representatives to ten. We didn't yet know which seat would be abolished but it meant that all seats would have substantial changes to their boundaries, and if my already marginal seat was moved even slightly east it would become a safe Liberal seat. I didn't want it to look like I was running scared if the boundaries became more unfavourable. But the main reason for my haste was because I was pregnant again. I thought it was fairest on Bill and the team if I told them immediately, rather than them temporarily covering my maternity leave only to then have to find someone to permanently appoint.

Even more importantly, it was the optics. I knew that, whatever my words, if I stood heavily pregnant announcing that I would not run again for family reasons it would send a clear message that I was hoping not to send.

After I told my family, I informed Senator Don Farrell of my decision. Despite the publicly held view that he is some sort of evil arch conservative, Don had supported me as a 26-year-old, pro-choice, socially progressive woman running for parliament. He would be the one left to deal with any preselection fights to replace me in the seat and the race that would be on to take my frontbench spot. It was an odd phone call, not least because I hadn't realised that he was actually on holidays in the Philippines and we had to FaceTime. He tried briefly to get me to reconsider or take some more time to think about it, but he knew that I meant it and I think he understood.

A few weeks later when parliament returned, I made an appointment to meet with Bill Shorten to 'discuss a personal issue'. I was terrified of telling him about my decision. I was conscious that Bill had both supported and promoted me, and I felt a deep guilt about what I was about to tell him. I thought I knew how the meeting would go. I thought he would be angry and let down, but would come around in a couple of days. I underestimated him.

Sitting down in Bill's office, I said that he had probably guessed that I wanted to tell him I was pregnant, but that wasn't the issue I had come to discuss. He looked surprised when I told him that I would not be running at the next election. He calmly comforted me, saying, 'I understand, you've been here for a long time now. You're over it?' I assured him that was far from the case. In fact, I felt more comfortable, better suited and ready to achieve real change than I had ever felt during my time as an MP. I just couldn't find a way to reconcile that with the mother I wanted to be. He instantly got it. Having a young daughter himself, he didn't question where I was coming from. He understood and was kind and supportive.

It was important to me that I announced my decision my way, and that meant telling my voters next. My local community was always my number one priority. I wanted to give the people who had repeatedly supported me the respect of informing them first. I knew what I had to do, and felt that quickly ripping the band aid off was the best way to do it. I drafted a letter to my community, and my staff worked tirelessly to print 65,000 addressed letters to every household in my electorate. Bill's staff asked me to give the story to the local paper first, but I refused.

So, on what would have otherwise seemed like a totally normal day, my letter started landing in mailboxes. I sat at home, frozen in fear, waiting. There was a moment when my phone beeped, and oddly enough it was from Liberal Minister and South Australian Senator Simon Birmingham; the word had quickly spread around Adelaide, he had seen my letter and was wishing me all the best. I went to my bedroom and just sobbed. My husband calls me the ice princess because I never cry, but all of a sudden my decision to leave was real and irreversible. I'd given it all up. I was instantly grieving; I felt broken and bereft.

A couple of hours later I was holding a press conference and Bill Shorten had flown into town to join me. I warned him that I felt so sad and lost that he might have a blubbering mess by his side in front of the cameras. He was very kind and told me a joke to think of if I felt I was about to cry. He tried to help me get through it.

I switched to work mode, put up the wall and just did what I had to do. But I knew that I was walking away from something truly extraordinary.

———

Four months later I gave birth to my youngest son, Charlie. (It was a much better birth, thank goodness. Easy and almost fun, even.) My interstate travel was greatly reduced due to the fact that I had moved to the backbench. That was probably lucky. I was now travelling back and forth to Canberra on my own with two children under three.

My boys are both amazing and adorable, although they are very different. While Sam is thoughtful, sensitive and an intro-vert, with Charlie you always know exactly how he is feeling. This is a great thing, as he is a happy child and normally shows this by singing and dancing for anyone who will watch. But when Charlie was flying, he was not a happy baby at all. And the whole plane would know it. He would get ear pain and then scream relentlessly from take-off to landing. It wasn't much fun.

We finally found a wonderful nanny, Georgia, who was able to start at stupid o'clock in the morning when Dave headed off to work, which meant that Sam no longer had to travel with me and I could concentrate on the little screamer, Charlie. It didn't really work though. Sam liked coming to Canberra and felt like he was missing out when he stayed home, so pretty soon he was back to travelling with me and Charlie most of the time. One day he summed up our problem perfectly. He said, 'Mum, when I stay home I miss you and Charlie, but when I go to Canberra I miss Daddy, Jimmy and Soph. I just want us all to be together.' That's what I wanted too. It's what was right for our family. How lucky are we that our biggest 'problem' is that the six of us like being together.

On 18 February 2019 I delivered my final speech to the parliament. I concluded it with a message to my beautiful children: 'I'm leaving a job that I love for me. I'm leaving because what you've given me is something that I love more than this excellent job, because there is nothing in the world that I want more than to be present and active in guiding you and supporting you and being with you as you grow into the amazing men that I know you'll be. There's nothing more rewarding, more entertaining, more important to me than being there for you two crazy, clever, kind and funny little people.'

Ultimately that was the very simple truth that I couldn't overcome.

In the time that has passed since I left the parliament I have had a moment or two of quiet contemplation about that decision. I now have the chance to work with some brilliant not-for-profits and organisations that I care deeply about. But I know that I will never again have the opportunity to affect the sort of change that I once did. For me, every time that I hear the comforting deep breathing of my sleeping children, every time I get a day to play their made-up games of 'baby bunyips' or 'battling bears', I know that I made the right choice for me.

Women can be mothers and MPs. I am positive of this – mainly because if you look to our parliament you can see the evidence in the form of countless women across the chamber.

It just wasn't right for me anymore.

CHAPTER 11

SHAKING UP THE PARLIAMENT

IT WAS ALMOST midnight in Canberra in 2004 and first-time mother Natasha Stott Despoja had a real problem. Parliament was sitting into the night so she had to be present in the House, but she also had to breastfeed her new son, Conrad. No one around her seemed to understand that her young baby needed to be fed regularly. 'No one was particularly supportive of that,' she said. 'My colleagues in my party room weren't.'

When she shared the story with me, even twenty years on, it still made me gasp.

'It was one of those parliamentary sitting nights when you go through the night,' she said. 'At about eleven o'clock, I said to the whip's office, "I'll need to go and feed Conrad." And she said, "You can't leave, we can't give you a pair, you've got to stay for the vote." I said, "A child needs to be fed. I'll have to get the nanny to bring him in.""

She went to see Comcar to get a driver to collect Conrad and his nanny, who would have to get him up out of his bed in the middle of the night and bring him in to the parliament to be breastfed. 'And Comcar just said, "Nope, that's a flagrant misuse of the rules because you're not in the car with him." Just incredible.'

She was stuck at Parliament House. Her hungry six-month-old son was stuck at her accommodation. It was almost midnight and there was still no end in sight for the parliament sitting. I cannot imagine the stress, frustration and rage that I would feel in such a situation. How are you meant to do your job and be a mum in those circumstances?

The most awful thing about this story is that absolutely nothing has changed to prevent it happening again today.

Workplaces across the world have found ways to modernise and adapt to the rise in female participation and double income families. Job-sharing arrangements, flexible work options, keep-in-touch days, working from home days, extra carer's leave – business has innovated and found a variety of measures to assist the work and family balance. But our parliament has failed to respond as quickly as the private sector. Change is both slow and often fiercely resisted. It seems to be due to a combination of the deeply entrenched masculine culture and the commitment to remain loyal to the Westminster traditions that underpin our parliament.

As Clare O'Neil remarked, 'I've worked in some of the most high-pressure environments in the private sector. The culture of politics, the total lack of concern for family bounda-ries, is unlike anything I have ever seen anywhere else that I've worked.'

It's not as if the issue isn't acknowledged. Every few years we start a conversation about how we could reform the parliament to make it more modern and family-friendly. Commentators raise the need for change; MPs sometimes informally debate options and possible reforms. More often than not the issue is then rapidly placed in the too-hard basket and everybody moves on. If we are to ever see real diversity and increase women's representation this is an issue that needs to be tackled head-on. It isn't just parenting responsibilities, which disproportionately continue to fall on the shoulders of women, it's about caring responsibilities more broadly, for elderly parents or for grown-up children. Real change, not just tinkering around the edges, would also hopefully lead to an increase in the number of women with health requirements or disability entering parliament.

There has been some progress. Within my years in parlia-ment I saw the staff bar transformed into an onsite childcare centre. It was an absolute godsend to me to have high-quality early education and care just metres from the parliamentary chamber. It came about after MPs, mainly but not exclusively women, lobbied for over a decade, persisting even when their pleas fell on deaf ears. Generations of parents will be in their debt. But it shouldn't have taken that long.

Natasha captures the impact of the development, telling me, 'When I went back to parliament for the first time and saw the childcare operation, I burst into tears. I just went, "Are you kidding me?" Because it literally would have changed my parliamentary life.'

I spoke to women across the political spectrum about what would help when it comes to modernising the culture of parliament. In some ways the visibility of parliament – from question time on TV to the dedicated reporting about politics from most media outlets – might actually help accelerate cultural change. It's not like parliament's a private organisation, where everything happens behind closed doors and change has to be driven exclusively from within. Change at parliament can be driven from the outside too – by the shifting norms and values of Australian culture. And Australians are increasingly embracing flexible working conditions that allow for a better work–life balance, particularly for those with children.

The women I spoke to suggested things like changes to parliamentary sitting hours and practices, changes to parliamentary standing orders (which are the rules that govern how parliament operates), changes to politicians' entitlements or rules around acceptable work expenses, and permanently adopting some of the parliament's responses to the COVID-19 pandemic. There is a range of more radical reforms that could also be considered.

There was a consensus across the board that in-person, face-to-face parliament was both vital and untouchable. There was also a view that simple changes could make the running of the parliament more efficient. Often weeks will be dedicated to debating one relatively straightforward change; this is to say nothing of the time spent discussing no concrete proposal at all but just people's views on any topic of the day. There was a conflict of view between mothers who travelled with their young babies and wanted more family-friendly sitting hours so they could take their children home at a reasonable hour each night, versus mothers who had older children back at home and would prefer longer sitting hours each day in return for fewer sitting weeks. All believed that reform was required.

Karen Andrews argued, 'I think you've got to start looking at some fundamental changes to the way parliament works. Could that period of time be used much more effectively? So we're discussing the things that matter, not just, we've got four days and this is what we're going to do to fill them up and run debates for a certain amount of time.'

There is often a sense in parliament that we should do things the way we've always done things. But questioning the status quo, especially when the status quo dates from one hundred years ago, is a vital part of what makes a democracy.

Marielle Smith pointed out, 'I think it is worth looking at how we use our time and how time can be used more effectively. If anyone's listened to a full day of parliament you know that there's a lot of time in the day which probably could be trimmed without having many consequences for our democracy or the future of our country.'

Parliament often sits from morning until late at night and all members need to be present in the building, if not the chamber, to be able to vote at any moment. Amanda Rishworth noted that the House of Representatives no longer has a period each night between 6.30 and 8 pm where there are no votes called. That used to mean that during that brief period in an otherwise twelve-hour day, you could at least briefly leave the building or have specific time that you knew would not be unexpectedly interrupted.

'That really helped in terms of getting my child bathed, getting him into bed and then going back to the parliament [for a vote or debate]. I think having defined breaks in the long day, not necessarily breaks but times when there are no divisions [times when votes are held], would be much more family-friendly and useful.'

Marielle expanded on the issue of sitting hours. 'I don't think in any workplace, the idea that you would work from 8 am to 11 pm as your stock-standard hours, not to mention all the work you do to prepare for those hours, is reasonable for people's mental or physical health. I mean, it certainly makes it extremely difficult for people who are trying to parent and participate at the same time.'

Outside of regular parliamentary activities, for two weeks three times a year senators hold interrogations of public officials, known as 'Senate estimates'. Marielle spoke of the practicalities of these sessions.

'During Senate estimates, my briefing starts at 8 am and Senate estimates doesn't close until 11 pm at night. Juggling that, even with a toddler, has been extremely hard. I'm about to do it with a newborn baby as well. It's all well and good to say that there's childcare at Parliament House. It's not open at eleven at night and, even if it was, I would not put my child in it for those hours. So there's still a long way to go in terms of the work environment out there.'

There are some basic changes that would drastically make being a member of parliament more family-friendly. Anika Wells suggested the introduction of a blanket rule that parliament not be scheduled during the first week of school, as this would stop parents routinely missing a child's first day, although there are challenges around different school terms in each state. For me, I would suggest a stronger stance is taken on last-minute changes to the sitting hours. On too many Thursday afternoons, when MPs have spent the whole week telling their children that they will be home on Thursday night, the government then decides that there is a law they urgently need passed and that the sitting will be extended into Thursday night or possibly Friday. MPs are then forced to make the awful phone call home. It disappoints children and partners, and puts plans in disarray. Effective time management becomes a victim of the sport of politics and, once again, it is families and children who are left to pay the price. Priorities.

The one thing that ensured that I didn't have any experiences like that dreadful night Natasha endured was people. I was lucky to have helpful people around me. I saw a change in parliament from people having strict attitudes and giving stern-talking lectures for daring to request any sort of flexibility to a greater awareness and understanding of the logistical issues that people faced. The support of my party whip was crucial in my ability to get my job done.

A whip's job is to make sure all of their party's MPs are present for every vote. They are in charge of who gets leave and who doesn't, who can leave the building and who can't.

They are notoriously strict and at times mean. Their decisions and attitudes make all of the difference to flexibility on parliamentary sitting days. For the whole time I was juggling being an MP and a mum, the chief whip of the Labor Party was the Member for Fowler, Chris Hayes. He is an incredibly wonderful man, a loving father and grandfather and someone with an understanding of the importance of family responsibilities. On countless sitting nights, he would tell me that it was okay to take my boys home at 6.30 because even though the parliament was still sitting, there were no votes expected that night. On other occasions, I would take my pyjama-clad children to his office with a pleading face. Chris would concede that there was a vote expected, but it was on a small technical issue of insignificance to my electorate. He would rationalise it by figuring that the numbers dictated that we were going to lose the vote anyway, so it didn't really matter if we lost by one more vote. I could take my children home to bed. He was supportive and considerate, and I will always adore him. But clearly that is not everyone's experience.

At the same time as I was breastfeeding Sam and working as an MP, Kelly O'Dwyer was juggling her parliamentary career and her first child. She seems to have had a very different experience with her whip. Scott Buchholz was the government chief whip. There is an infamous story that he once sent Kelly a note with some 'advice': perhaps she should just express more breastmilk so that breastfeeding didn't interfere with her duties in the parliamentary chamber. Her daughter was three months old at the time.

The attitudes of the person filling the role of party whip make a huge difference. This should be a consideration in selecting them. Surely though, we need better support and rules in place so people don't have to rely on the luck of getting a decent and understanding human being in that role to be able to make it work.

We don't need to turn the parliament on its head to make this easier. It doesn't have to be radical or controversial. Back in 2009, a parliamentary research paper by Dr Mark Rodrigues highlighted the importance of pairing to assist parliamentarians with children. One easy change would be for the parties to agree on a limited and specific new category of guaranteed night-time pairs available to parents also caring for babies. It would not be difficult to introduce. It would not alter our system or the result of debates.

It can't be left to the women – or men – who need these pairs to be the only ones to advocate for this. My conversations indicated that there are women who fear that advocating for change would create a backlash and create the impression they were trying to slack off. As someone who has travelled regularly back and forth to parliament with two small children, I can guarantee the effort required is far from slack. The question is whether the parliament decides that we actually value that effort and are prepared to recognise and help ease it.

Happily, there have already been significant changes to standing orders to accommodate breastfeeding mothers. The change to allow breastfeeding in the chamber received the most publicity, as did Greens Senator Larissa Waters when she became the first to do so in May 2017. But in fact, years before, there had been a much bigger and more helpful reform introduced in the House of Representatives. In 2008, for the first time since Federation, an individual's vote in the House of Representatives could be counted even if they were not physically in the chamber for the division. It was granted to women who were breastfeeding in their office at the time. The importance of this was momentous. You rarely know exactly when a vote is going to be called; it could be at almost any moment of any long sitting day and when it does you have four minutes of ringing bells throughout the whole of Parliament House before the chamber doors are locked and you miss the opportunity to record your say. The consequences of this can be immense. In a minority parliament it is much more than just recording your say – your vote, or lack of it, can determine the fate of an entire law. It can be a rush at the best of times, but markedly harder if you have to remove a hungry child from your breast first or even harder if you have to navigate the vast corridors of Parliament House with said child clinging to your boob. Now, women in that situation can ring the whip's office during those four minutes to claim their breastfeeding proxy. Bravo!

To this day the Senate has no such provision. Marielle Smith is about to become the first senator from a major party in almost twenty years to give birth while in office, and she is determined to see this addressed. 'The very least we could do is ensure that there is no longer such disparity between the House and the Senate when it comes to breastfeeding mothers.' The Senate has considered this matter before, but rejected the proposal for reasons that remain unclear. These aren't big changes but they make a very big difference. It's no longer acceptable to simply park simple but meaningful reforms in the too-hard basket.

There are many other areas where the parliament has not fully kept up to date with the modern requirements of the people now elected to it. I am well aware that nobody outside of the parliament wants politicians to have any entitlements (expenses for travelling, for example) at all. Even as an ex-MP it is with great trepidation that I raise this topic. You say the term 'politicians' entitlements' and people immediately think of Bronwyn Bishop swanning about in a taxpayer-funded helicopter. If entitlements are going to exist though, they should be focused on the most relevant areas of need. It's incredibly telling to look at the way that the entitlements are structured – it says a lot about the values and priorities that sit behind them.

Amanda Rishworth is a shadow minister who zips around the country. She was also a breastfeeding mother who relied upon family support to do her job. Whenever there is controversy or a politician misuses their travel entitlements the rules are tightened, the number of flights is stripped back, the access is restricted. This is understandable: the public don't want public funds rorted. But it also has consequences. There are currently allowances for politicians to travel to do their jobs. There are also more limited family entitlements to ensure that their family can join them on occasion. The people who most rely on those family travel entitlements are generally MPs travelling with small children. Whenever those entitlements are restricted, those women's capacity to undertake both roles becomes harder.

This was an issue that Amanda faced, caught in a tightening of the rules after yet another media scandal in 2015 about a politician misusing entitlements; she was forced to pay for trips so that her husband could support her to do her job and breastfeed her child. It has since been partly addressed, with an exception made for nursing mothers until their child is twelve months old. I no longer needed this entitlement and was on my way out when the reforms were made but I did point out that World Health Organization advice recommends two years of breastfeeding. I was told I was pushing my luck. If your child is over twelve months old and is still required to travel with you for any reason, you access support for that out of the same entitlement that members use to fly their spouses to join them to attend dinners or awards nights. And you get the same number of trips. I would strongly argue that they are not the same priority.

And if you access the entitlement you will often be criticised for it. As Amanda said, 'I feel very angry when I get journalists come to me and say, "What could we do to make parliament better?" And then two days later, the same people are bashing up people for taking their entitlements.' Worse still, breast-feeding mothers sometimes top the newspapers' shame lists of parliamentarians who claimed the most in travel entitlements, often without explanation. As Amanda said, 'It's those types of things that make you question whether you should do it or not. It's those sorts of things that actually make it really hard.'

We can decide that we think women should pay to make it work out of their own pocket, but we can't then simultaneously claim that we want more women in parliament, knowing that many of these women will be mothers.

There are lots of silly little examples of entitlement issues. I remember when I was getting my new work car. You get to select from a range of optional extras. I care nothing about cars and didn't really need any of the extras. No need for a tow bar or tinting, roof racks or whatever else might have been on that list. I did need an anchor point added so that I could safely install a child car seat. I was told, 'Sorry, you'll have to sort that out yourself, it's outside of entitlement.' I didn't care about the money or even the effort, but if you are going to cover some things maybe make it less obvious who wrote the entitlements and who they were written for. As with anything, money talks, and clearly shows what is prioritised.

If there has been any silver lining amid the horrors of the coronavirus pandemic, it has been the way it has forced stubbornly entrenched cultures and practices to adapt. The question for the parliament now is how much it returns to business as usual and how many of these innovations remain in place.

There was broad agreement that the culture around non-parliamentary travel needs to permanently change. As a minister I spent more days than I could count having each of my three main meals in different capital cities. Penny Wong explained, 'The number of times I've got up at 4.30 in the morning to go to Sydney for two meetings and try to get back in time to see the kids as they are going to go to sleep ... now I think, really, I probably could have done the meetings online. And I hope that some expectations around that are different now. I think it's really hard on women with young kids.'

Clare O'Neil was so optimistic about the permanent changes that would flow from the COVID-19 travel restrictions that she almost made me think I had made a terrible mistake leaving parliament. Especially for MPs who aren't based on the eastern seaboard, it is the constant travel that is often the most incompatible with parenting – as it was for me, and for Tim Hammond.

Clare observed, 'There is this practice in politics where it is a reflex to jump on a plane every time you want to speak to someone. That kind of travel was always unnecessary, and it will end now. If we can just get a bit more relaxation around the need to be there in person for every meeting and every event, then that is going to be a huge thing for working parents. It's going to reshape how we do our jobs as members of parliament, as it will for many professions.'

Beyond changes to travel, in response to COVID-19 the parliament introduced a temporary reform that would previously have been unthinkable: a virtual parliament. Members and senators could participate in the debates of the day and ask and answer questions in question time remotely, by video hook-up from their homes or offices in their electorates. It was a momentous change, and one that brought hope for some.

Anika Wells saw the potential that could be unleashed if some of these measures were made permanent. 'The people who we most need to hear from, the people who are most under-represented in parliament, like carers of people with a disability, are the ones who currently find it hardest to get here. There are people who could never manage what we have to do by way of federal travel. So virtual parliament would allow caregivers, not just people with babies, to contribute. And there's certainly a lot of us pushing for that. Hopefully we make some headway and lock down some permanent arrangements.'

Clare O'Neil also noted that there was already a pushback against any suggestion of not reverting exactly to prior arrangements. 'Remote options available to us should be continued for family reasons, and it's going to be an interesting debate because I think, surprisingly, a lot of members of parliament will say that that's not appropriate and that people do need to be present at the parliament to be at the parliament. Obviously, it would make a dramatic difference if you could continue to attend parliament, but not be in Canberra.'

Marielle Smith has a slightly different take, showing the diversity of opinion regarding future reform even among mothers of young children, let alone the broader parliament. 'I have heard people say that virtual parliament or virtual participation is the answer to all of this. I don't think it is. I think virtual participation is a useful addition to our democratic system to allow people who otherwise would not be able to participate, to participate. But I think the risk with ingraining virtual participation is that it will be used as an excuse to exclude people from physically participating in the job. And so much of parliament's work depends on being able to look someone in the eye, being able to have a debate in a public forum in full view of the public, and through all those different means. So I would be worried about saying virtual parliament should stay forever.'

I agree that face-to-face contact is critical to the way things actually get achieved in Australian politics. You will often achieve more from grabbing a minister as you pass them in a corridor than you ever will from lobbying through letters that get re-routed to departments, or phone calls that get handled by junior staff. You develop policy ideas and alliances through conversation and networking. It is crucial to making progress. I do find the lack of imagination on the part of our broader parliament disheartening though. Despite being handed a once-in-a-lifetime opportunity to truly change and modernise, I suspect that what we will instead see is a quick 'snapback' to business as usual.

Looking abroad though, even prior to COVID-19, we can see some more ambitious thinking. From time to time we speak of female MPs being on 'maternity leave'. The reality is that for most there is actually no such thing as real maternity leave; it just means a brief period without interstate travel. There aren't any 'acting MPs' who can step in and fulfil your electorate duties. You don't have a deputy who can temporarily fill in for you. In effect, any time that you have off is time when your electorate does not have an MP to attend their functions, recognise their achievements or address their problems. Your staff are without their employer. Maternity leave means not attending a few weeks of parliament. I'm sure I am not the only one who also spent much of that time dragging my newborn child around the electorate attending functions and events or working in the electorate office signing letters and forms.

The UK recently found a way to address this issue. British Labour MP and first-time mum Stella Creasy made history in 2019 when she became the first MP to be represented by a 'locum', the medical term for a stand-in doctor who can cover the duties of another physician when they are unavailable. In her case, the 'locum' was one of her own constituents, Kizzy Gardiner, who was hired to stand in for Creasy for six months to work on electoral and constituent work while Creasy gave birth to and raised her baby daughter. Creasy has long been a campaigner for maternity rights for women and believed her own case would be a watershed for other women who wanted to continue to have children without ending their political career. The role of the locum was limited to work in Creasy's Walthamstow electorate – Gardiner did not sit in the parliament, take part in question time or vote, but kept the electorate office running in the absence of the normal local member.

The BBC reported that Creasy said she hoped the case would set a precedent for politics and other workplaces. 'If the place that makes the law doesn't recognise the value of ensuring cover for the duties of MPs, then how can it advocate for the millions of parents across the country worried that if they take time out to care for newborn children they will suffer?

'As yet parliament has still to get its act together to come up with a policy on this area and has not yet even begun to consult on the issue as promised, but this post means residents in Walthamstow can be confident that when my child is born they will still have someone to take up their cases with ministers, local public services and an advocate for the causes they care about.'

I can see how this system could work. I always loved my electoral work – it was the most rewarding and satisfying part of the job – but the reality is that most constituents who come to see you just need a simple pointer in the right direction. It might be a problem with street lighting, a complaint about vandalism in a local park, a workplace issue where they are being underpaid, or a question about Medicare – it would be easy to train someone up to play that front-of-house role in providing valuable information to the public. The truth too is that, with parliament sitting twenty-odd weeks a year, this is exactly how electoral offices run anyway when the local member is in Canberra.

Julia Gillard said of the trial, 'You look at any other occupation, if you worked for the public service or one of our big publicly listed companies, if you went on maternity leave, someone would be doing your job and then you'd come back and you'd take your job back over. And things would have been done in the time you've been away. And we just don't do that for parliamentarians now. And why don't we?'

A more contentious and ambitious proposal, also out of the UK, is for MPs to be elected on a job-sharing basis. British MP Caroline Lucas struck a job-sharing arrangement with her parliamentary colleague Jonathan Bartley, with the two of them dividing the workload as joint leaders of the Greens Party of England and Wales.

While that arrangement was something that involved the two MPs sharing their role, Lucas pointed to a research paper by the University of Bristol entitled 'Open House', which advocated a more formalised system whereby electorates could even be held by two members at the same time.

'Job-sharing MPs could keep their caring responsibilities, they could keep voluntary work, they could continue part-time in their profession,' Lucas said. 'It would help more women into politics, more disabled people and more people for whom being an MP is currently unimaginable and inaccessible.'

There are, of course, significant logistical and cost issues that need to be addressed. What would happen in the event that one of the MPs became embroiled in a corruption scandal or had to be dismissed? How would remuneration be structured to ensure that the public did not baulk at the idea of paying for an increased number of MPs?

Two things are clear: the current arrangements for women in politics are less flexible than in the private sector, and they drive many women away from ever going into politics.

If we look to the future, and we aspire to a parliament that truly reflects the community that it represents – not just with women but with parents, carers, people with a disability, or people with health needs – it follows that we are going to have to think more radically at some point along the way. I have no doubt if there was the will, and the urging of the broader community, we have the wit to come up with more ways to make it work. The private sector has taken steps to modernise. When will the parliament?

CHAPTER 12

WHY IT'S WORTH IT

PHILOSOPHERS HAVE LONG argued about whether there is any such thing as pure altruism. Altruistic behaviour can result in positives for both the giver and receiver; in other words, we get something back from helping others. Whether it is a little thing like helping someone with their shopping or paying for someone else's parking, we're likely all familiar with the glow that you get in return for helping others. It feels good to help improve someone's day. It's not just a feeling; it's backed up by science. Published research has shown that helping friends, acquaintances or even strangers mitigates stress, boosts positive emotions and improves our mental health.

Now imagine that instead of helping a stranger with their shopping, you have an idea about how you could make Australia better. Imagine then being elected, becoming a minister and making your idea a reality, seeing your idea being implemented in every school, every hospital, or every workplace. Imagine your idea helping millions of people. And that is what actually happens in the job of a member of parliament. It is the reality that drives almost every person in politics. That is what makes being an MP worth it – that's the reason we put up with the sacrifices and demands along the way.

As I was writing this book, or more specifically procrastinating on social media when I should have been writing this book, a tweet popped up in my feed. The community campaigner and activist Sally Rugg had responded to yet another media report about the treatment of women in politics, on this occasion about a female staffer who resigned after false, anonymous allegations were published about her bullying other staff members. Sally wrote, 'I'm often asked if or when I'd go into politics, and this is always the first thing I think of. It seems that if political operatives want a woman gone and they're not bullied or harassed out of there directly, they'll say she is a bully herself.'

It was incredibly disheartening to read this, although I could understand where she was coming from. Once more the culture of politics was taking the attention away from the purpose of it. I don't know Sally, but I do know that she is a successful activist and an outspoken advocate, particularly upon issues of equality. She is exactly the sort of woman you would assume might consider parliament as a natural career progression.

Of course, I understand that bad news and controversy sell newspapers. I get that scandals grab people's attention, and that nobody wants to write a story about how a member of parliament had a particularly rewarding day. Yet if we don't balance this unrelenting negativity with the positive side of politics, we risk turning away people who might otherwise make amazing contributions to our country. We also turn off the general public, reinforcing the idea that Canberra is out of touch, parliament is a sleazy, unsafe, Machiavellian workspace, and that politicians are just a bunch of people who spend their days yelling at each other, driven by nothing but a quest for power.

So what does drive politicians? What brings meaning to their jobs and to their lives? Linda Burney explained it well. 'The thing that I truly believe is that part of our job whilst we're on this earth's surface is to leave it a little bit better. Parliament is where the very big decisions are made about the shape of society, the rules, the delivery of service. You're truly at the table.'

The truth is, despite the focus on conflict and division, at its very heart politics is about positivity. I'm yet to meet anyone who has entered politics because they like the idea of yelling at someone across the parliament and being yelled at in return. People enter the profession, almost without exception, because they believe in its purpose. It's about driving reform and improvements and making our country a better and fairer place. That is overwhelmingly what many women – and men – love about the job.

There are lots of jobs where you can get a sense of accomplishment, pride and reward. And lots of jobs give you the satisfaction of having helped someone. They range from the practical – nurses, teachers, doctors, counsellors – to the less obvious – designers, editors, lawyers, and the list goes on. So what makes politics different? Short of being the person who develops a cure for cancer, I can't think of many who can help more people than a successful parliamentarian. For me, and for many others, there is nothing that can ever compare to being a member of parliament.

There were two main reasons the women I spoke to thought it was worth it all: first, the capacity to create real change in Australia; and second, the magnitude of help you can be responsible for ensuring people in need receive. Instead of helping just one person, you can help thousands, or even millions.

Marielle Smith argued, 'There is no better mechanism to get changes for your community and changes to the way our nation works. I feel lucky every single day that I go in and get to be part of the debate and part of the decision-making, which governs so many fundamentally important things to our community and the people I think need the most support and most help.'

Clare O'Neil summarised it pretty succinctly: 'In politics, you can make change in one day that people outside the parliament will literally work their whole lives and careers for. There is just no other game in town if you care about trying to reshape your country's future.'

Amanda Rishworth had studied long and hard to become a successful clinical psychologist before she entered parliament. She was passionate about it and good at it, but she couldn't shake the feeling there was something more she could do. As she explained, 'With psychology, you're helping an individual and one individual at a time. That's rewarding. But there's a line-up of people at your door still wanting help and you're not changing the broader community. With politics, with one decision, you're able to change the outcomes for a whole community. And that is very rewarding. Sometimes it feels like you're bashing your head against a brick wall, but when you crash on through, you get to change lives, and no one can ever take that away from you.'

Meaningful change becomes even more possible when you're a federal minister. I remember taking my firstborn Sam for his induction at childcare. The educator explained to me that there was this new thing called the Early Years Learning Framework, which ensured that each activity the children did was guided by research on age-appropriate learning. It was like a curriculum for toddlers. I smiled and nodded, feeling like it would be really awkward and immodest to tell her that I was the minister who had approved and introduced it.

She went on to explain that there were also now nationally consistent standards for staffing and play spaces and quality. I nodded and smiled again as I thought back to how hard I had fought to get all states and territories of all different political persuasions to agree to the National Quality Standards. There were many days when I didn't know that we'd get there. We had many private operators vocally opposed to any measures to increase quality and they ran active scare campaigns on how it would affect prices. The federal Coalition were opposed to the reforms and threatening to undo them. Hardest of all, we had different states opposed to different parts of the reforms and threatening to walk away. Our public servants were constantly negotiating with their state counterparts, my chief of staff was regularly negotiating with different state staffers and I was talking to different state ministers, warning them of the political campaign they would face if they declared that children in their state would not receive the same levels of care and attention as children in the rest of the country. It was a slog.

Now, sitting in my son's childcare centre, I was a classic protective parent, adjusting to the idea of my beloved child being at childcare, and I felt incredibly comforted to hear all of this information. And what was important was not that I was being briefed on this, or that every parent across the country would be receiving that same information, but that each and every *child* would be receiving this improved quality of care and education. Their centres would be measured against these national standards, and the results would be publicly reported. As somebody who believes that the first five years of a child's life are critical to the future of that individual, this was overwhelming to me. I helped make that happen. How incredible is that?

When I asked Sussan Ley about the best moments of her job she was unhesitating in her reply: 'I'll always remember the billion dollars that I worked to find in the health budget so that we could list drugs for hepatitis C [on the pharmaceutical benefits scheme]. I knew that might not have happened if I hadn't really wanted to do it.' There are over 130,000 Australians living with chronic hepatitis C. Sussan continued, 'I remember one day I was outside a post office in a country town and somebody came up to me and said, "I just want to shake your hand. You were the health minister who listed the drug that saved my life." That was just amazing. It was such a rewarding moment.'

Jenny Macklin was behind the biggest increase to the base rate of the aged pension in Australia's history, when in 2009 she delivered a $60 a fortnight increase. As a local member I heard firsthand how important this was to older Australians who had previously been forced to keep their heaters off in winter to avoid the increased electricity bill, people who had sacrificed their own welfare just to be able to send their grandchildren a $10 note in their birthday card. I have no doubt that every local member all over the country had heard similar tales of hardship, and $60 a fortnight made an enormous difference. Jenny said, 'I am really proud of what we did for pensioners. It's just a massive improvement. We took a million people out of poverty. There's still a lot of older people living in very dire circumstances, especially if you don't own your own home, a lot of single women particularly. I think about that as it was a really great step, but there's a lot more work to be done for older Australians.'

Lifting a million pensioners out of poverty might have been hard to top as your most rewarding achievement but Jenny was also instrumental in the establishment of the National Disability Insurance Scheme in 2013. She told me how she and Bill Shorten worked for five years to make it a reality. She was driven, as she explained, because 'you couldn't look a mother of a severely disabled child in the eye and not think, "Well, we've got to do something about this."'

The NDIS isn't perfect, and its ongoing implementation has been difficult, but it's a huge improvement on the patchwork of systems in place before, and it sends an important message to the people it supports, and to the broader community. As Jenny said, the NDIS 'will be really, really profound because it's about saying that people with disability can have a different kind of life. That they're not going to be told what to do, that they can decide what they want their life to be like. If that happens over time that will be truly wonderful.'

It doesn't always get there, though. There was a piece of policy work that I was incredibly proud of, that only about three people in the world will have any memory of.

From 2010 to 2013 I was the Minister for Employment Participation. Following the Howard Government's move to disband the old Commonwealth Employment Service (CES) and outsource it to a variety of private and not-for-profit organisations, employment services was the biggest contract that the federal government procured outside of defence. Anyone finding themselves unemployed would be directed to the nearest service for help finding a new job. When we spoke with employers, the employment services and, most importantly, jobseekers, it quickly became clear that the system wasn't working well.

Rather than just blithely hand over another 8 billion dollars to the largely ineffective, bureaucratic and expensive system that had been in place since its outsourcing, I wanted to examine if there was a better way to do things. We went through a major consultation process with employment services, jobseekers, employer groups and welfare organisations. We came up with an entirely new system. A system that was based around the challenges of each distinct region of Australia. One that worked with local service providers to help people actually overcome the barriers that they faced to employment, whether that be homelessness, addiction, language barriers or other factors.

One that worked with local employers and addressed the skills, training or attributes they required in order to employ local jobseekers. It was innovative and adaptable. My colleagues were supportive, and I was so proud of the work.

This would be a significantly better story if I could then tell you about the millions of Australians who were helped out of unemployment as a result of this policy work. Unfortunately, it was not to be. The Labor government was heading towards the September 2013 election when Kevin Rudd resumed the prime ministership from Julia Gillard, and his office wanted to hold off on announcing the policy until his major campaign launch speech. As it turned out, they decided not to announce it and I eventually found myself six days out from an election that everybody could see we were going to lose without having announced this major policy that I had spent two years working on.

I was adamant that we needed to announce it. So in the week of the election, when I was desperately sick with what was probably pneumonia, we scheduled its public announcement. I stood in front of a group of very kind stakeholders who humoured me, each knowing full well that this was a fruitless exercise. In a voice no louder than a whisper, unable to speak longer than about three seconds before coughing furiously and gasping for air, I presented my beloved brainchild. Days later we lost the election and the proposal was never again heard of.

Winning elections is how you get the ability to improve millions of people's lives, which is why politics is necessarily a game you play to win. And where there are winners, there are losers, which makes for a competitive and often adversarial environment. This has always been the case, both in Australia and globally – some national parliaments can even descend into fist fights. But it seems that somewhere along the way the focus in Australia turned to the sport of politics, the optics, the squabbles and scandals, and away from the motivations, reasons and consequences that sit behind it all. It is the sport that turns a lot of people off, but the outcomes are the thing that makes it all worthwhile. The optimist in me still likes to think that one day a future government might decide to take a much-needed look at how our employment services work, or don't work, and someone will say, 'There was some work done on this a few years ago that we could dust off and take a look at ...'

Although there are huge benefits to being a minister, one of the best parts of the job is as a humble local member of parliament. Each and every day you have the chance to help local residents overcome challenges that impact their everyday life. As Tanya Plibersek put it, 'Helping someone with a Centrelink problem that sees them get a year's worth of backdated pay, that helps them deal with grinding poverty, that's a really good feeling. And it's kind of addictive. I can't imagine a job that didn't have that occasional win for someone else as the reward for your hard work. I find it extraordinarily emotionally rewarding.'

Every woman I spoke to listed local achievements as one of the highlights of their job. For Pauline Hanson it was securing funding for a driver education centre in Townsville; for Sussan Ley it was a highway upgrade; everybody had a story about infrastructure funding or a particular individual that they will never forget.

In my final speech in parliament, I spoke about how important and underrated the role of a local member of parliament is. It's something I myself was once in danger of forgetting.

In 2017 I had announced my upcoming resignation and moved to the backbench. After my first term, I had spent my whole parliamentary career as a minister or shadow minister. I was used to spending my days in Canberra in shadow cabinet deliberations about the issues of the day or working on our party's strategy. Now on the backbench, I was bored and restless, apprehensive about what I was giving up and nervous about what would follow for me.

Sometimes the universe delivers you exactly the person you need to meet, at exactly the right time. For me that person was Anna Pak Poy. I remember exactly where I was, walking through the corridors of Parliament House, scrolling through my emails when I came across one from someone called Anna who lived in my seat of Adelaide. She explained that she was the mother of a terminally ill one-year-old boy who had a disease called infantile Tay–Sachs. He was losing access to the supports that he relied upon as the state transitioned to the NDIS. She kept running into dead ends when desperately trying to get the situation resolved. I snapped out of my malaise, remembering all the things that I loved about being a local member, remembering the power we had to help. I emailed her back to tell her I was about to walk into the House of Representatives chamber, but would do all I could to help.

Coincidentally, my seat in the chamber was alongside the Member for Macarthur, Mike Freelander. He had spent the bulk of his career as a paediatrician. I asked him what he knew about Tay–Sachs disease and noticed that his face immediately dropped. He explained to me that it was one of the cruellest diseases imaginable. Your child is born and develops completely normally, meeting milestones as any other child might, until they're about six months old and you start to notice their development slowly regressing. Often it will take many months to get a diagnosis, as it is such a rare and largely unknown disease. Meanwhile the regression in your child's mobility, development and overall health continues. In the majority of cases the child will die before they reach four years of age. There is no cure.

Joe Cook from my office rang Anna so we could get more information and start making inquiries on her behalf. It turned out that her son Sebby required a registered nurse to make regular home visits, which they had in place, but the transition to the NDIS meant that the state government would no longer fund it and the NDIS team argued that it wasn't their responsibility. Anna and Sebby were slipping between the jurisdictional cracks.

I met with Anna when I was back in Adelaide. From the moment she walked in with her folders of background, information and research I could see that the authorities had picked the wrong woman to mess with. My first words to her were, 'We are going to fix this.' We didn't need to talk for long. She told me about Sebby, his condition and his likely life expectancy, but also about his smile, his sparkle and his charisma. I felt ridiculous that I was the one wiping away floods of tears when she was the one watching her darling child slowly die before her eyes. Together we made a plan.

Less than two hours later I had written to both the state and federal ministers responsible and rung their offices to speak to their chiefs of staff. While they were both from governments of a different political persuasion to me, I explained that I was coming to them directly to avoid it becoming a political fight. I didn't want to put the family through the stress of making this a media story. That being said, I also told them each that if it wasn't resolved in forty-eight hours, they would be seeing Anna and gorgeous Sebby on the front page of the newspaper. I wanted it fixed.

A couple of days later Anna rang to say she had been informed that Sebby's nurse would be returning. I felt a wave of relief. In fifteen years of parliament, I'd been emotionally invested in many cases, and the ones we failed to fix haunted me still. At least the case of Anna and Sebby would not be one of those. And somehow, in the midst of a situation that few of us could ever begin to imagine, Anna still had the time and energy for compassion for others. She said, 'Kate, I know that there are at least sixteen other families in South Australia who are in exactly the same situation. One of them barely speaks English. It's not enough that we have fixed it for Sebby when I know that nothing has been fixed for them.' We saddled up once more.

I fired off another round of letters, but I didn't have all the names and details. It was a more complex issue, and frankly I think people were a bit sick of jumping at my requests or threats. We needed a different approach. Senate estimates was coming up the following week. Senate estimates happen three times a year, and involve senior executives from all the government departments fronting up to the parliament to answer questions from senators and explain budget measures that they are responsible for implementing. We briefed Tasmanian Labor Senator Carol Brown on the situation, and she was on board.

Fronting up at estimates, Carol was fierce and direct with the National Disability Insurance Agency officials. 'What about the other sixteen families?' she asked. 'We'll fix them all,' the agency responded, I suspect having little idea what she was talking about. My staff and I were watching, gathered around a monitor back in my Adelaide office. Had that just even happened? It was over in a couple of minutes, but those minutes would change the lives of families who desperately needed help. When I sent the footage to Anna she had to watch it multiple times before she could accept that it was a result of her advocacy. Politics. It changes lives.

Following Sebby's tragic death in 2019, Anna established a foundation in his honour to ensure that other families going through this unthinkable journey have information, support and advocacy as they require. I am deeply honoured to serve as one of the inaugural directors of The Rare Find Foundation.

There are no winners when it comes to serious childhood illness but in Australia if your child was diagnosed with Tay–Sachs before 2019 you walked away with nothing more than the name of a rare disease written on a piece of paper. No information, no support services, nothing. That's changed: the Rare Find Foundation secured grants, researched and printed information booklets for physicians and families, and now offers support services. It is an organisation most worthy if you are looking for someone to throw a donation towards.

One of the great things about my job is that I met Anna, whose friendship I will always treasure. Her strength, determination and drive inspire me constantly, but I am also aware that no matter how hard I work now, I will never have the power and the platform to help her or the other families facing that grim reality anywhere near as effectively as I could when I was an MP. The platform that you have to speak out when you are in parliament, the contacts that you have, the authority that your position gives you – all are unrivalled. When you are an MP you hear stories like Anna's constantly, people placed in unthinkable situations, lost in the bureaucracy and unable to get a resolution. And you can help. That is remarkable and so incredibly rewarding. This is the work that MPs do every day, which very few people ever know about. In 151 electorate offices across the country, this is the work that is taking place. Is it worth the hard days, the unnecessary crap? Yes. Every. Single. Second. No question.

This is also the work that is almost completely invisible to most people. This part of the job, which most MPs would rate as among the most important, is barely known about by most of the community. I could not count how many times I met with a local resident and they began by saying, 'I've never met with a politician before. I had no idea that you could just ask for a meeting and they would sit down and listen to you and then help.'

It's not the fault of the community that there isn't a greater awareness of this important work that takes place every day. The culture of parliament has a lot to do with it, and the media play their part too. When I was first elected I was totally shocked at how inward-looking the Canberra press gallery could be. At the end of my first year, one of the newspapers offered annual report cards of how they thought MPs had gone that year. They gave one of my recently elected opponents a C, stating something like, 'he is highly regarded but is a marginal seat holder and has to concentrate his efforts on his local community which comes at the expense of making inroads in Canberra'. He was downgraded for working to help his local community! I thought that was the point of our jobs. But according to this member of the Canberra press gallery, working to be an active and effective advocate for your community and their issues was an impediment to being a high-rating politician because you were missing political hits and power-broking. Helping people, being effective at policy development, advocating on local issues – these things are the heart of our job. But somehow the twisted Canberra culture now seems to place greater value on attacking or humiliating someone in the parliament.

Being a politician is a complex, hard job, and it comes with complex, hard problems but also huge opportunities. As Penny Wong said, 'We have an opportunity to make change. And yes, it is an extraordinarily tough job at times. There's a big toll on your personal lives, on your relationships and, at times, your health. But there are not many jobs where you get that opportunity to actually shape the nation.'

The sport of politics is ugly, often unfair and no doubt off-putting. But the purpose of the profession is remarkable. If we could find a way to shift the focus away from the sport to the purpose, even a little, I suspect it would do great things for the reputation of the profession. It may even mean that some potential future members of parliament no longer question whether it is worth sticking their hand up at all.

My ten-year high school reunion happened to be held during my very first campaign for election, before I became an MP. I wasn't a particularly diligent student in high school, instead putting my efforts into misbehaving, smoking behind the school gym and experimenting with things I may one day deny to my children. At the reunion, I asked one of my former teachers, Mr Johnson, whether he was surprised to now see me running for parliament. He reminded me of a presentation that I gave to my Year 10 Australian Studies class, where I spoke of the Australia we were and the Australia that we could be, lecturing my fellow students about reconciliation, equality and the outdated notion of monarchy. He said something kind and generous that day: he thought I was exactly where I should be, and doing exactly what I should be doing. He was right. It's the best job in the world. Worth every second.

CHAPTER 13
WOMEN CHANGING THE NATION

IT IS A problem that women make up half the Australian population and yet still only a third of the parliament. And it is a problem that Indigenous people, people of colour, members of the LGBTQIA+ community, differently abled people and other important groups are also grossly under-represented in parliament. This isn't just about balanced representation being fair and equitable, though of course that is important. And it's not just about balanced representation being essential for cultural change in Canberra, although that's also important. This is about the fact that only when parliament is reflective of our community can it best prioritise and act on the issues impacting that community.

I have seen firsthand how women have changed our nation in ways that might otherwise never have happened. When I asked

Julia Gillard whether she knew of programs or legislation that wouldn't have existed without a woman sitting at the cabinet table she didn't hesitate for a millisecond. 'Without Jenny Macklin, we would not have paid parental leave. No doubt about that.'

Think about that for a moment. Over a million parents, mainly mothers, have had the chance to take paid leave to spend with their newborn child as a result of this policy. We can measure the impact of that in terms of the number of people who have accessed the scheme. We can extrapolate the impact of women's continued connection to the labour market and ongoing work-force participation. But how do you begin to measure the impact on the bond developed between those babies and their parents or the effect on family relationships of reducing that financial stress and assisting parents to find a way to make it all work?

None of that would have happened in 2011 without that one woman being elected to parliament. This is why it matters to all of us. Having more women in the parliament changes the nation for the better.

Paid parental leave is an example that shows that things don't just happen because 'their time has come'. Ten years ago, Australia was well behind in international comparisons when it came to paid parental leave. We were one of the last countries in the developed world without government-funded parental leave. The parliament was also well behind the business community, who had already begun to act on the issue, and the broader community, who largely saw it as a no-brainer. But it very nearly didn't happen at all. The politics were difficult and finding the huge sum of money to pay for it wasn't any easier.

Jenny explained how long and how hard she worked behind the scenes to make this policy a reality. 'I'd been working on that for more than ten years before we got into government. I worked on it through all the Howard years. He created this terrible culture war between working and stay-at-home mums, which just enraged me. I was trying to find a way through that at a time when there were still lots of Labor men – not so much in the parliament, although there were a few, but especially in the trade union movement and within our broader Labor movement – who didn't support paid parental leave. They thought mothers should be at home. I had to find a way for our policy to work inside that broader Labor movement.'

By the mid-2000s the politics around paid parental leave had become complex and divisive, but the Australian community had moved on, with a big cultural shift underway in parenting responsibilities. As Jenny acknowledged, 'The Labor Party, and certainly the Liberal Party, were actually a long way behind where the public were; more and more young women and men were saying, "Well, we want to take time off to be with our baby but we want to keep our jobs, we can't do both."'

Jenny worked hard to develop a policy that navigated the politics and controversy, and with the help of Tanya Plibersek gained the support of the broader Labor Party. As Jenny explained, 'Tanya and I really did it together at the 2007 election. If we hadn't pushed it at that point, it probably wouldn't have become an official policy.'

The federal election on 24 November 2007 saw a change of government after eleven years of John Howard as prime minister, and Jenny became the Minister for Family, Community Services and Indigenous Affairs in Kevin Rudd's Labor government. Even then the struggle was far from over. There was still the huge job of working out how to legislate and implement the policy.

'What I found as a minister is how long big reform takes. What that demonstrates is that if you're going to do something big like that, you have to start on the first day and you have to be ready, and then you have to try to hold the portfolio the whole time. That was the other thing. I was lucky enough, through all our turmoil, to hold that portfolio for six years.'

But an even bigger obstacle arose: the Global Financial Crisis. With a recession sweeping across the world in 2008, all priorities, policies and spending commitments had to be evaluated. The paid parental leave scheme was an enormously expensive spending commitment and very nearly ended up on the cutting room floor. With billions of dollars now unexpectedly having to be spent on stimulus measures in a desperate bid to save Australia from recession and prevent millions of workers from sliding into unemployment, the paid parental leave policy became precarious, to say the least. Many government members believed it had to be at least delayed if not abandoned altogether. It would have been, if Jenny Macklin didn't fight for its survival.

Jenny was certainly not the only woman working for this goal. She herself cites the work done by Pru Goward as Sex Discrimination Commissioner, the long-term advocacy of Natasha Stott Despoja, the influence of Heather Ridout as the head of the Australian Industry Group and trade union leaders like Jennie George, Sharan Burrow and many others. But without Jenny in parliament, it would not have eventuated. She was understated when she acknowledged, 'It was touch and go. We finally got there.' The lives of millions of Australians were changed as a result.

It's a two-way street – when parliament legislates changes, like paid parental leave, it can have an important influence on the broader community. After the Labor government introduced paid parental leave in 2011, the private sector lifted its game, with a 7 per cent increase in large companies offering paid parental leave since 2013. Almost 50 per cent of Australian workplaces now offer some form of paid parental leave separate to the government's program. Unions have also historically played a role in pushing for changes like this. And when the private sector begins to make changes, like introducing diversity targets, or gender-equitable parental leave schemes, this often creates a new norm that puts pressure on parliament to follow suit.

A decade on from the scheme's introduction in January 2011, we now find ourselves in dire need of the next steps of reform. Georgie Dent, Executive Director of parent advocacy group The Parenthood, recently described Australia's paid parental leave on Twitter as being 'woefully inadequate' and the 'second least generous scheme in the OECD'.

Jenny herself believes that her policy was just the beginning and that there is much more work to be done. 'If men and women really want to be equal, then we have to share the child-rearing. We've got to really move to the next stage with paid parental leave and really make it *parental* leave, not maternity leave. I called [the government program] parental leave on purpose but I'm not blind to the reality that it's mostly women who take leave. It's still a big cultural shift and financial shift, but it's happening. More and more men are staying home and more and more businesses are saying, "We'll give you the proper time off." I would say to the next generation the chance is there for you to take it to the next point.'

The likely champions of paid parental leave policy reform are our current and future female members of parliament, and, one hopes, our current and future male members of parliament, especially those with firsthand experiences of parenting. When they emerge, will they be supported by the people sitting around the cabinet table?

This is just one policy that would likely still be a pipe dream if not for women in parliament. As Julia Gillard said, 'There are many examples of how women have diversified and enriched the agenda and pushed things home.'

Of course without Julia herself we would not have seen half of the huge reform agenda that was put in place under her watch. We would not have seen the Gonski measures to increase the quality of every school across the nation. We certainly would not have seen the Royal Commission into Institutional Responses to Child Sexual Abuse. Thousands of survivors would not have received the comfort of their pain finally being acknowledged, nor would they have access to the financial redress scheme. Without Tanya Plibersek we would not have the first National Plan to Reduce Violence Against Women and their Children. Or, most likely, the follow-up plans. Without Nicola Roxon there is no question we would not have plain packaging tobacco laws, or health checks for four-year-olds. Without women in parliament we may never have had an NDIS and would not have seen national childcare reform and improvement of funding to ensure that every four-year-old across Australia has access to a quality preschool program, or funding for the promotion of women's sport. The list goes on and on. These reforms were all achieved within only one government, in just five years.

But women's influence and achievements in parliament stretch well beyond traditional 'women's issues'. Tanya Plibersek argued, 'It's about perspective on issues. When I had the housing portfolio and we were building public housing and emergency accommodation, I was aware of the need for emergency accommodation for women and children escaping domestic violence. You don't have to read the statistics to know that it has to be done. Your personal experiences as a woman change your perspective on what a homeless person looks like. It's not just a bloke sleeping rough, it's a woman sleeping with her kids in the car.'

Penny Wong said, 'I have no doubt that particularly in the Gillard Government from 2010 to 2013 many of the reforms we put in place would not have happened if we didn't have as many women around the cabinet table. I think having me in Finance and Jenny Macklin in Social Security meant that a lot of those reforms, which were mainstream economic reforms, recognised the differential gender impact and tried to improve the differential economic position of men and women strongly; that was really important.'

She cited particular economic reforms like the increase in the tax-free threshold and the low income superannuation contribution as assisting all low income workers but particularly benefiting Australian women, who are over-represented in the lower income percentiles and have less superannuation accumulated than men of a similar age.

The impact of different perspectives in policy formulation can be seen across the board but is perhaps best demonstrated by the Fair Work Act and the subsequent equal pay case. As Minister for Workplace Relations in the Rudd Government, Julia Gillard introduced the Fair Work Act in 2008. It replaced the Howard Government's 'WorkChoices' legislation, which the community had deemed to be too extreme. The Fair Work Act sought to restore workers' rights and modernise our workplaces and our industrial relations system. Importantly, the new laws contained a new provision on pay equity that ensured employers were required by law to provide 'equal pay to work of equal or comparable value'. The impact of this inclusion would soon be felt by over 150,000 of Australia's lowest paid workers.

Testing this new provision, trade unions led by the Australian Services Union put forward an equal pay case in 2010 for social and community service workers, who are overwhelmingly women. As a result of Jenny Macklin's work, the federal government assisted them by putting in a joint submission and pledging to fund its share of any resultant pay increases. It was argued that these workers, providing family counselling services, working in disability services, running homeless shelters and supporting victims of domestic violence, were undervalued and underpaid, the work they did traditionally being seen as 'women's work'.

In the most significant move towards equal pay in thirty years, the Fair Work Commission agreed. Over 150,000 workers, 120,000 of whom were women, received pay rises of between 23 and 45 per cent as a result. The federal government put forward $2.8 billion towards these increases. Imagine how big an impact a 45 per cent pay increase would have on your life. For these hardworking, low-paid people in difficult and extremely necessary jobs, it is almost impossible to imagine the effect that would have on their lives and the lives of their families.

Julia Gillard said of the equal-pay case: 'I don't think that we would have had the preparedness to back-in what was very costly, but very morally right, without women pushing for it and women arguing for it and being very much on the case about gender pay equality.'

It is not just as federal ministers that women have achieved change. Whether on the frontbench or backbench, in government or opposition, women in the parliament have changed the agenda, shone a spotlight on long-neglected issues and ensured action on a range of key issues. And they continue to do it every day.

Marielle Smith said, 'Politics isn't always about the big questions of macro-economic reform. It's also about the smaller changes we can make to our federal laws and regulations, which make life better, safer, easier, happier, healthier for Australian families. And I think women have done incredible work across a spectrum of health and economic issues to deliver that.'

There are endless examples to back this up. Liberal Member for Boothby Nicolle Flint and then Labor Member for Canberra

Gai Brodtmann teamed up in 2017 to form the bipartisan Parliamentary Friends of Endometriosis Awareness group. They sought to raise awareness of the condition, to advocate for greater research and investment and to call for government action. It is no coincidence that by 2018 Health Minister Greg Hunt had apologised to the Australian women with endometriosis who had suffered for too long. He pledged $4.7 million for research and education on the condition. In June 2020 Nicolle Flint announced that she had herself been diagnosed with stage 4 endometriosis and underwent major surgery. There is little doubt that her advocacy mattered to the staggering 700,000 Australian women who suffer from the condition. Hopefully the increased funding will lead to earlier diagnoses and less suffering for the next generation of women to face this crippling condition.

Labor Senator Kristina Keneally has been a champion for increased support for families who have a stillborn child, and for greater awareness of the warning signs. Each day in Australia six babies are stillborn, and there has been little improvement in overall stillbirth rates in the last thirty years. Kristina's daughter Caroline was stillborn in 1999, and she powerfully shared the story of her loss, telling the Senate that Caroline 'enlarged my understanding of love and loss. She taught me to survive. She made me brave'.

In early 2018 the Senate established a select committee to investigate stillbirth in Australia and make recommendations to prevent them. Kristina became a member of the committee, which was chaired by Malarndirri McCarthy. Kristina's lived experience was so important in informing the work that was being done, and ensuring that Australians had trust in the genuine commitment of the inquiry. In response to the committee's work, the government later announced $7.2 million in initiatives designed to reduce stillbirths. Kristina continues to advocate for greater support for grieving families.

Since being elected in 2019 Marielle Smith has campaigned heavily on the need to strengthen consumer laws governing the use of button batteries. She argues that while the law requires them to be secured behind a screw-fastened compartment on children's toys, there are no such requirements on other household appliances like remote controls. As she says, 'We've had multiple children die in Australia because of this. We have up to twenty children hospitalised, suspected of ingesting these batteries, each week. And yet it has not been a point of urgent consumer reform. It's something which can be easily fixed in the federal parliament. These sorts of issues might not be the big picture issues of the day, but they are seriously important to women and to families and are now being raised up through our federal parliamentary chambers. That's a really big and significant shift.'

Senator Jenny McAllister has focused her energy on women's retirement savings. Recognising that, on average, women currently retire with almost 50 per cent less superannuation than men, and 23 per cent of women retire with no superannuation at all, Jenny has worked tirelessly to shine a spotlight on the growing rates of poverty, housing stress and homelessness among retired women. She established and chaired the Senate

Inquiry into Economic Security for Women in Retirement in 2015, and her committee's report provided a roadmap to action, with nineteen recommendations to increase gender equality in retirement.

These are just examples of how women can affect policy that I personally witnessed during my time in the parliament. As Tanya Plibersek rightly pointed out to me, the influence of women in policymaking extends beyond the elected members and through to the efforts of women in senior staffing roles dating back to the Whitlam Government. Policy on women's shelters, early childhood and discrimination all came from women's voices being heard as key advisers.

———

It is well established that boards and organisations make better decisions when they have a more equal balance of gender. The Australian Government's Workplace Gender Equality Agency cites a mountain of evidence which demonstrates that gender equality in the workplace increases the productivity of the organisation and boosts the profits. It increases performance and improves culture. (The same has been shown in companies with a diverse workforce across gender, age, religion, education, ethnicity, sexual orientation and other attributes.) As businesses across the world act upon this research, it is confusing and short-sighted that all sides of our parliament have not also recognised or acted upon it, to the detriment of the Australian community.

Broader perspectives in the parliament mean better policies for all Australians, and a wider spectrum of issues considered.

There is also a case to be made for the importance of women in parliament influencing the numbers of future women in parliament. Research has shown that when women are exposed to powerful female role models, they are more likely to endorse the notion that women are well suited for leadership roles. So the more commonplace it is to see women in parliament, the more the average woman is likely to see it as normal. Equally, there's an argument that when boys grow up seeing women in positions of power alongside men, it normalises gender equality for all.

This is why it matters to all of us. It matters to every worker who now enjoys better protections and conditions at work thanks to the Fair Work Act. It matters to every family who has had precious time to bond with their child thanks to the paid parental leave program. It matters to every woman who has received the support she needs to flee domestic abuse; and hopefully to many of the future generations of girls who may be spared such violence as a result of the prevention programs put in place by successive governments. It sure as shit matters to those women who would still be slugging it out day after day working to deliver our community services for a measly wage nowhere near reflective of their worth.

A more diverse parliament that draws on a wider range of life experiences and perspectives will mean every Australian will benefit from better considered policies and programs. Gender equality is the first and most obvious step towards a better parliament and a better Australia. We need more than just women though. We need everyone who is elected to bring different attitudes and expectations of behaviour that also contribute to cultural change. And we need greater diversity across the board. There's plenty of evidence that both business and the community are once again ahead of parliament in this respect.

We need a fair, equitable and modern workplace in our federal parliament that does our country justice. The stakes are high; the standards should be too.

CHAPTER 14

WHERE TO FROM HERE?

I FEEL EXCITED about what lies ahead for women in politics. In my final term I noted that not only was there an increase in the number of women on my side, but that increase was already having an effect on culture. In conducting the interviews for this book I was genuinely inspired by the attitudes and outlooks of the new women elected to the parliament. They had an expectation that things would be better for them and for those who came after them. That's what happens. I want it to happen quickly.

I asked each woman I spoke with to predict how parliament might look in the future. Across the board women from all political parties had a sense of optimism. They believed that we would see an increase in female representation and that the culture would improve.

The general awareness of what constitutes sexist behaviour and of the power imbalances within organisations has risen in recent years. Millennials and Gen Z are coming into the workforce with new expectations, and they aren't content to sit quietly and suck it up. Both men and women are calling out what they see as unacceptable norms, and in doing so are helping to create momentum. And, as we've seen, there's structural change afoot, with arguably the biggest shifts in corporate culture in a generation at companies across the world accelerated by the impact of COVID-19, from Unilever to NAB to Microsoft to PwC. What this means is greater diversity in leadership positions, equal opportunities and transparent pay for men and women, and high-quality parental leave arrangements for all new parents, among other changes.

Women make up 60 per cent of university graduates in Australia, but the air is still thin at the top of the corporate ladder for women. In 2020 only 12 per cent of senior executives and 5 per cent of CEOs in the ASX200 were women. By contrast we can see that parliament has changed, however incrementally, with women making up 30 per cent of cabinet in the current government and 31 per cent overall across the whole parliament. Compare this to 1980, when only 2 per cent of federal parliamentarians were women. Perhaps this is another example of the way parliament and the private sector intersect and influence each other. We can only hope to see increasing numbers of women CEOs and executives in coming years.

Mothers who work are now the norm, rather than the exception, and this broader cultural change has been reflected in increasing numbers of MPs who are also mothers, particularly mothers to younger children. Thankfully, we've moved swiftly from a culture where Kelly O'Dwyer was told to 'just pump more breastmilk', to one where Greens Senator Larissa Waters calmly breastfed her daughter while speaking in the federal Senate in 2017.

Women are beginning to question the wisdom of keeping their heads down and just 'getting on with it' when they cop sexist treatment, as we've seen from Sarah Hanson-Young and Nicolle Flint. It's hard to focus on your job when everyone else is focused on your sex life, your appearance or your parenting ability. Clearly, women in parliament need to have tactics for working within the existing culture, but they also need to question the status quo and push for change when the opportunities arise. As Julia Baird wrote in *Media Tarts* about women politicians, 'They need to both learn to play the system as it is now, and attempt to transform it into a more human, diverse, accessible place.' Seventeen years later, it's still a work in progress.

Pauline Hanson believes we'll see an increase in the number of women in politics, and her reasoning was pretty straightforward. 'I hear from people, even children, students from schools, people from women's organisations, businesswomen, and they all say to me, "You are an inspiration to us." I hear that a lot.' She was confident that many of these women would seek to follow in her footsteps.

Others I spoke to had less simplistic reasons for optimism. Labor's affirmative action rules will continue to ensure an increase of women in the ranks, and there is a view that this will have flow-on effects across the whole parliament.

Julia Gillard has sensed a change on the other side of politics since Labor adopted its strident policy on quotas, saying, 'Now at least you get some leading Liberals who are prepared to say, "I don't know if I'm one hundred per cent with you, but I get that there's something in that to think about."'

Women now make up over 46 per cent of Labor's federal MPs. Tanya Plibersek said, 'Because we're at a critical mass in the Labor Party, I think we're slowly dragging the parliament with us. The conservative parties seem to have realised that in a marginal seat contest they're better off putting up a woman in many cases. So while they're not in any hurry to introduce targets, I think for purely electoral mathematics, they'll be continuing to preselect more women. And I think there's more demand from their rank and file members for something that looks more like a pathway to politics for more women.'

There was also a view that the community would drive change, that there was a desperate desire for our parliament to be better, more representative of who we are and more reflective of our values. After the Abbott years, after witnessing America divide itself in two during Donald Trump's reign, and after the COVID-19 pandemic turned people's lives upside down, there was a sense that the Australian people would demand a different way forward. COVID-19 has also demonstrated the value that people place on women's leadership styles during a crisis – such as that of Jacinda Ardern in New Zealand – and highlighted the importance of women contributing to policies in a time when women are shown to be economically vulnerable and shouldering even more of the burden of care.

Tanya Plibersek explained that the pendulum had swung too far towards brutal win-at-all-costs political game-playing and trickery. 'The temperature will need to be turned down in the coming years, or at least I hope it will, I hope that people will begin again to value civility in public discourse. I think the pendulum is coming back to something closer to valuing people and civility.'

Politics 'reflects us back to ourselves', as Annabel Crabb put it in her essay 'Men at Work'. The community's standards of behaviour, and expectations of women and men in parliament, are a kind of distillation of the community's expectations in general. And when those expectations aren't met, the community begins to view politics and politicians with cynicism and fatigue. The more our parliament is reflective of our community, the more likely we are to see everyday Australians who want to engage with, and perhaps even work in, our parliament.

As Penny Wong noted, 'I always say to younger women that you can make a decision not to be interested in politics, but you can never make a decision not to be affected by it. If you are going to be affected, you should engage. So we've got a job as women, as do the men in our parties, to say to women, to younger women, that your contribution is valued. Yes, it's hard, but it is about shaping the country. And that's important.'

In fact there wasn't just an optimism but an excitement about the future for women in parliament. Natasha Stott Despoja captured it by telling me, 'I love the fact that the future is going to be shaped by some of these activist, strong, younger women who are out there doing incredible things. I don't want them to eschew parliament. I want them to be a part of it.'

Julie Bishop saw the potential we have for women to step up and change the country too. 'I always encourage young women to consider politics as a career. Of course they have to be aware of the pitfalls, and they have to be aware of the nature of it. However, they should also be ambitious enough to hope that they can help effect change. The more women there are in parliament, the more likely it is that we will be able to effect change. You need a significant number of women to do that, a critical mass, and we can get there.'

We're not quite there yet. Structural change is usually about playing the long game. But it was unexpectedly supercharged in 2020 amid the COVID-19 global pandemic. So many of the unquestioning assumptions around work culture have been chucked out as companies that resisted working-from-home policies and flexible hours were forced to update their attitudes in a matter of weeks, and found that productivity remained stable despite the lack of 'bums on seats'. In the face of the deadly virus, structural and cultural changes that probably would have taken years if not decades to occur have happened with breathtaking speed. Now, companies in Australia and internationally are making working from home the new norm – Atlassian, Twitter and Facebook have all announced that their employees will never have to work in the office again. It's almost certain that other broader structural and cultural changes will come out of the upheaval of 2020.

In 2008, speaking about the GFC, Rahm Emanuel, Barack Obama's chief of staff, told a *Wall Street Journal* forum that 'you never want a serious crisis to go to waste', describing it as an opportunity to do things you thought you could not do before. 2020 presented a unique opportunity for structural change, to question the ingrained assumptions of what parliament has to be like, and what a politician looks like. Hand in hand with this is what we can do as individuals, in our own lives, to advance change. Every woman I spoke to had some advice for those who will follow, which is relevant for almost all women in their professional careers. Much of it came down to staying true to your values. Remember who you are and what you're there to do, back yourself, and make sure you have the support that you need.

Linda Burney was characteristically direct. 'Do not emulate the men. The most powerful person and the most important person is you. Be yourself, and listen to yourself.'

Penny Wong expanded on this. 'Find your own voice, because it has always been the most powerful. It has to be who you want to be. I think women are often taught to implicitly or explicitly respond to others' expectations. In politics, yes, be aware of the context and expectation. But you really have to find your path, your voice, how you dress, how you want to speak. You have to find that. That's the one piece of advice I always give people, because it was probably the most profoundly important advice I ever got.'

Sussan Ley shared a similar sentiment. 'Never lose sight of who you really are. If you can be yourself, whoever that is, and advocate, represent and be a force for change, then that's the best possible expression that you could give that role.'

Proving that perhaps it is true that if you search hard enough you can find some common ground with anyone, I agreed entirely with Pauline Hanson when she said, 'If you have a passion for your country and the people and you want to do the right thing by the people, we need good strong people in this place, so give it a go. What I say is, don't underestimate yourself because a lot of these other people in this parliament wouldn't have a clue.'

It remains true that women often believe that we have to be the very best before we can throw our hat into the ring; we have to meet every requirement and have every qualification. Men are much more likely to believe that they are good enough, close enough and back themselves, which has led to the saying that women should 'carry themselves with the confidence of a mediocre white man'.

On this topic, Clare O'Neil said, 'I think impostor syndrome is a perennial problem for women in politics. We live in a world where women are just not rewarded for being super confident and sure of themselves. And that's important in politics. You've got to make yourself heard and make yourself known and remind everyone that you're there. So I think once you do get into parliament, you need to own it and realise you're entitled to be where you are and your voice is important. I think the quicker you realise that, the more impact you're going to be able to have.'

Ultimately, the women I spoke to believed that one of the most important pieces of advice is the one that Julia Gillard regularly gives to young women: make sure that you are clear on your purpose. Marielle Smith explained how important this was to her. 'Julia told me that purpose is everything and that you need to be absolutely resolute in your mind about why you're doing it and what you want to achieve. There will be difficult days and there will be dark days. People will come after your family, people will say terrible things about you. People will ridicule you. You will make sacrifices in your family. I know every day what I want to achieve for my community. And if you know that, you can get through anything. If you put your hand up for parliament because you're looking for celebrity or you think it might be an interesting thing to do, or someone suggested it and you thought, why not? I don't think that's enough to sustain you through the difficulty. And the difficulty does take on a different nuance and I think a different nastiness when you're a woman, so you really, really need to be clear on what drives you and why you're there.'

Some of the advice offered actually has nothing to do with what happens in the workplace. Anika Wells said, 'I got some advice from one of my mentors many years ago, and she said that this sounds counter-intuitive to us, but the best decision you can make for your career is your choice of partner, because ultimately it's they who help you do everything you want to do, particularly if you also don't have family support. And I think that's true. Nothing I have done would have been possible without my husband Finn understanding what it would involve and signing up to it as well.' The importance of choosing the right partner was something Sheryl Sandberg, the chief operating officer of Facebook, wrote about in her 2013 book *Lean In*. After her husband died unexpectedly in 2015, she wrote a second book, *Option B*, where she acknowledged the privilege she had enjoyed as someone with a supportive partner, and the fact that for many people this isn't an option. This remains true for many women.

Amanda Rishworth spoke of the importance of maintaining friendships that are far removed from the workplace. 'Politics can become all consuming. I've got a couple of friends who are not a hundred per cent sure what I do, but are supportive nonetheless, and I think that's really good. And then I've got friends who will be brutally honest with me. Having outside friends stops your whole identity from becoming the politician as opposed to just Amanda. I'm very passionate about my job and I care about it, I spend many hours thinking and working on it. But I don't want to be the politician. I want to be Amanda. So having those friends who knew you before is really, really worthwhile.' For me, this was also particularly true. Nothing offers better perspective than catching up with a group of people who love you and who couldn't care less who asked who what in question time last week. My group of friends were my rock.

Natasha Stott Despoja is clear with those who ask her advice. 'We've got to be honest about the reality of politics. And I haven't glossed over it, I haven't tried to sugarcoat it. I've been really upfront about the fact that politics is a brutal profession at times and it's particularly difficult for women. And it's even harder for women who are young, from a diverse background, Indigenous, from CALD [culturally and linguistically diverse] communities.

And someone like [South Australian MP] Kelly Vincent can only begin to give you an idea of what it's like being a woman with a disability and the youngest ever woman to get into a parliament. Try to make sure that you have support networks. Politics is so often about disunity and division that if you don't have a support basis or a network, then you can't function.'

No matter who it is – an individual, a group, an organisation – make sure you know where you turn to get your batteries recharged, to boost your confidence or just to put your work into wider perspective.

There were many other tips offered. Don't define yourself by other people's views of you. Do work out where you will get your sense of resilience from. Don't take to heart the cruel comments on social media. Do focus on the positive elements of the job as well as challenging the negative. Do find a mentor who you trust and can rely on. Do speak up about bad behaviour, discrimination or bullying, no matter whose side is doing it or to whom. I would add, do bring others with you. Ensure that part of your legacy is supporting the women who will follow you.

And maybe it's best to stay well clear of the Parliament House prayer room.

I share the sense of optimism for the future. It feels like we are on the cusp of the next wave. Women seem determined to stand up and be heard. We have a generation of girls now entering adulthood who grew up seeing a woman at the top. We have a broader understanding of the benefits of greater gender equality and the consequences of women not being well represented around the cabinet table. We have more men being elected who don't fit outdated stereotypes and who are willing to join the push for change.

I don't want to just see more women in parliament though. I want it to be better for them. Mainly, I want it to be better for all of us.

We can't be complacent. More women in the parliament will have an impact on improving the culture but we also need to improve the culture to attract more women and ensure that they are able to succeed at the job. It is a case of the chicken and the egg.

In a recent discussion with a high-achieving, successful and articulate friend, I asked if she would consider a career in politics. She dismissed the idea instantly, saying, 'I have far too many skeletons from the past to ever even contemplate it.' Many women saw the way Julia Gillard and others were crucified over their personal lives as a huge disincentive to enter politics. Men, on the other hand, see ample precedents of male MPs brushing off their youthful (or recent) indiscretions as 'locker room talk'.

It's exactly what Marielle Smith feared. She spoke about women watching Julia's experience: 'The nastiness reached such a peak that in terms of putting your hand up for federal political life, there are a lot of women who would wonder if they could do it. I think most of us would look at the sorts of things she copped criticism for, including things in her past, and look at our own lives and think, if you put a certain lens over almost anything everyone has done in their life, it can look a certain way. And am I prepared to put myself or my family through that?'

In a recent conversation with a senior MP, he confirmed that there still aren't any agreed rules of what is off limits in parliament except that you don't go after people's staff or their families. Even those small conventions are regularly challenged by MPs eager to land a hit. If we are to successfully attract broad representation from the community, there needs to be more firmly agreed conventions around rules of engagement, and they will need to be fiercely protected. Less muck raking, less character assassination, less rumours and sleaze. The parliament will always be a combative place, I'm not suggesting we all link arms and sing 'Kumbaya', but there are respectful ways that you can challenge your opponent.

It is unclear whether this kind of change is likely to be driven from within the parliament, where MPs are focused on the immediate battles before them. It may need to be enforced from outside, by the community and particularly the media demanding better standards and treatment and punishing those who they see as playing too hard.

I spent my entire adult life working in politics. I knew that it was a tough environment. I didn't know how out of whack it was with the rest of Australia until I re-entered normal society. I think it's reasonable to say that I didn't have a huge reputation for aggression or being a political attack dog while I was in parliament, yet since entering the real world I have had several occasions where I've had to check myself and my impulses. I've had to remind myself that normal people don't speak to each other around a board table like we would around a cabinet table. Normal people don't engage with their opponents in the vicious way that we would pursue our political enemies. People are less blunt, more civil, more interested in listening to and giving credit for other people's ideas. They are more decent, compassionate and connected to each other as humans, rather than treating each other as combatant. The private sector does crazy things like setting meeting times well in advance and not expecting you to drop everything at a moment's notice. It seems to recognise that people have lives and families and that their work is not their entire reason for existence. The culture of parliament is not just failing to lead the culture of Australian workplaces, it is desperately outdated and unpleasant in comparison.

We tell ourselves that it's because the stakes are so high, because we believe so passionately in what we're doing. Yet lots of people are passionate about their work. Surely the fact that the stakes are so high means our standards should be higher? It should be a battle of ideas and solutions for the Australian community, not a race to the bottom to besmirch your opponents. We all deserve better than the manner in which our parliament currently works. Imagine what these women could achieve if they weren't also spending hours, days or years having to protect their reputation from made-up sexual slurs, making sure the colour of their shirt or their appearance wasn't going to distract from their message, or handling abuse or threats that their male colleagues wouldn't dream existed. Imagine the outcomes that could be achieved for all Australians. Imagine the example it could set for the nation.

In my first ever speech, I conceded that I was young and

idealistic. Maybe I am just old and idealistic now. But I am something more than that: I'm determined. Our parliament has to be better, for all of us.

It will only change if we demand it.

SOURCES

Most of the quoted material included in this book comes from my conversations with Australian MPs. I have also drawn on other sources, as outlined below.

INTRODUCTION: TIME FOR CHANGE

Former Prime Minister Malcolm Turnbull said ... Ben Doherty, 'Malcolm Turnbull says Liberal Party definitely has a woman problem', *The Guardian*, 9 March 2019, theguardian. com/australia-news/2019/mar/09/far-too-blokey-turnbull-says-liberal-party-has-gender-inequality-problem

CHAPTER 1: WHERE HAVE WE COME FROM?

In 2019, 51 per cent of Australia's population was female ... Australian Institute of Health and Welfare, 'The health of Australia's females', 10 December 2019, aihw.gov.au/reports/ men-women/female-health/contents/who-are

As at December 2020 the number of ALP MPs ... Anna Hough, 'Composition of Australian parliaments by party and gender: a quick guide', Australian Government Department of Parliamentary Services, 2 December 2020, parlinfo.aph. gov.au/parlInfo/download/library/prspub/3681701/upload_binary/3681701.pdf

At its worst, to co-opt that infamous line ... Jenna Price, 'The hashtag that shook the foundations of Alan Jones' power', *The Sydney Morning Herald*, 13 May 2020, smh.com.au/national/the-hashtag-that-shook-the-foundations-of-alan-jones-power-20200512-p54s8p.html

While people with a disability make up a whopping 18 per cent ... The McKell Institute, 'Representative government: Diversity in the next parliament', April 2019, mckellinstitute. org.au/research/articles/representative-government-diversity-in-the-46th-parliament

In an interview after her election she answered ... 'The rise of Kelly Vincent', ABC News, 9 April 2010, abc.net.au/news/2010-04-09/the-rise-of-kelly-vincent/2585022?nw=0

CHAPTER 2: WEAPONISING SEXUAL GOSSIP

Ben Smee wrote an explosive report ... Ben Smee, '"Extreme" Queensland LNP vetting allegedly focused on female candidates' sexual histories', *The Guardian*, 23 July 2020, theguardian.com/australia-news/2020/jul/23/extreme-queensland-lnp-vetting-allegedly-focused-on-female-candidates-sexual-histories

CHAPTER 3: SLUT SHAMING

Sarah told Radio National at the time ... RN Breakfast, 'David Leyonhjelm "slut shaming me" with "stop shagging men" remark, Sarah Hanson-Young says', ABC News, 3 July 2018, abc.net.au/news/2018-07-03/david-leyonhjelm-sarah-hanson-young-slut-shaming-shagging-men/9934114

The judge found that Leyonhjelm's claims ... Michael McGowan and Paul Karp, 'Sarah Hanson-Young awarded $120,000 in damages in defamation case against David Leyonhjelm', *The Guardian*, 25 November 2019, theguardian.com/australia-news/2019/nov/25/sarah-hanson-young-awarded-120000-damages-defamation-david-leyonhjelm

The story leaked claims about ... Michael McGowan, 'BuzzFeed apologises to Emma Husar for distress caused by "slut-shaming" article', *The Guardian*, 30 July 2019, theguardian.com/media/2019/jul/30/buzzfeed-apologises-to-emma-husar-for-distress-caused-by-slut-shaming-article

She told Leigh Sales on ABC's 7.30 ... Gareth Hutchens, 'Emma Husar says "vicious slut shaming" ended her career', *The Guardian*, 29 August 2018, theguardian.com/australia-news/2018/aug/29/emma-husar-says-vicious-slut-shaming-ended-her-career

... with editor Neil Breen stating in *The Daily Telegraph* at the time ... 'Nude photos not of Pauline Hanson', *The Advertiser*,

17 March 2009, adelaidenow.com.au/news/national/nude-photos-not-hanson-ex-husband-says/news-story/963be207250fdd603f48762347861080

It is now widely believed that they were instead ... 'Porn scorn for paper', *The Sydney Morning Herald*, 23 March 2009, smh.com.au/national/porn-scorn-for-paper-20090323-971m.html

The newspaper's public apology to Hanson ... Nick O'Malley and Erik Jensen, 'Valuable lesson from Pauline', *The Sydney Morning Herald*, 19 May 2009, smh.com.au/national/valuable-lesson-from-pauline-20090519-bd70.html

CHAPTER 4: SHE'S WEARING WHAT?

The Telegraph **chose to celebrate this momentous occasion** ... Sonia Haria, 'Why Kamala Harris is the modern beauty icon the world needs', *The Telegraph*, 7 November 2020, telegraph.co.uk/beauty/news/liner-lashes-lip-gloss-youthful-beauty-tricks-behind-kamala

'It's getting worse not better,' ... James Purtill, 'Media's gendered stereotyping was worse for Gillard than Thatcher 30 years earlier, research shows', Triple J Hack, 25 February 2020, abc.net.au/triplej/programs/hack/media-gender-stereotypes-worse-for-gillard-than-for-thatcher/11996326

The Age **ran a piece which stated ...** 'Dress code formal for the first day of school', *The Age*, 17 November 2004

The Daily Telegraph **wrote that ...** 'Some new hats as pollies step to it', *The Daily Telegraph*, 17 November 2004

The American Psychological Association characterises imposter syndrome ... Kirsten Weir, 'Feel like a fraud?', American Psychological Association, 2013, apa.org/gradpsych/ 2013/11/fraud

I sat down with *Grazia* **and did an interview ...** 'I'm horrified by how we see ourselves: Kate Ellis, federal Minister for Youth gives her verdict on our body survey results', *Grazia*, 19 April 2010

When I was approached by *Sunday Life* **...** 'The female network: Kate Ellis on women in leadership roles', *Sunday Life Magazine*, 26 June 2011

The Business Council of Australia's stated position ... Business Council of Australia, 'Submission to the Department of Families, Housing, Community Services and Indigenous Affairs on Reporting Matters under the Workplace Gender Equality Act 2012', February 2013, d3n8a8pro7vhmx.cloudfront.net/bca/ pages/3539/attachments/original/1532038424/sub_to_fahcsia_ on_wge_act_2012_reporting_final_4-2-2013.pdf?1532038424

A few weeks after the story, *Sunday Life* **ran a follow-up.** Natalie Reilly, 'What's wrong with this picture?', *Sunday Life*, 24 July 2011, dailylife.com.au/news-and-views/dl-opinion/whats-wrong-with-this-picture-20120130-1qpb7.html

That piece … was followed by another … Rebecca Reid, 'Don't call me a bad feminist for wanting to know about Kamala Harris' makeup', *The Huffington Post*, 8 November 2020, huffingtonpost.co.uk/entry/kamala-harris-makeup-telegraph_uk_5fa80913c5b67c3259b02457

CHAPTER 5: SOCIAL MEDIA MADNESS

Australia Institute research commissioned by Ginger Gorman … Ginger Gorman, *Troll Hunting: Inside the world of hate online and its human fallout*, Hardie Grant Book, 2019

As journalist Andrew Marantz wrote … Andrew Marantz, 'Facebook can't fix itself', *The New Yorker*, 19 October 2020, newyorker.com/magazine/2020/10/19/why-facebook-cant-fix-itself

CHAPTER 6: THE 'SISTERHOOD'

… Julia told parliament at the end of one particularly murky question time … Alexandra Kirk, 'Gillard: I did nothing wrong', ABC PM, 26 November 2012, abc.net.au/pm/content/2012/s3641211.htm

... the Coalition Government voted to abolish the Family Court despite expert evidence ... 'Put families over politics, abandon flawed family court merger', Law Council of Australia, 20 November 2020, lawcouncil.asn.au/media/media-releases/put-families-over-politics-abandon-flawed-family-court-merger

CHAPTER 7: FIRST TO THE TOP

There was the menu at an LNP fundraiser ... Bridie Jabour, 'Julia Gillard's "small breasts" served up on Liberal Party dinner menu', *The Guardian*, 12 June 2013, theguardian.com/world/2013/jun/12/gillard-menu-sexist-liberal-dinner

David Farley, CEO of Australian Agricultural Company, called her ... Richard Willingham and Natalie O'Brien, 'CEO compares PM to an old cow', *The Sydney Morning Herald*, 4 August 2012, smh.com.au/politics/federal/ceo-compares-pm-to-an-old-cow-20120803-23l4j.html

... Senator Bill Heffernan's comments labelling her ... Dan Harrison, '"Barren" Gillard blasts Heffernan', *The Age*, 2 May 2007, theage.com.au/national/barren-gillard-blasts-heffernan-20070502-ge4so2.html

On different occasions, radio host and shock jock ... Heath Aston, 'Gillard's father died of shame: Alan Jones', *The Sydney Morning Herald*, 29 September 2012, smh.com.au/politics/federal/gillards-father-died-of-shame-alan-jones-20120929-26soa.html

'I will not be lectured about sexism and misogyny by this man.' 'Transcript of Julia Gillard's speech', *The Sydney Morning Herald*, 10 October 2012, smh.com.au/politics/federal/transcript-of-julia-gillards-speech-20121010-27c36.html

Journalist after journalist lined up to slam her. Amanda Lohrey, 'A matter of context', *The Monthly*, November 2012, themonthly.com.au/gillard-abbott-and-press-gallery-s-dwindling-relevance-matter-context-amanda-lohrey-6771#mtr

As Tory Shepherd wrote eight years later ... Tory Shepherd, 'I was wrong about Julia's speech. It was misogyny', *The Advertiser*, 15 July 2020, adelaidenow.com.au/news/opinion/tory-shepherd-what-matters-about-the-misogyny-speech-now-is-how-it-resonated-around-the-world/news-story/c66e870f01e4e61a61a4890ec340ed7d

CHAPTER 8: THE POLITICS OF MOTHERHOOD

Court transcripts from early 2020 show that ... Ben Smee, '"Extreme" Queensland LNP vetting allegedly focused on female candidates' sexual histories', The Guardian, 23 July 2020, https://www.theguardian.com/australia-news/2020/jul/23/extreme-queensland-lnp-vetting-allegedly-focused-on-female-candidates-sexual-histories

SOURCES

CHAPTER 9: CHOOSING TO MAKE IT WORK

In Julia Baird's 2004 book ... Julia Baird, *Media Tarts: How the Australian press frames female politicians*, Scribe, 2004

CHAPTER 10: GIVING IT ALL AWAY

'I am seething with anger ... Jamila Rizvi, 'Kate Ellis shouldn't have had to resign', News.com.au, 9 March 2017, news.com. au/jamila-rizvi-kate-ellis-shouldnt-have-had-to-resign/ news-story/bbe726b7c39623813e6c75cd7703453a

'More than anything, I wonder how disheartening ... Katy Hall, 'In Kate Ellis, we are losing so much more than just a politician', Mamamia, 9 March 2017, mamamia.com.au/kate-ellis-resignation

As Julia Baird wrote in her book ... Baird, *Media Tarts*

CHAPTER 11: SHAKING UP THE PARLIAMENT

There is an infamous story that he once sent Kelly a note ... Glenday, James, 'Frontbencher Kelly O'Dwyer asked by Chief Whip Scott Buchholz's office to express more milk to avoid missing parliament', ABC News, 16 September 2015, abc.net.au/ news/2015-09-16/odwyer-asked-to-express-milk-to-avoid-missing-parliament/6781218

The BBC reported that … 'Stella Creasy: UK's first "locum MP" to cover maternity leave', BBC News, 3 October 2019, bbc.com/news/uk-politics-49922613?intlink_from_url=http://www.bbc.com/news/politics/constituencies/E14001013&

'Job-sharing MPs could keep their caring responsibilities … 'Caroline Lucas: job sharing could invigorate an archaic Westminster', Green Party, 5 September 2017, greenparty.org.uk/news/2017/09/11/caroline-lucas-job-sharing-could-invigorate-an-archaic-westminster

Back in 2009, a parliamentary research paper … Dr Mark Rodrigues, 'Children in the Parliamentary Chambers', Parliament of Australia Research Paper no. 9 2009–10, 19 November 2009, aph.gov.au/About_Parliament/Parliamentary_Departments/Parliamentary_Library/pubs/rp/rp0910/10rp09#_Toc246394477

CHAPTER 12: WHY IT'S WORTH IT

Published research has shown that helping … Elizabeth Raposa, Holly Laws and Emily Ansell, 'Prosocial behaviour mitigates the negative effects of stress in everyday life', *Clinical Psychological Science* 4.4, 10 December 2015, doi.org/10.1177%2F2167702615611073

There are over 130,000 Australians living … 'Hepatitis statistics', Hepatitis Australia, 24 July 2020, hepatitisaustralia.com/hepatitis-statistics

CHAPTER 13: WOMEN CHANGING THE NATION

... the private sector lifted its game, with a 7 per cent increase ... Almost 50 per cent of Australian workplaces ... 'Parental leave and support for caring', Australian Government Workplace Gender Equality Agency, 2019, wgea.gov.au/ data/wgea-research/australias-gender-equality-scorecard/ 2018-2019-gender-equality-scorecard/employer-action-on-gender-equality/parental-leave-and-support-for-caring

Over 150,000 workers, 120,000 of whom were women ... 'Locking in funds for historic equal pay rises', Ministers' Media Centre, Department of Education, Skills and Employment, 9 October 2012, ministers.dese.gov.au/gillard/ locking-funds-historic-equal-pay-rises

... 700,000 Australian women who suffer from the condition. 'What we're doing about endometriosis', Australian Government Department of Health, 4 June 2020, health.gov.au/health-topics/ chronic-conditions/what-were-doing-about-chronic-conditions/ what-were-doing-about-endometriosis

... Australian women, who are over-represented in the lower income percentiles ... 'Gender indicators, Australia', Australian Bureau of Statistics, 15 December 2020, abs.gov.au/statistics/ people/people-and-communities/gender-indicators-australia/ latest-release

... and have less superannuation accumulated than men ... 'The gender gap in retirement savings', Australian Human Rights Commission, humanrights.gov.au/our-work/gender-gap-retirement-savings

Each day in Australia six babies are stillborn ... 'Stillbirth facts', Stillbirth Centre of Research Excellence, stillbirthcre.org.au/resources/stillbirth-facts

... on average, women currently retire with ... James Dunn, 'Women less than equal in retirement', *Australian Financial Review*, 8 December 2020, afr.com/companies/financial-services/women-less-than-equal-in-retirement-20201203-p56khb

Research has shown that when women are exposed ... Nilanjana Dasgupta and Shaki Asgari, 'Seeing is believing: Exposure to counterstereotypic women leaders and its effect on the malleability of automatic gender stereotyping', *Journal of Experimental Social Psychology* 40.5, September 2004, doi.org/10.1016/j.jesp.2004.02.003

The same has been shown in companies ... David Rock and Heidi Grant, 'Why diverse teams are smarter', *Harvard Business Review*, 4 November 2016, hbr.org/2016/11/why-diverse-teams-are-smarter

CHAPTER 14: WHERE TO FROM HERE?

Women make up 60 per cent of university graduates ... 'Higher education enrolments and graduate labour market statistics', Australian Government Workplace Gender Equality Agency, 9 August 2019, wgea.gov.au/data/fact-sheets/higher-education-enrolments-and-graduate-labour-market-statistics

In 2020 only 12 per cent of senior executives ... '2020 CEW Census reveals women in leadership positions has flatlined', Chief Executive Women, 17 September 2020, cew.org.au/wp-content/uploads/2020/09/200917-MR-2020-CEW-Census-reveals-women-in-leadership-posoitions-has-flatlined-FINAL-BUSINESS-1-1.pdf

COVID-19 has also demonstrated the value ... Jack Zenger and Joseph Folkman, 'Research: women are better leaders during a crisis, *Harvard Business Review*, 30 December 2020, hbr.org/2020/12/research-women-are-better-leaders-during-a-crisis

Politics 'reflects us back to ourselves' ... Annabel Crabb, 'Men at Work: Australia's parenthood trap', Quarterly Essay 75, September 2019

In 2008, speaking about the GFC, Rahm Emanuel ... Gerald Seib, 'In crisis, opportunity for Obama', *The Wall Street Journal*, 21 November 2008, wsj.com/articles/SB122721278056345271

INDEX

Abbott, Diane
    target of online abuse 90
Abbott, Tony 28, 85
    legacy of Gillard conflict 113–14,
        238
    the misogyny speech 127–30
    opposition to Gillard 110
    sexist attacks on Julia
        Gillard 121–2
affirmative action policies 13–14,
    105, 238
Aged Pension increases 209
Aly, Anne 116
    on the impact of online abuse 90
Amnesty International
    research on online abuse 82, 89–90
Andrews, Karen 30, 115
    on a family-friendly
        parliament 187
    motherhood and politics 155–7
    need for a women's caucus 107–8
    preselection and
        motherhood 139–40
    on social media abuse 87–8
Arndt, Bettina 85
Australian Labor Party
    affirmative action policies 13–14,
        105, 238

engagement with gender
    issues 115
Labor Women's Network 105
Status of Women Caucus
    Committee 105
Australian Services Union
    equal pay case 228

Baird, Julia 149, 167
    on women in politics 237
Banks, Julia 2
Bartley, Jonathan (UK)
    job-sharing MPs 200–1
Berejiklian, Gladys 101
Bird, Sharon 104
Birmingham, Simon 44, 179
Bishop, Julie 2, 134
    on cross-party groups 108
    diversity of women's views
        117–18
    on the future of women in
        politics 240
    opposition to Gillard 111
    personal appearance 61, 65–7
    RU486 debate 116–17
    sexist culture of parliament 16
boys' clubs in the workplace 38
Breen, Neil 49, 50

Brodtmann, Gai
  Parliamentary Friends of
  Endometriosis Awareness 230
Brough, Mal 121
Brown, Bob 31
Brown, Carol 216
Burke, Anna 17
Burke, Tony 29, 37
Burney, Linda 22–3, 116
  advice to young women 241
  on political motivation 205
Burrow, Sharan 224
button batteries consumer
  laws 231

Canberra press gallery
  narrow view of politics 218
carbon price 131
childcare 3, 183, 205–6
Clare, Jason 46–7
Clinton, Hilary
  personal appearance 65
Collier, Paul 23
Cook, Joe 214
COVID-19
  impact on parliamentary
  business 195–6
  impact on women 3
  women shouldering the burden
  of care 239
Cowan, Edith 12
Cox, Jo 94–5
Crabb, Annabel
  'Men at Work' 138, 239
Creasy, Stella
  locum use in UK
  parliament 198–9

Credlin, Peta 28, 32
  opposition to Gillard 111
  RU486 debate 117
Crowley, Rosemary
  cross-party lunches 106–7

Democrats
  leadership contest 100–3
  RU486 debate 117
Dent, Georgie
  paid parental leave reform 225
Dignity Party 23
disability advocates in
  parliament 23–4

Early Years Learning
  Framework 207
Element AI
  research on abusive
  tweets 82
Elizabeth Reid Network 105
Elliot, Justine 104
  candidacy and
  motherhood 139–42
Ellis, Kate
  advised on personal
  grooming 58–9
  Australia's youngest
  minister 34–5
  backgrounded 33–4
  becomes a parent 167–70
  on being a local member 213–14
  campaigning with a child 172–3
  Christmas cards 92–4
  friendships with other women
  MPs 103–4
  Grazia story 71–4

loss of friend to suicide 145–6
as Minister for Childcare 137
resigns from parliament 149,
  165–6, 177–82
on the role of social media 89–90
rumours of pregnancy 142–5
scrutiny of personal
  appearance 63–4
Sunday Life interview 73–6
target of sexual rumours 29–30,
  51–5
trolled on Twitter 81–2, 83–4
Emanuel, Rahm 241
Emily's List 105
employment services reform 210–11
Endometriosis Awareness 230
entitlements and parenting 193–5

Facebook's role in online abuse 96–7
Fair Work Act 228, 233
Fair Work Commission
  ASU's equal pay case 229
'fake news' 91
Family Court abolished 118–19
Farley, David
  sexist attacks against Gillard 121
Federal Women's Committee (Liberal
  Party) 105
Flint, Nicolle 77–8
  Parliamentary Friends of
  Endometriosis Awareness 230
Follett, Rosemary 12
Freelander, Mike 214

Gardiner, Kizzy
  locum use in UK parliament 199
gender diversity 18–22

gender equality across the
  workforce 232–3
George, Jennie 224
Gichuhi, Lucy 2
Gillard, Julia 7, 12, 30–1, 68–9
  ASU's equal pay case 229
  on the boys' clubs 38
  on clarity of purpose 243
  on cross-party groups 108
  Fair Work Act 228
  legacy of Abbott conflict 113–14
  legacy of sexist abuse 246–7
  locum use in UK parliament 200
  the misogyny speech 127–30
  on motherhood and politics 135–6
  online abuse and its impact 84, 90
  the positive impact of women in
    politics 222, 226
  role model for young women 1
  scrutiny of personal
    appearance 60, 61, 64–7, 70–1
  on sexism in the media 130–1
  target of sexist attacks 121–3
  on women leaders 118
Gillard Government
  achievements 131
  reforms 227–8
  success as a minority
    government 143–4
'Gonski' school reforms 131, 226
Gorman, Ginger 80
gossip as a weapon 27–39
Goward, Pru
  paid parental leave campaign 224
Grattan, Michelle
  reaction to the misogyny
    speech 129

Grazia magazine 71–4
GST legislation 101–2

Hammond, Tim 166
Hanson, Pauline
  advice to young women 242
  on being a local member 212–13
  Family Law review 109
  on the future of women in
    politics 237–8
  target of slut shaming 48–50
Hanson-Young, Sarah 2, 31–2, 32
  and Christine Milne 100–1
  defamation case 45
  need for a women's caucus 106–8
  scrutiny of personal
    appearance 61, 62–3, 69–70
  on slut shaming 2
  socialising triggers sexual
    rumours 37–8
  target of sexual rumours 36–7
  target of systematic slut
    shaming 41–6
  on women working together in
    parliament 99–100
Harradine, Brian
  foreign aid and family planning
    debate 116
Harris, Kamala 132–3
  treatment by the media 57–8, 77–8
Harris, Lachlan 52–4
Hartcher, Peter
  reaction to the misogyny
    speech 129
Hayes, Chris 176, 190
Heffernan, Bill
  sexist attacks against Gillard 121

'Her Rights at Work' by Anne
  Summers 122
Hockey, Joe 121
Howard, John
  'WorkChoices' legislation 228
Hume, Jane 115
Hunt, Greg
  endometriosis research and
    education 230
Husar, Emma 2
  impact of slut shaming by
    media 50–1
  on slut shaming and sexual
    rumours 39
  target of slut shaming 46–8

imposter syndrome 67, 242–3
Indigenous representation 22–3
Inquiry into Economic Security for
  Women in Retirement 231–2
'Inside the Canberra Bubble,' *Four
  Corners* program 24–5

job-sharing MPs (UK) 200–1
Jones, Alan 15
  personal attacks against Gillard 122
Jones, Tony 85
Jordan, Alister 53

Kanck, Sandra 102
Kelly, Ros 17
Keneally, Kristina
  select committee into
    stillbirths 230–1
Kernot, Cheryl 59, 100
Kirner, Joan 12
  Emily's List 13–14

Labor Women's Network (ALP) 105
Lawrence, Carmen 12
Leigh, Andrew
  'The Motherhood Tax' 138
Ley, Sussan 14, 106
  advice to young women 241–2
  on being a local member 212
  on political motivation 208–9
  preselection and
    motherhood 139–40
  scrutiny of personal
    appearance 68–9
Leyonhjelm, David
  defamation case 45
  slut shaming activities 41–2
LGBTIQ+ representation 20–2
Liberal Party
  disengaged from gender issues 115
  lack of affirmative action 14–15
  sexist attacks against Gillard 121
  support of women
    politicians 105–6
LNP Coalition
  normalisation of sexist
    attacks 125–6
locum use in UK
  parliament 199–200
Lucas, Caroline (UK)
  job-sharing MPs 200–1
Lyons, Dame Enid 12

Macklin, Jenny 104
  ASU's equal pay case 228–9
  foreign aid and family planning
    debate 116
  paid parental leave 222–6
  on political motivation 208–9

Marantz, Andrew
  Facebook's role in online
    abuse 96–7
Marriage Equality Law Postal Survey
  (2017) 20
May, Theresa 59–60
McAllister, Jenny
  Inquiry into Economic Security for
    Women in Retirement 231–2
McCarthy, Malarndirri
  select committee into stillbirths 230
Media Tarts by Julia Baird 149
'Men at Work' by Annabel
  Crabb 138
Menzies Centre
  female participation 14
Merkel, Angela
  personal appearance 64
Miller, Rachel 24
Milne, Christine 100
Milne, Glenn 51, 54
the Misogyny Speech 127–30
Morrison Government
  female participation rate 14
  response to 'Inside the Canberra
    Bubble' 25
motherhood
  politicisation 139–42

'Name It. Change It' project 76–7
National Disability Insurance
  Scheme 131, 209–10, 213–16
National Plan to Reduce Violence
  Against Women and their
  Children 226–7
National Quality Standards
  policy 207–8

O'Dwyer, Kelly 114, 115, 190–1
  resigns from parliament
  149
O'Dwyer, Michael 137
O'Neil, Clare 114–15
  advice to young women 242
  on family-friendly
  workplaces 184–5
  impact of COVID-19 on
  parliamentary business 196
  motherhood and politics 150–4
  the need for social media
  strategies 95–6
  on political motivation 206
van Onselen, Peter
  reaction to the misogyny
  speech 129
'Open House' by the University of
  Bristol 200

paid parental leave 131
  campaign 222–6
  need for reform 225–6
Pak Poy, Anna 213–16
Pak Poy, Sebby 213–16
Palaszczuk, Annastacia 101
parliament
  as a family-friendly
  workplace 183–201
  legacy of the attacks on Julia
  Gillard 113–14
  as a male domain 15–16
  predatory sexual culture 24–6
Payne, Marise
  women's support network 106
personal grooming requirements for
  female politicians 58

Pickering, Larry
  sexist attacks against Gillard 122
plain packaging tobacco laws 227
Plan International Australia survey
  (2017) 2
Plibersek, Tanya 8, 33, 103, 119
  being a local member 212
  on civil public discourse 239
  on cross-party groups 109
  on double standards 17–8
  influence of Labor's affirmative
  action policies 238
  Labor's Deputy Leader 35
  motherhood and politics 157
  paid parental leave campaign
  223
  scrutiny of personal
  appearance 61, 64, 70
  on the sexist attacks against
  Gillard 124
  Whitlam Government legacy
  232
  on women's perspective on
  issues 227
Porter, Christian 24
predatory sexual culture in
  parliament 24–6

Rare Find Foundation 216–17
Rees, Shannon 51
retirement savings of women 231–2
Reynolds, Linda 113
Reynolds, Margaret
  foreign aid and family planning
  debate 116
Richards, Kate 137
Ridout, Heather 225

INDEX

Rishworth, Amanda 32
  on entitlements for
    politicians 193–5
  on a family-friendly
    parliament 187–9
  motherhood and politics 157–8
  online abuse 80, 87
  on political motivation 206–7
  scrutiny of personal
    appearance 61
  supportive personal
    networks 244
Rodrigues, Dr Mark
  on a family-friendly
    parliament 191
Roxon, Nicola 226
Royal Commission into Institutional
  Responses to Child Sexual
  Abuse 131, 226
Rudd, Kevin 34
Rugg, Sally
  on women and politics 204
rumour as a weapon 27–39

Sales, Leigh 47, 81
Sandberg, Sheryl
  on supportive partners 242–3
Senate
  slut shaming in question
    time 43–4
sexist attacks
  normalisation of sexist
    behaviour 125–7
sexual politics 24–6
sexual rumours
  triggered by socialising 36–8
sexual weaponisation 34

Shanahan, Dennis 145
  reaction to the misogyny
    speech 129
She Should Run 76
Shepherd, Tory
  reaction to the misogyny
    speech 129
Shorten, Bill 173, 176
  'Death Taxes' Scare
    campaign 91–2
slut shaming 2, 39
  definition 41
Smith, Marielle 133, 229
  breastfeeding provisions for the
    Senate 192–3
  button batteries consumer laws 231
  on clarity of purpose 243
  on a family-friendly
    parliament 187
  impact of COVID-19 on
    parliamentary business 197–8
  legacy of Gillard's sexist
    abuse 246–7
  on the misogyny speech 129
  motherhood and politics 159–60
  on political motivation 206
  on the sexist attacks against
    Julia Gillard 123
social media
  abuse of women 79–98
  and sexual gossip 32
social media companies,
  lack of responsibility 95
Speers, David 81
Status of Women Caucus Committee
  (ALP) 105
stillbirths select committee 230–1

Stott Despoja, Natasha 28, 30, 184–6
  advice to young women 245
Stott Despoja, Natasha *continued*
  cross-party lunches 106–7
  Democrats leadership contest 100–3
  on the future of women in politics 239–40
  paid parental leave campaign 224
  scrutiny of personal appearance 60–1, 69–70
  on women working together in parliament 100, 117
Sturgeon, Nicola
  scrutiny of personal appearance 60
suffragettes 11
Summers, Anne 122

Tangney, Dorothy 12
Thatcher, Margaret 59–60
'The Motherhood Tax' by Andrew Leigh 138
Troll Hunting, by Ginger Gorman 80
Trump , Donald 91, 96, 162, 163
Tudge, Alan 24
Turnbull, Malcolm
  on Australian cultural attitudes 6
Twitter
  use and abuse 83, 87–8

Victorian Women's Trust 133
Vincent, Kelly 23–4, 245

Waters, Larissa
  breastfeeding in parliament 191
Weatherill, Jay 32
Wells, Anika
  impact of COVID-19 on parliamentary business 196–7
  motherhood and politics 160–3
  supportive partners 243
Whitlam Government legacy 232
Williams, Blair
  the scrutiny of women's appearance 59–60
women in corporate Australia
  under-representation 236–7
women in parliament 12–13
  cross-party caucus 106–8
  diversity of views 117–18
  the future 235–49
  positive impact on Australian life 222–34
  as proxies for men's attacks on women 109–13
  under-representation 221
  working together 99–119
women's appearance
  in political settings 59–78
Women's Media Centre (US) 76
women's suffrage 11
Wong, Penny 19–22, 30, 32, 127
  advice to young women 239–40, 241–2
  dealing with online abuse 97–8
  on Gillard Government reforms 227–8
  impact of COVID-19 on parliamentary business 195–6

on the impact of online
 abuse 90–1
the need for social media
 strategies 95–6
the positive impact of women in
 politics 227–8
on the sexist attacks against
 Gillard 124–5
on social media abuse 84–5

Workman, Alice 48
Workplace Gender Equality
 Agency 73, 75–6, 232–3
Wright, Tony 36–7

Zaetta, Tania 52

ACKNOWLEDGEMENTS

I CANNOT BEGIN to adequately express my gratitude to the women who agreed to be interviewed for this book: Julie Bishop, Natasha Stott Despoja, Tanya Plibersek, Linda Burney, Sarah Hanson-Young, Penny Wong, Anika Wells, Pauline Hanson, Amanda Rishworth, Karen Andrews, Jenny Macklin, Marielle Smith, Sussan Ley, Clare O'Neil, Justine Elliot, and of course Julia Gillard. I thank each one of them for their time, their trust and for their insights.

I am incredibly lucky to have had the chance to work with the great team at Hardie Grant Books. This book would not exist were it not for the belief of Arwen Summers, who persisted after twice approaching me to write it and twice receiving a polite decline. I thank Arwen for her advice and her support; she always made me feel better when I was doubtful, and this is without question a better book because of her input. I'm so grateful to Emily Hart, who was given the task of informing me that I really needed to submit this book and remained good humoured even as I resisted because I didn't want anyone to read it. She also never once complained about my crippling IT knowledge limitations. Deonie Fiford enthusiastically took on the task of editing. I thank all of the Hardie Grant marketing, publicity and sales teams for their hard work. It has been a delight to work with them all.

My life became better when I became friends with Tim Watts. He and Joe Cook went so far above and beyond in supporting me throughout this process that I will remain forever in their debt. From volunteering to transcribe interviews to reassurance and ideas, these are two very good people whom I adore.

I thank wholeheartedly those that have offered me support, assistance and advice along the way, particularly Shannon Rees, Marielle Smith, Jamila Rizvi, Suzanne Kellett and Amy Ware.

I am so blessed to have my beautiful family. My thanks go to Sophie, Jim, Sam and Charlie for their tolerance and understanding, and to my mum Ros, my mother-in-law Carolyn and my father-in-law Lloyd for all that they do, but in particular the extra babysitting shifts as deadline loomed.

Mostly, though, I thank my husband Dave. I cannot imagine how frustrating it must have been for someone who writes well and writes quickly to have to sit and witness me procrastinate and um and ah over single sentences for hours at a time. He never judged or displayed signs of irritation. Instead, somehow Dave always knew the moments when I needed encouragement, the moments I needed advice and when I just needed a cheerleader – and played each role to perfection. I am so very grateful. It has been a really hard time to write a book. We've experienced not just a pandemic and the associated lockdowns and craziness, but sudden deaths in the family, serious health issues among those closest to us and a range of additional hurdles. Dave has been the rock that kept our show on the road throughout and made it possible for me to complete this book. There is no one else I would ever want by my side as we navigate life's adventures, and I am so grateful that I get to spend every day with someone who I love with all of my heart.